THE SUBORDINATE SUBSTITUTE

THE SUBORDINATE SUBSTITUTE

Another Wrong Turn on Carillon Avenue

PETER CARNLEY

CASCADE Books • Eugene, Oregon

THE SUBORDINATE SUBSTITUTE
Another Wrong Turn on Carillon Avenue

Copyright © 2024 Peter Carnley. All rights reserved. Except for brief quotations in critical publications or reviews, no part of this book may be reproduced in any manner without prior written permission from the publisher. Write: Permissions, Wipf and Stock Publishers, 199 W. 8th Ave., Suite 3, Eugene, OR 97401.

Cascade Books
An Imprint of Wipf and Stock Publishers
199 W. 8th Ave., Suite 3
Eugene, OR 97401

www.wipfandstock.com

PAPERBACK ISBN: 978-1-6667-6521-2
HARDCOVER ISBN: 978-1-6667-6522-9
EBOOK ISBN: 978-1-6667-6523-6

Cataloguing-in-Publication data:

Names: Carnley, Peter, author.

Title: The subordinate substitute : another wrong turn on Carillon Avenue / Peter Carnley.

Description: Eugene, OR: Cascade Books, 2024 | Includes bibliographical references and index.

Identifiers: ISBN 978-1-6667-6521-2 (paperback) | ISBN 978-1-6667-6522-9 (hardcover) | ISBN 978-1-6667-6523-6 (ebook)

Subjects: LCSH: Atonement.

Classification: BT265.2 C40 2024 (paperback) | BT265.2 (ebook)

01/08/24

Cover design: A photograph of the ruins of the first-century synagogue at Ostia, the ancient Port of Rome. Jewish workmen were involved when the Emperor Claudius undertook a major reconstruction of the port facility. The ruin of the synagogue at Ostia is located on the ancient waterfront, at the edge of the city, just a little to the East of the Porta Marina through which Paul would have passed when he arrived in custody around the year 58. Although it is extremely likely, whether Paul actually visited the synagogue is one of the unanswered questions of history.

For
those who have difficulty
in coming to terms with the belief
that God required the death of his Son
as the remedy for the sin and evil of the world.

CONTENTS

Preface		ix
1	Introduction	1
2	Penal Substitutionary Atonement	27
3	The Sydney Doctrine Commission Report 2010	55
4	Pierced for Our Transgressions?	73
5	Penal Substitution and the Caricature of God	106
6	"The Good News of God's Wrath"	131
7	God's Justice: Punitive, Retributive, or Restorative?	152
8	Metaphors and Mystery	182
9	Persons in Communion	216
Bibliography		235
Author Index		253
Subject Index		259

PREFACE

I started writing this book, along with its companion volume, *Arius on Carillon Avenue*, in the month of May 2020. This was a time of worldwide lockdowns caused by the unwelcome spread of the highly infectious (and scarily sinister) coronavirus. The strictly enforced confinement created by the need for "social distancing" certainly disrupted the accustomed patterns of life. Among other things it put an end to travel beyond a few kilometers from home; for a time even this was allowed only for the explicit purpose of purchasing "essentials for living." International travel was of course entirely impossible.

Despite the frustrations and inconveniences of successive enforced lockdowns they did, however, at least have the positive outcome of creating time and space for some quiet self-reflection in retreat from the business of life in the world. Happily, this in turn led to what seemed to be a windfall opportunity to begin to do something unscheduled. I decided to tackle a project that would otherwise not have been attempted—the writing of some memoirs.

I chose to begin with the last years of my working life as archbishop of Perth, during which I served concurrently as primate of the Anglican Church of Australia. These happened to be the first years of the present century, from 2000 to 2005. This seemed an easier option than starting a memoir at a perhaps more predictable beginning, with accounts of the arrival of the first Carnleys on Australian shores from Yorkshire in the mid-nineteenth century, and the early twentieth-century struggles of my parents through the years of the Great Depression. This could then have been followed by my own earliest childhood memories, which coincided with the years of the Second World War. The more proximate "primatial" years of just two decades ago begged attention, however, given that I still retained an abundance of vivid memories of them, and also had immediate access to a good deal of archival material relating to them that was stored away in my study filing cabinet, where it awaited sorting pending its eventual dispatch to the diocesan archive.

My memories of those years were also informed by a consciousness of the fact that there were some unresolved issues arising from theological controversies in which I had been very much involved. This unfinished business had tended either to be put in the "too-hard" basket, or was simply bumped aside by the pressure of whatever else it was that needed to be done at the time. The enforced lockdowns under the shadow of COVID provided a welcome opportunity to revisit and carefully unravel some of the logical entanglements of the conflict of ideas that, even after some quite intense public debate, had tended to be left hanging in the air. There is always the hope, of course, of achieving some clarity about the real nature of the issues involved, and even the prospect of finding a possible way of resolving some of them. As I began to work on this postretirement project, I soon found that I was writing much more than a memoir.

The result was, first, a study of the doctrine of the Trinity with a focus on the popular conservative evangelical belief in the "eternal functional subordination of the Son to the Father." Over the last two decades this has attracted the charge of being sub-Trinitarian, and even of constituting a contemporary form of the ancient heresy of Arianism.[1] It can fairly easily be discerned that this novel subordinationist Trinitarianism is of far-reaching importance, for it leads to a package of quite distinctive and interrelated beliefs. It has important implications, for example, for the discussion of contemporary gender-related issues relating to the alleged interpersonal subordination of women to men. It also has as a role in the formulation of a highly distinctive understanding of the theology of human redemption that is said to have involved the payment of the penalty of death by Christ whom God is said to have sent into the world as the "subordinate substitute" to suffer and die for its sin and evil *instead of* sinful humanity.[2]

This package of interrelated beliefs was brought to the life of the Anglican Church of Australia in a very well-defined and confident way primarily as a result of the appointment of T. C. Hammond, who came from Ireland to be principal of Moore Theological College in Sydney in 1936.[3] Since then it has become domiciled in the Anglican Diocese of Sydney, with its epicenter at Moore College, which has historically been located on Carillon Avenue

---

1. A debate introduced and tenaciously pursued by Kevin Giles. See *Trinity and Subordinationism, Jesus and the Father*, and *Rise and Fall of the Complementarian Doctrine of the Trinity*. Arius was judged to have been guilty of calling into question the full divinity of Christ by arguing that he was not eternally equal with the Father in authority and dignity but rather, as the creature of the Father, essentially the Father's subordinate.

2. The "penal substitutionary theory" of the atonement.

3. For a detailed account of Hammond and theological federalism, see Carnley, *Arius on Carillon Avenue*, chapter 2.

in the suburb of Newtown, although it has spread much more widely and is now found dispersed around Australia. I speak of it as Australian "Carillon Avenue" theology, though closely related versions of essentially the same theological ideas are found elsewhere in the world, particularly in Britain and very noticeably in the United States of America.

In Australia there is no doubt that the pioneering influence of T. C. Hammond at Moore Theological College in Sydney has been of enormous significance in relation to this theological phenomenon. Hammond was a "federal" theologian who became fervently committed to a kind of Scholastic Calvinism inherited from the great James Ussher of Ireland and the Westminster tradition of English Puritanism, with roots going back to Zacharius Ursinus of Heidelberg in the sixteenth century. Ursinus held that God had made a contract[4] with Adam on condition of obedience, which Adam broke. Because penalties attach to broken contracts generally, a penalty for Adam's disobedience and for all humanity after him naturally had to be paid to satisfy the just demands of a righteous God. Contractual presuppositions of this kind naturally underpin the "penal subordination theory" of the atonement that explains human reconciliation with God as a result of the payment of the penalty of death by Christ *instead of* sinful humanity. Obviously, the obedient "*eternal* functional submissiveness" of God the Son in the internal life of the Trinity is foundational to this approach to the understanding of God's redemption of humanity by sending his ever-obedient Son to die upon the cross in the historical context of this world of space and time.

In the United States, a parallel standout and definitive contribution to this style of theology was made by the nineteenth-century theologian Charles Hodge, who taught theology at Princeton for fifty years, and his son A. A. Hodge, who studied under his father and in fact published much of the notes he took in the course of his father's lectures. Both the Hodges were card-carrying "federal" theologians. Both were Trinitarian subordinationists and both naturally promoted the soteriological implications of this belief in the form of the penal substitutionary doctrine of the atonement in a systematized theological package. It is not a surprise that T. C. Hammond acknowledged the agreement of his own "federalist" theology with that of the Hodges.

I somewhat clumsily got drawn into public controversy over this issue of Trinitarian subordinationism in 2004/05 by daring publicly to declare

---

4. Hence "federal" from "foedus"="contract."

a hand in sympathy with the assessment of its problematic status when measured by the standard orthodox belief in the doctrine of the Trinity.[5] The more recent COVID-related opportunity to revisit and reconsider the key issues of nearly two decades ago and to submit them to much closer scrutiny has confirmed me in the view that the belief in the "eternal functional submissiveness of the Son to the Father" deviates seriously from the traditional norm of the church's Trinitarian faith. This has eventually resulted in the production of the companion volume to this—*Arius on Carillon Avenue*.

Then, second, the opportunity of the lockdowns of these last years has provided the opportunity further to explore the outworking of the doctrine of the Trinity in the theology of redemption, which has resulted in the writing of this book, *The Subordinate Substitute*. In this case, a debate about the "penal substitutionary theory" of the atonement in the year 2000 was triggered, not so much by something that was actually said, but by the fact that I had dared to publish some thoughts on the meaning of the cross of Christ in an outlet of the Australian secular press *without* so much as mentioning "penal substitution"! Chapter 2 of this book relates something of the story of what was in fact an even more intense public controversy than that relating to the "eternal functional submissiveness" of the Son in the inner or immanent life of the Trinity, which was to follow it some four years later.

As with the discussion of the subordinationist doctrine of the Trinity itself, this book's reflection on the theology of redemption from a Trinitarian perspective is therefore very much grounded in the experience of publicly expressed disagreement and, indeed, spirited theological debate. Apart from assisting in unpacking and understanding the detailed logic of this specific approach to atonement belief, the value of revisiting the public discussion of it is that it helps appreciate something of the fervor and passion with which it is believed, and why it is that some conservative evangelical people are of the view that it is in fact quite essential to an authentic proclamation of the Christian gospel. Once again, although this book began its life by my revisiting a historical debate, it has also therefore become much more than a memoir.

Very early in the life of this writing project I came to the view there is little point in raking over the coals of a debate of the past, unless some effort is made to further the debate and, indeed, to make a concerted attempt to deal with it by bringing the relevant issues to some kind of conclusion. This is obviously particularly so when the issues by and large remain unresolved.

---

5. In Carnley, *Reflections in Glass*, chapter 7.

PREFACE

The outcome of this study is that the "penal substitutionary theory" of the atonement is found to be as problematic as the alleged interpersonal subordinationism of the immanent life of the Trinity to which it is so closely related.

As in the case of the production of *Arius on Carillon Avenue*, I am duty bound to acknowledge my profound gratitude to those who have helped and supported me in the course of the writing of this book. First, I am enormously appreciative of the constant help and support of my loving wife, Ann, not least for putting up with me around the house without relief during these COVID years. Somebody has said that it is one thing to pledge one's life to another "for better, for worse" but it is quite another thing when it is for lunch as well. I am well aware, furthermore, that Ann has not just had me "around the house," but around the house with theological preoccupations of mind persistently clouding the atmosphere. In and through it all she has managed to sustain us—both in the challenging business of mere human survival and very importantly in the love of God.

I am also grateful to others who have contributed specifically to the production of both these books. Marianne Dorman and David Wood have generously read portions of the manuscripts and valiantly persisted with the technicalities of Trinitarian description that have necessarily to be engaged if truth is to be found, while at the same time watching out for typographical and grammatical errors. On the other hand, I am greatly indebted to Bill Leadbetter who, as one who has had a Sydney background before his escape to Western Australia, happens to be well acquainted with "Carillon Avenue theology." I am enormously appreciative of his willingness to bring his theological mind and acute scholarly skills to the painstaking review of the draft text and for "fact-checking" his experience of the historical context, while sharpening the grammar and improving the expression of the argument. I do not deserve to be the recipient of the prodigious gift of Bill's time and energy and scholarly precision.

I also wish to thank Lauren Pickering, the library manager of St Mark's Library in Canberra, for her helpful assistance in sending on-loan volumes across the country, and especially for scanning and emailing pages of articles that were not available to me in Perth.

Needless to say, I am also enormously grateful to the editor in chief, K. C. Hanson, and the staff at Wipf and Stock, for the splendid professional help and skill that they have brought to the production of both these books. I want particularly to thank those with whom I have had direct dealings—Matt Wimer, George Callihan, and Jorie Chapman on the administrative side, Rodney Clapp who was assigned to me for the work of editing, and Jesselyn Clapp for her format checking, Savanah N. Landerholm for typesetting, and no doubt many others whose names I do not know who have been involved in bringing this project to completion. It has been a pleasure to deal with such congenial people and with such an impressively proficient publishing house.

+ Peter Carnley, Fremantle, January 1, 2023

1

INTRODUCTION

It may come as something of a surprise that theological debate in Australia and North America in the first two decades of this century[1] that was specifically focused on the "eternal functional subordination of the Son to the Father" was pursued in tandem with a somewhat unlikely traveling companion. This debate about the rather abstract nature of the internal relation of the Persons of the Trinity (with the Son's obedience being said to complement the Father's command) was understood to bear upon a parallel contemporary discussion of the divine intention for gender relationships in the living of human lives. Whether for good or ill, or whether it was even legitimate for an analogy to be drawn between the internal relations of the Persons of the Trinity and human inter-gender relationships, the notion of the "eternal submissiveness" or "eternal subordination" of the Son was perceived to be a kind of paradigm of the nature of interpersonal relations more generally conceived. Antagonists lined up against one another either as "subordinationists" or "egalitarians." Subordinationists treated the complementarian doctrine of the Trinity as being of specific relevance to the question of the subordination of wives to their husbands in the home, and women to men in society at large, not least in the ministry and authority structures of the church. Trinitarian egalitarians, on the other hand, appealed to the orthodox definition of the Nicene *homoousion* to insist that the requirement of the full and equal sharing of the very same substance and nature by all three identities of the Trinity pointed in the opposite direction.

1. This debate was triggered in Australia by the publication of a report in 1999 of the Sydney Doctrine Commission, entitled "The Trinity and its bearing on the relationship of men and women." In the United States a debate over essentially the same issues was triggered by a blog of Liam Goligher in 2016. These debates are fully discussed in Carnley, *Arius on Carillon Avenue*, chapter 1.

Either way the doctrine of the Trinity was drawn into a foray in the arena of contemporary gender politics.

We should not be oblivious of the fact that, at the same time, apart from the analogous operation of interpersonal subordination in the internal life of the Trinity and in the gender-based relationships of human life, belief in the "eternal functional submissiveness of the Son to the Father" was already assumed by many of the very same subordinationists (if not by the egalitarians) to have important implications for the understanding of the doctrine of redemption.

It is not difficult to see, for example, that the alleged "*eternal* functional submissiveness of the Son to the Father" in the internal (or immanent) life of the Trinity may be understood to play out in historical time in the specifics of the penal substitutionary theory of the atonement. According to this theory the timelessly eternal and unwavering obedience of the Son is said to have come into play in the economy of salvation in space and historical time when the Son, by dying on the cross, is said to have paid the just penalty for the rebellious disobedience of Adam and all sinfully disobedient humanity after him. And this is not to mention the flow-on effect that the redemption of humanity has for the restoration of God's good purposes for all creation. Thus, God the Father is understood to have exercised his commanding will by sending his obediently submissive Son to die upon the cross as the "subordinate substitute" for the rest of humanity. In turn, by the willing exercise of his eternally obedient submissiveness to the will of the Father, the Son may thus be said to have died "for our sins."[2]

While issue may rightly be taken with the validity of belief in the "eternal functional subordination" of the Son as fundamentally flawed and falling short of the norms of Christian orthodoxy,[3] this in turn appears *prima facie* also to render its flow-on in the penal substitutionary theory of the atonement also problematic. Even so, the basic assumption that cognizance should be taken of the intimate logical relation between the doctrine of God the Holy Trinity and the understanding of God's work of human redemption may be positively endorsed. These two topics—the theology of the Trinity and the doctrine of redemption—are in fact more intimately related than is often imagined.

In other words, we can embrace and even celebrate the fundamental theological premise that *any* doctrine of the redemption wrought by God, as a matter of general principle (as distinct from the specifics of the penal substitutionary theory), should properly be consciously developed from a

---

2. 1 Corinthians 15:3.

3. This is the thesis of the companion volume to this one, *Arius on Carillon Avenue*.

Trinitarian perspective. There is an unavoidable logical connection between the understanding of the nature of God, as God *is*, and the understanding of the outworking of the good purposes of this same God in the drama of human redemption.

This means we can enthusiastically accept the importance of a necessary focus upon the saving significance that Christianity has discerned in Christ's death on the cross and resurrection from the dead as providing the raw material of human experience in the economy of salvation for the development of the doctrine of the Trinity. But it also means that, *vice versa*, the doctrine of the Trinitarian nature of God may be brought to the church's work of explaining how the human consciousness of imperfection, and the ensuing religious experience of alienation in the face of the righteousness of God, may be understood to have been overcome by the deliberate action of God. The Trinitarian nature of God and theories of the atonement go hand in hand.

As it happens the pursuit of the implications of Trinitarian subordinationism that had been initially triggered by the need to address gender-related moral and ecclesiological issues over the last two decades, and that could also, by a similar kind of logical extension be brought to the theology of redemption, has tapped into a new wave of interest in the theology of the Trinity in its own right. Indeed, a resurgent theology of the Trinity had been attracting the lively interest of scholars right through the second half of the twentieth century.

This renewal in Trinitarian theology had originally been initiated by Karl Barth in the years between the two world wars. In the course of the production of his *Church Dogmatics*, the first volume of which appeared in 1936, Barth expressed his disenchantment with nineteenth-century liberalism, to which he found himself reacting by developing an uncompromising commitment to the serious pursuit of the implications of the category of revelation for all Christian theology. This began to shine a startling new light on the inherited doctrines of Christian orthodoxy, a development which was to be of enormous benefit in relation to the doctrine of the Trinity.

That something of importance was at that time beginning to grip the interest of the entire Christian theological world was confirmed by the fact that Barth's contribution to a revival of interest in the Trinity in Reformed theology was soon matched by the notable work of thinkers of caliber and impressive originality across the denominational spectrum—such as, for example, the German Jesuit theologian Karl Rahner in the Roman Catholic

Church and, perhaps even more notably, John Zizioulas, who worked very self-consciously from the perspective of Eastern Orthodoxy and the fourth-century discoveries of the Cappadocian fathers. In the Reformed tradition Thomas Torrance soon became their dialogue partner, at the same time sustaining a continuing interest in the original insights of Barth.

These great minds of the twentieth-century theology of the Trinity were soon joined by innumerable interpreters, some of whom enthusiastically celebrated and promoted the work of their adopted mentors, while others felt the need to take serious issue with them. As a consequence the subject of the Trinity, which had suffered a degree of neglect, if not almost even a passive kind of disdain as something of an unnecessary theological oddity, inevitably began to reclaim its rightful place at the center of the Christian theological curriculum.

It is not a coincidence that the flourishing of the ecumenical movement occurred concurrently with this scholarly development. Following upon the creation of the World Council of Churches in 1948 and the convening of the Second Vatican Council between 1962 and 1965, the mainline Christian churches and other ecclesial bodies entered into serious bilateral conversations. A succession of formal dialogues on topics that had historically been divisive across Christian denominations was matched in the theological world more generally by the collaborative work of revitalizing the centrally shared affirmations of the Christian faith. At the head of the list was the distinctive understanding of the Christian God. In reviewing this renewed interest in the doctrine of the Trinity through the second half of the twentieth century, the Melbourne evangelical theologian Kevin Giles could observe from the perspective of Australia in 2002 that "No other doctrine has gained so much attention from so many first-rate theological minds in the last thirty years. Now it is agreed that the doctrine of the Trinity, as Athanasius and Augustine saw so clearly, is the primary and foundational doctrine of Christianity."[4]

If we were to be invited to conduct a poll to identify the stand-out publications on the Trinity of this period, one of the most influential would surely be *Being as Communion*, which John Zizioulas published in 1985, and which quickly became a "must read" for all of us who at the time became captivated by the discovery that the Trinitarian vision of God as a communion of Persons in one unity of being could inform the ecumenical quest for the reintegration of the churches. Zizioulas's articulation of an ecclesiology

---

4. Giles, *Trinity and Subordinationism*, 94.

of "persons in communion" that was less formal and institutional than that to which most of us had been accustomed, offered the vision of the local eucharistic community drawing its identity from the historical fact that it was *instituted* by Christ, but *constituted* by the life-giving gift of the Spirit. And so the church was understood as a communion of human persons that actually participated by grace in the communion of God by being called to share in God's very own life. The conditioning relevance of Zizioulas's contribution to the understanding of the theology of the Trinity and its ecclesiological implications in relation to the doctrine of human redemption will be found in chapter 9 of this book.

A little over twenty years earlier, in 1967, Karl Rahner had already made a significant contribution to this burgeoning new wave of interest through the publication of a monograph, which appeared in English in 1970 under the title of *The Trinity*. In this slim volume Rahner defined a methodological principle that his interpreters quickly discerned to be of signal importance for guiding the international and interdenominational theological conversation. This principle was widely celebrated and acclaimed, and soon became known as "Rahner's Rule."

Rahner pointed out that it is a grave mistake to approach an understanding of the Christian God in an entirely abstract and theoretical way, as though it might simply involve the unveiling of the hidden logical secrets of the inner life of the divine reality. His thesis was that Trinitarian description should ideally be grounded in a treatment of the Christian perception of the action of God in the history of the world, and more specifically in God's management of human redemption—through what has become known as the "economy" or "management" of salvation. In this way, Rahner's contribution to the theology of the Trinity meant that a good deal of the revitalized interest in the world of Christian theology through the second half of the twentieth century had, somewhat fortuitously, to do with the very theme of the perception of the Trinity in the economy of salvation and *vice versa* on the relevance of the doctrine of the Trinity for developing an understanding of the atonement.

Rahner's chief complaint was that the theology of the Trinity is often treated in a self-contained and timeless way, as though entirely divorced from human life. He argued by contrast that Christian reflection on the nature of God as Father, Son, and Spirit arises out of the fundamental experience of salvation in Christ. Hence, a statement for which Rahner is now famous: "The Trinity is a mystery of *salvation*, otherwise it would never have been revealed."[5]

---

5. Rahner, *Trinity*, 21.

Rahner began his methodological discussion with the startling remark (for which he is now equally famous) that "should the doctrine of the Trinity have to be dropped as false, the major part of religious literature could well remain virtually unchanged."[6] In other words, he drew attention to the fact that in Christian piety and "textbook theology" there has been a historical failure to appreciate the relevance of the truths of salvation history for an understanding of the doctrine of the Trinity, and, *vice versa*, also a failure to appreciate the fundamental importance of the doctrine of the Trinity to the truths of salvation. Indeed, his contention was that the church's theologians have not only tended to isolate reflection on the Trinity from its proper source, but have separated it from its proper controlling function in relation to other doctrines as well. As a consequence of this, by concentrating on the eternal relations of the Persons in the internal life of the divine, the doctrine of the Trinity had become detached not only from the primary Christian focus on salvation history that he laments, but from other Christian doctrines that can only really be properly understood from a Trinitarian perspective.

To Rahner's mind there are some fundamental reasons that explain this mistaken historical tendency to treat the doctrine of the Trinity as a self-contained enterprise. He argued in the first instance that since Thomas Aquinas, the doctrine of the Trinity has been accommodated to a logically prior discussion of theism more generally conceived. In effect this has subordinated it to the doctrine of the unity of the one God. In his historical review of this development, Kevin Giles noted that "Karl Rahner lays the blame for this retreat in the history of Western theology at the feet of Aquinas, who discussed first and separately *De Deo uno* (The one God) before discussing *Deo trino* (God the Trinity)" and furthermore that "This order suggests that the trinitarian nature of God is a secondary feature of the Christian understanding of God."[7] In relation to this specific point, Rahner may well have been anticipating the sentiments of John Zizioulas, who regularly drew attention to this kind of shortcoming in the characteristically Western approach to the theology of God by way of contrast with Eastern Orthodoxy's (to his mind) correct starting point of the interpersonal relations of the Trinity. Zizioulas discerned that Eastern Orthodoxy was privileged in this respect as a consequence of its inheritance from the Cappadocian fathers of the fourth century, whose Trinitarian reflection began with the role of the

---

6. Rahner, *Trinity*, 10–11.

7. Giles, *Trinity and Subordinationism*, 94.

Father, as the eternal "origin" and "cause" of the Son and Holy Spirit rather with a discussion of the one "substance" of divinity and its divine nature.

The problem to which Rahner drew attention was not, however, narrowly focused on the opposing starting points that were alleged to seed differences of style between the theologians of Eastern and Western Christendom. If anything, the difference between the Western focus on the unity of the Godhead and the "substance" of divinity, as opposed to Eastern Orthodoxy's focus on the Person of the Father as the "origin" and "cause" of the other two Trinitarian identities, is often somewhat overexaggerated.[8] Rahner's concern was in methodological terms rather more broadly based and fundamental than this. For, apart from different "starting points," what has become known as "classical theism," which in the West took a set course from Aquinas onwards, may be said to suffer from an ahistorical concentration on the work of the philosophy of religion, by drawing out the logical implications, for example, of the "absolute ontological independence" or *aseity* of God. This focus upon the logical implications of philosophical categories rather than on the historical and exegetical work on the scriptural texts, in turn explains how reflection on the doctrine of God tended to become divorced from the biblical narrative of the history of salvation.

Other recent commentators on the twentieth-century revival of interest in the doctrine of the Trinity, and specifically on Rahner's self-conscious advocacy of the need to engage with the "economy of salvation," have observed that the Western "turn" away from a primary focus on the doctrine of the Trinity cannot be attributed to Aquinas alone. The discussion needs to be broadened to include additional contributing factors. Fred Sanders, for example, has noted that the medieval church as a whole, both in the East as well as in the West, further encouraged theology to drive a wedge between the eternal being of God and the perception of God's action in the world by working with a distinction between the "essence of God" and the "energies of God." This kind of distinction then eventually became solidified in the modern period, particularly under the influence of Immanuel Kant's clear epistemological division between the *phenomenal* and the *noumenal* as a way of signaling the difference between things "as they appear to us" and things as they actually are "in themselves." As Sanders says, "Theologians in the nineteenth century presupposed that Kant had, at the very least, problematized any speculative move from the phenomenal realm to the noumenal."[9] In a sense this encouraged a mode of thought that presupposed

---

8. See Derrick Peterson's trenchant critique of this as an oversimplification in his Multnomah Biblical Seminary thesis, "Forgetfulness Which Appears as Memory."

9. Sanders, *Image of the Immanent Trinity*, 48.

a kind of barrier between the essence of things as they are "in themselves" and the way they are known through human experience—and, we might add, interpreted with conceptual linguistic tools that are always in some sense relative to a specific historical context. As a consequence, one way or another, the Christian theology of revelation had to face the challenge of finding a way of smashing through this barrier from God's side into the world of time and change.

In any event, it was by way of providing a corrective to this inherited theological problem that Rahner pointed out that in the history of salvation we see the incarnate Son relating to the Father in the Spirit. This is the "economic Trinity," or better the Trinity revealed in "the economy" or management of salvation, which he therefore contends should properly be the ground of reflection on the internal nature of God as God is in God's self, which is usually referred to as the "immanent Trinity." Insofar as it has become possible for Christians to claim in faith that, as a consequence of the life and work of Jesus Christ, humanity now enjoys the possibility of living in reconciliation and peace with God the Father, not least by sharing in his very own life through the gracious gift of his Spirit, then in giving an account of this experience it is necessary to speak in Trinitarian terms. Rahner therefore says that "it is a fact of salvation history that we know about the Trinity because the Father's Word has entered our history and has given us his Spirit." Thus, he famously declared that *"The 'economic' Trinity is the 'immanent' Trinity and the 'immanent' Trinity is the 'economic' Trinity."*[10]

Now, the perceptive reader may well have noticed already that "Rahner's Rule" is in fact exemplified in the making of a theological connection between a specifically complementarian and subordinationist doctrine of the Trinity by which it is held that the Son is "eternally subordinate" at least in a relational sense to the Father, and the outworking of this notion in historical time in the economy of salvation in the specific terms outlined in the theory of "penal substitution." The eternally obedient Son is sent into the world of space and time as a requirement of the Father in the interests of achieving the redemption of humanity. Indeed, this highly specific expression of the doctrine of salvation is not only an exemplification of Rahner's Rule; there is a sense in which Rahner's Rule has played a positive role in the development of it.

Robert Doyle as the most vocal defender of the subordinationist thinking of Australian Carillon Avenue theology, specifically as it is found in the 1999 Report of the Sydney Doctrine Commission on "The Trinity and

---

10. Rahner, *Trinity*, 22, italics added.

its bearing on the relationship of men and women," appealed to Rahner for support in contending that the perception of the obedience of the historical Jesus even unto death on the cross is of a piece with his "eternal relational submissiveness" to the Father in the internal or immanent life of the Trinity. In doing so, Doyle had no qualms in citing Rahner on the Trinity precisely in order to argue that the obedience of the incarnate Jesus, which is discerned in the economy of salvation, refers us immediately to the *eternal obedience* of the Son to the Father in the immanent life of the Trinity.

Without qualification or restriction, Doyle appears to be committed to the defense of the proposition not only that the immanent Trinity *is* quite simply the economic Trinity, but that the economic Trinity *is* the immanent Trinity. And not only that, he also seems comfortable with the view that the content of what is revealed in the life of the historical Jesus in the economy of salvation is not to be understood as something of the *divine nature* that is equally shared by Father, Son, and Spirit (as defended by the Nicene definition of the *homoousion*), but something that manifestly distinguishes the several uniquely individual identities, specifically *as* the Father and the Son, but also the Spirit, in their internal functional complementarity. This is, of course, entirely contrary to the reluctance of the early fathers to give positive content to the *hypostases* of the Trinity in terms of individually and uniquely possessed properties beyond the fundamental identifying properties of the Father's begetting of the Son, the Son's being the only begotten of the Father, and the Spirit's proceeding from the Father. Apart from these incommunicable properties relating to "origin" that are unique to the personal identities of each of the three Persons of the Trinity, orthodox Trinitarianism affirms that all other properties are equally and fully shared (the *homoousion*).

In defending belief in the "functional" or "relational" subordination of the Son to the Father in the immanent Trinity, Doyle effectively contends that we do not need Christ to reveal the nature of God, "which we already knew anyway."[11] Rather, what is in fact revealed in the economy of salvation is said to be something about the incommunicable properties of each of the individual divine Persons over and above the traditionally accepted appeal of the early church fathers to the originative properties of "begetting," "being begotten," and "proceeding" for this purpose. Although Doyle believes this is what Rahner has in mind in declaring that "the economic Trinity *is* the immanent Trinity," this application effectively of Rahner's Rule is therefore theologically problematic when measured by the norms of Christian orthodoxy. Insofar as what is revealed of the Trinity in the life, teaching, death, and resurrection of Jesus in the economy of salvation is

---

11. Doyle, "Use and abuse," section on Barth and Rahner.

defined by the *homoousion* it is the full and equal sharing of the very same divine nature by all three Persons in one unity of being, not something that is personally unique to each of the three identities.

Doyle made this view transparently clear by insisting that it is not just the *shared divine nature* that is revealed in and through the humanity of Jesus, but allegedly something about the *hypostatic* nature of the eternal Word of God in relation to *and by contrast with* the eternal Father. As with the proponents of Australian Carillon Avenue theology generally, he is a complementarian, not a Trinitarian egalitarian. Instead of Christ revealing something about the equally shared divine nature of God, what is said to be revealed therefore as Doyle would have it actually *distinguishes* the Son from the Father. Unfortunately this seriously fractures the unity of the Trinity.

This proposition is defended by Doyle in his review article entitled "Use and abuse of the fathers and the Bible," written in reply to Kevin Giles's *The Trinity and Subordinationism*. In this long article Doyle claims Rahner's support for his own subordinationist position while insisting that Kevin Giles entirely misrepresents Rahner's position: "Rahner affirms that the incarnation reveals not only something about God generally (which we already knew anyway), but particularly about the Person of the Son or the Logos, his own relative specific features within divinity." At this point Doyle cites Karl Rahner, *On Trinity* (sic), page 28. Whether this appeal to the support of Rahner's Rule is legitimate remains to be seen.

Exactly the same point was rehearsed again by Doyle in his review article of chapter 7 of my 2004 book *Reflections in Glass*. In challenging a point I had made about the divine freedom, Doyle argues that

> for divine freedom to be genuine there must be the possibility of the Father not sending the Son, but the Father being sent by the Son instead, for the Father to take flesh and die for us. Implicit in this is the possibility of a divine "no" by the Son which is accepted by the Father.[12]

Doyle's response to these hypothetical heavenly transactions is that they are "totally abhorrent," and that "the sending of the Father is roundly rejected, for example, by a long tradition stretching from Augustine, through Aquinas, to Karl Rahner." In claiming Rahner's support, Doyle makes the point that there is no possibility of the Father being the Sent One, for because he is Father he is the Sender. He says, furthermore, that "If every divine member of the Trinity could become man, become incarnate, that would 'create havoc with theology' and be against the whole sense of holy

---

12. Doyle, "Reflections in Glass, Chapter 7."

Scripture."[13] The same point is made by the Sydney Doctrine Commission in its report of 1999, section 4.5/paragraph 21, which reads:

> In fact, it was not the Father but the Son who was the incarnate Mediator, and it could not have been other. We never read, for example, that the Father obeys the Son or that the Son sends the Father, or that the Spirit creates through the Father.

Doyle also points out that Rahner's work on the Trinity also strongly insists that the Father could not die. This grounds his conviction that these roles/functions/operations of the Persons of the Trinity are not interchangeable, but eternal. "What happened in the economy," he says, "is rooted in the eternal differentiation of the three Persons."[14]

Once again, Doyle quite explicitly also repeats his argument that we are not to understand that Jesus revealed something of the Trinitarian nature of God that is equally shared by all three Trinitarian identities (in a way that is governed by the requirements of the *homoousion*). Rather, Doyle mistakenly, although very confidently, defends his interpretation of Rahner's Rule specifically in relation to this: "Rahner also affirms that the incarnation reveals not only something about God generally (some of which we already knew from the Old Testament), but particularly about the Person of the Son or the Logos."[15] Instead of revealing something of the divine nature, Jesus is said to reveal "his own relative specific features within divinity," as asserted by Rahner himself in *The Trinity*, on page 28.

In this way, Doyle specifically contends that what is said to have been revealed in the economy of salvation is the obediently submissive will that is said to be unique to the identity of the Son—which in turn implies the commanding will that is said to be unique to the identity of the Father.

By appealing to Rahner's Rule in support of this it is as though the human experience of Jesus' obedience in history simply maps on to a corresponding reality in the inner nature of the eternal divine Word that preexists the incarnation. Thus, Doyle claims quite unequivocally that "Rahner ties the obedience of the Son in the economy back into the immanent Trinity."[16]

---

13. Doyle, "Reflections in Glass, Chapter 7."
14. Doyle, "Reflections in Glass, Chapter 7."
15. Doyle, "Reflections in Glass, Chapter 7."
16. Doyle, "Use and abuse," section on Barth and Rahner. Although Doyle cites Rahner, *On Trinity*, (sic). 62–63, Rahner explicitly insists that when we speak of Jesus' "obedience to the Father, his adoration, his submission to the Father's unfathomable will" the reference is to the sense "of the sonship" of the historical Jesus and not "'metaphysical' sonship" (i.e., sonship in the eternal life of the Trinity). Clearly, Doyle has seriously misinterpreted Rahner on this important point.

This appears simply to be based on Rahner's dictum that the economic Trinity *is* the immanent Trinity in the specific sense that the obedience of the historical Jesus, humanly revealed in the economy of salvation is in effect said quite simply to be understood as being *continuous with* the obedience of the eternal Son in the inner life of the immanent Trinity. Hence, Rahner's Rule is fundamental to this understanding of things insofar as it is effectively used to prove, at least to Doyle's satisfaction, the legitimacy of belief in the "*eternal* functional subordination" of the Son to the Father.

It has to be admitted that in the process of facing up to the task of pursuing the connections which show "how the mystery of the Trinity is for us a mystery of salvation,"[17] Rahner himself unfortunately falls into some fundamental ambiguities. It is certainly the case, for example, that he tends to drift from epistemological concerns about the way in which the nature of God is humanly perceived through being revealed in salvation history to ontological statements that seem to suggest that the eternal being of God as a Trinity of Persons was actually being defined or even actualized in the events of salvation history. Certainly, Moltmann, Pannenberg, and Jenson have tended to read him in this radical kind of way. Rahner argues, for example, that in the economy of salvation, as we see the incarnate Son relating to the Father in the Spirit, we come to appreciate the individual identities and roles of each of the Persons. He points out that only the Son is incarnate in the economy of salvation, for example, not the Father nor the Spirit. Likewise, the Son alone dies upon the cross, and so on. The functional identities of Father, Son, and Spirit, become clear both in creation and in the "economy of salvation." Hence, the "economic Trinity *is* the immanent Trinity."

Rahner himself even goes on to argue that this "division of labour" amongst the Persons of the Trinity as we know them in the economy of salvation gives the lie to the standard interpretation of the traditional claim of the church fathers, not least Athanasius and Augustine, about the indivisibility of the divine acts, and hence the volitional agency of a single equally shared divine will. This unfortunately suggests that Rahner's proposals imply a multiplicity of individualized wills within the life of the Trinity, rather than a single divine will, which thinkers like Athanasius and Augustine relied upon so heavily to ensure the indivisibility of the divine action in the world—and, indeed, to argue against polytheism. For them a commitment to the indivisibility of a single divine will is essential.

---

17. Rahner, *Trinity*, 21.

Despite the fact that individual Persons are understood to be involved in specific ways in the economy of salvation, in the tradition of orthodox Christian theology the divine unity of willing has also to be expressed in the economy of salvation, otherwise we would be in danger of falling into tritheism.

As Stephen R. Holmes understands Rahner's proposals, particularly when he says that the affirmation "he is incarnate" is a claim that can be made of the Second Person of the Trinity only, not of the Father or of the Spirit," are easily susceptible of being misconstrued:

> Rahner's invitation to read the gospel histories as accounts of inner-triune relations has invited others to go further than he would in reinterpreting technical Trinitarianism. In particular, it is very tempting to read the gospel narratives as describing relations between persons who are precisely distinct "centres of consciousness and activity"; when the incarnate Son prays, "yet, not my will but yours be done" (Luke 22:42 NRSV), the assumption that the Son has a different centre of consciousness and volition from the Father is invited.[18]

This kind of misinterpretation of Rahner's original intentions in articulating his rule appears to be exemplified in Doyle's appeal to Rahner's views as a support for his own contention of the validity of belief in the "eternal relational subordination" of the Son to the Father. Instead of the nature of divinity being revealed in the economy of salvation in terms of the equally shared properties of the *homoousion*, not least including the shared property of a single divine will, Doyle tends to push Rahner in the direction of suggesting that something is revealed about the individual *hypostatic* identities of the eternal Father, Son, and Spirit. This is over and above the usual appeal to the identifying criteria of begetting, being begotten, and proceeding from the Father (precisely as the "origin" and "cause" of the other two Trinitarian identities). For example, the fact that, as Rahner observed, the Son becomes incarnate and the Father does not, may appear to suggest not just a difference of role but some kind of ontological distinction between them. Rahner himself may not have intended this, but his emphasis on the grounding of the doctrine of the Trinity in the economy of salvation is open to being exploited so as to take his thinking in that direction. The fact that the Son

---

18. Holmes, *Quest for the Trinity*, Kindle ed., loc. 223. The root problem here is that this prayer, as a prayer of the incarnate Son, is an expression of his human nature in relation to God the Father, not an expression of his divine nature.

as the eternal Word of God and not the Father becomes incarnate in the historical Jesus, and that he dies upon the cross whereas the Father does not, does not necessarily mean, however, that what is revealed in the economy of salvation is *not* the nature of divinity that is equally and fully shared by the eternal Word with the Father and the Holy Spirit. It is important to note that, when Rahner's contends on page 28 of *The Trinity* that it is not just that Jesus revealed "something which we already knew" in the economy of salvation, the "something already known" that he has in mind is explicitly identified. What is *already* known is said to be "that in general God is a person." Clearly, Jesus did not just reveal *that* in the economy of salvation! Rather, Rahner's point is that through the incarnation of his Word and the gift of the Spirit in the economy of salvation, the *Trinitarian nature of God* was initially revealed and that this was eventually formulated in terms of a "very special differentiation of persons."[19] In other words, what is revealed in the economy of salvation is not some general truth about the personal nature of divinity, but, explicitly, something that warranted the development of the threefold interpersonal communion of the church's Trinitarian belief. Rahner is in fact concerned to underline the Trinitarian importance of the role of the Word in becoming incarnate in Jesus as the only begotten Son of the Father, as distinct from the personal nature "of God generally" that might be said to have been revealed in Jesus, for this was indeed "something which we already knew."[20]

Rahner is admittedly not always easy to understand, but we may be certain that in Rahner's mind what is "already known" about the nature of God is not complemented by the additional knowledge that "the Son is subordinate to the Father," as Doyle would have us believe, but by the knowledge that God is a Trinity of Persons. Indeed, Rahner's commitment to Christian orthodoxy entails that what is revealed in the economy of salvation has to do with the equally shared divine nature of the three Persons of the Trinity in one unity of being. The suggestion that the Son might be "eternally subordinate to the Father" is not an element of Rahner's theological understanding of things.

It is already clear that the reception of Rahner's Rule has not been all plain sailing. The theological response to it has in fact been various, and certainly not always positive. Indeed, while some, like Robert Doyle have sought to extend Rahner's basic insights in what has to be said appears to be a far

19. Rahner, *Trinity*, 28.
20. Rahner, *Trinity*, 28.

more radical direction than Rahner himself may have intended, others have found the theological implications of Rahner's thesis particularly troublesome, with the result that some of his critics have actually dismissed his contentions as only superficially impressive; indeed, some have said they are actually incoherent.

It is not possible here to review the entire range of responses to Rahner's Rule. Given that others have monitored these responses and developments of Rahner's original notion over time, often with trenchant criticism, I do not plan to attempt to unpack these often challenging arguments again here.[21] However, a good deal is obviously to be learned from the last seventy-five years since the revival of interest in the doctrine of the Trinity, not least from the protracted story of responses in the wake of Rahner's articulation of his rule, that is of direct relevance to the examination specifically of the logical coherence of the penal substitutionary theory of the atonement and its legitimacy when measured both against the biblical traditions relating to the economy of salvation and its theological orthodoxy when measured against the doctrine of the Trinity. Certainly, a number of traps have surfaced from which we may usefully learn.

It has become customary to speak of this division of opinion over Rahner's Rule in terms of "radicalizers" and "restricters." Those who are now regularly referred to as "radicalizers" are said to develop Rahner's axiom by concentrating on the human perception of the Trinity in the drama of redemption (the "economic Trinity") at the expense of sustaining *any* real interest in the immanent Trinity. The complaint in general terms is that the "radicalizers" over-concentrate on the epistemology of the knowing of God in the economy of salvation in a way that minimizes any interest in the ontology of the being of God as God *is*. The list of the most notable thinkers who are said to be guilty of this theological misdemeanor includes such internationally eminent theological thinkers as Jürgen Moltmann, Wolfhart Pannenberg, Robert Jenson, and Rahner's Roman Catholic colleagues Piet Schoonenberg, Hans Küng, and Catherine Mowry LaCugna.

It is important to appreciate that though these "radicalizers" are said to push Rahner's thought beyond the original intentions of Rahner himself, as a general rule they push it in the opposite direction from that already discussed in relation to Robert Doyle. Instead of using Rahner's axiom to make radicalizing (ultimately ontological) statements about the inner relations of the immanent Trinity, they are said to be guilty of so emphasizing the revelation of the Trinity in the economy of salvation as to minimize or

---

21. Reviews of these radical developments of Rahner's axiom may already be found in Molnar, *Divine Freedom and the Doctrine of the Trinity*, and in Sanders, *Image of the Immanent Trinity*.

even to eliminate any interest in the ontology of the Being of God. In other words, the emphasis on epistemological questions relating to the perception of the Trinitarian experience of God in the economy of salvation is at the expense of any real interest in drawing conclusions about the internal life of the eternal Trinity (the "immanent Trinity").

If it is a mistake to render the immanent Trinity hostage to the human perceptions of the economy of salvation in the way exemplified by the work of Robert Doyle, then the second trap is the reverse of this. It has to do with the methodological problem of the "radicalizers" of Rahner's Rule of focusing on epistemological issues relating to the perception in faith of the economic Trinity in the history of salvation with so much single-minded enthusiasm as, in effect, to minimize or even dismiss the ontological reality of the eternal being of the immanent Trinity. In this regard, the contributions of Wolfhart Pannenberg and Catherine Mowry LaCugna to the Trinitarian discussion will suffice to illustrate something of the problems that Rahner's Rule has raised and which we might profitably seek to avoid. By attending to them, we may hopefully avoid falling into them again.

In the case of Wolfhart Pannenberg, given an overriding focus upon the revelation of God in the history of salvation and its eschatological implications that is characteristic of his systematic theology, an ontological interest in the immanent Trinity tends to disappear from view, even if inadvertently. In the case of Catherine Mowry LaCugna, by contrast, a quite deliberate methodological decision has been taken to dismiss ontological considerations relating to the immanent Trinity. In the context of her exclusive focus on "God for us" in the history of salvation this is seen as an irrelevance.

Pannenberg tacitly accepts the general principle articulated by Rahner's Rule that the theology of the immanent Trinity is not to be separated from the history of salvation, and that therefore what is known of the immanent life of the Trinity is what is revealed in the economy of salvation. Indeed, in a recent cautious reworking of his historical position,[22] he declares, "Whatever can be said about the eternal Trinity is to be found in the historical revelation of God, in the economy of salvation." However, this does not mean that it can be assumed therefore that there is a one-to-one correspondence between one and the other. Pannenberg remains uncompromising in insisting that he is equally prepared to acknowledge that "there

---

22. Pannenberg, "Divine Economy and Eternal Trinity" in 2007.

are differences between the eternal Trinity and the particularities of the history of salvation."[23]

Pannenberg helpfully points out that any knowledge of God that is derived from the divine self-revelation in the economy of salvation is subject to its eschatological fulfillment. However, this necessarily entails that what is revealed in the economy of salvation must be understood to be partial and indistinct. He accounts for this by pointing out that from a Christian perspective "our historically conditioned experience of meaning and truth remains provisional."[24] The other side of this penny is the "role of anticipation in the historical process and historical experience." An anticipatory knowledge entails that a "difference occurs as a qualification of our possession of truth and meaning." "This is true," he says, "for the life of faith, in contrast to the eschaton. In the act of faith we embrace the ultimate truth of God, but the final vindication of our faith is still to come in the eschatological vision."[25]

From a biblical point of view it is difficult to take exception to this eschatological emphasis, for which Pannenberg is famous. Though Pannenberg does not refer us to St. Paul at this point, he could profitably have done so. As St Paul says, this side of the eschaton we see as "though a glass darkly"—what is discerned of God in faith in the economy of salvation is like a somewhat indistinct reflection in an ancient polished metal mirror, "not face to face" (1 Cor 13:12). This must surely mean that what is revealed is sufficient to allow it to be discerned in faith but insufficient to rule out the possibility of greater clarity of insight to come. Indeed, it is because what is perceived in faith is subject to further fulfillment that faith is the ground of hope—and we do not hope for what is already the object of present experience, we hope for more clarity to come. In other words, what is known in faith is the ground of Christian hope, and Paul reminds us that we do not hope for what we already see, but for what is yet to be seen.[26] Pannenberg therefore reminds us that he more cautiously speaks in terms of a provisional epistemology: we must recognize "this provisional status of our knowledge of God in a history that is not yet complete."[27]

In allowing for the hope of eschatological fulfillment in this way, however, Pannenberg effectively but perhaps inadvertently puts an emphasis on what is revealed of the Trinity in the economy of salvation, but as a

23. Pannenberg, "Divine Economy and Eternal Trinity," 85.
24. Pannenberg, "Divine Economy and Eternal Trinity," 85.
25. Pannenberg, "Divine Economy and Eternal Trinity," 85.
26. Rom 8:24.
27. Pannenberg, "Divine Economy and Eternal Trinity," 85.

practical consequence very little emphasis is put on the being of God as God *is*. Given that he seems prepared to acknowledge that there is more to the transcendent Being of God than what is provisionally known of God in the economy of salvation "this side of the eschaton," his interest in this is necessarily minimized. In a sense it tends to be omitted from view by default. While on the basis of his publications through the 1990s his interpreters tended to corral him with the "radicalizers" of Rahner's Rule, there is a sense in which it might now in fairness be more appropriate to think of him as a "restricter" whose main concern is simply to qualify what is known of God in the economy of salvation by emphasizing its partial and incomplete nature. The charge of those who see him as a radicalizer is that he allows the immanent Trinity to recede into obscurity.

By contrast, Catherine LaCugna as a matter of methodological strategy quite deliberately abandons any interest in the immanent Trinity in the course of pursuing her account of "God for us" in the economy of salvation, and even suggests that to devote an interest in the being (or ontology) of the inner nature of God in the eternal Trinity is a waste of time.

Some critics therefore fear that LaCugna and others like her have unfortunately tended to leave themselves open to the charge of ending with a form of pantheism. It is as though the divine becomes a component of the natural order that is understood in terms of a kind of monism. This is seen as the inevitable concluding point of her methodological commitment of privileging epistemology (the knowledge in faith of the revelation of God in human experience), over ontology (an account of the eternal Being of God, albeit grounded in the experience of salvation). In fairness, her concluding position may perhaps be more accurately described as a kind of pan-en-theism—the belief in a God whose existence is relative to the created universe and so known *in and through it* rather than being equated with it as in classical forms of pantheism.

Somewhat ironically, LaCugna herself consciously resorted to her uncompromising commitment to pursuing an exclusively epistemological method so as to sidestep this very charge. That is to say, she was alert to the fact that Rahner's concentration on the revelation of the Trinity in the economy of salvation could lead to a kind of pantheism. Her initial contention was that in making the distinction between the immanent Trinity and the economic Trinity Rahner was not speaking ontologically but only epistemologically, for if he were speaking ontologically he would be speaking of two Trinities, two Gods.[28] She believed, on the other hand, that if his identification of the immanent Trinity with the economic Trinity (so as at least to have one Trinity!) were to be understood ontologically this really *would* amount to a kind of pantheism. The being of God would be inextricably associated with the material creation to which God was related and in which God operated. Hence, she opted for an epistemological reading of Rahner as a preferred alternative to an ontological reading.

Even so, from an epistemological perspective it has to be observed that a claimed knowledge of the presence and being of God in and through the created order and the events of human history at the expense of making an ontological claim for the eternal Being of God outside of space and time, would also appear to be in danger of falling, if not into pantheism, at least into a kind of pan-en-theism by reducing belief in God to belief in a being who is confined to the arena in which he is known. Although not identified with the created order itself (as in pantheism) such an approach suggests a God who in a sense is *only* found there.

In other words, in the course of her treatment of "God for us," LaCugna herself unfortunately appears to deny the existence of a transcendent God. In this case, as she herself says, she has moved well beyond the position espoused by Rahner: "It is on this point that we part ways with Rahner."[29] Indeed she forthrightly says, "The God conceived as a self-enclosed exclusively self-related triad of persons does not exist. . . . These are all false gods, fantasies of the imagination that has allowed itself to become detached from the rule of God's life disclosed in Jesus Christ."[30]

Perhaps her meaning is that a desired privileging of the God known in the economy of salvation might acknowledge the existence of a God "beyond" what is known, but never in a totally detached, inactive, and uninvolved kind of way separate from the created order in which that God is known. In this case her point about the importance of epistemology and the revelation of the Trinity in the economy of salvation might be accepted without necessarily suggesting the rejection of the doctrine of the immanent Trinity. However, while ever it is suggested that God is fully revealed as the God who "outstrips the human capacity to receive or explain this self-communication," then this God tends to recede from view.[31]

We can appreciate LaCugna's methodological transposition of Rahner's Rule in a purely epistemological direction, but given that God is said not

---

28. LaCugna, *God for Us*, 231.
29. LaCugna, *God for Us*, 221.
30. LaCugna, *God for Us*, 397.
31. LaCugna, *God for Us*, 217.

to be known beyond the God actually revealed in the economy of salvation, she tends to end by denying even the possibility that distinctions known in the economy of salvation may be thought to be grounded in distinctions of the inner life of God and *vice versa*. LaCugna herself, while acknowledging that Rahner did not mean to deny the immanent Trinity, nevertheless herself calls for a moratorium on ontological speculation about the nature of God as God is in God's self. It is understandable that some have expressed concern about the apparent demise of the transcendence that allows God the freedom to be God in the privacy of God's self. It is understandable that LaCugna's attempt to make God accessible and relevant to human experience has led to some alarm about the fact that the end outcome of this appears to be a kind of pantheism or at best a kind of pan-en-theism.

The alternative interpretation of Rahner's Rule offered by the "restricters" has to do with the articulation of a kind of median position between those who tend to render the immanent Trinity hostage to the economic Trinity by assuming that the ontology of the being of God is subservient to the epistemological concentration on the perception in faith of the economy of salvation, and those of Rahner's interpreters who have taken a course that tends to be dismissive of the immanent Trinity. Whether this is unwittingly and by default as in the case of Pannenberg, or quite deliberately as in the case of LaCugna, the concern is that any real interest in the immanent Trinity is removed from the theological picture.

Broadly speaking, those who are usually classified as "restricters" therefore seek to affirm the revelation of the immanent Trinity in the economy of salvation, but nevertheless express serious reservations about an overconfident identification of what is perceived to have been revealed in the economy of salvation quite simply with the immanent Trinity (as in the case of Robert Doyle), without registering some cautionary qualifications or restrictions on what is said. Among those of this general view are some of Rahner's contemporary Roman Catholic colleagues (Yves Congar, Walter Kasper, and Hans Urs von Balthasar), as well Reformed theologians, some of whom work from a Barthian perspective. These include T. F. Torrance, Paul D. Molnar, and Fred Sanders. Generally speaking, as we shall see, these thinkers are anxious to preserve an *apophatic* reserve in relation to the ontological transcendence of God that inhibits any unthinking suggestion that the limited human perception of God the Holy Trinity in the economy of salvation may quite simply be said to describe the inner being of God as God is, without some careful qualifications.

One of Rahner's early critics, his Roman Catholic colleague Yves Congar, understandably suggested that Rahner's Rule should therefore be unidirectional—the economic Trinity is a reflection of the immanent Trinity, but not *vice versa*. The immanent Trinity does not conform to the perceptions of the Trinity in the economy of salvation in a one-to-one kind of way. In other words, Congar found it necessary to argue that the human perception of the presence and activity of God in the economy of salvation must be understood as a flickering and inadequate perception of the immanent Trinity. What is perceived in faith is certainly understood to be a perception of the immanent Trinity, but for the very reason that it is a finite and human perception it is not to be thought that the immanent Trinity conforms to it. The humanly conceived conclusions that are based on the human experience of salvation in Christ must therefore be recognized to be subject to limitations. There is a sense in which Pannenberg's concluding position is very similar to this, though with an eschatological coloring.

For this reason, many of those who have responded to Rahner's Rule have, in the light of Congar's critique, subsequently found it necessary to qualify it or to place restrictions upon it. After all, if the immanent Trinity (or God as God is in God's self) were simply thought to be the economic Trinity, in the sense of being thought to conform without qualification to the human perception of God discerned in the course of the economy of salvation, this would be to fashion God in a human image by failing to acknowledge that God as God is in God's self is beyond all humanly formed images of him. The outcome would in fact be a kind of idolatry—for mental images of God can be just as troublesome as metal ones. At best the human experience of God in Christ through the gift of the Spirit points us towards the nature of the eternal being of the divine, which would be entirely unknown without it, but it is not to be imagined that God himself, as God is, salutes in obedience to humanly conceived images of him.[32]

By and large, the majority of critics of Rahner's Rule have therefore tended accept the first half of the rule, but to insist upon imposing some qualification of the second part.[33] What is claimed to be known of God in the economy of salvation may be acknowledged to constitute a legitimate claim in faith to the knowledge of God, but how God *is* does not necessarily conform only

---

32. See Congar, *I Believe in the Holy Spirit* III, 12–15.

33. This is the emerging consensus represented by the impressive work of such theologians as Stephen R. Holmes (*The Quest for the Trinity*, 2012) and effectively by Michael Bird and Scott Harrower (*Trinity without Hierarchy*, 2019).

or strictly to the human perception of him. The immanent Trinity cannot be said, quite simply and without qualification, *to be* the economic Trinity.

Fred Sanders, who regards himself as a "restricter," has constructively sought to build a bridge between the eternal relations of the divine Persons of the immanent Trinity and the perception of these relations as they are understood to have been revealed in the "economy of salvation," by appealing to the scriptural notion of the "image of God." He notes that a christological recentering of the Genesis treatment of God's creation of humans "after his own image" was part of the New Testament witness at least insofar as Christ was declared to be "the image of the invisible God" (Col 1:15). He might well also have noted that the same Letter to the Colossians appeals to this notion in a soteriological context when those who "have been raised with Christ" and who have "stripped off the old self" are said to have clothed themselves "with the new self, which is being renewed in knowledge according to the image of its creator" (Col 3:10).

Paul D. Molnar pursues an alternative strategy in order to safeguard the priority and integrity, and ultimately the eternal transcendence, of the immanent Trinity. In this case the operative concept is the notion of the "freedom of God." The significance of the divine freedom as Molnar speaks of it is that it safeguards the logical priority of the immanent Trinity in relation to what may be known of God through his saving action in history. In this way Molnar ensures that Rahner's Rule is not misused by generating a kind of reductionism that suggests that what may be known of God in the economy of salvation is somehow exhaustive and that nothing more is to be known of God—or rather, that there *is* nothing more *to be known*. In this sense God is "free" from the restraint of conformity to human perceptions of him.

Molnar appeals to the theology of Karl Barth to assert the ontological priority of the immanent Trinity as the ground of the revelatory action of God in the world. At this point Molnar holds Rahner himself responsible for radicalizing interpretations of the rule. It is not so much the radicalizing interpreters who are at fault for misconstruing it; rather, Molnar's view is that they have simply drawn out the actual logical implications of what Rahner himself has said. Rahner himself is the culprit. Indeed, Molnar is inclined to dismiss the rule by rejecting it altogether.[34]

Molnar's complaint is that, by suggesting that the immanent Trinity simply *is* the Trinity as known in the economy of salvation, Rahner is responsible for initiating an abandonment of the divine transcendence, which in turn is said to have led to a widespread historical defection from the orthodox doctrine of the Trinity. As a consequence, Molnar insists that the

---

34. Molnar, "Function of the Immanent Trinity in the Theology of Karl Barth," 367.

immanent Trinity must retain an essential priority, which he tends to equate with a divine freedom from confinement to proportions imposed by the necessarily limited perceptions of God derived from the divine self-revelation. These perceptions must be limited because they are formulated by using the only available tools of a finite language within the finite dimensions of human history. Although this is unavoidable because the self-revelation of God takes place within the finite constraints of human history, God as God *is* continues to be free to be as he chooses, and to be *for us humans* in ways that go beyond anything that has been perceived to have been so far revealed of God in the economy of salvation. Whereas Pannenberg has argued that the partial revelation of God in the economy of salvation has yet to be eschatologically fulfilled, Molnar argues conversely that the personal freedom of God entails that he may not legitimately be expected to conform to the (necessarily limited) humanly perceived perceptions of him. The immanent Trinity thus has a logical priority over humanly formed notions of the divine Being, even though these are based upon the perception of his self-revelatory action in the world.

What is of concern to the "restricters" of Rahner's Rule applies precisely to the kind of thinking of Australian Carillon Avenue theology, of which Robert Doyle has been a representative spokesperson. The "restricters" are reluctant to equate properties that are said to have been revealed in the life and death of the human Jesus (such as submissiveness) quite simply with eternal properties of the eternal Word (and the Spirit), along with a different and complementary property to the Father, without attending to some carefully formulated qualifications. The suggestion that the obediently submissive character of the historical Jesus as this may be discerned in his life and manner of dying simply maps on to the eternal Word of God so as to introduce a relationship of domination and submission into the immanent life of God is precisely what needs to be carefully scrutinized in the light of the norms of the orthodox belief in the full and equal sharing of the very same nature by all three Trinitarian identities (the *homoousion*). The second half of Rahner's Rule, that the economic Trinity quite simply *is* the immanent Trinity, should not be applied without careful qualification.

Obviously, even the best insights into the nature of God based upon the economy of salvation are necessarily subject to qualifications imposed by the finite limitations of the minds that perceive and appropriate them. While in the economy of salvation God exercises his "freedom *for* us" and our salvation, in the immanent life of God he therefore retains a necessary "freedom *from* us"[35]—God is not constrained by our image of him. Thus,

---

35. Molnar, "Function of the Immanent Trinity," 398 (my italics).

what we know of God is revealed to us through the economy of salvation, but God retains his transcendence even when revealing himself—indeed he reveals himself precisely as "wholly other" and transcendent. The ultimate mystery of God thus remains even when he makes himself known in self-revelation, for when he reveals himself he necessarily reveals himself *as* mystery. As Paul Tillich never tired of saying, "God is always beyond our images of him."

This means that Rahner's Rule has to be handled with a good deal of care. While it may readily be acknowledged that the raw material for the development of the doctrine of the Trinity must necessarily be drawn from the economy of salvation, the reverse cannot be asserted, however, without qualification: God cannot be required to conform to human perceptions of God. On the other hand, it can be accepted that the doctrine of redemption cannot be allowed to fall victim to flights of speculative thought without being grounded in, and informed by, the doctrine of the Trinity. A doctrine of the redemption wrought by God the Holy Trinity of Three Persons in One Unity of Being is bound to take on a distinctive form.

It follows that what may be learned from the Trinitarian debates of the twentieth century obviously have to be kept in mind in the course of the examination of the logical coherence of the penal substitutionary theory of the atonement. We are faced with the question of whether penal substitution may legitimately be judged to be viable in the light of a careful reading of the biblical tradition and in the light of orthodox Trinitarian belief.

If the theology of the Trinity is intimately related to the theology of redemption in the sense that a viable theology of redemption involving reconciliation and peace with God should be understood from a Trinitarian perspective, then it seems to follow that a defective or unorthodox theology of the eternal relations of the Persons of the immanent Trinity, may be expected in all likelihood to surface in the form of a problematic theology of redemption. If, as is argued in *Arius on Carillon Avenue*, a subordinationist and complementarian understanding of the nature of God is not only defective, but essentially sub-Trinitarian and even neo-Arian and ultimately heretical (i.e., to be avoided at all costs), then we should not be surprised to encounter difficulties in relation to a possibly noxious impact on the theology of redemption.

Obviously, we must necessarily seek to understand the thinking of the proponents of the penal substitutionary theory of the atonement and carefully assess the arguments that are most regularly advanced in defenses of it, specifically in the light of the orthodox doctrine of the Trinity. Right at the outset, it is not difficult to sense that a theology of salvation based on the role of the "subordinate substitute," who is held to exercise his alleged eternally subordinate and obedient willing in compliance with the commanding authority of the Father in a moral relationship of domination and submission, appears to fracture the simplicity and unity of willing of the Godhead.

It is important, however, not to preempt the serious discussion of the actual arguments that are most regularly advanced in support of the theory of penal substitution. To this end, in the following chapter, we will first turn to the genre of memoir in order to ground the discussion of penal substitutionary atonement in an account of its operation in the concrete living experience of faith—in the form of my own experience of actual encounter, and indeed of hand-to-hand engagement, with its articulation and defense by some of its most ardent proponents in Australia in the year 2000. Hopefully this account of a local Australian controversy will not only assist the cause of coming to a clearer understanding of the arguments of the proponents of the theory, and hence the judgement of their logical force or otherwise, but also inform an appreciation both of the fervor and passion with which this specific doctrine of atonement is held to be true. This will help us understand why it is that some conservative evangelicals are so firmly of the view that it is in fact the only possible explanation of atonement and thus quite essential to an authentic proclamation of the Christian gospel.

As it happened, an echo of this local Australian controversy was heard in Britain between 2003 and 2005, when some forthrightly critical and widely publicized remarks of the Baptist leader Steve Chalke, the senior minister of Oasis Church in London, triggered a passionate discussion of "penal subordination." In the expression of these sentiments Chalke was followed by Jeffrey John, the Anglican dean of St Albans at the time, who made very similar comments in a BBC Easter broadcast in 2007. This too was widely discussed.

Naturally, spirited defenses of the theory in response to the criticisms of the kind mounted by Chalke and John quickly ensued in Britain. At a symposium in London in 2005, Garry Williams mounted a spirited defense of the theory, which he published in 2007. Similarly, Steve Jeffery, Michael Ovey, and Andrew Sach came to the party with a significant book entitled *Pierced for Our Transgressions* in the same year. Meanwhile, N. T. Wright in a forthright response both to Jeffrey John and the authors of *Pierced for Our Transgressions* occupied a kind of median position: while expressing serious reservations about the way in which the theory of penal substitution is often presented, both by its critics in caricatures of what is really involved, but equally in the defenses even of many of its proponents, Wright presents his own version of a "penal" understanding of the atonement which he believes is more in keeping with the biblical traditions of the love of God and his steadfast covenant promises.

These theological disturbances of 2007 in Britain were picked up in that same year at the Synod of the Anglican Diocese of Sydney, which resolved to refer the question of the penal substitutionary atonement to its Doctrine Commission. This eventually led some three years later to the production of what is in fact a paradigm defense of penal substitution in a report of the commission that was tabled in 2010. This is heavily dependent on the presentation of Garry Williams at the London Symposium of 2005. The fundamental difficulties and shortcomings of the thinking of this report, specifically from the perspective of the biblical traditions and the orthodox belief in the Trinity of three Persons in one unity of being, will be carefully examined in chapter 3. This will form the basis of a more stringent examination in chapters 4, 5, 6, and 7 of key arguments that have been mounted both in criticism and in defense of the theory by contributors to the debate from wider afield.

To my mind, none of these attempted defenses appear to acknowledge the importance attaching to theological language relating to the transcendence of God, not to mention the essential limitations of the metaphorical nature of the New Testament atonement traditions and their problematic ability to furnish propositions that are clear and distinct enough to form the basis for the development of the theories that so often are built upon them. This makes the development of a coherent *theory* of atonement a risky undertaking right from the outset.

In the closing chapters of this book an attempt will be made to outline an alternative approach to an understanding of the reconciliation of humanity with the righteousness of God and his good purposes, with a clear consciousness of the relevance of the doctrine of the Trinity in view. Instead of speculative doctrinal *theories* that tend to focus on the way in which God may be said to have turned his hostility to sin away from those deserving of punishment through the obedience of Christ in self-offering upon the cross, this results in a less theoretical and more experiential understanding of reconciliation and atonement with God of a more incorporative and participative kind. This will be achieved by bringing the theology of the Trinity to bear upon the theology of redemption so as to avoid an exclusive concentration on the cross of Christ alone by taking account also of the resurrection and glorification of the raised Christ and the gift of the Spirit as equally essential elements in the economy of the salvation of humanity.

2

PENAL SUBSTITUTIONARY ATONEMENT

I was elected to the office of Primate of the Anglican Church of Australia on February 3, 2000, having acted in that capacity for the previous three months or so.[1] The date for the formal inauguration of this ministry was set for April 30, 2000. This act of liturgical recognition was to occur in St. Andrew's Cathedral in Sydney, given a standing convention of the National Anglican Church that this kind of event should be synchronized with a scheduled annual meeting of all Australian bishops in Sydney, which was usually also immediately preceded by a regular meeting of the Standing Committee of the Church's General Synod. This strategy was simply designed to ensure the presence of a modestly sized but appropriately representative gathering of the national Anglican community.

Even though, as a known "progressive" and as an enthusiastic supporter of the ordination of women, I was hardly a popular choice as primate from the ultraconservative theological perspective of the Anglican Diocese of Sydney, it was thus Sydney, of all places, that was put upon by the National Church to host the event. It has to be acknowledged that there may even have been a little mild resentment in the Sydney air, given that the local archbishop, Harry Goodhew, was the runner-up in the final round of the primatial voting. Goodhew carried a handicap that probably hindered

---

1. Following the retirement of the previous primate, Archbishop Keith Rayner of Melbourne, I was the next most senior metropolitan and therefore became the acting primate pending the election of a new primate. Primates of Australia are elected by an electoral committee comprised of all diocesan bishops, and an equal number of clerical and lay representatives of the National Church, who in turn will themselves have been appointed to this committee at a previous General Synod.

his election, basically because his actual retirement from ministry loomed over the horizon of the near future, too soon to make him a viable choice.[2] On the other hand, I was sixty-two and, though I had myself planned on retiring well before the statutory retiring age of seventy years, once elected, had to put this on hold for at least the next five years.

In any event, as it happened, between these two dates—election on February 3 and the formal primatial inauguration on April 30—I was approached by the editor of an Australian news magazine called *The Bulletin*, to write an article on the meaning of Easter. It was Lent so this was a perfectly appropriate topic. *The Bulletin* was at that time an enormously prestigious Australian platform for political, business, and social commentary, in format and style not unlike *The Spectator* in Britain or *Time* in the United States. It had a long and proud history behind it and could boast of a significant nationwide circulation.[3] I regarded this invitation not only as a privilege, but as a welcome opportunity to communicate some modest Christian reflection on the meaning of Easter to a wide and largely secular audience. It was not only a missiological opportunity that was too good to miss, but a pleasure to be able to break free of the straitjacket of writing for in-house church publications, and to speak to more than just the already converted. This *Bulletin* article appeared in April 2000 under the title of "The Rising of the Son."[4]

The Australian bishop and church historian Tom Frame has since questioned my perception of the missiological importance of this opportunity to communicate to the general community through the columns of a secular publication, basically because of his perception of the attendant danger of triggering unproductive public controversy.[5] Frame lumped the article together with my publication four years later of *Reflections in Glass* with this same complaint in mind. Rather than being aimed at a general and predominantly secular audience, this book was a more theologically technical in-house review of "trends and tensions within the Anglican Church" as I had perceived them in my time as primate. Even so, in this case Frame

---

2. Goodhew retired in 2001, and was succeeded by Archbishop Peter Jensen.

3. *The Bulletin* was first published in 1880. Unfortunately, it went out of publication in 2008.

4. It was in fact followed by a series of contributions to *The Bulletin* in subsequent years: "King on a Cross" on April 17, 2001; "Godfellows" on May 22, 2001; "The Ultimate Sacrifice" on April 2, 2002; "Such is Life" on April 16, 2002, and "In the Beginning" on September 3, 2002.

5. Frame, "Dynamics and Difficulties," 142–43; *Anglicans in Australia*, 4–8.

questioned its presumed purpose of "provoking debate via a commercially published book."[6]

It may readily be conceded that, in a world of theological and moral pluralism, somebody is bound to take exception to the published expression of ideas with which they happen to disagree, even if others might judge the very same ideas to be mildly innocuous. Frame, however, was of the view that the public debate of theological issues, if engaged in by a head of church, called for a prolegomena to address questions about *how* public debate should be conducted, what rubrics or constraints are imposed by high ecclesiastical office, how the mission and ministry of the church would be advanced by such debate, and whether some issues did not lend themselves to this kind of debate.[7] This catalogue of requirements might well devolve

---

6. Tom Frame, "Dynamics and Difficulties," 143. I am not convinced that *Reflections in Glass* was written simply to "provoke debate," or to "set the public agenda for the Australian Anglican Church" as the somewhat overenthusiastic publisher's blurb on the back cover had it. It was rather a retrospective attempt to identify "trends and tensions in the contemporary Anglican Church" by way of explaining them and then attempting to respond to them, thus contributing to the debate.

7. Frame, "Dynamics and Difficulties," 142–59. The same complaint is repeated almost verbatim in *Anglicans in Australia*, 4–5. It was happily not the case that the mission and ministry of the church could not successfully use the secular media, however, particularly with regard to matters relating to moral theology canvassed in *The Bulletin* and *Reflections in Glass*, even despite the often technical and scientifically subtle nature of the issues involved.

For example, "Such is Life" in *The Bulletin* on April 16, 2002 was followed by a rational and useful public discussion. The chief point of that article was the contention that, in the fourteen days or so between the fertilization of an ovum and the conception of a human individual (at implantation), the harvesting of embryonic stem cells for scientific purposes was ethically acceptable from a Christian point of view. This distinction between fertilization and conception has to be made for logical reasons: within this fourteen-day period twinning may occur, which means that only at implantation, about fourteen days after fertilization, is it logically possible to say that "a human individual has been conceived." For this reason, at this same time we are able to speak of a woman "conceiving a child."

Archbishop Peter Jensen even contributed to this debate. Although Jensen passed over the important semantic distinction between fertilization and conception, he called on scientists to look to other sources of stem cells. According to a report of Staff Writers of Labonline that was posted on March 25, 2002 under the heading "Religions Split on stem cell issue," Jensen argued: "We are against the destruction of embryonic life in order to extract stem cells, particularly when there are perfectly ethical means of extracting the necessary cells from umbilical cord blood in newborns, and from the brain and bone marrow in adults . . . . Destroying embryonic life to heal ourselves builds such a society, where the vulnerable are commodities to be used up by the powerful." (The difficulty with adult stem cells, however, is that cells "remember their age" as was demonstrated in the case of the cloned sheep "Dolly," which developed arthritis and died well before its time).

Similarly, Cardinal Theodore McCarrick of Washington was reported to have argued

into a recipe for a kind of paralysis in communication, or worse a pathetic set of excuses for dereliction of a bishop's specific duty as a leader at least to try to articulate theological truth and challenge error.[8] But Frame appeared to think that trying to engage in the public discussion of theological issues could quite easily lead to controversy with a potential negative effect. In my case, he observed that it "might hinder or debilitate the discharge of his responsibilities as head of the national Church."[9]

Whether *Reflections in Glass* was productive or unproductive as a stimulus to some self-critical Anglican debate is hard to tell without some sophisticated market research, though Frame does not hesitate to pronounce that the book was unable to help Australian Anglicans "gain a better understanding of Anglicanism or an appreciation of the critical issues members of the Church need to tackle for the sake of its mission and ministry in the twenty-first century."[10] Rather, it was alleged to have simply driven people back into the burrows of their own set positions.[11]

Even though the identification of "trends and tensions" within the life of the church, along with some attempt to contribute to their clarification, was designed to stimulate some self-critical debate amongst its believing

---

that the procedure of harvesting embryonic stem cells "beckons scientists to take on the role of God and reduce humans to mere spare parts." (Reported by Staff Writers, "Religions Split on stem cell issue.") McCarrick also seems to have been oblivious to the important fertilization/conception distinction.

On April 2, 2002, the editorial of *The Australian* newspaper, 8, picked up and commended the point about conception being a fourteen-day process following upon fertilization. However, the opposite view was expressed by Anthony Fisher, *The Bulletin*, April 30, 2002, 34. Fisher tried to defend a definition of a single "moment of fertilization/conception" (that was effectively articulated by Pope Pius IX in 1869, even before the discovery of the nature of conception as the "docking" of sperm and ovum by Edouard von Beneden in 1875). Fisher supported the contention that fertilization and conception were synonymous terms denoting a single moment in time, even to the point of arguing, in the face of the possibility of twinning in the fourteen-day period between this alleged moment and the implantation of the resulting blastocyst, by declaring "one conceived human individual can become two."

Finally, in December 2002 the Australian federal parliament passed appropriate legislation (*The Research Involving Human Embryos Act 2002*) enabling the harvesting of stem cells for medical research purposes from excess-to-need IVF embryos produced within fourteen days after fertilization.

8. I have in mind the ordination promise to "drive away all false doctrine" or to "correct and set aside teaching that is contrary to the mind of Christ."

9. Frame, *Anglicans in Australia*, 5.

10. Frame, *Anglicans in Australia*, 7. The same complaint is repeated almost verbatim in "Dynamics and Difficulties," 142–59.

11. In Frame's judgment, participants in the debate that the book prompted were led by its alleged "combative style" to withdraw "to their traditional corners" (Frame, *Anglicans in Australia*, 6–7).

members, *Reflections in Glass* was in fact a quite different exercise from the earlier journalistic attempt at communicating something of the meaning of Easter to the wider secular world via *The Bulletin*. In any event, Tom Frame is clearly of the view that this initial primatial foray into the world of journalism did not achieve anything helpful either. Rather, to his mind it already illustrated the danger of expressing theological ideas through public media outlets. Indeed, in 2006/7 when Frame published these remarks he was not engaging in some idle theoretical speculation plucked from the miasma of abstract thought, but writing from his actual retrospective experience, knowing full well that *The Bulletin* article in particular, which appeared ahead of Easter in 2000,[12] and to a less degree *Reflections in Glass* in 2004, had actually provoked an enormous amount of very lively public interest and controversy.

No sooner had "The Rising of the Son" hit the newsstands than some Sydney folk began publicly to express their disagreement with it in unmistakably hostile terms, and even to announce that they planned to boycott the primatial inauguration on April 30 because of it. In one case a Sydney Carillon Avenue theologian who happened to have been overseas, and who confessed that he had not actually read the article, declared that he would be staying away simply on the basis of what his wife had relayed to him over the telephone! Some, who had long before sent in an apology for their inability to attend on April 30 because of "other commitments," suddenly switched the excuse to the subject matter of *The Bulletin* article. Others declared that primates were hardly of crucial importance in the life of the Church anyway; a primatial inauguration was not a big deal and should not be thought of as something "not to be missed."[13]

The secular press made merry with all this furor in its reporting and even in cartoons, which generally showed little mercy in their apparent quest to give protesters a hard time. The caption of one cartoon in the *Sydney Morning Herald* read: "Aren't they supposed to be resurrecting the Church not burying it?" Another portrayed heaven with "Sydney Anglicans" divided by a wall from "The rest of the World."

---

12. "Rising of the Son," *The Bulletin*, April 25, 2000, 40–43.

13. For example, Dr. John Woodhouse, who was then rector of the Parish of St Ives in Sydney, declared on national television that the primatial inauguration "was never going to be a big event anyway." Sydney people were said not to be "much interested in primates."

The net outcome of all this was that, far from the inauguration being a modest and fairly insignificant gathering that might at best have attracted a congregation of a few hundred people, the Sydney protesters unwittingly succeeded in whipping up a Sunday afternoon congregation of something closer to a thousand people. This obviously came as a surprise to the perspiring cathedral sidesmen who were to be seen frantically hurrying in with stackable chairs to accommodate those overflowing the pews. As the procession entered the cathedral perhaps a hundred people spilled outside into the square, some carrying signs dutifully witnessing to "biblical truth" in response to garbled news reports. When we talked with them after the service, some turned out not even to be Anglicans, but card-carrying members of a fundamentalist sect from outer-suburban Sydney.

The details of the service of inauguration had been negotiated by my chaplain, Sean Mullen, with his uniquely personable skill, and with the ever-courteous help of Bruce Kaye, who, as the general secretary of the General Synod, shouldered the unenviable responsibilities of the permanent representative of the National Church in its office, which is permanently based in Sydney. But it must be said that the Sydney Cathedral authorities, archbishop Harry Goodhew himself, the dean, Boak Jobbins, precentor Lawrence Bartlett, and Mark Quarmby, the cathedral's assistant organist, were all graciously welcoming and unfailingly helpful.[14]

The former governor general of Australia, Sir Zelman Cowen, read the first lesson from Ezekiel 37 and another of my good friends, the Australia actor Jacki Weaver, read a section of the resurrection discourse from St. Paul's First Letter to the Corinthians. The Cathedral Singers, directed by Eric Petersen, combined with the choirs of the Sydney parishes of St. Mary's, Waverley, and St. Anne's, Strathfield, to make the music, and backed a splendid soprano, Christine Beasley, in the singing of an anthem: "Rejoice, the Lord is risen!," Mascagni's wonderful "Easter Hymn" from *Cavaliera Rusticana*. I preached the sermon.[15]

The band of St Mark's Anglican Community School, Australia's first low-fee, coeducational Anglican community school, had come across from Perth to play in the cathedral square before and after the service, and three indigenous Kimberley boys, Gideon Mawaljarlai, Luke Mawaljarlai, and

---

14. All of these had shaken free of the received idiosyncratic stereotype that the press labeled "Sydney Anglicans." A petition organized by the Revd. Deryck Howells of St. Matthias's Church, Centennial Park, had gathered one hundred signatures, apparently in the hope of having the event banned from the Sydney Cathedral, but Harry Goodhew, to his credit, resisted.

15. This was subsequently published in a collection of sermons, *Yellow Wallpaper*, Sermon No. 32, 251–60.

Neil Maru, whom I was helping to educate in Perth in a new Aboriginal educational initiative, blew through their primordial didgeridoos to create some appropriately mystical vibrations as the assembly processed out into the sunlight. Members of the congregation were invited to visit an exhibition of icons that had been set up across the square in the foyer of St. Andrew's House by Marice Sariola, an expatriate Finnish Lutheran deaconess and gifted icon painter, who had brought samples of her work across the country from Busselton in the south of Western Australia.

In due course the crowd moved to a gathering space in the adjacent St. Andrew's Cathedral Choir School, which had been made available through the kind hospitality of the headmaster, for a celebratory drink and the usual speeches of welcome, especially to those who had come from afar, including neighboring primates from New Guinea, Polynesia, Japan, Southeast Asia, New Zealand, and a representative of the Primate of the United States. And I think a happy time was had by all.

It all made for a reasonably worthy and suitably buoyant event that, undoubtedly, was made all the more self-consciously exuberant than it would otherwise have been through the determination of many of those present to counter all the static that had been heard in the lead-up to it from Carillon Avenue. Certainly, I personally felt very well supported.

But what exactly was it in *The Bulletin* article that had triggered all the preceding public furor? Those who monitor such things in the world of journalism reported that, in the wake of "The Rising of the Son," over three hundred separate press articles, cartoons and comments, including significant numbers of letters to the editor had appeared in media outlets scattered across the nation. I was not able to read more than a portion of these, but a substantial wad of collected press cuttings, plus about fifty letters of protest that had come directly to me, confirmed something that I had already discerned in the ten days or so before the inauguration.

Somehow, the chief focus of public debate had quickly come to center on the uniqueness of Christ in the context of the competitive diversity of the religions of the world. This was something of puzzle, for in "The Rising of the Son" the chief point was to suggest that Easter could be understood as "the event of concrete forgiveness," following some insights of the Belgian Jesuit Edward Schillebeeckx. In the course of this article I made the point that the experience of forgiveness is most poignantly felt precisely when forgiveness is concretely received from one's very own victims. We can appreciate the significance of the fact that in the early Easter proclamation that is reported in the first couple of chapters of the Acts of the Apostles, the crucified and raised Jesus is said to have returned victoriously from the grave, not condemningly and vindictively, but with the proffer of forgiveness even *to the very ones who had crucified him*. Thus, the early Christian proclamation was: "God has made . . . this Jesus, *whom you crucified*, Lord and Christ" (Acts 2:36). In making this point, I drew attention to the fact that, when Luke, the author of Acts, wrote that "only through Jesus can you be saved" (Acts 4:12), he was not just saying that only through Jesus among the religious leaders of the world can you be saved, but also that only through Jesus "your very own victim" can you be saved. The article then went on to say that, likewise, we all know something of the concrete impact of this divinely poignant forgiveness when those whom we tend to victimize, whether intentionally or unwittingly, forgive us. Furthermore, we ourselves make people our victims, or victimize people, not just when we are perpetrators of some kind of insult or violence at their expense, but when we put them down for whatever reason, write them off, or dismiss them as just "plain fools." And that is also why, when we ask for God's forgiveness of our sins in the Lord's Prayer, we are careful to add the words "as we forgive those who sin against us." Only so will those who victimize us know something of the divine forgiveness in human reconciliation and peace.

In other words, the point of *The Bulletin* article was that Luke was not *just* saying in Acts that only through Jesus as a religious leader can humanity be saved from its wretched divisions, but also something about the meaning of Easter as the return of Jesus from the grave with the proffer of forgiveness even for those who had crucified him, and about the possibility of our receiving of forgiveness, not just in an entirely abstract sense detached from our own actual experience, but in a concrete sense, from those whom we victimize.

I soon discovered, however, in the week prior to the primatial inauguration that *The Bulletin* text was regularly being quoted with the crucial word "just" missing. My alleged statement then became the bald declaration that the New Testament "did not (. . .) say that salvation came only through Jesus." This obviously implied a questioning of the uniqueness of Jesus amongst the religious leaders of the world. In this way the article was given a meaning that was seriously at variance with that of the original text.

When I eventually tracked down the source of this misrepresentation, I found to my astonishment that it had apparently been perceived by Anglican Media Sydney that many church people were tuning into the public controversy but had not actually seen *The Bulletin*, which was in fact a sell-out. It was therefore decided that "The Rising of the Son" should helpfully be reproduced on its own diocesan website. All this was well-intentioned, but done without permission either from me or the editor of *The Bulletin*, and thus with breathtaking disregard for copyright law. Unfortunately, just to compound this indiscretion, Jeremy Halcrow, a staffer of Anglican Media Sydney, had edited the article and, in seeking to shorten it a little, had inadvertently omitted the crucial word "just" in the process. When I protested this disaster to Margaret Rodgers, who directed Anglican Media Sydney and whom I counted as a good friend, she became very defensive of "her staff" but at least immediately agreed to correct the website text, with a footnote explaining that the word "just" had unfortunately been omitted in the first posting. Eventually she wrote to the National Meeting of Bishops to apologize. It was an "honest mistake." But the damage had been done.

It was clear that, because the major proportion of those who registered negative reactions and protests in the press and in correspondence directly to me[16] were in fact responding not to *The Bulletin* article itself but to a corrupted and misleading text,[17] the debate had thus come to center on the question of the uniqueness of Jesus in the context of the religions of the world, rather than on the nature of forgiveness, especially when it is received from one's very own victims. This certainly illustrates Tom Frame's point about how easy it is for unproductive controversy to be whipped up in relation to passionately held religious beliefs. Whether this can be elevated into an excuse for not trying to communicate at all through the secular media outlets of the world is, of course, another matter. On the other hand, even if Jeremy Halcrow's mistake was not intentional, it was understandable; it demonstrated how easy it is for people to jump to conclusions that inadvertently project their own religious perceptions on to somebody else. This was a good example of the unwitting and nonchalant pitfall of misquoting statements so as to fit them to a preconceived outcome that may have been assimilated by osmosis from the cultural and intellectual environment. In this case it seemed to have been incorrectly assumed that I was the kind of Christian who did not believe in the uniqueness of Jesus.

Meanwhile, I was a little bemused to find that I was being supported and complimented in the secular media for not making exclusivist Christian claims, and for admitting that there were "other paths to heaven"! Even though that may well be so, for we cannot presume to preempt the judgments

---

16. The great majority of which came from postal addresses in Sydney.

17. Including Archbishop Harry Goodhew himself, who was coaxed by the media to register his disagreement with what I was alleged to have said, not knowing that he had been misled into responding to a corrupted text produced by his own media staff. I also received about fifty letters from Sydney addresses expressing dissent in very hostile, and indeed sometimes abusive terms, on the basis of what they had read on the website of Anglican Media Sydney.

that rightly belong to God alone, I myself would be more comfortable to affirm the more obvious truth of St. John's Gospel that we can only come *to the Father* via Jesus *the Son*, the One who uniquely called God "Father" in a way that has certainly become uniquely characteristic of Christianity.[18]

However, it has to be acknowledged that very negative and hostile reactions to "The Rising of the Son" were in fact being registered long before the development of this frenzied focus on the uniqueness of Jesus in the context of the religions of the world. Exactly what the furor was initially all about remained something of a mystery, until the reverend Phillip Jensen of the Parish of St. Matthias, Centennial Park in Sydney, spilled the beans.[19] Jensen posted a response to "The Rising of the Son" on the website of his church in which he declared that the root cause of the article's alleged shortcomings was its omission of explicit adherence to the substitutionary theory of the atonement—the view, particularly characteristic of federal theology, that the payment of a penalty (death) for sin and rebellion against God was borne by the sinlessly innocent Jesus, acting voluntarily as a substitute for the sinful descendants of Adam, thereby making it possible for them to be reconciled to God. Jesus may therefore be said to be our Savior because he quite literally died as a substitute for sinful humanity, for, though himself sinless and entirely undeserving of punishment, he accepted punishment *in the place* those who really deserved to be punished. This is usually said to have achieved a double effect. First, it is said to satisfy the demands of retributive or "deserved" justice (for it is said that the sins of humanity could not just be overlooked by a righteous God, as though with a shrug of the shoulders they were of no consequence: somebody had to pay the penalty for them). And, second, it is said at the same time to act as a salve to neutralize the "wrath of God," who, being righteous, must necessarily display his abhorrence and condemnation of sinful disobedience by "hating the sin while loving the sinner."

Although *The Bulletin* article certainly did not refer to this particular theory of the atonement, Phillip Jensen rightly guessed that it is a theory that has very little appeal to me.[20] I would certainly not have dreamed of

---

18. John 14:6

19. Phillip Jensen is the brother of the Sydney Archbishop Peter Jensen. His very lively parish of St. Matthias, Centennial Park at the time seemed to become an epicenter of outrage over "The Rising of the Son."

20. In fact, I had publicly questioned the theological viability of the penal substitution theory of the atonement in a brief article which was published in the Perth *Anglican Messenger* in March 1991, under the title "Theory of the Atonement Makes God

commending it to the general public, let alone try to persuade people into believing it. Given the obvious morally dubious principle expressed in it, that a righteous and loving God would impose a harsh punishment on his innocent Son for the crimes of others just to satisfy his own righteous anger or to meet the alleged contractual demands of a kind of justice that he was himself responsible for establishing, it is surely a big ask. After all, by setting himself at sufficient epistemic distance to allow human creatures the cognitive freedom either to respond to him in genuinely uncompelled love, or not to acknowledge his sovereign presence at all, God was the creator of a world in which self-centered, all-too-human disregard of his sovereign creative presence was always likely to be a factor from the outset. Nevertheless, even if Phillip Jensen judged that I was not a proponent of the penal substitutionary theory of the atonement, he was not just guessing when he lamented that there was no mention of it in "The Rising of the Son." This was a fact.

At first sight it might seem somewhat odd that issue might be taken over the content of a press article, not so much because of what it actually said, but on the basis of what it did *not* say. After all, it is never possible to say everything that could be said. One has necessarily to be selective, particularly in a brief press article. The absence of some reference to a single specific theory of the atonement seems fairly innocuous, furthermore, when we remember that the Christian church has never defined any particular theory of the atonement as a required dogma, and that when the first Christians sought to express something of their experience of the felt meaning of the death and resurrection of Christ, they clearly had recourse to a variety of descriptive metaphors. The New Testament record shows that, in order to express just something of the meaning of the surpassing mystery of the cross and of the experience of reconciliation and peace with God that was believed to have been initiated by the crucified and vindicated Jesus, the first Christians had recourse to a variety of images.[21] Whether these metaphorical images are amenable to development into a systematized "theory of the atonement" is a good question.

Curiously, the theory that a penalty had been paid for human sinfulness may in fact be amongst the least compelling of them, for this theory

---

Look Cruel." This triggered a lively debate of this topic in Perth through the second half of that year. My stance in relation to the issue was already well known across Australia by the year 2000.

21. For example: the payment of a penalty, release from prison, freedom from capture by the paying of a ransom, being bought and released from slavery, the making of satisfaction by propitiatory sacrifice, victory in battle.

raises a number of questions. For a start, whether someone else can make atonement as a substitute for the sins of another may be problematic; one who suffers instead of me for my crime, may pay a penalty in some substitutionary sense, and "get me off the hook," but that does not free me from guilt. Furthermore, the payment of a penalty by another is in principle called into question both in Jeremiah 31:29–30, and Ezekiel 18, where it is held that no one can be judged to be guilty and to suffer the penalty for the sins of another (explicitly the sins of parents or their children). As a consequence of this kind of questioning, not to mention the disturbing imagery of an apparently cruel, vindictively "punishing God" that is often said to be implicit in it, the "penal substitution theory" has understandably diminished in its popularity in many quarters of the Christian church, very noticeably so over recent years.

Moreover, other New Testament atonement possibilities are more easily identified: the first believers declared that Jesus had died vicariously, *for the benefit* of others—"for us" (Rom 5:8), or for "the ungodly" (Rom 5:6), "for a weak brother" (1 Cor 8:11), or "for all" (2 Cor 5:14). It was as though they had been "bought" as slaves might be commercially bought or redeemed and released from their slavery, the release of Israel from slavery in Egypt being a model (Exod 6:6–8, 13). Or it was as though they had been released from bondage to sin as from a kind of imprisonment, for a ransom had been paid to secure the release "of many" from the hands of an enemy (Mark 10:45).[22] Alternatively, a victory had been won over the "principalities and powers" of evil by the *Christus Victor* (Col 2:15).

Perhaps most importantly, the author of the Epistle to the Hebrews, in the most extended New Testament treatment of the theme of the reconciliation with God that was understood to have been won by the death and resurrection of Jesus, argued very forcefully that the ancient religious practice of imagining that an alienated God could be placated or propitiated by the offering of animal sacrifices had been replaced and fulfilled by the once-and-for-all self-sacrifice of Christ.

However, from the perspective of Hebrews, the cross and resurrection are viewed as a composite whole, so that reconciliation with God is not made to depend upon the cross alone (sometimes referred to as *crucicentrism*).[23]

---

22. Like the penal substitution theory, the ransom theory also raises some troublesome questions: if a ransom has been paid in return for the release of prisoners, the question is, to whom is a ransom paid for the sins of the world, and if it was paid to the devil, why could not God have dealt directly with the devil by giving him his just deserts and sending him packing?

23. This is sometimes the focus of criticisms of the penal substitution theory that are leveled by theologians of the Eastern Orthodox tradition. For example, see Lossky,

Rather, as the victim of those who manhandled him, Jesus was uniquely equipped to do what no other human being could do, given that he was not only entirely innocent, but understood to be without sin, and was thus able, in offering himself even unto death on the cross, to make a *perfect* self-offering. Also, as the raised and exalted one, whom God vindicated by resurrection from the dead, he could make an offering of perfect worship, no longer as victim on the cross in historical time, but as the raised and exalted "great high priest" for all eternity (Heb 7:25).

If it was not Paul himself, then it was an author in the Pauline tradition who already expressed essentially the same idea in Ephesians 5:2 and also in Colossians 3:1–4.[24] Then, developing a metaphor that was foreshadowed in the form of a contracted formula by Paul in Romans 8:34, the author of Hebrews portrays Jesus both as the perfect victim, who is vindicated by God, and also as the great high priest who "passed through the heavens" (Heb 4:14) and entered the holy of holies to sit at the right hand of God, forever to intercede on behalf of all humanity, and to make good their sporadic and inadequately feeble offerings of worship to God.

The author of Hebrews then proceeds to affirm that, as a result of this pioneering achievement of the crucified, raised, and exalted Jesus, people of faith are set on "a new and living way" through "the veil of his own body" (Heb 10:20) and transported to sit with him in reconciled communion in the nearer presence of God, an image that is also found in Ephesians, Colossians, Romans, and elsewhere in the New Testament, with Psalm 110:1 in the background.[25] It is understandable that the later Gospels also preserved a tradition that the veil of the temple in Jerusalem through which the high priest entered into the holy of holies to effect reconciliation with God[26] had been torn apart at the time of Jesus' crucifixion.[27] The understanding of

---

"Redemption and Deification," 99: "The final goal of our union with God is, if not excluded altogether, at least shut out from our sight by the stern vault of a theological conception built on the ideals of original guilt and its reparation. The price of our redemption having been paid in the death of Christ, the resurrection and ascension are only a glorious happy end of his work, a kind of apotheosis without direct relationship to our human destiny. This redemptorist theology, placing all the emphasis on the passion, seems to take no interest in the triumph of Christ over death. The very work of the Christ-Redeemer, to which this theology is confined, seems to be truncated, impoverished, reduced to a change of the divine attitude toward fallen men, unrelated to the nature of humanity."

24. The Pauline authorship of Ephesians is sometimes disputed.

25. See Eph 1:20, 2:6, 5:2; Col 3:1–4; Rom 8:34; 1 Pet 3:22; Acts 2:33, and Matt 22:44.

26. By sprinkling the blood of the sacrificial victim on the mercy seat, the golden lid of the ark over which the *shekinah* of God's presence hovered.

27. Matt 27:51.

atonement won by Christ by placing it in the general context of the cult of the Jewish temple is thus well grounded across various books of the New Testament.

In any event, given the rich diversity of this metaphorical language and imagery, one might be forgiven for thinking that the lack of a specific reference to the substitutionary payment of a penalty and its rationale specifically in a presupposed juridical context can hardly be thought to be scandalously reprehensible. It seems that some kind of hidden agenda appears to have been operating in the minds of those who felt this lack so strongly as to be propelled into an orchestrated display of public hostility and protest, even to the point of foot-stomping refusals to attend a primatial inauguration. In order to understand the obvious emotional depth of this reaction we have to try to stand in their shoes.

The fact that the omission of any reference to the penal substitution theory of the atonement in a press article could be viewed with such strongly felt disapproval may be explained, to a very considerable extent, by the fact that in some evangelical circles this particular theory of the atonement is thought to be a quite *necessary* requirement of faith. In other words, the gospel of Jesus Christ is not good news without it. In fact, in some evangelical circles this confessional belief appears to have been elevated almost to the status of a required dogma, even though there has never been an ecumenically agreed and authorized dogmatic definition of the atonement in the entire history of the Christian church. The early ecumenical councils of the church spelled out the basic requirements of belief in relation to the incarnation and divinity of Christ, and then followed this up by producing an authorized and precise formulation of the doctrine of the Trinity. However, the church has resisted the temptation to pronounce on exactly how Christ's death on the cross accomplished reconciliation with God. It has simply been content to work with the rich diversity of the New Testament's metaphorical language and imagery.[28]

---

28. Thus, John McIntyre cautioned that: "Anyone approaching the study of the death of Christ, and seeking for a definitive understanding of the classical words of St Paul (1 Cor 15:3), 'Christ died for our sins in accordance with the scriptures', encounters an immediate stumbling block." McIntyre noted that the manner in which the death of Christ, particularly in relation to the forgiveness of sins, is referred to in the credal and latter confessional statements of the church "is singularly frugal, very varied, and nowhere approaches the sophistication which the doctrines of God and of the Person of Christ achieve at the hands both of the orthodox and heretical expositors." See McIntyre, *Shape of Soteriology*, 1.

Nevertheless, for some evangelical Christians, and certainly for many in Australia whose thinking is formed on Carillon Avenue, this has become a nonnegotiable item of faith and piety. For them, Christ's payment of the penalty for human sin is not just the *preferred* way of understanding and explaining the alleged reasons behind God's provision of the remedy for Adam's disobedience; it is central and necessary.

This elevation of the penal substitution theory of the atonement to the status of a required belief may be illustrated anecdotally from a very irate letter dated November 14, 1991, that I recently came across as I sorted through collected papers in an old file marked "The Atonement." It had come from one of my former clergy of the Diocese of Perth, who had written in the wake of some concerns about the inadequacy of the penal substitution of Christ that I had published in the Perth diocesan monthly newspaper of March of that year.[29] At the time we were embarking upon a "Decade of Evangelism" in which members of the church were being encouraged to communicate the essentials of their faith as intentionally, and with as much enthusiasm, as possible. The issue of whether the penal substitution theory of the atonement was more of a hindrance than a help to our mission therefore put this doctrine under some scrutiny. In this letter, my correspondent of 11/14/1991 included a draft "Open Letter to the Archbishop of Perth" that he said he intended to publish, in which he insisted on his own authority to teach what "years of study of God's word" had taught him. He remonstrated that, because the penal substitutionary explanation of the atonement "lies at the very heart of the gospel," he had "no alternative" than to "go on preaching the doctrine which above every other lies at the heart of so many Christians' love for God." Moreover, he insisted that the New Testament doctrine that Jesus "was offered (by God) once and for all to bear the sins of many, annulling sin by the sacrifice of himself (Hebrews 9.26–28)" *had* to be understood in penal and substitutionary terms because "God has chosen to deal with us in a framework of legal justice."[30]

---

29. This was "Theory of the Atonement makes God look cruel," *Perth Anglican Messenger*, March 1991, 12, in which I had in fact pointed out that a visiting evangelist to Perth who had recently addressed a group of tertiary students on "why Jesus was their Saviour" made it all sound as though "God the Father should be charged with child abuse."

30. Very predictably, T. C. Hammond provides a clear precedent for this view. In a way that is characteristic of federal theology's treatment of the exercise of God's grace from the perspective of justice and legal principle, he was quite adamant that the in use of the Latin word "*justificare*" "we are moving in the region of law and justice" . . .

It is important, however, to make it clear that this is not just a passing perception of Australian Carillon Avenue theology based on anecdotal experience. Archbishop Peter Jensen in an address to an Anglican Evangelical Conference in Britain, which was published by Anglican Media Sydney on January 30, 2003, declared, "Whatever else we may and must say about the cross of Christ, for evangelicals the central feature of its effective power lies in the sin-bearing penal substitution of the Saviour." Likewise, at the National Evangelical Anglican Congress in September of that same year he reiterated this declaration: "The doctrine of penal substitution is inherent to evangelical religion; it is part of the logic of it. That is why in days gone by, evangelicals have been in the forefront of the fight to preserve it. And that is why it is at the very center of evangelical piety."[31] As the central feature of what must be said about the cross, it is clearly not to be taken lightly by conservative evangelical Christianity; still less, when something is said publicly about the meaning of Christ's death and resurrection, can its omission simply to be overlooked. The same centrality was affirmed by Jensen's brother, Phillip, in an article in definition of the evangelical Christian: "The centrality of the saving work of Jesus in the Gospel that we preach means that our identification is as Evangelicals rather than as Catholic, Orthodox or Charismatic."[32]

From this self-consciously conservative evangelical point of view it is perfectly understandable that to talk about the forgiveness of God, and the experience of concrete forgiveness when it is proffered by one's very own victim, is unacceptable without *first* talking of the penal substitution of Christ. We should not be surprised to find specific examples of theologians of this same persuasion who have actually ventured to argue for the "primary controlling status" of penal substitution in the context of all other New Testament metaphors for expressing the Christian experience of reconciliation and atonement with God. In other words, it is explicitly contended that, while the rich plurality of atonement images and New Testament metaphors may be acknowledged, it is nonetheless the case that the penal substitution theory in particular provides a basic interpretive framework of a juridical kind that warrants it being accorded a "primary controlling status." Without

---

"we can go further and assert that it is redolent of the law courts" (*New Creation*, 67). "We must therefore find a place for law in the very heart of God" . . . "a man is declared righteous before the tribunal of God" (69).

31. Jensen, "Good News of God's Wrath."

32. Jensen, "Defining the Evangelical" (2008).

this overriding and controlling juridical framework, the other models and metaphors are said to be inadequate.

The British evangelical Steve Jeffery, for example, has maintained that other models and metaphors of the atonement only make sense if penal substitution is first affirmed,[33] for it is central and essential to the affirmation of Christ's victory over evil powers, and to his achieving of reconciliation between sinners and God. There would be no liberation from captivity to sin and Satan through recourse to the models of redemption or ransom, for example, without it. This means that, far from being peripheral to a theology of human reconciliation with God, this specific approach, based upon juridical values and legal principles, must be regarded as central, with other alternatives avenues of approach being said to be dependent upon it. The same line of argument has been pursued by Roger Nicole, who argued that the "penal substitution of Christ is the vital centre of the atonement, the linchpin without which everything else loses its foundation."[34] Likewise, James Packer, in "What Did the Cross Achieve?," was anxious to affirm that we must not focus exclusively on penal substitution, for we must not define atonement in single-category terms.[35] However, even while making a place for other models for understanding the human achievement of reconciliation with God, he nevertheless argues that penal substitution is the foundational category: "It is evident that this category explains all the others."[36]

Without wanting to produce a catalogue of essentially the same views, it is pertinent to note, as a final instance of this, that, in his address at the opening of a London Symposium on the atonement in July 2005, David Hilborn echoed this approach of Packer. Hilborn argued that, though historically "atonement has been explained by various theories drawn from a wide range of biblical imagery, and Evangelicals have characteristically acknowledged that orthodox understanding of it depends on a combination of such theories, rather than on any one in isolation. . . . Yet . . . amidst these and other theories penal substitution has long been regarded as the 'controlling model' within mainline evangelicalism—the *sine qua non* of our soteriology."[37]

Insofar as it is assumed that this particular doctrine of God's redemptive grace must be worked out on the basis of a prior commitment to the consideration of juridical values and legal principles of the kind said to

33. Jeffery, Ovey, and Sach, *Pierced for Our Transgressions*, 211.
34. Nicole, "Postscript on Penal Substitution," 451.
35. Packer, "What Did the Cross Achieve?," 112.
36. Packer, "Atonement in the Life of the Christian," 416.
37. Hilborn, "Atonement, Evangelism and the Evangelical Alliance," 4.

govern the payment of a penalty in order to rectify the broken contractual arrangement first made between God and Adam, it is difficult not to hear a persisting echo of the methodology of federal theology in this insistence on this basic significance of penal substitution as the controlling model for the theology of reconciliation and atonement.

This theological dynamic is amply illustrated in the work of T. C. Hammond, particularly in *The New Creation*, which he published in 1953. In outlining his theology of human redemption T. C. Hammond naturally laid an important emphasis on the objective achievement of the work of Christ. He accepts that justification before God cannot be won by human works, for no matter how sincerely pious or dedicated the motivation behind them, such works remain inherently defective. Even with the best of intentions sinners remain imperfect; by their own efforts they are incapable of shaking entirely free of natural selfish desires and self-interest and are therefore said to be deserving of punishment. Christ alone is the Savior of sinful humanity through the perfect obedience of his self-offering, whereby the punishment justly deserved by others is said to be borne by him *in their stead*.

Faith in Hammond's view is in turn the gift of God to those who are moved by the Spirit to throw in their lot with Christ by appropriating what he has done in their behalf—or more accurately what he has done "in their stead." What humans cannot achieve themselves, Christ achieves for them by the perfect offering of the shedding of his own blood on the cross. In this way Hammond believed that "God found a means of reconciling His justice and His mercy, honouring His law and ransoming the sinner."[38]

By contrast with this emphasis on the objective achievement of Christ, Hammond is persistently critical of what he speaks of as "liberal" and "modernist" approaches to the understanding of Christian faith, which he characterizes as falling into the error of seeing Christ purely as an ideal to be imitated. In this case, he declares that nothing objective is achieved by Christ apart from providing the ideal for others to emulate. Therefore, he argues, without penal substitution this approach to the significance of Christ is inadequate. "Regretfully, we have to say that it transforms Christ into an ideal Example and adds little except the historic content of His great life to the conception of the idealists."[39]

This is roundly condemned as a form of Pelagianism. "The Pelagian conception," Hammond says, "is that we attain justification by imitating

---

38. Hammond, *New Creation*, 78.

39. Hammond, *New Creation*, 72. He has in mind F. H. Bradley and T. H. Green.

the life of our Lord, just as we fall into sin by imitating the life example of Adam."[40] He regrets that modern theologians have been affected by this kind of presentation "but in so far as it lays aside any reference to the atoning work of our Lord and depends on an inherent ideal . . . it must be classed as a modern form of Pelagianism."[41]

When it comes to explaining just how the sacrifice of Christ's self-offering has its atoning effect, Hammond naturally goes to Paul's references to justification. This term is said to be understood notably by reference to what Paul says in Galatians 3 and Romans 3 and 5: "justification" is a matter of being accounted or declared righteous by God by virtue of the payment of the required penalty through Christ's sacrifice. However, whether this is to be understood as the production of some change of attitude on the part of God (a form of propitiation), or the blotting out of sin (more properly expiation), or merely as effecting some kind of cleansing[42] has been a matter of sustained theological speculation. This is because the precise meaning of the key Greek word (*hilasterion*) in Romans 3:24, which is usually translated as "propitiation" but sometimes "expiation," is very difficult to pin down. It is a word, unfortunately, that is used very rarely in ancient writing, possibly owing to the fact that it was only really needed when Christians like Paul had to grasp for words as they faced the challenge of explaining the mystery of the cross.

Where *hilasterion* is used elsewhere in Scripture it is found only in the Septuagint (e.g., Exod 25:16–22) and in the Epistle to the Hebrews 9:5, where its literal meaning as a neuter noun is "lid of the arc," the golden mercy seat physically located in the inner sanctuary of the temple, symbolic of the divine presence. To this the high priest went as part of the ritual of the Day of Atonement to sprinkle the blood of the sacrificed victim as a symbol of the offering of its life so as to achieve reconciliation with God. In this case, the atoning effect of the sacrifice of Christ is somewhat obliquely referenced by Paul in Romans 3:24, speaking apparently metaphorically of Christ, using the image of the mercy seat—a material object. For this reason this is often thought to be somewhat awkward, and does not really explain how the sacrifice of Christ actually had its effect.

There is a possible alternative suggestion that the clue is found not in *hilasterion* but in *hilasterios*, an adjective meaning "propitiatory" as in "propitiatory sacrifice," but used with the force of a noun meaning "that which

---

40. Hammond, *New Creation*, 71.
41. Hammond, *New Creation*, 71.
42. The suggestion of Kirk, *Commentary on the Epistle to the Romans*, 65–66.

propitiates" or "one who propitiates." In this case Paul's meaning is that God has set forth Christ as "a propitiator."

In any event, just how Christ *is* the propitiator remains unclear until, in Hammond's case, this discussion is placed in the context, not of the temple and its cult of sacrificial offerings, but in the entirely different forensic context of the administration of justice and the application of legal principle—what he speaks of as "the tribunal of God."[43]

An invitation to a forensic explanation of propitiation is provided by Paul's constant use of forensic language in relation to justification. For example, the concept of justification itself is taken from the procedures of a court of law in which a person is acquitted by being pronounced "not guilty" or, in other words, as "having been justified." The argument is that because of Christ's perfect obedience through to his self-offering on the cross, it is not just that Christ was himself "accounted righteous" but that in him as representative head all humanity was "accounted righteous" or "justified" on condition that they appropriated it to themselves by faith.

When read through the forensic lens of Hammond's inherited federal theology this leads to the full-blown theory of propitiation won by Christ, explained in terms of the penal substitution theory of the atonement. Because Adam is said to have entered into contractual obligations with God "on condition of obedience" as the federal or contractual head of all humanity, all humanity became implicated when he defaulted. Similarly, Christ dies as the substitute for all humanity by paying the penalty, not just for Adam's disobedience but for the disobedience of all for whom Adam acted as their representative or federal head. He is, as Hammond says a number of times, the federal head of the new humanity.[44]

It has to be acknowledged, however, that an entirely contrary case has been put forth by very eminent theologians and New Testament scholars. Colin Gunton, in a pioneering and magisterial study of the diverse images and metaphors of the atonement in the New Testament, concluded that the penal substitution theory could not be elevated to a position of superiority over the rest.[45] James Dunn likewise concluded that because such a variety of metaphors is employed in the New Testament to explain the reconciling

---

43. Hammond, *New Creation*, 69.

44. Hammond, *In Understanding Be Men*, 79, 84, 97, 116. A more detailed account of Hammond's "federal theology" and its historical origins may be found in the companion volume to this, *Arius on Carillon Avenue*, chapter 2.

45. Gunton, *Actuality of Atonement*, 160–67.

significance of Jesus' death and resurrection, "It would be unwise, . . . to make any one of these images normative and to fit all the rest into it."[46] On the other hand, Dunn is of the view that *if* there is a preeminent model amongst the others in the New Testament, it is the more remarkably prominent metaphor of cultic sacrifice,[47] which is not only a feature of the Epistle to the Hebrews, but also of the theology of Paul. Dunn argues, "One of the most powerful images used by Paul to explicate the significance of Christ's death is that of the cultic sacrifice, or more precisely the 'sin offering' which could be offered up by individuals or groups in the Jerusalem temple (*Leviticus* 4) and the annual Day of Atonement sacrifices (*Leviticus* 16:11–19)."[48]

N. T. Wright has also maintained that one of the main reasons for rejecting the proposal of the primary controlling status of penal substitution is the fact of the fundamental logical incompatibility of the various New Testament images of atonement. Wright correctly observes that the proposition that the penal substitution and sacrificial images could be seen to be somehow logically connected and interdependent has to face the reality that juridical and cultic language are actually wholly different. He is personally prepared to acknowledge that in Isaiah 53 the notion of sacrifice is present alongside language that may be interpreted in substitutionary terms, but it is a mistake to coalesce them into a single univocal discourse, because the sacrificial imagery is significantly different from the juridical and equally powerful.[49] On the other hand, in *Jesus and the Victory of God*, Wright suggested "that we give priority—a priority among equals, perhaps, but still a priority—to those Pauline expressions of the crucifixion of Jesus which describes it as the decisive victory over the . . . principalities and powers. Nothing in the many other expressions of the meaning of the cross is lost if we put this in the centre."[50] Understandably, in a review of Wright's *Evil and the Justice of God*, D. A. Carson therefore observed that Wright has effectively elevated the Christus Victor model to a "controlling status."[51]

---

46. Dunn, *Theology of the Apostle Paul*, 231.

47. Dunn, *Theology of the Apostle Paul*, 166.

48. Dunn, *Theology of the Apostle Paul*, 212. Dunn sets out his reasons for believing that Paul's sacrificial atonement metaphors should be understood as distinct from others in an extended discussion.

49. Wright, "Cross and the Caricatures": "Part of the problem, of course, is that Paul never says the same thing twice when discussing the cross. The cross plays a thousand different (though interlocking) roles within his various arguments. Taking these references effectively out of their exegetical contexts and making them speak within a different context, a different line of thought."

50. Wright, *Jesus and the Victory of God*, 47.

51. Carson, "Review of *Evil and the Justice of God*," para. 13.

In the thought of Gunton, Dunn, and Wright we have a carefully considered and powerful convergence of views that should at least cause us to hesitate before uncritically accepting the proposition that the penal substitution theory *must* be accorded a kind of privileged status amongst the variety of New Testament images and metaphors used to communicate something of the theological significance of Jesus' death on the cross. Fortunately, we do not have to decide the issue of the comparative importance of models here, for there are many more telling reasons why we should question the legitimacy of the penal substitution theory, as we shall see.

The point at the moment is simply that, though this is clearly a matter of serious theological dispute and therefore somewhat problematic, the conservative evangelical belief in the "primary controlling status" of the substitutionary theory helps enormously to explain why it was that a press article on the meaning of Easter that was entirely without reference to it, could be judged to be seriously wanting, even to the point of being threatening and disturbing to so many who obviously found it difficult to think outside of this particular theological mindset.

Clearly, the penal substitutionary doctrine of the atonement has been elevated in terms of its dogmatic status so as to become a core belief in the construction of a particular kind of evangelical identity. In the light of this, it is thus at least understandable that the absence of this passionately held belief from "The Rising of the Son," as the absence of something held to be foundational and essential to the proclamation of the Christian gospel, particularly when combined with the (mistaken) perception that the uniqueness of Jesus was being denied, was able to trigger the hostility that certainly made Anglican Church life interesting in Australia through the first half of the year 2000.

Follow-up articles which I was invited to write, especially for Easter editions of *The Bulletin* over the next few years, produced nothing of the hostile and negative kind of response triggered by the publication of "The Rising of the Son." A further reflection on the revelatory significance of Christ's death on the cross, entitled "King on a Cross," appeared prior to Easter in 2001.[52] As it happened, as in the case of "The Rising of the Son," this article also did not make reference to penal substitution, but even so, and for whatever reason, the appetite for public controversy had apparently already evaporated from Carillon Avenue at that time.

---

52. *The Bulletin*, April 17, 2001.

The same may be said in relation to the reception of successive *Bulletin* articles. There were six of them in all. Despite Tom Frame's negative assessment of these forays into the public airing of theological and ethical issues using an outlet of the secular media, responses to this corpus of articles were by and large maturely considered, temperate, and appropriately respectful in their language. Indeed, for the most part they drew very appreciative support. Some *Bulletin* readers would undoubtedly have disagreed with at least some of the content of them; especially, for example, those that dealt with homosexuality and particularly with bioethics, which was passionately debated across Australia at the time. Even so, there were no displays of public hostility of the kind triggered by "The Rising of the Son." I think it is clear that the problems raised by this article did not have to do with the use of the secular media for the discussion of theological topics as Tom Frame has conjectured; rather, the controversy triggered by this article clearly had to do specifically with its lack of interest in the penal substitution theory of the atonement and the uniqueness of Jesus Christ.

The relatively uneventful calm in the years immediately following the controversy triggered by the publication of "The Rising of the Son" proved, however, to be short-lived when controversy was ignited again in 2004 by the publication of *Reflections in Glass*.

As we have already seen, exception was taken to a passing remark in a chapter on the "Admission of Women to the Episcopate" about the apparent Arianism involved in the promotion of Trinitarian complementarianism in the 1999 Sydney Doctrine Commission Report, and the problematic orthodoxy of belief in the "eternal functional subordination" of the Son to the Father. This time round, however, public reactions to the discussion of the penal substitutionary theory of the atonement, in a chapter on "The Death and Resurrection of Christ,"[53] were relatively muted.

The discussion of penal substitution in *Reflections in Glass* devoted some time to the examination of St. Anselm's explanation of the atonement in *Cur Deus Homo* by appealing to the theme of the making of "satisfaction." The question at issue is whether this is, as is often said, rightly regarded as a precursor to the more recent development of the explicitly juridical approach to the substitutionary payment of a penalty. The conclusion was that, in the thought of Anselm, notions of "satisfaction" for sin were colored by the social arrangements and obligations of feudal society of which Anselm was part, and that this was in fact significantly different from the more

---

53. *Reflections in Glass*, chapter 4.

recent concentration of evangelical interest in the more juridical theory of penal substitution. Insofar as Anselm drew an analogy from the lord/vassal relationship of the feudal ordering of his own society, in which "satisfaction" for default of an obligation was made good by renewing the oath of fealty and the restoration of the social arrangements that held that kind of society together, he appealed to notions of justice significantly different from retributive justice. The notion of making "satisfaction" in default of a feudal obligation is less centered on the payment of a penalty and more on the restorative justice expressed in the recovery of the lord's honor and the renewal of social bonds, whereby, for example, the lord promised accommodation and protection in return for some days each year of service from his vassals. Sometimes this took the form of farmhand service but often military service.

In Anselm's day an additional stratum of meaning was given the notion of satisfaction from the context of medieval penitential practice in which "a penance" is performed as a "satisfaction" by a sinner to attract the mercy of God (following Tertullian), rather than something to do with "substitution" in which one person pays a penalty of another. This means that the usual temptation to corral Anselm with proponents of the penal substitutionary theory becomes very problematic. It may be that the discussion of these aspects of Anselm's satisfaction theory in *Reflections in Glass* was found to be convincing enough following its publication in 2004, to discourage public expressions of dissent on Carillon Avenue. This may explain the apparent lack of enthusiasm for stirring controversy on this topic at that time.[54] As we shall see in the next chapter of this book, it is significant that in a report of the Sydney Doctrine Commission on the penal substitutionary theory of the atonement that was presented to the Diocesan Synod in Sydney in 2010, no appeal is made to St. Anselm or the notion of "satisfaction" in *Cur Deus Homo*.

This report was the outcome of a quickening of interest that had once again returned to the question of the penal substitutionary theory of the atonement at the Sydney Diocesan Synod three years earlier, in 2007. In moving a motion in the course of a passionate debate to request the Sydney Doctrine Commission to produce a report on the penal substitutionary understanding of the death of Christ, the then vice principal of Moore Theological College, the Reverend Dr. Bill Salier, expressed his concern at attacks on this

---

54. As we shall see, Anselm's satisfaction theory is not so much as mentioned by the Sydney Doctrine Commission in a report on penal substitution in 2010.

particular understanding of Christ's atoning death that had been made by "some high profile Anglican leaders: 'The understanding of the cross that is expressed in the motion has been consistently under attack from a variety of voices,' he said, citing Archbishop Peter Carnley's book *Flaws in the Glass* [sic]"[55] and very significantly, "recent comment by the Dean of St Albans."[56] Though the reference to *Reflections in Glass* was little more than tangential, this reference to the dean of St Albans alerted me to the fact that I was in good company in questioning the theological and moral acceptability of a penal and substitutionary understanding of things.

Jeffrey John, the dean of St Albans in England, had launched an attack on the penal substitutionary theory by questioning the propriety of the image of God that it unfortunately tends to project; indeed, in a *Lent Talks* broadcast on BBC Radio Four in April of 2007, Dr. John very provocatively suggested that those who insisted that God required Jesus to die for the sins of the world are portraying God as a "psychopath." "What sort of God was this," he asked, "getting so angry with the world and the people he created, and then, to calm himself down, demanding the blood of his own Son?" In Dean John's judgment, the traditional theological theme of substitutionary atonement is to be condemned outright as insane and illogical.[57]

Apart from "high profile Anglican leaders," Dr. Salier also noted that a similar attack had been mounted some years earlier by the British Evangelical leader Steve Chalke when he likewise, though perhaps unwittingly, raised questions about the image of God that was implied by the theory. Chalke, a member of the Baptist Church, had authored *The Lost Message of Jesus* with Alan Mann in 2003.[58] This book was not designed to be a considered theological treatise on the atonement, but rather an attempt to present what the authors believed was at the heart of Jesus' gospel—God's love and concern for the most marginalized in society. They insisted that those whom society might forget are not forgotten by God, and that God calls upon people of faith to demonstrate a similar love and concern.[59] Though

---

55. This should have been *Reflections in Glass*, but this may have been a journalistic flaw of the reporter, Jeremy Halcrow, rather than an accurate reporting of Dr. Salier's own words.

56. This reference is to a BBC Radio talk delivered by the Very Reverend Jeffrey John, dean of St Albans, at Easter 2007: Lent Talk Broadcast on BBC Radio 4, Wednesday April 4, repeated Saturday and Sunday April 7–8, 2007.

57. N. T. Wright responded to John by arguing that he had produced nothing more than a caricature: "To throw away the reality because you don't like the caricature is like cutting out the patient's heart to stop a nosebleed." See "Cross and the Caricatures."

58. Chalke and Mann, *Lost Message of Jesus*, 182–83.

59. Chalke and Mann, *Lost Message of Jesus*, 91–92.

neither Chalke nor Mann had explicitly mentioned the penal substitution theory, in a brief passing comment in which Chalke emphasized the love of God as the primary divine characteristic in the Christian revelation, and its importance for the care of the poor and marginalized, he happened to say: "The fact is that the cross isn't a form of cosmic child abuse—a vengeful Father, punishing his Son for an offence he has not even committed."[60] In the furor that followed he was charged with positively denying the penal substitutionary theory.

The Lost Message of Jesus thus unwittingly provoked considerable controversy, and in fact division, in British evangelical circles, undoubtedly because of Chalke's high profile as an evangelical leader and his perceived rejection of what up to this time had been thought to be a quite fundamental evangelical understanding of the gospel. This British controversy naturally reverberated amongst Australian Carillon Avenue theologians; hence the felt need in 2007 to have the Sydney Doctrine Commission set to work on the renewed study of the penal substitution theory of the atonement, obviously with a view to restoring its damaged reputation.

Even though Chalke had actually originally said that the cross of Christ "*isn't* a form of cosmic child abuse," in the course of the ensuing debate he did not back off from the charge that the image of "cosmic child abuse" *was* what the penal substitutionary theory often raised in peoples' minds, not only in the minds of evangelical believers, but in the understanding of many prospective Christian believers who, in his experience, were positively repelled from the gospel because of it. Indeed, Chalke's critique, if anything, became even more insistently condemning of a theory that he argued was "flawed, unbiblical and destructive to the proclamation of the Gospel."[61] This heated debate so divided evangelical Christianity in Britain that the Evangelical Alliance convened a symposium in London in July 2005 to canvass differences of opinion with a view to healing the wounds that Chalke's critique of penal substitution had opened up.[62]

---

60. Chalke and Mann, *Lost Message of Jesus*, 182.

61. See Chalke's follow-up article "Cross Purposes." N. T. Wright had agreed with Chalke, but hoped that a rehabilitated meaning content would make it possible to retain the language of "penal substitution."

62. This symposium was held in London in July 2005. The collected papers delivered at it were edited by Derek Tidball, David Hilborn, and Justin Thacker, and published as *The Atonement Debate: Papers from The London Symposium on the Theology of Atonement* in 2008.

In the Sydney Synod debate of 2007 Dr. Salier thus singled Chalke out for special mention, as a fellow evangelical Christian: "My point is that the issue is one of controversy within our circles ... The recent comments of Steve Chalke in his book equating the penal substitutionary view with cosmic child abuse being a particularly emotive example."[63] The missiological importance of this particular understanding of the atonement for evangelical Christians as an essential and foundational matter that should be acknowledged to go to the "very heart" of the gospel was also not lost on Dr. Salier. In finally moving the motion after some attempts to amend it, he said that the issue was worthy of discussion "in the light of the Diocesan Mission": "... what is the substance of our gospel presentation?" he asked. "Is this an element that will find a place?" Clearly, he was well aware that the evangelical understanding of its crucial missiological importance as the central meaning of the gospel and thus as a fundamental key to evangelical identity, was at stake. Towards the end of this debate, another member of the 2007 Sydney Synod, Tony George, who was a teacher at Pacific Hills Christian School, spoke passionately about this theory of the atonement as a "critically important issue in Christian education, especially in evangelism amongst teenagers." As Peter Jensen had said in 2003, it is a doctrine that is of "central importance" for evangelical Christians.

At the end of this debate, the Sydney Synod resolved to ask its Diocesan Doctrine Commission to write a report on the importance of penal substitution in understanding the Bible's teaching on the atonement.[64] After three years of deliberation the Sydney Doctrine Commission produced the requested report, which was finally presented to the Diocesan Synod in 2010.[65] Unsurprisingly, this report is quite unequivocal in its affirmation of the evangelical commitment to the central importance of the penal substitutionary understanding of the atonement, declaring that "Christ's bearing of sin's penalty of death as our substitute is the central achievement of the

---

63. In his historical account of this episode, Maxwell Wood makes a similar point: "What appeared to have made this perceived attack even more serious was that it was being made from within. Steve Chalke was regarded as a very high-profile and successful evangelical leader. He was also considered to be a longstanding and prominent member of the Evangelical Alliance (UK)." See Wood, "Penal Substitution in the Construction of British Evangelical Identity," 129; also, Hilborn, "Atonement, Evangelism and the Evangelical Alliance," 18.

64. This was Sydney Diocesan Synod Resolution 36/07.

65. This report entitled "Penal substitutionary atonement," signed by Mark Thompson, chairman, on behalf of Peter Bolt, David Hohne, Robert Forsyth, Robert Smith, and John Woodhouse, may be found online at: https://www.sds.asn.au/sites/default/files/PenalSubstitutionaryAtonement.DocCommission.%2836.07%29%20%282010%29.pdf?doc_id=NDE1NTA=.

cross . . . the basic reality that undergirds and integrates the other ways in which the wondrous achievement of the cross is described" (para. 16). This means that "penal substitution is not just one image among many. It has a foundational role to play in a holistic biblical description of the atonement and relates in a particular way to the other elements of their account" (para. 25). As a consequence, "it is essential that a Christian doctrine of the atonement be *penal* in the first instance" (para. 26). Hence, it is even declared that "Penal substitution is an indispensable element in the Christian proclamation of the cross" (para. 45).

This makes it amply clear that, for some evangelical Christians, the penal substitutionary theory is something that lies at the "very heart" of the gospel; its omission from any public reflection on the meaning of the cross cannot be contemplated. In an important review of "penal substitution" or "penal satisfaction" as it is called in *Recovering the Scandal of the Cross*, Joel Green and Mark Baker observe that "for many American Christians 'penal satisfaction' interprets the significance of Jesus' death fully, completely, without remainder."[66] Alas, this is not an exclusively North American phenomenon. We shall turn to an examination of the arguments of the 2010 report of the Sydney Doctrine Commission in the next chapter.

---

66. Green and Baker, *Recovering the Scandal of the Cross*, 32.

3

THE SYDNEY DOCTRINE COMMISSION REPORT 2010

Despite its affirmations of the central importance of the theory of penal substitutionary atonement, it has to be said that this report is very lackluster and disappointing. Indeed it contains so much that is theologically problematic that it is difficult to know where to start. It must suffice to focus upon some of its chief difficulties.

First, however, it is important to acknowledge, as of some significance, that this report entirely omits any discussion of St. Anselm's thought with regard to the atonement in *Cur Deus Homo*. In fact, it is somewhat surprising that the term "satisfaction" does not feature as an important concept in the course of this report. We may celebrate this omission as a point in its favor. It may well be that some serious questions about whether Anselm's appeal to the feudal concept of "satisfaction" that have been raised by the contemporary assessment of *Cur Deus Homo*, and whether it is rightly understood as a precursor to the theory of penal substitution, have been heard and judged to be, if not compelling, then sufficiently challenging, to deflect the authors of the report from the temptation to venture into that territory.[1]

---

1. For a detailed discussion of the problematic nature of the association of Anselm's thought with later theories of penal substitution, see Green and Baker, *Recovering the Scandal of the Cross*, 38–41, 117–19, 151–69.

This specific issue had already been pursued in *Reflections in Glass*, chapter 4. Aquinas rehabilitated Anselm's satisfaction theory insofar as he argued that God could have freed humans from sin without the need of any satisfaction, and that in so doing God would not have been acting against principles of justice (*Summa Theologiae* 3a.46.2, ad 3). However, Aquinas sought to improve on Anselm's theory, although he thought of his improved theory as a sacrificial theory: "Christ's passion was a true sacrifice" (*Summa Theologiae*, 3a.48.3).

Second, it may be said that the report understandably devotes a good deal of time to outlining the *need* for reconciliation and atonement with God, because of the parlous and sinful state of the human condition. By and large it is not necessary to take issue with these introductory paragraphs (paras. 1–14), though it will be necessary to question the understanding of the alleged biblical view of death as this is set out in paragraph 11.[2]

Third: that said, when the report finally addresses the theory of penal substitution (in paragraph 15) it immediately plants the seeds of a good deal of subsequent confusion by failing to make some fundamental semantic distinctions that are clearly required. The obvious distinction between speaking of Christ's death "instead of us" as against its being "on behalf of us," for example, or "for the sake of us," or "for our benefit" is passed up, in the apparent belief that all of this language is univocal. After first affirming that the death of Christ makes a definite atoning difference as an act by which the reconciliation of sinful humanity with God is achieved, the report baldly affirms that "it was an act of *substitution*." The term "substitution" is then explained by saying that "Christ acted in the place of others *for their benefit*" (para. 15; my italics). This conflation of the notion of Christ's dying "in place of others" with the concept of his dying "for their benefit" is thus made without so much as pausing to consider the obvious semantic distinction that should be observed between them. This means that, though the often-stated biblical affirmation that Christ died "*for* us" may simply mean "for our benefit," "for our assistance," "for our sake," or "on our behalf," paragraph 15 of the report plunges into complete confusion by blandly telling us in relation to Christ's death "for us" that this is what is meant by "substitution":

> Substitution is a broad term that covers the idea of someone acting on behalf of another (or others) and doing what they would otherwise have to do themselves; acting "one instead of another." This is what is meant by such statements as Christ died "for us" (Rom. 5.8) or "for the ungodly" (Rom. 5.6) or "for a brother" (1 Cor. 8.11) or "for all" (2 Cor. 5.14), or, with even stronger language, Christ's death as a "ransom in the place of many" (Mark 10.45).[3]

2. See page 63–71 below.

3. The inherent assumption that the phrases "on behalf of" and "instead of" are semantic equivalents appears to be endemic in much conservative evangelical reflection on the atonement. For example, Peter Jensen is obviously reluctant to attend to any possible distinction of meaning when he says that "to act on our behalf is to act as our substitute, to act in our place: 'Very rarely will anyone die for a righteous man,' says Paul, '. . . while we were still sinners, Christ died for us.' To die for another person requires that one must die in the place of that person—it is the only way my death for him or her can make sense." Jensen, "Good News of God's Wrath."

It is clear that, while other theories of atonement may outline an understanding of the nature of the divine initiative as a grace, or as *a help* to humans in achieving something of benefit in the form of reconciliation with God, as for example in the sacrificial theory, the notion that Christ died "*instead* of us" introduces something significantly different. In the case of the sacrificial theory, for example, Christ's offering of himself, beginning in historical time with his life of obedience even unto death on the cross, and leading to his eternal pleading of his self-offering at the right hand of the Father, may be said to be a help to humans by accomplishing something of significance for their ultimate benefit that they could not possibly achieve for themselves. In this case it may be understood to be a work of God-in-Christ "*on their behalf*" or "*for their sake.*" For example, by making good their feeble offerings of worship, the perfect offering of loving obedience of Christ to God, and his eternal intercession for sinful humanity, it may be said to achieve something "for their benefit," but this is not achieved by *replacing* their own continuing obligation to respond to God themselves, both in living morally obedient lives and in loving worship. In other words, the divine grace or help does *not* mean that humans are no longer called to the sacrificial offering of prayer and praise to God. He is not their "substitute" in this sense. Rather, his gracious help in the perfecting of the worship of Christian believers in reconciled peace before the throne of God, and their dutiful response to God, is not to be thought of as a substitute for their need to worship God with all their heart, and all their mind, and all their strength—pathetically inadequate and sporadic though it may be. Christ's eternal pleading of the sacrifice of the cross at the right hand of the Father is not *instead* of the human response of offering worship to God. Rather, as something "full, perfect, and sufficient" that transforms halting and feeble offerings into offerings "acceptable to God," it may justifiably be said that something was and is achieved for imperfect humans "on their behalf" or "to their benefit" as a help, a grace.[4] This means that, even if the notion that Christ died "instead of us" might be said to be essential to the *penal substitutionary* theory, this is not necessarily so with regard to the sacrificial theory. If anything, in the case of the sacrificial theory Christ's self-offering might be said to be a "substitute" for the sacrificial offerings of animals in the rituals of the temple in Jerusalem rather than as a substitute for the humans for whom it is intended to "benefit."

In the Epistle to the Hebrews the "once and for all" sacrificial offering of Christ may be understood to be in place of or *instead of* the ancient

---

4. See Richard Swinburne's very clearly argued contribution to this aspect of the grace or help of God in the sacrificial work of atonement in "Christ's Atoning Sacrifice," 27–29.

offering of bulls and goats in the temple in Jerusalem, and to have rendered those ancient practices obsolete and no longer necessary.[5] By contrast, with respect to humans, however, it is not *instead* of their offering of "themselves, their souls and bodies" but something done by Christ *on their behalf*.[6] Christ's self-offering "for others" does not replace a human obligation, but perfects the performance of it. Just as, while each of us must make our own apology and reparation to those whom we wrong, another may help us to make amends and even provide the means by which reparation may be made. So, Christ's self-offering of himself before God may be said to be a help to us (i.e., a grace), without substituting for us in such a way as to render it unnecessary for us to make amends ourselves.

Thus, in Mark's understanding of the Christian gospel the true disciples of Jesus are called to "take up their cross" and follow him in the same way (Mark 8:31; 9:31; 10:32–34). In this sense Christ's self-offering in the service of others is a model, not a substitute. Rather, as the author of Hebrews put it: Christ is the "pioneer and perfecter" of our faith "who for the joy that was set before him endured the cross, despising the shame, and is set down at the right hand of the throne of God" (Heb 12:2).[7] Christ's death, resurrection, and ascension, are therefore "for others," in the sense that they are a help in achieving something that human beings could not achieve by their own effort alone. As the author of the Epistle to the Ephesians put it, "by grace you are saved through faith; and that not of yourselves: it is the gift of God, not a result of works, so that no one may boast" (Eph 2:8–9). Clearly, something done "on our behalf" cannot simply be assumed to be something done "instead of us" or "as our substitute" in the sense of bearing a punishment that rightfully should have been imposed on all sinful humanity. This imposition of a penalty on Christ *instead of* on those who deserved punishment is what, unfortunately, invites the judgment that this would be both immoral and unjust.

Fourth: The next basic problem with the report is that the same failure to observe even basic semantic distinctions leads its authors to jumble together the various New Testament models and metaphors of atonement by ignoring the subtle differences between them. This confounds the entirely disparate contexts from which these metaphors emerge, and within which they draw their meaning. This tendency to conflate and confuse texts

---

5. Hebrews 9:12: "He entered once for all into the Holy Place, not with the blood of goats and calves, but with his own blood, thus obtaining eternal redemption."

6. Hebrews 9:24: "Christ . . . entered into heaven itself, now to appear in the presence of God on our behalf."

7. Some translations have Jesus as "the author and finisher of our faith."

inevitably invalidates the possibility of drawing uncontested logical entailments from them.

The New Testament language expressing something of the experience of reconciliation with God that was understood to have been achieved by the death and resurrection of Christ involves a rich confluence of models and metaphors. This means, as Colin Gunton noted in his magisterial examination of this rich cache of language, that "As we move from one family of metaphors to another, we must be aware that they do not operate in self-contained worlds."[8] This means that we should not just focus upon a single isolated model, but endeavor to hold various models together. Some caution is needed, however, before uncritically assuming that a single univocal meaning may be drawn from this variety of images, particularly in the absence of any reference to nuances that arise from the differences of contexts from which they come.

The contexts of the New Testament's atonement metaphors range from juridical, to commercial, to cultic, to the field of battle and the enjoyment of military victory. The tendency of this report is to imagine that it is methodologically possible to produce a single composite biblical theory of atonement even in the face of this variety, so as to construct an uneasy harmony. Unfortunately, this fails to appreciate the complexity of the richly different and sometimes logically competing models that are presupposed in the New Testament's witness. This leads to the illusion that it is possible to produce something approaching "*the* biblical view of the atonement," by following a method reminiscent of the now discredited methodology of the "biblical theology movement" of the period immediately following the Second World War. This unfortunately in fact violently distorts and misrepresents specific atonement models by hopelessly mixing the various families of metaphors.

For example, the penal substitutionary theory tends to focus on the cross, and on a sin-annulling transaction that is said to have gone on *behind* the cross in a way that is crucicentric.[9] As a way of dealing with sin, or more

---

8. Gunton, *Actuality of Atonement*, 83

9. It is noteworthy that J. I. Packer rightly seeks to avoid a narrow crucicentrism by insisting that the resurrection is an important element along with the cross in the consideration of the doctrine of the atonement ("What Did the Cross Achieve?," 112). However, when he comes to expound penal substitution as his preferred theory, the discussion is entirely without reference to the resurrection ("What Did the Cross Achieve?," 127). See the observation of Joel Green and Mark Baker on the inconsistency of this aspect of Packer's theology in *Recovering the Scandal of the Cross,* 179–80: "he argues that the resurrection is essential and an organic element, and offers a brief explanation to support that point. . . . It is telling, however, that when he turns to describe penal substitution he does not include the role of the resurrection, nor does he mention

accurately with "our sins," it is understood in a juridical sense to have paid the penalty that satisfies any further need for punitive or "deserved justice" to be done. At the same time this is said to neutralize or absorb the "wrath of God." In this case, the resurrection and ascension tend to be confirmatory, as a kind of heavenly reward for the obedience of Christ in the wake of his entirely undeserved passion and death on the cross.

The sacrificial theory, however, tends by contrast to regard the death of the victim only as a necessary preliminary to the taking of the blood by the high priest through the veil of the temple to sprinkle it on the mercy seat (*hilasterion*)—the act of pleading the sacrifice. On analogy with this, Christ's death on the cross may be understood as the preliminary action of a more composite whole, involving the resurrection and the ascension and the eternal heavenly offering of the raised and exalted Christ, *subsequent to* his death on the cross. All are essential components of Christ's reconciling work when the sacrificial model is employed. By contrast the penal substitutionary theory is almost exclusively centered upon the saving significance of Christ's suffering and death on the cross, understood not in a sacrificial but a juridical context.

Moreover, Paul's reference in Romans 3:25 to the cultic ritual of the temple may be understood entirely without the juridical overtones that are applied in the case of penal substitution. The reference is to Christ's being set forth, significantly, not out of God's wrath so much as "in the forbearance of God" for the propitiation/expiation (*hilasterion*) of our sins "by faith in his blood." This appeal to the analogy of the "*hilasterion*"[10] draws its meaning by association with the mercy seat as the "place" or "means" of "propitiation" and clearly belongs in the cultic context of the temple. As N. T. Wright has correctly observed, "you cannot easily align sacrifice and lawcourt."[11]

Throughout the report, however, there is a tendency to conflate logically competing and subtly different atonement metaphors and the contexts from which they are drawn, and even to speak not of penal substitution and its juridical context, and then of Christ's atoning sacrifice and its altogether different cultic context, but to conflate the two by referring to "substitutionary sacrifice"![12]

Once again, we note that, while it may be true that God's surprise provision of a goat may be understood as a substitute for Isaac as the originally

---

it as one of the main ingredients of the penal substitution model."

10. This is a hapax for Paul, for it appears here but not elsewhere in the Pauline corpus. But see also 1 John 2:2, where the related word is *hilasmos*.

11. Wright, "Cross and the Caricatures."

12. Sydney Doctrine Commission, "Penal substitutionary atonement," para. 17.

intended sacrificial victim in the story of Abraham's proposed sacrifice (Gen 22), a little care must be exercised before assuming that Christ's offering of his blood on the cross might be thought to substitute eternally for the punishment by death of all humanity. It may possibly be thought of as a substitute for the offering of the blood of bulls and goats in the temple in Jerusalem. But the substitution of Christ's death for the deserved punishment of death for all humanity is another thing altogether. It is understandable that a juridical model has to be drawn upon to explain this. On the other hand, the substitution of a goat for Isaac is no warrant for importing the concept of substitution into the juridical context of the payment of a penalty, or the commercial context of the payment of a debt, or the military context of the exchange or freeing of prisoners on payment of a ransom.

Fifth: We have already noted that it is to the credit of the authors of the report that they appear to be aware of the difficulties of working with Anselm's feudal concept of "satisfaction." As in the case of the report's avoidance of Anselm's satisfaction theory, any *direct* association with federal theology seems also to have been avoided. Indeed, the members of the Doctrine Commission may have done their work without being conscious of the need to keep a prudent distance from any suggestion that they were presupposing Ursinus's belief that God had made a contract (or covenant of works *with conditions*) with Adam, as against the gracious covenant *without conditions*, as in the case of God's covenant with Abraham. Certainly, when the report begins to outline the Old Testament history of God's covenants with the people of Israel, it does not to speak of a "covenant" of any kind with Adam. Instead, it speaks of "God's promises" to Adam (para. 15). Then, after passing up the possibility of using the term "covenant" altogether in relation to God's dealing with Adam, the report moves on to speak of the "covenant" made with Moses and the giving of the law, and so on.

However, even while avoiding the *language* of a "covenant" between God and Adam, the *substance* of federal theology's *ordo salutis* is unfortunately retained in the report. As in federal theology, and specifically, as in the Heidelberg Catechism of Ursinus itself, the juridical nature of *contractual* covenants (with conditions attached to them in the form of the provision of penalties should they be broken) is simply assumed, as against genuinely free and unconditional covenants of grace (without contractual strings attached). As a result, God's covenant with Abraham and his seed—when he promised to be "their God" while the people of Israel would be "his people"—and the guarantee that God would be faithful to his promise "come what may," exercises no methodological control in the theological discussion as it is pursued in this report. Instead, as in federal theology, the report moves from talk of God's "promise" to Adam directly to God's "covenant" with Moses, *without any reference to the covenant of grace with Abraham in between*. It is not without significance that this is entirely missing from the discussion.

Thus, the foreshadowing of Christ's covenant of grace in God's unconditional promises to Abraham, and the divine promise to be faithful to his promise to all people, which St. Paul so famously said was, as in the case of Abraham, because of their faith (like Abraham's) rather than works of the Jewish law, is effectively bumped out of active theological play. Instead, the report begins to work on the basis of the mistaken assumption that covenants are conditional or contractual by nature, and therefore automatically involve the imposition of a penalty should they be broken. They are "penal" in the immediate sense that they involve a penalty. Hence punitive justice is said to be something that is *deserved*. As in the case of Adam's disobedience, the penalty for the sinful disregard of God and his will for humanity is said to be death. By this maneuver an unwitting assumption of juridical values and legal principles takes over as the primary context for working out a theology of atonement. This contrasts with the possibility of considering an *entirely free* operation of grace in achieving reconciliation and atonement with God (as in the covenant God made with Abraham). The *language* of federal theology may be studiously avoided at least with respect to Adam, but as in Ursinus's Heidelberg Catechism of 1563, it is presupposed. In this report the *substance* of federal theology continues to live on, surviving like the grin of the Cheshire cat, even though the form to which it belongs has long since been conveniently shuffled out of view.

The report never recovers from this methodological commitment. Rather, a covenant of a contractual kind allegedly made by God with Adam, which is understood to have brought with it the conditional provision of the imposition of a penalty should the covenant be broken, tends constantly to be presupposed. In the Westminster Confession this is not just a presupposition, for it is explicitly enshrined in the Westminster Confession VII. ii. However, when the report, at the beginning of its argument in support of penal substitution in paragraph 15, speaks of the juridical necessity that it must be "penal" it is significant that this is simply asserted, but not one biblical reference is cited to demonstrate *why* this *must* be so. This is simply assumed as a given. This *presupposition* exactly echoes the federal theology of the Heidelberg Catechism itself. The shadow of federal theology may thus be detected right through the report, which even assumes a penal and moral understanding of death, though this is missing from the Old Testament, as we shall see.

❖ ❖ ❖

The implications of this methodological commitment flow specifically into the report's discussion of death in paragraph 11, where it is declared that death must be understood in penal terms. As in the Ursinus's Heidelberg Catechism, Genesis 2:17 is cited in support of the contention that death is the penalty imposed by God on all subsequent humanity for the sinful disobedience of Adam. Thus, the report says:

> God's response to sin has been clear from the very beginning. When the first human beings, out of envy of God's sovereignty, chose to grasp at equality with him, the penalty was death (Gen. 2:17).[13]

Federal theology's assumption that this verse from Genesis warrants the conclusion that God made a contractual arrangement with Adam and Eve of a conditional kind, with death as the penalty for breaking the contract, is however problematic. Apart from the fact that Eve has yet to come on the scene at this time, it assumes that Adam and Eve were created immortal, and only became subject to the limitations of mortality as a consequence of the fall. But there is nothing in the Genesis story to suggest that Adam and Eve were not created mortal in the first place, or to suggest, in other words, that they would not one day die. They are mortals. Mortality is not imposed on them as a punishment. The tree of life at the center of the garden of Eden holds the prospect of unending life, but for Adam and Eve that is a possibility, not a possession.

Upon their disobedience, furthermore, the punishment that they receive, according to the story in Genesis 3, is not death, but expulsion from the garden, by which they forfeited the possibility of reaching the tree of life at its center. It is also clear that they did not die *on the very day* that they ate of it, as Genesis 2:17 warns. Likewise, the punishment of the serpent is not death, but thenceforth to go "on his belly," slithering on the ground.[14] The notion that death is the penalty imposed upon all humanity for the

---

13. Sydney Doctrine Commission, "Penal substitutionary atonement," para. 11.

14. For those who mistake this creation myth for historical fact, this raises the question of how snakes moved about *before* being condemned to slither on the ground. This is a question that stumped William Jennings Bryan in the course of the fundamentalist prosecution of the evolutionist teacher John Thomas Scopes, in the infamous trial that occurred in Dayton, Ohio in July 1925. Though Bryan was prosecuting the trial, on day seven, he was called to the stand by Clarence Darrow, who defended Scopes. Darrow proceeded to a line of questioning that rendered the historical factuality of the story patently problematic. The mode of the ability to move of the snake prior to being condemned to slither on the ground becomes a problem for those intent upon a historical and factual reading of the story.

disobedience of Adam is a fond invention that is missing not only from Genesis but from the Old Testament generally.

In other words, if the penalty of disobedience in the Genesis myth is not death (as the Sydney Doctrine Commission Report mistakenly assumes) but rather, expulsion from Eden, then Adam and Eve may be understood to be mortals from the beginning. They are finite creatures who must live their lives under limitations imposed by space and time, and who must therefore eventually face death as a natural outcome. In this case, as with the rest of the created world, death is not a moral but an ontological reality, a natural accompaniment of all created life, whether animal or vegetable. As St. Paul so aptly put it, "the whole creation groans in travail up till now" (Rom 8:22). Death is not confined to humans as a penalty for their moral disobedience.

This means that Genesis 2:17 is not to be understood, as in federal theology, in a contractual sense, so much as a simple warning.[15] Instead of signaling a contractual arrangement or "covenant of works" with the penalty of death as the condition for not keeping it, God simply warns Adam of what he will naturally have to face by foolishly seeking to live a life of self-centered, self-reliant independence in the world. It is as though God created Adam and Eve as innocent children who had to learn obedience and the wisdom of accepting the tutoring of God, by living in fellowship with God, with the warning that otherwise, by trying to "go it alone," they would come to grief.[16] In other words, by cutting loose of the tutoring of God, in the mistaken belief that they could successfully live autonomously and survive though their own power of self-assertion, they will in fact be living dangerously, naturally forfeiting the possibility of life.

In this context, the injunction not to eat of the fruit of the tree of the knowledge of good and evil is not to be interpreted narrowly as some kind of sexual or moral prohibition, but as a much more board and general cautionary prohibition. Its warning is of the danger of going it alone in the world in independence of life-giving communion with God. As Von Rad has made clear, the injunction is to avoid being obsessed with worldly wisdom, as hostage to an infatuation to know all things whether they be good or bad. The serpent, as the most subtle and cunning of the creatures, thus

---

15. Ursinus's Heidelberg Catechism cited Genesis 2:17 in assuming that God had made a "covenant of works" with Adam, which in turn required the death of his Son. (Lord's Day 16, question and answer 40).

16. As in the tradition of classical Anglican theodicy since William King, *De Origine Mali*, 1702, (which was translated into English with extensive notes by Edmund Law in 1731 as *An Essay on the Origin of Evil*). King's work was the subject to a well-known critical discussion by Gottfried Wilhelm Leibniz, published as an appendix to Leibniz's *Théodicée* (1710) that, indeed, introduced the term "theodicy." It is also the inspiration of John Hick's magisterial *Evil and the God of Love*.

represents the desire to become immersed in the natural order, by seeking to know all things, whether good or bad, and being so beguiled by what we would today call the inquiring and scientific intelligence, as entirely to forget the sovereign presence of God and the tutoring of his will for the living of life well. The command not to eat of the tree of the knowledge of good and evil is thus a general warning of the natural consequences of the foolhardiness of trying to live autonomously without the help of God. In a sense this is tantamount to attempting to be as God is—absolutely ontologically independent. Instead they had to learn to "know their place" in the ultimate scheme of things, as mere mortals in need of God's help.

Instead of being narrowly focussed on moral inhibitions of a sexual kind, the brash quest to know things whether good or bad without heed to their possible life-threatening consequences, may be thought of as being of a piece, for example, with the specific warning not drink too much alcohol, or not to eat certain kinds of poisonous mushrooms, or not to eat porridge that has been stirred with the stick of the Oleander bush (which is poisonous), or to eat only the stalks of rhubarb but not to eat the leaves (which are likewise poisonous), for all this is to live dangerously; it will naturally cause death. In other words, by rejecting the guidance of God, they will forfeit the possibility of continuing life in the broadest of senses. A *premature* death will be their natural and inevitable destiny, for having been created out of nothing they will return to nothing. It is in this same sense that St. Paul warns that "if you live according to the flesh, you will die; but if by the Spirit you put to death the deeds of the body, you will live."[17] As in the case of God's warning to Adam in Genesis 2:17, "you will surely die," the warning of death is here also the warning of the natural consequence of forsaking the life-giving Spirit and living according to the flesh. It is not necessarily some kind of juridical punishment as in federal theology.

I am suggesting, in other words, that death is not a punishment but the natural outcome of seeking to live in self-centered independence in separation from God as the source of all life. As with the rest of created life, Adam and Eve, having been created *ex nihilo* so as to live in the created order under the limitations of space and time, therefore face the possibility of death as a return to nothingness. Hence, having been expelled from the garden, thereby forfeiting the possibility of reaching the tree of life at its center, Adam and Eve have to make their way in the world as the mortals they are with the forlorn prospect of having to face death as the ultimate natural consequence of fractured communion with God. As Athanasius put

---

17. Rom 8:12–17.

it, the consequence of eating of the tree of the knowledge of good and evil, was that the

> transgression of the commandment turned them back into the state *in accordance with their nature* . . . just as they had come into being out of non-being, so they were now deservedly on their way to returning, through corruption, to non-being again . . . Man is mortal by nature, since he is made out of nothing.[18]

In this theological tradition death is not a penalty imposed by God on beings whom he had originally made immortal, but a natural consequence of their mortality. As St. Paul was to declare in writing to the Romans, the fault of those of the pagan world was to immerse themselves in the created order in independence of God, worshipping the creature rather than the Creator: "They exchanged the truth of God for a lie; and worshiped and served created things rather than the Creator—who is forever praised. Amen" (Rom 1:25).

This understanding of things is fully in accord with the basic thrust of the Wisdom of Solomon on which Paul obviously relied, where the foolish are warned "not to invite death by the error of your life" (Wisdom 1:12) for "the ungodly by their words and deeds summoned death" (Wisdom 1:16)—not least by forsaking the pursuit of wisdom and the worship of the Creator by becoming infatuated with created things, as exemplified in the pursuit of idolatry—a theme which Paul also explicitly picked up in *Romans*.

The authors of the Sydney Doctrine Commission Report insist, however, that "the presence of death in the human race is not natural but penal" (paragraph 11). By mistakenly assuming that death *must* be understood as a penalty on the slender basis of Genesis 2:17, in which we may certainly hear the echo of the federal theology of Ursinus's scholastic Calvinism, and blind to a more careful reading of Genesis, the report is instead content to rely upon some words of John Stott:

> The Bible everywhere views human death, not as a *natural* but as a *penal* event. It is an alien intrusion into God's good world, and not a part of his original intention for human kind.[19]

There is a sense in which it is true that death is alien to the life-giving good purpose of God, but whether this makes it "everywhere" in the Bible

---

18. Athanasius, *On the Incarnation*, 4.4–6.
19. Stott, *Cross of Christ*, 65.

a penal and not a natural event is entirely fanciful. The fact is that, generally speaking, the Old Testament does not refer back to the creation myth of Adam and Eve and an alleged conditional contractual arrangement that specified death as the penalty for the failure to keep it, according to which God was led to impose death on all humanity as a punishment.

In looking for a biblical warrant for this contention, the best the report is able to do is to refer to the repeated refrain relating to the patriarchs in Genesis 5: "and he died"! Surely this is grasping at straws. This refrain appears in a catalogue of those who had lived unusually long lives, *and who eventually died*; but there is no shred of evidence in Genesis 5 to suggest that death was anything other than a natural phenomenon. On the contrary, the suggestion is that it is what is to be expected at the end of lives of longevity. This is to be accepted and embraced as part of the natural process of living. What is to be feared is a *premature* death.

Rather than simply accepting John's Stott's ill-disciplined assertion that "the Bible everywhere" views death as a penalty, and the assumption that this means that it is a penalty explicitly for the disobedient infringement of contractual obligations imposed by God, we would do better to turn to Stott's preaching. For here we find instances of Stott's appeal to God's graciously unconditional promises to Abraham, and to the affirmation of God's faithfulness to his promise *despite* human disobedience and failure, and to the ultimate fulfilment of those promises by Christ. Accordingly, if we wish to access biblical truth, we must attend to its promise that those with a faith like Abraham's, irrespective of identity or the keeping of the Jewish law, by faith and baptism "in Christ" are justified or accounted to be "in the right" as inheritors of the very promises made to Abraham.[20] The promises to Abraham provide the primary and paradigm example of the utterly free and *unconditional grace* of God's (noncontractual) covenant promises.

When we look to the report's use of the New Testament in search of support for the penal substitutionary view of Christ's death, it becomes clear that it relies heavily on Paul's words when he passed on the Easter tradition (which he says he had himself received) in 1 Corinthians 15:3: "Christ died *for our sins*, according to the scriptures." Whether these words "for our sins" can be made to mean more than "Christ died in order to free us from our sins" rather than specifically "he died in order to bear the punishment we deserve for our sins" is a good question.

---

20. See for example the sermon entitled "The Patriarch."

On the other hand, it may be significant that, on Paul's own admission, these words derive from an original Christian tradition *that he had received*. If they ultimately derive from the very band of the first disciples who had been with Jesus and who fled from the cross to save their own skins, this raises the question of whether in the first instance they can be understood to mean that Christ was punished and died while the original band of disciples escaped that fate and therefore lived to bear the guilt of deserting him. In addition, it also seems clear that Christ died as an innocent victim. The crime for which he was found guilty was the crime of being "King of the Jews" or at least of claiming to be King of the Jews. This was charged against him, even though he himself appears to have been careful *not* to claim to be a king—certainly not of this world. Hence in reply to the question of Pilate, "Are you a king?," he is reported to have said "You say that I am." This means there is a sense in which Jesus died because *it was claimed by others* to be their king, or it was claimed by others that he was the long-awaited messiah who would deliver his people from oppression who would thus become their king. In this case, can it be that it was explicitly because his original disciples were aware that Christ died because *they* claimed him as their king, rather than something he claimed for himself? If in this immediate sense he died "because of their sins," the tradition that he died "for their sins" may have initially been triggered by their own sense of guilt, given their own unwitting contribution to the cause of his death. In this case, it is at least thinkable that this was the original experience that led to the New Testament's subsequent more theologically reflective processing of the reasons for Christ's death at a more universal and indeed metaphysical level.

Though this can be little more than speculative, what is certain is that by Paul's time the sense that Jesus died "for our sins" can no longer be given the same original meaning that it might have had for those who felt the guilt of being responsible for his death by claiming him as their king. Indeed, Paul hardly ever speaks of "our sins" in the genitive plural. Instead, by contrast with this original tradition that he had received (1 Cor 15:3), when Paul himself speaks on this theme it is not "our sins," as in the tradition which he is quoting, but simply "sin." Instead of speaking narrowly of the sinful misdeeds of humanity (for which death might be thought to be a penalty imposed by God on sinful humanity), sin is, for Paul, an all-pervading gone-wrongness with the entire created order, a "missing of the mark" in the sense of a failure of a kind that is observable throughout the whole of creation to achieve its promised potential. Creation itself does not reach the fulfillment intended for it by God. In this case death is a consequence of sin, not in a narrowly human moral sense, but once again in a broad ontological sense. Hence, Paul is able to say, not that "the penalty for *our sins* is death" but that "the wages *of sin* is death" (Rom 6:23).

The report, however, blithely insists, "It is not just that death came into the world through sin, but human death is God's punishment for sin" (paragraph 11). Moreover, this is said to be what is declared by Paul when he says "The wages of sin in death" (Rom 6:23)! This interpretation of Paul's meaning is then rooted back to Genesis 2:17: the warning to Adam not to eat of the tree of the knowledge of good and evil, "for on the day that you eat it you shall die." Indeed, this appeal to Genesis 2:17 is even made notwithstanding the fact that on the day of eating Adam (and Eve) *did not die*, and in the face of the clear fact that, in the Genesis story, the punishment of Adam and Eve takes the form not of death but expulsion from the garden.

It is also important to note that when Paul wrote that the "wages of sin is death" he was not directly referring to the story in Genesis, but, as is now well known, was drawing his theological inspiration from the Wisdom of Solomon. However, even Wisdom does not see death as a punishment inflicted on humanity as a whole or as a punishment for Adam's failure to keep his contractual obligations. Rather, it is seen as a punishment explicitly of the wicked, an expression of the belief that the wicked will come to a premature end, while the righteous who pursue the wisdom of God will be blessed with what Wisdom calls "the prolonged old age of the righteous" (Wisdom 4:16). Insofar as Wisdom sees death as a punishment, at least of the wicked, while the enjoyment of life is seen as God's blessing of his faithful ones, Wisdom is able to assert that, by contrast with the wages of sin, the "wages of holiness" (Wisdom 2:22) is the prize of immortality for blameless souls "created in the image" of God's own eternity.

For Wisdom the possibility of continuing life is often said to be forfeited, not through the juridical or moral imposition of a penalty in order to fulfill the requirements of a kind of retributive or deserved punishment, but often as a natural consequence of human foolishness—the failure to seek wisdom. A dissolute life, lived selfishly and wantonly, is bound to reap an unwelcome reward in the form of a premature death; the blessing of a life lived in accordance with the dictates of wisdom achieves God's blessing, manifested in "length of days."

For Wisdom, a premature death, by being cut short in the midst of life, is the earned consequence, or just deserts, of the wicked, by contrast with the reward God has in store as a blessing for his faithful ones. Thus, the view of premature death is rather more nuanced than the all-inclusive and bald assertions of the penal view of death of the substitutionary theory of the atonement. That death is a punishment on all humanity because of Adam's contractual failure is a theme that is simply not present at all in the Book of Wisdom. Rather, the very opposite is the case. Far from being an imposition of God, it is explicitly affirmed that "God created us for incorruption" (Wisdom 2:23) and it was "through the devil's envy that death entered the world" (Wisdom 2:24). Thus, "God did not make death, and he does not delight in the death of the living" (Wisdom 1:13). It could hardly have been made more clear.

Given that Paul's thought suggests that he was well tutored in the Book of Wisdom, a great deal has to be imported into Romans 6:23 in order to achieve the interpretative outcome in which death is understood as a penalty imposed by God on all humanity because of the disobedience of Adam. There is a sense in which, for Paul, death is a natural or ontological consequence of human sinfulness: "sin came into the world through one man, and death came through sin, and so death spread to all, for all have sinned" (Rom 5:12). Even so, the Sydney Doctrine Commission Report goes so far as explicitly to insist, in a way that is contrary to this statement from Paul, that death did not spread naturally from Adam's attempt to live in independence of God, so as to embrace all humanity, but rather, was imposed on all humanity by God as a penalty for Adam's sin: Thus, the report is actually bold to say "it is *not* just that death came into the world through sin" (para. 11), and then goes on to generate the fiction that death is not just a natural consequence of sin, an unavoidable concomitant of the human condition, and as a form of life lived in foolish independence of the life-giving goodness of God, but rather that "consistency with his own goodness and the goodness of his creation, God justly required that these rebellious human beings forfeit the gift of life that he had extended to them" (para. 11).

We may be forgiven for thinking, however, that this penal view of death is entirely generated as a residual influence of the federal theology of T. C. Hammond, which became domiciled on Carillon Avenue from 1936 onwards. The penal view of death has its attraction because of the need to justify belief in the payment of the penalty imposed by God on all humanity by the death of God's own Son on the cross. In other words, the penal substitutionary view of the atonement is brought to the exposition of Scripture, rather than vice versa.

It is not necessary to claim infallibility with regard to the conclusions that have ensued from this examination of the Sydney Doctrine Commission's

Report into the penal substitutionary theory of the atonement. It is enough to say that the basic methodological commitments that are either made or fail to be made so condition the argument of the report as to render its conclusions highly problematic. The report's theological defects are obviously of such fundamental importance that they need to be taken into account with the utmost seriousness. In summary, they are:

1. The report fails to make any clear distinction between the phrases "instead" of" and "on behalf of" or "for the sake of" in relation to the human benefits received as a result of work of Christ.
2. The report confuses the rich diversity of the atonement metaphors in the New Testament, and fails to consider the logical competition of meanings arising from the diverse contexts in which these metaphors should properly be placed, in an apparent highly questionable quest to articulate "the" biblical view of atonement.
3. The report fails to distinguish between a contractual agreement which brings with it a penalty for the failure to keep it (of the kind that, historically, the federal theology of scholastic Calvinism claimed was made with Adam), and the graciously unconditional covenant made by God with Abraham, and his promise to be steadfastly faithful even in the face of the failures of Abraham and his descendants.
4. The unquestioning assumption of a moral and penal rather than an ontological view of death.

Unless these basic issues are addressed we may be forgiven for concluding, at the very least, that the exposition of penal substitution in the 2010 Report of the Sydney Doctrine Commission leaves a great deal to be desired.

In seeking to pursue theological truth in relation to these questions, we cannot underestimate the influence in what I have called Carillon Avenue theology of T. C. Hammond as the conduit of a more general inheritance from federal theology. The fundamental commitment of the penal substitution theory of the atonement to belief in the need for a penalty to be paid, allegedly in accordance with legal principle for Adam's disobedience, and the contention that this is demanded by the Father's righteousness, strongly suggests that the Son was sent into the world by God for this specifically juridical purpose. It is understandable that the two doctrines, the complementarian view of God which holds that the Son is eternally obediently subordinate to the Father, and the penal substitutionary theory of the atonement that holds that the obedient Son pays the penalty required by the Father instead of disobedient humanity, as the "subordinate substitute," are inextricably linked. The highly problematic complementarian doctrine of God, involving the subordination of the Son to the Father within an interpersonal dynamic of domination and submission that is implicit in the exercise of the Father's commanding will in sending the Son for this salvific purpose and the Son's eternal willing response of obedient compliance with it, might be thought to lend credibility to this particular theory of the atonement. However, in his case, if the eternal subordination of the Son seems problematic as fundamentally Arian and therefore theologically unacceptable, then this also has highly negative implications with regard to the penal substitutionary theory of the atonement that is so closely associated with it.

4

PIERCED FOR OUR TRANSGRESSIONS?

The Sydney Doctrine Commission's Report of 2010 on penal substitutionary atonement appears to have been significantly influenced by the thinking of Michael Ovey and his colleagues, Steve Jeffery and Andrew Sach, as this is found in their 2007 book *Pierced for Our Transgressions*. The commission's report cited this book with approval in its initial review of recent relevant publications of the time, noting it as "an extended defence of penal substitution."[1] Indeed, Mark Thompson, the chair of the Sydney Doctrine Commission in 2010, had already joined a veritable "who's who" of nearly fifty international evangelical scholars who commended the publication of *Pierced for Our Transgressions* (in its first ten pages!) when it originally appeared. As it turns out, in doing so he appears unwittingly to have let an unacknowledged federalist cat out of the bag,[2] for as in many expositions and defenses of penal substitutionary atonement, the distinctive theological stance of this book presupposes the basic identifying elements of federal theology.[3]

---

1. Sydney Doctrine Commission, "Penal substitutionary atonement," note 1.

2. Also included in these ten pages of commendations at the beginning of Jeffery, Ovey, and Sach, *Pierced for Our Transgressions* is the name of the Australian New Testament scholar Peter O'Brien, who is identified as senior research fellow in New Testament at Moore College in Sydney. O'Brien was not a member of the Sydney Doctrine Commission in 2010; however, it is significant that his discussion of Paul's alleged "covenantal nomism" is relied upon at significant points by the authors of *Pierced for Our Transgressions*. (See O'Brien's essay "Was Paul a Covenantal Nomist?")

3. For a full discussion of some of the modern manifestations of historical federal theology see the companion volume to this book, *Arius on Carillon Avenue*, chapter 2.

The authors of *Pierced for Our Transgressions* immediately (though perhaps unwittingly) reveal their latent federalist sympathies by tracing the theological pedigree of penal substitution back through the English Puritanism of John Owen (1616–83) and the Great Awakening and Enlightenment preacher, George Whitefield (1714–70), both of whom were exponents of the federal theology of their day. Indeed, Whitefield is explicitly quoted with reference to the alleged "covenant of works" said in federal theology to have been entered into by Adam as the contractual head of the human race, "the representative of all his seed."[4] This alleged "covenant" is clearly understood from the perspective of federal theology to have been conceived in contractual terms, with God's continuing favor being understood to be conditional upon the obedience of Adam and all those whom he represents.[5] According to an unquestioning historical reading of the Genesis creation story this presupposed contractual arrangement was of course understood to have been fractured by Adam's disobedience, and so Christ, "the head, the representative of the elect" is in turn said by Whitefield to have fulfilled the penal implications of Adam's broken covenant through suffering a "painful, cursed and ignominious death" by his perfect obedience, thus paying the penalty of human disobedience and sin inherited from Adam, and initiating the "covenant of grace."[6]

The residual influence of the inheritance of federal theology may in turn be detected insofar as the authors of *Pierced for Our Transgressions* apparently see no difficulty in importing contractual obligations into their understanding even of God's gracious covenant with Abraham. There is no question that Paul focuses directly on God's covenant promise to Abraham in Galatians and Romans in articulating his appeal to faith as against "works of the law" as the basis of the justification of both Gentiles and Jews. A federalist understanding of the alleged legal terms of God's covenant with Abraham is in keeping with their discussion of the generic concept of a covenant, in which they effectively accommodate their understanding of God's free gift of grace to matters of legal principle. This is made very clear insofar as they argue that "The biblical idea of covenant, so prominent in scripture, embraces both personal and legal aspects."[7] The special relationship that the people of Israel inherited from Abraham as a man of faith is

---

4. See Jeffery, Ovey, and Sach, *Pierced for Our Transgressions*, 193; Whitefield, "Sermons Preached," 9.

5. This identifying token of theological federalism became enshrined in the Westminster Confession of Faith (1646), 7.2

6. Jeffery, Ovey, and Sach, *Pierced for Our Transgressions*, 193, quoting Whitefield, "Sermons Preached," 9.

7. Jeffery, Ovey, and Sach, *Pierced for Our Transgressions*, 110.

acknowledged to have been "intensely personal" as a "people belonging to God" (1 Pet 2:9). Even so, they argue, "it also carried obligations." Somewhat surprisingly, they then jump forward some centuries from Abraham to the legal traditions of Deuteronomy in order to make their point. They argue that Deuteronomy 28–31 makes it especially clear that "there were blessings for obedience and curses for disobedience."[8] "Expulsion from the Promised Land was threatened if the people of Israel turned from the Lord to other Gods (Deut 30:17–18)."[9] In this way the covenant promise unconditionally made to Abraham that Paul proclaimed as having been fulfilled in Christ by the "free gift of grace" (Rom 5:15) and that he insisted extended to Gentiles as well as Jews on the basis of their faith as distinct from "works of the law," is made to conform to a kind of contractual arrangement in which the provisions of law also play an important continuing role.

Apart from the damage that all this does to the rhetorical force of the contrast that Paul draws in Galatians and Romans between "justification by faith" and "works of the law," it is important to note another fundamental difficulty. This is immediately posed by the fact that Paul explicitly dates the coming of the regime of the law to some 430 years *after* Abraham! (Gal 3:17). Furthermore, Paul's argument in Galatians is that the "coming of law" did not annul the promises that God had made previously to Abraham on the basis of faith in a period that was yet to experience the regulation of life by law. Sin and rebellious disobedience of the kind that ultimately ends in human tragedy and death "was indeed in the world before the law" (Rom 5:13), but the promises made to Abraham were based unconditionally on an interpersonal relationship based upon trusting faith. God for his part promises to be *steadfastly* faithful to his covenant people; they are to be his people "come what may" and he is to be their God. Clearly, to import legal principles into this retrospectively, and to make God's promise to Abraham conditional upon the keeping of the law, is illegitimately anachronistic. It is also logically vicious and inimical to Paul's fundamental message about justification on the basis of a "faith like Abraham's" rather than "works of the law."

But worse is yet to come. A presupposed understanding of "covenant" in contractual terms in the manner of historical federal theology, which makes it conditional upon keeping the law, and imposes a penalty in accordance with the normal requirements of the law of contract for behavior that is in breach of it, is also imported by the authors of *Pierced for Our Transgressions* into the story of God's dealing with Adam in Genesis 2 and

---

8. Jeffery, Ovey, and Sach, *Pierced for Our Transgressions*, 110.

9. Jeffery, Ovey, and Sach, *Pierced for Our Transgressions*, 110. See also 93–95.

3. As Paul points out, though sin and death was in the world before the coming of the law (Rom 5:13), it was a world in which God's dealing with humans was based on interpersonal trust between God and those whom he had made in his image, and involved God's exhortation to them to live in fellowship with him and in accordance with his will for them. Despite God's regular warnings of the tragic consequences of willfully seeking to "go it alone" by living autonomously and self-assertively in independence of him and his will for them, Adam and Eve set their faces on a road of self-reliance and self-determination and this meant that sin came into the world with death as the unavoidable outcome. Hence Paul says that "death exercised dominion from Adam to Moses" (Rom 5:14). Paul understands that the "coming of the law" some 430 years after Abraham was needed "because of transgressions" (Gal 3:19). This legal strategy of "reckoning with sin" was apparently understood to have been designed to deal with transgressions (Rom 5:13). Paul points out that previous to this, in the world in which there was no law, "there was no reckoning with sin." In other words, Paul's point seems to be that prior to the coming of the law there was no identification and codification of sins with specified penalties and hence no legal processes of the administration of law. It seems to follow that "until the law came" there was no interest in the kind of reckoning that involved the allocation of specific penalties and appropriate punishments of human transgressions in the manner of distributive justice. Paul characterizes the regime of the law in which sin exercised dominion in death "until Christ came" as a period in which life was lived in the consciousness of the law acting as a "disciplinarian" (Gal 3:34). All the while Paul seems to be at pains to distinguish the character of the relationship of God to those whom he had made in his image *before* "the coming of the law" from the relationship to those "whose sins were not like the transgressions of Adam" after "the coming of the law." Paul understood the state of affairs created by the wilful rejection by Adam of the tutelage of God's will (Rom 5:14) as having been essentially different from this regime following the "coming of the law."

Even so, the authors of *Pierced for Our Transgressions* apparently see no difficulty in importing the same Deuteronomic contractual and legal obligations that they anachronistically believe were a feature of God's promises to Abraham (in Genesis 12–13) into their understanding also of an alleged legal arrangement said to have also been made between God and Adam. The biblical warrant for this is said to be a contractual arrangement with Adam that is alleged to be *presupposed* in Genesis 2:17. Thus, it is argued that the "loving, personal nature" of the relationship that God had with those whom he had created in his image, was also "a 'legal' relationship in the sense that he set a law for them (Gen. 2.17)."[10]

As in historical federal theology, this effectively imports a presupposed "covenant of works" of a legal and contractual kind into the reading of Genesis 2:17. This contention is justified not by citing any biblical evidence but simply by asserting that as a matter of principle, "There is no inherent conflict between a *personal* relationship and a *legal* relationship"[11] and by pursuing this discussion in the context of a general understanding of covenants that assumes that all covenants involve a legal and contractual element.

It is important to emphasize that the authors of *Pierced for Our Transgressions* simply *presuppose* this alleged "covenant" with its legal component and contractual obligations even with Adam. They simply assert that the arrangement with God was a "legal arrangement" and that God "set a law" for Adam and Eve. This echoes the very same presupposition of Ursinus in the Heidelberg Catechism of 1563, which relied upon his more technical and legally explicit Major Catechism of 1562. Though this was not actually published until his death in 1584, from then onwards this presupposed contractual covenant, which Dudley Fenner referred to in England as the "covenant of works," was understood to carry the burden of a penalty should its contractual obligations be fractured. When God warned Adam and Eve that they "would surely die" should they opt for faithlessness in Genesis 2:17 this is assumed to have presupposed this legal obligation effectively of the "covenant if works." Given the contractual nature of the obligation that God had allegedly made with them, God's warning is interpreted as an explicit threat of the punishment of death. This set the fundamental propositions of subsequent federal theology even in the absence of any clear or specific reference to a covenant with Adam in Genesis 1–3. Indeed, save for a passing reference to a covenant with Adam ("at Adam") in Hosea 6 this theme is in fact absent from the entire Old Testament. It is pertinent to note also that even in Hosea the reference is to Adam's fracturing of his covenant relationship with God simply by his "faithlessness."[12] There is no suggestion, let alone anything explicit, relating to a contractual arrangement with legal obligations that Adam is said to have broken.

That all this is based on a presupposition in the absence of any clear biblical evidence is often openly acknowledged. D. A. Carson, for example,

---

10. Jeffery, Ovey, and Sach, *Pierced for Our Transgressions*, 109.
11. Jeffery, Ovey, and Sach, *Pierced for Our Transgressions*, 109.
12. Hos 6:7.

whose work is clearly important for Ovey, Jeffery, and Sach, tacitly accepts the problematic nature of this appeal to alleged legal and contractual obligations from a scriptural point of view. Carson admits that there is no explicit mention of a covenant with Adam in Genesis 1–3. "Yet," he says, "there is in some sense what some theologians have called a 'covenant of works.' . . . Those chapters lay a kind of seed bed of notions that are developed in much richer detail farther on in the Bible. The Bible doesn't talk of God as King in those chapters. But he is clearly reigning. The Bible doesn't talk about the church in those chapters, but there is the beginning of his own elect, covenant people."[13] This reasoning is sufficient to allow Carson to speak of an *implied* covenant with Adam also in Genesis 1–3, which is then described as an "agreement made by a sovereign—in this case, God—with human beings where there is worship and adoration on one side, and blessing and protection and privilege granted by God on the other side—*on condition of certain* obedience with threat of certain judgment if there is disobedience" (my italics).[14]

Likewise, S. J. Gathercole in his contribution to the 2004 work edited by Carson and others, entitled *Justification and Variegated Nomism*, is openly prepared to acknowledge that "forensic and juridical imagery" may be missing from the text of Genesis 2:17, but he nevertheless confidently declares that an implicit threat of the punishment of death grounds an alleged legal tradition of "transcendent retribution" that is to be found in the Old Testament and also in Paul.[15] This unstated but presupposed Edenic principle of "transcendent retribution" is then said to have been *recapitulated* in Deuteronomy 28 and 30:17–20.[16] As we shall see, Gathercole relies on this presupposed understanding of things to ground a penal understanding of death as "God's active punishment" on human sin that gives rise to the need of Christ's penal and substitutionary death.

While a divine threat to impose a penalty upon Adam should he fracture an alleged presupposed contractual arrangement with God may be required as the logical underpinning of the theory of the penal substitutionary death of Christ, it is clearly not explicit in the story of creation in Genesis and may not even be implicit there. Alas, there is no virtue in making a certainty out of something that is in fact less than certain. We have frankly to admit that the introduction of notions of a threat of retributive punishment for an alleged breach of contract in Genesis 2:17 as against God's warning

---

13. Carson, "Little Introduction to Covenants."
14. See Carson, "Little Introduction to Covenants."
15. Gathercole, "Justified by Faith, Justified by His Blood," 173.
16. Gathercole, "Justified by Faith, Justified by His Blood," 174.

to Adam of the pitfalls of "going it alone" in the world without his guidance and help may in fact actually be speculatively fanciful. Even so, the authors of *Pierced for Our Transgressions*, who are certainly reliant on Carson at a number of points in their argument, uncritically articulate essentially the same derivative of this federalist position, even despite its problematic nature as something at best "presupposed" and hence without a clear and uncontested biblical warrant.

An additional presupposition of the penal substitutionary theory of the atonement is that physical death itself must be understood in penal rather than in purely natural terms. Physical death is, after all, said to be the penalty for faithless disobedience that is alleged to have been threatened by God in Genesis 2:17. The suggestion is that Adam and Eve enjoyed an immortal life in the garden of Eden but were punished by the imposition of death and hence mortality as a penalty. They thus forfeited their original immortality because of their disobedience. From then onwards all sinfully disobedient humans after them suffered the same penalty of having to live with the anxiety of the mortal condition. Death therefore is not just a natural outcome of a sinfully disordered world; rather, death is a punishment quite deliberately imposed on humanity by God. This means that Christ's death is not something to be accommodated to the permissive will of God. As Gathercole insists, death is always "God's active punishment." And: "Death is by definition a penalty."[17] The theory of Christ's payment of the penalty of death instead of all humanity for the sinful disobedience inherited from Adam obviously assumes, and in fact logically relies upon, this penal understanding of death. It is alleged that this explains why it was necessary for Christ to come into the world and why the "penal substitution is foundational and the heart of the atonement."[18] An explicitly penal understanding of death accounts for the need of Christ to suffer and die, thus bearing the punishment necessary to save humanity from the sad implication of its mortal condition. If, as Thomas Schreiner says, in a helpfully succinct definition of penal substitution, "The punishment and penalty we deserved was laid on Jesus Christ instead of us, so that in the cross both God's holiness and love are manifested,"[19] then clearly this only has logical traction if death as such is understood as the continuing penalty imposed upon humanity for Adam's transgression. As the mechanism of its reversal Christ's death

---

17. Gathercole, "Justified by Faith, Justified by His Blood," 179.
18. Schreiner, "Penal Substitution View," 67.
19. Schreiner, "Penal Substitution View," 67.

therefore necessarily presupposes that death itself must be understood as a penal rather than a purely natural phenomenon.

Given that the phenomenon of death as an element of the experience of sinful humanity generally must therefore necessarily be understood in penal rather than in natural terms, it is not surprising to find that proponents of the penal substitutionary theory therefore allege that a penal view of death is a nonnegotiable teaching of the biblical tradition as a whole, starting with the Old Testament. In the first instance this is of course said to be a presupposed implication of the alleged contractual arrangement said to have been made with Adam in Genesis 2:17. This means that the words of this text cannot be construed merely as a *warning* of the unavoidable natural consequence of Adam's sinful decision to reject the proffer of life with God. It is not just that Adam and Eve are the victims of the self-inflicted natural consequences of their sin of living faithlessly. In other words, it is not that death is bound up with sin in a relation of cause and effect. Rather it must be understood explicitly in a retributive sense as the delivery of a divine threat to deprive the first humans of the privilege of immortality and to reduce them to the condition of mortality. This means that Genesis 2:17 is more than just a warning of the ultimate natural consequence of the sin of trying to live autonomously and independently, entirely separated from fellowship with God, but embodies an implicit and quite deliberate threat to carry out a divine punishment. It is said to have been imposed by the explicit retributive decision of God.[20] As we shall see in chapter 7, among proponents of penal substitution this required punishment is said to have been necessitated by God's justice. Thus, the punishment of death was imposed upon Adam and Eve as a consequence of their disobedience, and thereafter all humanity is said to have been deprived of immortality by being reduced to a mortal condition because of the dictate of God's justice. Furthermore, this unfortunate state of human affairs is said to have been initiated "in the day" that Adam and Eve ate of the fruit of the tree of the knowledge of good and evil. Having threatened the punishment of death, there is a sense in which God must be faithful to his promise: God's justice means that sinful humanity faces the inevitability of death as the explicit imposition of God.

It is something of a puzzle, however, that according to the Genesis tradition itself, despite this alleged threatened imposition of the punishment of death "in the day" that they ate of the fruit of the tree of the knowledge of good

---

20. Hence the authors of *Pierced for Our Transgressions* simply speak of "the 'death' threatened in Genesis 2.17" (118).

and evil, Adam and Eve *did not* die. In other words, it seems that this alleged threatened punishment was not actually carried out by God. If it was in fact a threat then *prima facie* it appears to have been an idle threat. The story of Genesis itself indicates that their actual fate was not death but exile from the garden of Eden.[21] This meant that *as mortals* they forfeited access to the tree of life that was said to have been located at the center of the garden, and hence they forfeited the *possibility* of immortal life in fellowship with God, but they did not physically die. Indeed, *Genesis* reports that Adam went on to live for a total lifespan of 930 years!

If the punishment that God allegedly threatened would befall Adam and Eve "in the day" that they ate of the fruit of the tree of the knowledge of good and evil does not appear to have been physical death after all, we clearly have a problem insofar as the alleged "penal" understanding of death is concerned. This is not new. It was noted already early in the fifth century by Augustine in *City of God*,[22] and even before him in the second century by Irenaeus in *Against Heresies*.[23] But it certainly poses an awkward question for the authors of *Pierced for Our Transgressions*. They acknowledge that God must by nature be true to his promise: having threatened the punishment of physical death, the divine truthfulness means that this is a threat that must be carried out. Thus, they readily admit that "for God to fail to punish sin would mean denying his own truthfulness."[24] Indeed, they argue that eventually the truthfulness of God explains the necessity of Christ's substitutionary death, for according to the theory of penal substitution, Christ's death is said to fulfill the requirements of this threatened punishment for all disobedient humanity in the wake of the sinful disobedience of Adam and Eve. In this way, indeed, his penal substitutionary death is said to demonstrate that God is true to his promise. Even so, God does not appear to have been true to his original promise in relation to Adam and Eve themselves, for whom the punishment "in the day" that they ate of the fruit of the tree of the knowledge of good and evil was not death but simply expulsion from the garden.

Obviously, this raises an important question for the authors of *Pierced for Our Transgressions*: "What is the nature of the 'death' threatened in Genesis

---

21. This is actually conceded by Gathercole in his exposition of Genesis 2:17. See "Justified by Faith, Justified by His Blood," 173.

22. Augustine, *City of God*, 13.12.

23. Irenaeus, *Against Heresies*, 2.33; 5.27.

24. Jeffery, Ovey, and Sach, *Pierced for Our Transgressions*, 125.

2:17?"²⁵ Their basic answer is that, insofar as Adam and Eve were cut off from open fellowship with God they were in a metaphorical sense "dead" even while in a physical sense being still alive. In other words, the authors of *Pierced for Our Transgressions* seek to sidestep the confronting difficulty that Adam and Eve did not die "in the day" of their disobedience by arguing that their expulsion from Eden may nevertheless be said to have been a "kind of death."

This in effect means that the authors of *Pierced for Our Transgressions* seek to handle the awkward fact of Adam's longevity by arguing that Genesis 2:17 does not actually mean to threaten "death" in the natural or biological sense "in the day" of Adam's disobedience, but refers instead specifically to a spiritual kind of death that results from having to live in a fractured relationship with God. This alleged threatened punishment of "spiritual death" rather than physical death itself was therefore what was imposed upon Adam and Eve "in the day" of their disobedience, even if their physical death was delayed.

This metaphorical or "spiritual" death that was visited upon Adam and Eve "in the day" of their disobedience is in turn said to be what is "now experienced by unbelievers," citing Ephesians 2:1. Here Paul reminds believers that they were once "dead in their transgressions and sins." This means that the punishment of God threatened in Genesis 2:17 may also legitimately be thought to be not biological or natural death but a metaphorical or "spiritual" kind of death. In other words, the penalty of death is really to be understood, not as physical death, but in fact as life—but a life of "exclusion from the loving presence of God."²⁶ This is the penalty that comes into effect immediately, and that is said to be a kind of "death." Even so, physical death is not to be treated as a natural phenomenon, but as a kind of "delayed" sentence that by extension is also envisaged in the threat of Genesis 2:17! It too is part of the penalty. It is just that the punishment of physical death is postponed for actual execution at a future time.

The interpretation of Genesis 2:17 by appeal to this kind of double effect is not peculiar to the authors of *Pierced for Our Transgressions*. The avid creationist and arch-critic of evolutionary theory Terry Mortenson also argues this.²⁷ First, Mortenson points out that the phrase "you shall surely die" does not necessarily mean to suggest that this is to happen instantaneously. He

---

25. Jeffery, Ovey, and Sach, *Pierced for Our Transgressions*, 118.
26. Jeffery, Ovey, and Sach, *Pierced for Our Transgressions*, 119.
27. Mortenson, "Genesis 2:17—'You Shall Surely Die.'"

points out that this is an English translation of a Hebrew idiom that literally reads "dying you will die," which does nothing more than intensify the impact of the verb. It means "you will most certainly die." Then the phrase "in the day" (*beyôm*) is said not necessarily to mean "on the very day" or "instantaneously," but simply "when," without strict temporal specification. So the meaning is "when" or "once" you disobediently eat of the tree of the knowledge of good and evil then you will (eventually) die (physically) . . . but meanwhile you are already spiritually dead.

Mortenson is able to include a natural or physical understanding of death in the meaning of Genesis 2:17 by referring to Paul's understanding of the inextricable relation of sin and death as this is expressed in Romans 5, where Paul "is clearly speaking of physical death" first in relation to Christ (verses 8–10) and "other men's physical death" (in verse 14). From these Pauline references Mortenson concludes that the constructions "dying you shall die" and *beyôm* ("in [the] day") implicitly include physical death as well as a kind of spiritual death. Thus he declares that Genesis 2:17 does not "require us to conclude that God was warning that the very day you eat from the tree is the exact same day that you will die physically." The Hebrew wording of Genesis 2:17 allows for a time lapse between the instantaneous spiritual death on that sad day of disobedience and the later physical death (which certainly did happen, just as God said, but for Adam some 930 years later). Mortenson's conclusion is that "As Scripture consistently teaches, both kinds of death (spiritual and physical) are the consequence of Adam's rebellion."[28]

It is pertinent to note that what is held to be what "Scripture consistently teaches" appears to be achieved by combining a text implying one thing with a text implying something at variance with it and then rationalizing the resulting awkward discrepancy so as to produce a kind of harmony. Thus, the absence of a reference to the immediate death of Adam and Eve "in the day" of their disobedience despite the alleged threatened punishment of Genesis 2:17 is combined with a reference of Paul to physical death as a consequence of sin in Romans 5:12 in order to produce the theory of spiritual death and delayed physical death; it then becomes "the consistent teaching of Scripture" that both kinds of death, physical as well as spiritual, are consequences of Adam and Eve's disobedience!

The struggle of the authors of *Pierced for Our Transgressions* to sustain a specifically penal understanding of death by combining talk of an immediate

---

28. Mortenson, "Genesis 2:17—'You Shall Surely Die.'"

metaphorical or spiritual death with an alleged delayed physical death is even further complicated insofar as they argue that God's alleged threatened punishment of sin is not just "death" as such but specifically "an *untimely* death." This is a punishment that is reserved specifically for the very wicked.[29] In this case "length of years" might naturally be judged to be a reward of God to the righteous. Even so, this kind of blessing is not said to have been extended to Adam despite his reported longevity. Rather, Adam's delayed death is said also to be a punishment. While an expedited and untimely death is brought forward for the exceedingly sinful, even a delayed physical death is said to be understood also in penal terms as the punishment for Adam's sin and for the sin of all humanity descended from him.

Furthermore, a penal understanding of death is also said to be implicit in biblical references to "the fate of those who are without Christ at the final judgment." The book of Revelation is said to speak of death as a synonym for the eternal suffering of hell. This "second death" (Rev 2:11; 20:6, 14; 21:8) is also declared to be a punishment.[30] But then the authors of *Pierced for Our Transgressions* immediately revert to the contention that "the very fact of our mortality" is a punishment.

When all this is added together as a conglomerate the firm conviction of the authors of *Pierced for Our Transgressions* is that "It is impossible to escape the conclusion that death is God's punishment for sin."[31] D. A. Carson is likewise able to convince himself that Genesis 2:17 is to be interpreted to refer to "death in all its forms."[32] Clearly, however, we might be forgiven for thinking that all this involves a degree of special pleading in which every possible biblical reference to death is pressed into service for use as evidence to secure the *penal* view of death. Given the lack of an unequivocally direct and clear evidential warrant, the alleged threat of death said to be implied in Genesis 2:17 and the delay in its execution, we are compelled to scrutinize the arguments for a penal rather than a natural understanding of death with great care.

---

29. Jeffery, Ovey, and Sach, *Pierced for Our Transgressions*, 124. As we shall see Romans 1:32 might well be cited in support of a belief in the retributive use of death for deserved gross evil deeds. Whether death is always to be experienced by humanity as a punishment is another question.

30. Jeffery, Ovey, and Sach, *Pierced for Our Transgressions*, 125.

31. Jeffery, Ovey, and Sach, *Pierced for Our Transgressions*, 123.

32. Carson, "Little Introduction to Covenants."

In defending the view that a penal view of death is sustained through the Old Testament, the authors of *Pierced for Our Transgressions* contend that this is supported by the appearance of the words "and he died" which are repeated as a refrain in Genesis 5 in relation to the succession of patriarchs. As was noted in the previous chapter, the Sydney Doctrine Commission Report apparently follows the argument of *Pierced for Our Transgressions* specifically at this point.[33] It also contends that a penal understanding of death is *implicit* not just in Genesis 2:17, but in the Old Testament generally, and particularly in the repetition of this refrain. The argument is that a specifically penal understanding of death is communicated insofar as this refrain may be read as a lament. After quoting Paul in Romans 5:12 in relation to the causal connection between sin and death (to which we shall return), the authors of *Pierced for Our Transgressions* appeal to the list of those patriarchs who had lived long lives and "who died" and then boldly assert that "The very fact of our mortality, *then*, is a penalty for sin. Indeed, 'the wages of sin is death' (Rom. 6.23)."[34]

The word "then" is printed in italics here given that it seems to be suggested that the logical force of a "lament" is that it signals God's punishment. Clearly, however, this does not follow as a logical entailment. There is no implicit logical connection between the lamentable sadness of death and the explicit punishment of God. Even a lament upon the death of someone, whether a friend or a revered personality of civic importance, does not mean that his or her death was imposed by God as a penalty rather than being a natural occurrence. Similarly, the use of the words "and he died" as a refrain in relation to the eventual demise of the patriarchs may be designed to signal nothing more than the bare historical fact of their passing.

On the other hand, Paul's use of the metaphor of "wages" (Rom 6:23), significantly quoting the Book of Wisdom rather than relying on the creation story in Genesis, may be understood to mean simply that death is a consequence of a *causal* kind that naturally results from the sin or fallenness of the world. It is an inevitable implication of sin as an all-pervasive failure of the creation to reach its divinely intended purpose rather than a punishment explicitly and intentionally imposed by God *ab extra* as a kind of divine fiat.

This understanding of a kind of causal or natural connection between sin and death as something inbuilt or immanent in fallen creation, rather than as the explicit imposition of a punishment by God that is expressive of his retributive justice has also been forthrightly challenged by

---

33. See page 67 above.
34. Jeffery, Ovey, and Sach, *Pierced for Our Transgressions*, 122.

S. J. Gathercole in his concerted defense of penal substitutionary theory.[35] Gathercole acknowledges that immanentist proposals have been in circulation right through the last century, often being entertained with enthusiasm and at times achieving considerable popularity. In the period between the world wars, C. H. Dodd championed the view, for example, that the notion of a God of retributive justice was in fact a pagan aberration. In his influential commentary on Romans Dodd tried to argue that "instead of being interpreted in a personal sense as the expression of 'the wrath of God' understood as a divine attribute, death is rather a kind of inevitable, almost automatic, consequence of sin. Sin *works itself out* in death."[36]

Dodd's proposals had been anticipated a decade earlier by the eminent Danish Old Testament scholar Johannes Pedersen, who had contended that the principle of retribution is not the heart of the biblical religion, but rather that the dominant position is a widely held emphasis on a direct causal connection between all human behavior and its corresponding consequence.[37] Pedersen argued that in the Hebrew tradition the language for divine punishment for sin had been worked out in an immanentist, cause-and-effect manner[38] so that "goodness bears blessings within itself, and that wickedness entails curse and misery."[39] While Pedersen almost certainly overplayed his thesis by insisting that this was not only a very early tradition but that it was in fact central to Hebrew thought, there is no doubt that this approach to sin and death is to be found in the Old Testament. It is notably most evident in Proverbs, where the paradigm example is Proverbs 26:27: "If you dig a ditch you will fall into it." We might also cite Jesus' own teaching: "Those who live by the sword will die by the sword."[40] In neither case is it necessary to suggest that God must be understood to be the active agent of retribution. Rather, a consequence of "curse and misery" is in a sense already immanently inbuilt as an inevitable outcome of evil behavior.

---

35. In his essay "Justified by Faith, Justified by His Blood."

36. John Knox's summary of Dodd's thesis in *The Death of Christ*, 155. Knox was himself of the view, however, that "actually there is no way to eliminate the evidence that Paul also thought of death as a punishment of sin and of 'the wrath' as the righteous judgment of God upon those who have disobeyed his will." Likewise, Käsemann observed in his *Romans*, 96, that "The argument that legal terminology is unsuitable for the ethical relation of God and man, and that it can be used only paradoxically (Dodd), is a relic of what is now an illegitimate liberalism."

37. Gathercole, "Justified by Faith, Justified by His Blood," 172.

38. Pedersen, *Israel*, I–II, 434.

39. Pedersen, *Israel*, I–II, 437.

40. Matt 26:52.

Similar proposals have in more recent times been pursued with vigor by Ulrich Wilckens and Klaus Koch. Wilckens followed Pedersen and others in arguing that God does not respond to human sin by resorting to active punishment; rather, the consequences of sin work themselves out in what he referred to as a *"Tat-Ergehen-Zusammenhang."*[41] Koch in turn argued that this understanding of the "impersonal" nature of the consequences of sin and evil tended to be lost and replaced by a more retributive understanding of things particularly in the process of the translation of Hebrew texts into Greek at the time of the production of the Septuagint. This tended to introduce an understanding of punishment in a retributive sense with God as the active agent of punishment.[42]

In arguing against this alleged immanentist understanding of the relation between sin and death in the Old Testament Gathercole naturally attempts to take issue with both Wilckens and Koch. For example, he questions Koch's conclusions about the extent of the cause-and-effect motif in the Old Testament, citing as a specific example Koch's contention that the LXX translation of Psalm 62:12 wrongly introduces a retributive sense through the use of the Greek word *apodidomi*. Gathercole seeks to counter this by observing that Paul acquiesces in the use of this very word in Romans 2:6. From this he concludes that "it is questionable whether Paul conforms to the reconstruction of OT theology proposed by Wilckens."[43] Whether the use of a single Greek word inherited from the Septuagint is sufficient to demonstrate that Paul consciously accepted a retributive sense of death and the rejection of an original Hebrew immanentist tradition that it was used to translate is surely problematic. We cannot assume that the subtle distinctions of a modern debate were as clearly in the forefront of Paul's mind as Gathercole would have us imagine. It is not possible to claim to know with confidence that Paul rejected an immanentist understanding of the consequences of sin and evil purely on the basis of his use of this word alone. On the contrary, it is pertinent to observe that in the preceding verse there is in fact a suggestion of a more immanentist understanding of things when Paul actually warns his readers that "by your hard and impenitent heart you are storing up wrath for yourself" (Rom 2:5), with the implication that the ultimate eschatological judgment of God will be a revealing of a state of affairs that is in some degree humanly self-inflicted.

Curiously, Gathercole is prepared to acknowledge that the immanentist theme is "strong in *Proverbs*" and also that retributive notions may certainly

---

41. Wilckens, "Exkurs: Das Gericht nach den Werken I."
42. Koch, "Is There a Doctrine of Retribution in the OT?"
43. Gathercole, "Justified by Faith, Justified by His Blood," 173.

have crept into the theology of the Old Testament as something acquired in the translation of the LXX. Indeed, he even admits that Klaus Koch might be "right to argue that Greek forensic language entails something of a shift in meaning from the Hebrew."[44] Somehow, however, these concessions get lost in his enthusiasm to highlight the continuing importance of divine retribution in his understanding of the biblical tradition. Even though he first speaks of a "*parallel* tradition of transcendent retribution both in the OT and Paul,"[45] he is in the end able to persuade himself that God's explicit imposition of the punishment of death is in fact the controlling understanding of things. This is said to be what is referred to by Paul, for example, in Galatians 3, where the "curse" is understood to have been transferred by God to the sinless Jesus "instead of" sinful humanity at large. This is said to be understood by Paul explicitly as the imposition by God of the punishment of death on the crucified Jesus. Thus, Gathercole concludes that "the thought of an impersonal curse" is "surely as foreign to Paul as it is to the OT."[46] The end result is that, despite his earlier concessions relating to the organic natural connection between sin and death, he categorically declares, "Death is by definition a penalty."[47]

Gathercole's method of argument in reaching this conclusion is instructive. First, he assumes that a pattern of divine retribution is rooted in the Old Testament where the "divine promise of life for obedience to the commandments is counterbalanced by God's threat of death for those who disobey."[48] This is said, somewhat surprisingly, to be already present in God's alleged "threat of death" to Adam in the garden of Eden should he disobey the command not to eat from the tree of the knowledge of good and evil. At this point Gathercole cites Genesis 2:17! But, as we have already noted, this is to assume exactly what needs to be proved from this text. Indeed, Gathercole himself has argued that we are to understand Genesis 2:17 as a threat containing an implicit penal understanding of death, even despite his own admission that forensic and legal imagery is actually missing from this text.

In order to arrive at this reading of Genesis 2:17 he therefore draws on Deuteronomy, arguing that the alleged Edenic command with its threatened punishment is "recapitulated" in Deuteronomy 30:17-20. In this text

---

44. Gathercole, "Justified by Faith, Justified by His Blood," 173.
45. Gathercole, "Justified by Faith, Justified by His Blood," 173. My italics.
46. Gathercole, "Justified by Faith, Justified by His Blood," 177.
47. Gathercole, "Justified by Faith, Justified by His Blood," 179.
48. Gathercole, "Justified by Faith, Justified by His Blood," 173.

infringements of God's command result in active punishment.[49] In other words, Gathercole reads Genesis 2:17 in the light of Deuteronomy's teaching that the administration of the law means that blessings and curses will accrue according to behavior.

Apart from the anachronism of introducing "commandments" into God's dealing with those made in his image long before "the coming of the law," this is problematic. As we have already noted, the idea that the promise of life to Adam is assumed to be conditional upon a juridical requirement is effectively a residual echo of the alleged "covenant of works" of historical federal theology. It suffers from the problem that this unfortunately logically assumes that Adam was already immortal in the garden of Eden and that he was deprived of immortal life by this alleged imposition of the punishment of death; the absence of any suggestion in the Genesis story that Adam and Eve were originally immortal poses a difficulty. Though Adam is warned of the dire consequences of his faithlessness, in fact Adam is mortal and will one day naturally die. Adam's fate is not death but banishment from the garden, and so entails that he is denied access to the tree of life at the center of the garden. Indeed, Gathercole himself effectively concedes that death is *not* imposed as a punishment on the day of Adam's disobedience by himself citing (in Hebrew) the tradition that Adam was in fact expelled from the garden on that day.[50]

Perhaps more important than Deuteronomy in Gathercole's interpretation of God's warning to Adam in Genesis 2:17 is his appeal to Paul's understanding of things in Romans. In contending that "the pattern of death as the consequence of sin is integral to Paul's thought"[51] it is explicitly a penal understanding of death that Gathercole has in mind. In relation to this he cites Romans 1:32; 5:12–14; 6:23; 7:5, and 7:11 as proof that Paul thought of death as the penalty intentionally imposed by God for sin, thereby transferring a curse from all humanity to Christ.

It is important to note that the first of these references is in a context in which Paul speaks initially of culpable misbehavior among the gentiles that is "worthy of death." Paul cites a catalogue of gross sins of those "filled with all manner of wickedness" (in Romans 1:29–31), and speaks of their knowledge of a decree to the effect that such people "deserve to die."[52] This is prob-

---

49. Gathercole, "Justified by Faith, Justified by His Blood," 174.
50. Gathercole, "Justified by Faith, Justified by His Blood," 173.
51. Gathercole, "Justified by Faith, Justified by His Blood," 175.
52. Romans 1:32

ably not a knowledge and rejection of the Jewish law among the gentiles, but a kind of moral awareness of the will of God that is acquired as self-evident truth that has been revealed in their hearts and in their consciences in accordance with a kind of natural law.[53]

In chapter 2 of Romans, even Jews, who are in possession of the Torah, are likewise castigated for their manifest failures. In this case, just as those committed to the well-doing are deemed to be worthy of a reward of glory and honor and peace in view of their good deeds, so the wickedly sinful are exhorted to repentance with the reminder of the prospect of having to face the wrath of God on the day of judgment.

In this context of talk of the revelation of the wrath or condemnation of God on all sinful behavior, first amongst the gentiles who well know that they deserve to die, and the equally apparent prospect of the revelation of the wrath of God both to them and to Jews on the day of eschatological judgment, belief in the immanentist view of the relation of sin and death is not possible, at least in Romans chapters 1 and 2. As Käsemann has observed, given the focus on the ultimate judgment and the threat of the exercise of the wrath of God, an impersonal or immanentist view of the relation of sin and death is hard to sustain.[54]

It has to be observed, however, that Paul's writing in these opening chapters of Romans is persuasively rhetorical in tone.[55] It is not just that the list of twelve offenses of the gentiles in Romans 1:29–31 is stylistically rhetorical rather than logical, as Käsemann has noted. Paul's writing is *persuasively* rhetorical in chapters 1 and 2 in the sense that he is at pains to emphasize the enormity and gravity of willfully sinful behavior in the context of highlighting the need for repentance (Rom 2:4). Furthermore, this exhortation to repentance is given heightened urgency by reminding both his gentile and Jewish hearers of the threat of apocalyptic judgment. On that day when God's righteous judgment will thus be eschatologically revealed their reprehensible behavior will be dealt with, along with the good deeds of those who in well-doing seek for "glory and honor and immortality." In this explicitly rhetorical context an implicit understanding of the meaning of references to death as a penalty for grossly sinful behavior is naturally appropriate; those involved in such gross behavior know that they "deserve to die." Clearly, the tone of these chapters invites a penal coloring to references to death. Gathercole is therefore justified in his belief that those who

---

53. See Käsemann's very detailed discussion of this in *Romans*, 36–52.
54. Käsemann, *Romans*, 37.
55. As Käsemann perceptively points out in *Romans*, 50–51.

through the twentieth century championed a purely immanentist understanding of the causal relation of sin and death were guilty of overplaying their hand.

Unfortunately, however, Gathercole then treats the principle of the retributive punishment of deeds worthy of death which he discerns in Romans 1 and 2 as a kind of heuristic paradigm to which references to death in the rest of Paul's writing are made to conform. This includes the very references from Romans 5:12–14; 6:23; 7:5, and 7:11 which he has already cited as proof of an understanding of death as a retributive punishment. A careful reading of these very texts, however, fails to reveal any explicitly retributive understanding of death as a penalty. Indeed, it is significant that, as Paul shifts his emphasis from speaking of the catalogue of specific sins of which both gentiles and Jews are personally guilty, he begins to reflect not upon "their sins" but on "sin." In a sense "their sins" are symptoms of an underlying invidious force to which he refers simply as "sin" (in the singular). When Paul speaks not of the "sins" of culpable individuals and of the societies to which they belong (as he does in Romans 1 and 2) but of "sin" in a more general sense as in Romans 5:12–21, for example, he thinks of an all-pervading gone-wrongness of the whole created order. As Käsemann puts it, in this context "death is a force which shapes the cosmos."[56] It is precisely at this point that death tends to be less a punishment that is justly imposed on individuals and more the natural outworking through all creation of "sin."

As a result, in Romans 5 Paul's language is less accusative of those whose sinfulness is deserving of death and more reflective of the sorry condition of the whole created order, which is characterized by "sin" as a falling short of its intended goal, ultimately with death as an integral element of its sorry condition. Curiously, Gathercole is himself not unaware of this. He in fact admits, "Often Pauline sin language is of sin as a power, and death personified as 'entering' and 'reigning' as in Romans 5.12–21."[57] Furthermore, he acknowledges that this is a "different model" from the model of Romans 2:6 where the reference is to the "God who repays each person according to his deeds." If there is difficulty in depersonalizing God's wrath and the thought of the imposition of the punishment of death as the explicit expression of God's condemnation of sins "worthy of death" in Romans 1:18–32, this is not the case in Romans 5:12–21. This effectively pulls the rug from Gathercole's own argument that death is *always* to be understood in a penal rather than a natural sense, not to mention the argument of Carson that

---

56. Käsemann, *Romans*, 141.
57. Gathercole, "Justified by Faith, Justified by His Blood," 179.

"death *in all its forms*" is to be regarded as a punishment imposed on all humanity in the wake of Adam's disobedience.

Likewise, it is significant, that it is not said in Romans 6:23 that death is the wages of "your sins" but that death is the wages of "sin." As has already been noted, the notion of the exercise of an explicitly retributive justice imposed on all humanity by God has to be brought to this text. Furthermore, in the next text cited by Gathercole in support of a retributively penal understanding of death, Romans 7:5, it is made clear by Paul that the sinful passions "were at work in our members to bear fruit for death." And a few verses later, in 7:11, he says that "sin deceived me . . . and killed me." It is clear that sin is a force that exercises a kind of agency leading to death. This does not necessarily mean that God is not secretly at work within this process, and a systematic theologian would almost certainly urge us to make a distinction between God's permissive will and the intentional exercise of his active will. However, notions of death as something *ab extra* from outside of human existence as a consequence of the operation of the agency of a retributive God exercising judgment and imposing a penalty on errant behavior have to be imported into Paul's language at these points.

These texts certainly speak of death as "a consequence of sin" but in none of them is there an explicit reference to God as the immediate agent of death as such, with death being explicitly understood as a punishment. An honest reading of Romans 5:12–14, 6:23, 7:5, and 7:11 will therefore reveal that a clear and unequivocal reference to the retributive agency of God is simply missing. At the same time, a careful reading of these four texts in fact suggests that a causal or immanentist connection of sin with death appears more likely to be the correct interpretation of them. Even if Wilckens and Kock, in the wake of the work of Pedersen and Dodd in the first half of the twentieth century, applied this insight more extensively and with more confidence than they should have, this is effectively to recognize at least the partial validity of their arguments.

Clearly, it is a mistake to over-systematize Paul at this point. Paul sometimes speaks of "our sins" or "your sins" but his more characteristic language is not to speak of a plurality of "sins" in this sense but of "sin" in the singular as a more general, all-pervading defect of the whole created order.[58] Death is an integral part of life in created space and time, whether animal or vegetable life; in the processes of living cells die and are replaced as organisms grow and develop and age in maturity and eventually die. In this natural context Paul's language is less rhetorical; it is not directed at the

---

58. Indeed, it is pertinent to note that in one of the key instances when Paul speaks of "our sins" in the genitive plural in 1 Corinthians 15:4 he is quoting a tradition that he had in fact received.

specific acts of wickedness of those whom he addresses and the societies of which they are part, and their consequent need of repentance, but is more generally reflective of the sorry state of the human condition as a whole—the condition in which he finds himself.

Death in this context is less a penalty and more a regrettable misfortune. The whole created order is not in need of additional punishment; it is already in the thrall of death. Paul sees clearly that it is not in need of punishment; it is in need of correction and redemption. And while a retributive understanding of behavior "worthy of death" might be understood to attract punishment in the form of a *premature* death, the death that comes naturally to all living things because of "sin," regardless of the reckoning or counting of transgressions of the law, is spoken of less as a penalty and more as a regrettable defect that necessarily affects all mortals. In this sense death comes to everyone without discrimination, whether wickedly sinful and destined to be punished or committed to well-doing and worthy of blessing. As the natural result of "sin," death in this sense eventually catches up with all mortals, even those who have lived long and blameless lives and who have been blessed by God with "length of days." Furthermore, when Paul reminds both gentiles and Jews of the gross sinfulness that attracts the judgment of the wrath of God among those "who deserve to die" (by contrast with the rewards of good deeds that apply to others), he naturally highlights their need of repentance; however, death as the consequence of "sin" that eventually comes to everyone is not a fate that might be avoided by repentance.

Clearly, it is a mistake to seize upon a retributive and penal understanding of death in the explicit sense of the punishment of a *premature* or *untimely* death that may be discerned in Romans 1 and 2, or in Deuteronomy 28, and assume that it is used in the very same sense elsewhere. In a context that is less focused on the rhetoric of persuasion, and therefore less conditioned by the need for repentance, death is understood as the more general natural consequence of "sin" and is therefore less a punishment and more a regrettable misfortune of the human condition that is to be overcome.

Gathercole himself warns of the danger of failing to attend to nuances of meaning that arise when words are used in different contexts. For example, he rightly says "we should not automatically import Pauline concepts from elsewhere into Romans 3–4..."[59] Following this principle, it would seem that we should therefore not automatically import notions of death as a

---

59. Gathercole, "Justified by Faith, Justified by His Blood," 177.

retributive punishment from Romans 1 and 2 into the interpretation of Romans 5:12–14, 6:23, 7:5, and 7:11, where, indeed, an immanentist interpretation of the relation of sin and death seems more appropriate. However, Gatherole himself falls into this very methodological trap, not only in relation to these four texts, but in places where the outcome is even more disastrous.

In his exposition of Romans 3:25–26, for example, there is a sense in which he abandons this principle by arguing the reverse—that these verses "should at least be seen in the context of the general picture elsewhere."[60] As a consequence the view of death as a retributive punishment that he finds in Romans 1 and 2 is brought from the forensic context of the law court to the interpretation of what Paul has to say in Romans 3 about what clearly belongs in the sacrificial context of the temple in Jerusalem. First, Gathercole simply assumes that, when Paul says that God's justification by grace as a gift through the redemption of Jesus Christ was achieved "by his blood," this phrase is simply a synonym for "a death." The same may be said of the use of this phrase in Romans 5:9. However, in Romans 3:25, where this phrase is found, it appears in association with a reference to God's putting forth Christ as a *hilasterion*.[61] However this much discussed word is to be understood, this is an unmistakable allusion to the temple cult of the Day of Atonement in which the high priest sprinkled the blood of the sacrificial victim on the lid of the ark of the covenant, the symbolic token of the divine presence. This cultic act operated as a *hilasterion* to effect the expiation of sin so as to renew the covenant with God.[62] This is obviously not the context of a law court from which the term "justification" originally derived. The reference to "the shedding of blood" signals that this is not just a reference to "a death." It is in fact an explicit reference to a *cultic* death.

Even so Gathercole, in speaking of the justification of sinners by the "shedding of blood" simply as "a death" then contends, "This reference to Jesus' death . . . should be understood in the general Pauline framework of sin leading to death."[63] He then assumes that this "leading to death" continues to presuppose the forensic framework appropriate to a court of law in which distributive justice is administered and in which death takes its place explicitly as the retributive punishment of transgressions.

At the beginning of his discussion of "Justification and Atonement in Romans 3.21–4.25," Gathercole warns, "There is not space here to deal with

---

60. Gathercole, "Justified by Faith, Justified by His Blood," 177.
61. This is the transliteration into English of the Greek ἱλαστήριον.
62. See also 1 John 4:10, where the word is *hilasmon*.
63. Gathercole, "Justified by Faith, Justified by His Blood," 179.

Christ's death as sin offering . . . still less to discuss at length the meaning of much discussed terms such as ἱλαστήριον."[64] Alas, this is a notoriously difficult text to interpret, but Gathercole's decision of methodological self-denial leaves him free to upload his own forensic understanding of death as a retributive punishment drawn from the forensic context of the exercise of God's wrath and judgment in a law court as the meaning of the essentially cultic term *hilasterion*.[65]

The explicit allusion to Christ's death as a *hilasterion*, in the very same verse as Paul's reference to the "shedding of Christ's blood," makes it imperative, however, that we acknowledge that this "shedding of blood" is not just a synonym for "*a* death" understood forensically as a retributive punishment. Its meaning belongs not in the law court but in the ritual of the temple. Whether it is to be translated as "expiation," "propitiation," or simply "mercy seat" as the place of reconciliation and atonement where the high priestly act of sprinkling of the blood of the sacrificed victim occurred, this is not the language of a law court. As Käsemann has pointed out explicitly in relation to Romans 3:25: "Cultic language can hardly be contested." Significantly, Käsemann therefore goes on to observe categorically, "The satisfaction theory cannot be based upon it."[66] Alas, this is not to mention satisfaction specifically as this is proposed by the penal substitution theory as the means of demonstrating God's own righteous condemnation and wrath in the exercise of his judgment of sin.

Even so Gathercole does not hesitate to import forensic language into this radically different context of the sacrificial cult of the temple in Jerusalem. At this point in his discussion of Romans 3:25–26 he even dares to cite Paul's catalogue of reprehensible sins of the gentiles in Romans 1:18–32, noting the forensic coloring of this passage that ends with the statement that "those who do such things are worthy of death." He then goes on: "The whole context of 3.21–26 is of course how people are saved through the work of Christ from this divine decree of death and divine action of judgment. Death is by definition a penalty."[67]

This is a remarkably promiscuous way of doing theology. The elision of essentially different contexts in this kind of way, without attending to the

---

64. Gathercole, "Justified by Faith, Justified by His Blood," 168. Transliterated into English, ἱλαστήριον as *hilasterion*.

65. Paul uses this term here at Romans 3:25 but it is not found anywhere else. It is open to be interpreted as an "expiation" (of sin), "propitiation" (of the divine wrath), or simply as "mercy seat" (the lid of the ark as the token symbol of the presence of God where sacrificial blood was sprinkled to renew the covenant on the Day of Atonement).

66. Käsemann, *Romans*, 97.

67. Gathercole, "Justified by Faith, Justified by His Blood," 177.

importance that a change of semantic context has on the precise meaning of words, is bound to lead to a confused and distorted understanding of things. The assumption that the forensic language of the law court and the cultic language relating to the sacrificial offerings of the temple is simply univocal, so as to articulate a single allegedly coherent explanation of Paul's understanding of the way in which justification and the experience of reconciliation and atonement with God had been achieved, must therefore be very seriously challenged.

It is important to say that Gathercole is not alone in assuming the methodological validity of interpreting the meaning of language without observing the significance of the impact of differences of context in which such language is used. If anything he is simply a paradigm illustration of the promiscuous elision of contexts that abounds in many expositions of the penal substitution theory of the atonement. Gathercole's fellow contributor to *Justification and Variegated Nomism*, Peter T. O'Brien, for example, also nonchalantly assumes that the penal substitutionary death of Christ is quite simply to be understood as what is meant when Paul uses the term *hilasterion*, thereby also dropping a forensic and juridical understanding of death as a punishment into the context of the sacrificial system of the temple. O'Brien in fact quotes yet another fellow contributor to the same volume (Douglas Moo) when he speaks of "the substitutionary death of Christ Jesus as a ἱλαστήριον for sinners" and then unpacks the meaning of ἱλαστήριον' in parenthesis as ("mercy seat"; "propitiation").[68] It is almost as though it is a self-evident truth that is not in need of explanation or defense that the sacrificial death of a victim as a temple offering and Christ's substitutionary death understood on analogy with the punishment imposed in a court of law need not to be differentiated. Indeed, O'Brien's omission of the term "expiation" along with "mercy seat" and "propitiation" in his parenthetical explanation of the meaning of *hilasterion* speaks volumes: it suggests that we are not to think in terms of the expiation of sin by a sacrificial offering; instead we are to think in terms of the propitiation of God's wrath in the exercise of his righteous judgment upon sins that are "worthy of death." Death is not so much an offering that expiates sin, it is a juridical punishment that satisfies a wrathful God.

The forensic and juridical language appropriate to a court of law cannot, however, simply be imported into the cultic context of the temple and its sacrifices. It would be bizarre, for example, to speak of a sacrificed animal being pronounced guilty, or of an animal being judged to be "worthy of death" *as a punishment*. We may have to acknowledge that we do not really

---

68. O'Brien, "Was Paul a Covenantal Nomist?," 291.

understand how sacrifices were understood to have worked in the cults of the ancient world, but we can be sure that the procedures of the temple and those of a court of law belong in different worlds. Likewise, it makes no sense to speak of the transfer of God's wrathful condemnation of sin to the crucified Christ from the animal victims of temple sacrifices. If there is any notion of substitution in Paul's appeal by way of analogy to the "shedding of blood" in the temple it is the *ideal* substitution of the eternal Christ "who ever lives to make intercession for us," who is in a sense the eternal substitute for the passing particulars in space and time of the animal victims of the sacrifices of the temple in Jerusalem. At this point it is significant to remember that Paul does not just inherit the culture of Hellenistic Judaism but, as a citizen of the intellectual world of Middle Platonism, almost certainly shared its epistemological commitment to an amalgam of Stoic insights with an otherworldly Platonism. A kind of Middle Platonic epistemological dualism seems to be reflected, for example, in the analogy that Paul draws between the high priest and the temple in Jerusalem and Christ as the heavenly high priest in the sanctuary of heaven, as well as in the contention that we humans are able to participate by faith in the eternal life of the raised Christ through the gift of his Spirit, which is accessed in space and time.

It is clearly a mistake to conflate the meaning of the forensic language of the law court and the cultic language of the temple in a forlorn effort to create a single coherent theory of atonement. If the language from one context is allowed to creep into the other, then it is important to be alert to the inevitability that a significant nuance of meaning will result. John Knox once perceptively observed that we have in the New Testament "two stories" relating to humanity and its redemption: "In the one, Man is the helpless slave of Sin, who uses the Law to keep him in subjection and finally rewards his victim by turning him over to Death."[69] In the other story "man has sinned against God's holy law and has incurred the penalty of death."[70] The story of the sacrificial Lamb who takes away the sins of the world, and the story of the conqueror of the slavery of sin are two different stories. "Each story," he says, "is coherent and consistent in itself, and each story is profoundly true; but the two stories cannot be mixed, with anything like a coherent result. In both stories Man, Sin, Law, Death and Christ appear. But the role which each plays varies with the story."[71]

---

69. Knox, *Death of Christ*, 155–56.

70. Knox, *Death of Christ*, 156.

71. Knox, *Death of Christ*, 155.

The pity is that Gathercole's concentration on Paul's reference to the "shedding of blood" simply as "*a* death," and then its assimilation at his hands to the penal view of death as always a punishment, privileges the concept of death in his exposition of Paul's understanding of justification to the exclusion of an interest in the saving significance of Christ's resurrection.

It has already been noted that Paul's reference to the shedding of Christ's blood in close association with his appeal to the cultic concept of a *hilasterion* is based upon the drawing of an analogy between the taking of the blood of the sacrificial victim by the high priest through the temple to sprinkle it on the lid of the ark, the mercy seat, understood as the symbolic token of the place of the presence of God. In addition, it has to be noted that this temple analogy also invites a shift of focus from the death of Christ to the imaginative contemplation of the passage of the *raised and glorified Christ*, who, "passing through the heavens" as the great high priest, now sits victoriously at the right hand of God, "where he ever lives to make intercession for us."

While this theme is of course central to the Epistle to the Hebrews, where its saving significance is drawn out in detail (especially in Hebrews 9 and 10), it is clearly a motif that was already well known to Paul. And we may say, that this was with the notion of justification obviously not far from his mind. In Romans 8:34 he says: "Who is to condemn? Christ Jesus is the one who died—more than that, who was raised—who is at the right hand of God, who indeed is interceding for us." It seems clear enough that Paul is thinking of justification not only as a release from condemnation that was achieved in a single moment, at the time of Jesus' death by the shedding of his blood, but as a continuing reality that is integral to the eternal work of the raised and glorified Christ at the Father's right hand. Hence the righteousness of God is understood by Paul to have been demonstrated in the composite event of Christ's death *and* resurrection: Christ "died for our sins *and was raised* for our justification" (Rom 4:25).

We have also to appreciate the importance of the fact that the Christ who was raised and glorified "at God's right hand" is also the Christ who is known by faith in space and time through the gift of his Spirit. Indeed, given that Paul understood the raised Christ to have become a "life-giving Spirit" (1 Cor 15:45), it is understandable that his continuing work of representing humanity by interceding on its behalf "at the right hand of the Father" can, from the point of view of human experience in space and time, also be said to be a continuing work of the Spirit. Thus, it is not just that the raised Christ, understood on analogy with the high priest entering the holy of holies is understood by Paul to be at the right hand of the Father making intercession for us as our representative or priestly advocate; in Christ's presence with us as Spirit he is understood also as a priestly or representative person "interceding" for us (Romans 8:26–27). This aspect of his redemptive work is understood to be timelessly eternal and an ever-present happening in time as a consequence of the resurrection. Clearly, this should not be excluded from the total picture of Paul's understanding of justification and the achievement of reconciliation and peace with God. In a sense, the justification of sinners may be accessed in space and time by faith because of the eternal reality of this redemptive work of Christ *on their behalf*.

Unfortunately, a treatment of the significance of the resurrection falls by the wayside in Gathercole's exposition of Paul's understanding of justification, which he preferentially pins instead to Jesus' death, even despite Paul's statement in Romans 4:25, in which he declares that Christ "died for our sins and was raised for our justification."[72] Gathercole apologetically explains his failure to devote time to a consideration of the possible saving significance of the resurrection simply because of the want of space. This is the same reason that he has already cited for not entering upon a discussion of the meaning of *hilasterion*, though it has to be conceded that it may also be that he believed that the term *hilasterion* had already been adequately discussed in the literature. In any event, we may well sympathize with the challenge of having to come to terms with want of space; it is not possible to deal with everything. In this case, however, the plea of lack of space to deal with the resurrection conveniently allows Gathercole the freedom to focus exclusively on Jesus' death in a crucicentric way as that which accomplishes reconciliation and atonement; hence, the justification of sinners is said simply to have been achieved "by his blood" (Rom 3:25; 5:9). In this way he is able to isolate Jesus' death so as then to permit the explanation of its significance in penal terms as the payment of the penalty required by retributive justice. Justification is understood to have been achieved therefore by Christ's payment of the penalty of death *instead of* humanity at large; but this is unfortunately to the exclusion of a consideration of the positive saving and life-transforming impact upon humanity at large of Christ's resurrection and the continuing impact of the gift of his Spirit.

---

72. Thomas Schreiner likewise acknowledges the importance of resurrection: "God's people are impoverished if Christ's triumph over evil powers at the cross is slighted, or Christ's exemplary love is shoved to the side, or the healing bestowed on believers by Christ's cross and resurrection is downplayed." ("Penal Substitution View," 67.) However, as Gregory A. Boyd observes: "Schreiner asserts that the resurrection is necessary for us to be forgiven and thus is part of the penal substitutionary dimension of Christ's work. Unfortunately, Schreiner nowhere explains why this is so." ("Christus Victor Response," 99). In fact, in Schreiner's account of the penal substitution theory the resurrection is seriously marginalized.

In a balanced and carefully argued article on "Paul's Use of Righteousness Language against Its Hellenistic Background" (also in volume 2 of *Justification and Variegated Nomism*), Mark Seifrid is careful to point out, however, that the event in which God's righteousness is demonstrated is the event of Christ's death *and* resurrection.[73] In other words, Christ's death and resurrection form a composite redemptive event, as two sides of the one penny. There is obviously an inextricable causal relation between death and resurrection, for example, given that death is necessarily logically prior to resurrection. It is not possible to have the latter without the prior occurrence of the former: resurrection is resurrection *from the dead*. On the other hand, the significance of Jesus' death cannot be understood other than in the light of the experience of the resurrection, which ensured that Christ was understood to have been vindicated by God, thereby becoming victorious over death. If the resurrection of Christ is integral to the demonstration of the righteousness of God in this way, then this composite saving event, inclusive of the resurrection and not just his death alone, is what grounds the conviction in faith that "God shows his love for us in that while we were yet sinners Christ died for us" (Rom 5:8). If we are justified by the shedding of Christ's blood, we are at the same time justified by his resurrection.

At this point we also encounter another aspect of Paul's understanding of justification, and the concomitant experience of reconciliation and the achievement of atonement and peace with God. This is precisely its essentially experiential face. Paul is not just a theorist. He is essentially an empiricist whose talk of justification is grounded in, and flows out of, his experience of a sense of freedom and release from bondage to sin, which in faith he acknowledged to have resulted from the redemption won by the death and resurrection of Christ. Thus, in celebrating the new life in Christ Paul declares in Galatians that Christ redeemed us (perhaps significantly, Paul says here from "the curse of the law " rather than from "the curse of God") in order that "in Christ Jesus the blessings of Abraham might come to the Gentiles." He then very significantly adds "so that we might receive the promise of the Spirit through faith" (Gal 3:13–14). The vindication of Christ by God and the demonstration of the righteousness of God is through the event of the death and resurrection of Christ *and the gift of the Spirit*. Just as the righteousness of God is not just an abstract divine virtue, but something demonstrated by God in the actuality of human experience in the event of

---

73. Seifrid repeats this phrase regularly and systematically in "Paul's Use of Righteousness Language."

Christ's death and resurrection, so it is as a humanly experienced reality that continues to be concretely known to faith through the actual gift of the Spirit and not just abstractly as a theory to be understood.

Paul is very clear that it is participatively "in Christ Jesus" that the blessing of Abraham might come upon the gentiles and that the promise of the Spirit might be received through faith. In contending that those who "set their mind on the flesh" are those for whom the law is a regulatory disciplinarian, he declares by contrast that those who set their mind on the Spirit enjoy the freedom of the children of God. What frees them from the burdensome obligation of trying to keep the law is not so much the theoretical awareness of a legal fiction, involving the notional transfer of God's wrathful condemnation of sin from humanity at large to Christ, as the actual gift of Christ's Spirit *to* humanity at large. Those who are justified by faith rather than "works of the law" are those who are "in the Spirit, since the Spirit of God dwells in (them)" (Rom 8:9). Though "the body is dead because of sin, the Spirit is life because of righteousness" (Rom 8:10). It is in the Spirit that they are freed from the obsessive burden of law-keeping by their personal commitment in trusting faith to abide by the loving will of God. This means that the justifying effect of Christ's death and resurrection is not speculative and theoretical, but in an important sense, empirical and descriptive. Justification and the achievement of human reconciliation and peace with God is in this way not just something to be understood, but something to be concretely encountered as a reality that is entered into by faith and known by actual acquaintance. Paul is thus often at pains to remind his hearers of their initial experience of the proffer of the possibility of new life in the form of gift of the Spirit that he describes as something that they actually knew. It was something concretely experienced in faith and celebrated as an object of thanksgiving "in Christ" through the gift of the Spirit.

Among other things this means that the transforming impact of the gift of the Spirit is not to be thought of as something subsequent to faith, but in fact as logically prior to faith. Faith is the awareness of it that is itself logically, though not necessarily temporally, prior to placing one's trust in it. This means that the life of the Spirit is a matter not of trying but of trusting. It is not, for example, that love tries to be kind; rather love *is* kind. It wells up spontaneously as the gift of grace, like a "spring of living water." As Paul says: "Love has been poured out into our hearts by the Holy Spirit who has been given to us" (Rom 5:5). The new life "in Christ" then becomes a matter not of trying to achieve righteousness by doing the "works of the law" but of a trusting faith in the God who in the death and resurrection of Jesus has demonstrated his righteousness and is always faithful to this promise to deliver the gift of the Spirit to his faithful ones.

If atonement is not a theory but an actual experience of reconciliation and peace with God "in Christ," it is a mistake to submit it to the kind of reductionism in which it is treated simply as a kind of legal maneuver in which God is said notionally to have accepted the death of Christ as the satisfactory payment of the penalty of death for Adam's transgression instead of humanity at large. The justification of humans by faith in Christ is not just an abstraction of thought about the redirection of the oppressive burden and guilt of sin away from humanity. It is not just something about which Paul can simply theorize, leaving generations of Christian theologians to try to understand. Rather, justification, reconciliation, and peace with God is something to be apprehended in faith and entered into as a form of life, a concrete living experience.

John Knox, in *The Death of Christ*, perceptively observed, "The meanings . . .which the images of victory and sacrifice were created to express were empirical meanings. They were realities known, at least in principle, or in their first fruits, within the life of the Church, and among those who participated in the Spirit. . . .The realization of this deliverance belonged, and of course belongs still, to the very existence of the new community of the Spirit."[74] What was inherited as a consequence of the promises originally made to Abraham by those of faith in Christ and that freed them from the burden of the "curse of the law" involved much more than a notional awareness of a kind of legal maneuver in the mind of God focused narrowly on Christ's death, but the living reality of the experience of grace through the transformative gift of the Spirit.

It seems clear enough that attempts to defend the penal substitutionary theory of the atonement have to face very considerable hurdles. Not least among these is the problematic nature of the view of Adam and Eve as originally immortals, and of the penal view of death itself and mortality as the punishment imposed by God on all humanity in the wake of their disobedience. Adam and Eve were mortals whose disobedience resulted not in death but in their forfeiting of access to the tree of life in the center of the garden. In relation to this story the redemptive work of Christ may be understood, not so much in terms of the payment of an alleged penalty in the form of the punishment of death, but in terms of the restoration of access to the tree of life, which, in the light of his resurrection from the dead, may be perceived to be located on the hill of Calvary.

---

74. Knox, *Death of Christ*, 156.

In addition to this fundamental problem, however, we have to take note of the fact that an overconcentration on Christ's death as such, and the reductionist attempt to develop a theory of atonement effectively on the basis of it alone, with only a perfunctory reference to the resurrection, and indeed frankly without serious consideration being given to the resurrection, does not do justice to the New Testament witness to the mystery of God's redemption of humanity.

Unfortunately, the crucicentric linking of the justification of sinners to the death of Jesus and the understanding his death as the payment of a penalty, effectively to the exclusion of a consideration of the significance of the resurrection, leads methodologically to some problematic theological conclusions in relation to the role of God in redemption. Ultimately this impacts our perception of the immanent nature of God. In the first instance, the preferential focus on the death in achieving God's saving purpose gives rise to some language that is suspiciously univocal. S. J. Gathercole, for example, tends to equate the human actions of those who crucified Jesus with the divine action of God in achieving his own redemptive purpose. Thus, it is said that insofar as Paul used the language of the "handing over" of Jesus as an alternative to the language of death, this "has the double sense both of the divine 'handing over' and the human act of Judas."[75] It is almost as though the language of the "handing over" of Jesus is to be understood univocally regardless of whether the grammatical subject of the handing over is God or Judas. "Thus," Gathercole says, "Paul emphasises the *unity* of the act of God in dealing with sin and the human act of judgment upon Jesus."[76] In this case there is an ironic sense in which the handing over of Jesus to arrest and execution somewhat uncomfortably suggests that Judas performed the role of a messenger of God's good purpose as a kind of "evil angel." And this is not to mention the role of Caiaphas, Pilate, and the crowd baying for blood. According to the logic of the penal substitutionary theory of the atonement all human players are portrayed as unwitting agents of the good purposes of God insofar as they are said to have carried out his plan of salvation. Judas, Caiaphas, Pilate, and the crowd are humanly responsible for crucifying Jesus, but from the divine point of view this is deliberately intended to achieve the just punishment for humanity's sins, as though the end justifies the means. Hence, Jesus undergoes the curse of a cruel death. As Paul says, "Cursed is the man who hangs upon a tree." But this is not just a humanly contrived curse. According to the proponents of the penal substitutionary theory of atonement it is also the "curse of God" that is normally

---

75. Gathercole, "Justified by Faith, Justified by His Blood," 182.
76. Gathercole, "Justified by Faith, Justified by His Blood," 183.

directed towards the condemnation of human sin, but now transferred to the innocent Jesus *instead of* humanity at large.

This understanding of the role of God in the work of human redemption, with its focus almost exclusively on the death of Christ, is to be contrasted with what transpires in relation to the role of God when this redemptive event is thought of as the composite justifying event of death-and-resurrection. In this case, Jesus' crucifixion and death occurs unequivocally at the hands of evil men; God's active role is to vindicate and justify Jesus by resurrection. God's active role is understood in terms of the vindication of the unjustly persecuted Jesus through his being raised from the dead by God and exalted to glory as Lord and Christ. This is the pattern of argument, for example, in the paradigm early post-Easter sermons now found in Acts 2 and 3: "This man Jesus whom you crucified, God has raised up and designated to be Lord and Christ."

All this may be understood to have occurred in the foreknowledge of God, and to have been indirectly in accordance with his *permissive will* without suggesting that it occurred as a consequence of an explicit decision of God acting *ab extra* to exercise retributive punishment. There is no necessary implication that what transpired on Calvary was in accordance with the active will of God in achieving his alleged redemptive purpose. It is positively not as though God the Father is complicit in the gross miscarriage of justice perpetrated by the betrayal by Judas and the manipulation of law by Caiaphas, Pilate, and the crowd.

If the evil action of those who persecuted and crucified Jesus is to be accommodated as a matter of the permissive will of God this is because God gives humans the freedom to do evil as the other side of the penny of the freedom necessary for them to become morally responsible human persons. But talk of the active will of God in achieving his own plan of salvation by sending his Son, not just into the world "that others might live," but explicitly that he might die, and not just to die as the natural end of his temporal existence in space and time, but to die prematurely in great pain upon the cross as the divinely intended way of bearing the penalty for the world's sin, is quite another matter. In this case it was not just that God was able to achieve his ultimate purpose by turning the tables on those who had unjustly treated and crucified Jesus thereby vindicating him in resurrection and exaltation to glory. Rather, the death itself is the central "moment" of the divine plan and purpose. In this way, the immediate agents of Jesus' death—Judas, Caiaphas, Pilate, and the crowd—unwittingly become the earthly instruments through whom God is said to have achieved his salvific purpose of the justification of sinners.

It is clear that, insofar as the immanent nature of God is necessarily understood on the basis of what is revealed to our understanding in the economy of salvation, then the witness of the New Testament to God's redemption in Christ though the composite saving event of his *death and resurrection* cries out for attention. Otherwise, it is highly likely to lead to a conception of God and of God's dealing with his people that, to say the least, we may find distinctly uncomfortable if not morally objectionable. Given that the penal substitutionary theory of atonement logically leads to a theology of the kind that S. J. Gathercole has laid out with great candor in the form of his account of the role of Judas as the active human agent of God's redemptive purpose, thus portraying him as a kind of "evil angel," we may rightly regard it as questionable and highly problematic.

In other words, the concentration on Jesus' death by arguing that the justification of sinners was achieved simply by "the shedding of Jesus' blood," to the effective exclusion of a consideration of the vindicating role of God in Jesus' resurrection, leads to an unwelcome set of implications in relation to our understanding of the redemptive action of God and hence our understanding of the immanent nature of God. Indeed, as has been argued at length in the companion volume to this book, *Arius on Carillon Avenue*, insofar as the Father is said to have sent his ever-obedient Son into the world to suffer the punishment of death in order to achieve the good of his own ultimate salvific purpose, we may perceive a troublesome congruence of this theory of atonement with the neo-Arian belief in the "eternal subordination of the Son to the Father."

This is an ample illustration of Karl Rahner's contention that the understanding of the immanent nature of God is grounded in the revelation of God in the economy of salvation, but care obviously has to be taken to ensure that what is revealed of God is rightly understood. On the other hand, as Rahner has also observed, a doctrine of redemption cannot satisfactorily be worked out independently of the doctrine of the Trinity. We may wisely be open to the possibility that a more orthodox Trinitarian view of God may helpfully inform an alternative approach to the doctrine of human redemption that is in accordance with "the love of the Father, the grace of the Lord Jesus Christ, and the fellowship of the Spirit." Meanwhile, in the following chapters of this book we shall examine some further problematic implications of the penal substitutionary theory in relation to the understanding of the immanent nature of this Trinitarian God.

5

PENAL SUBSTITUTION AND THE CARICATURE OF GOD

If the failure to address the fundamental theological considerations that were raised in the previous chapter is sufficient to trigger some serious questioning, which makes the 2010 Sydney Doctrine Commission Report's exposition of penal substitution appear somewhat problematic, this is not to be compared with the seriousness of the theological problems that flow from the report's handling of the criticisms that have been leveled against the theory.

Apart from its earnest attempt to expound a biblically and morally acceptable account of penal substitution, there is a concerted attempt at pushback in the 2010 Doctrine Commission Report insofar as it explicitly seeks to answer criticisms of the theory that have been publicly expressed on regular occasions, but very notably in Britain in 2003 and 2004 by the Baptist leader Steve Chalke, and in 2007 by Jeffrey John, who at the time was the Anglican dean of St Albans. This is the charge that penal substitution misrepresents God the Father as the perpetrator of a cosmic form of child abuse, or as a psychotic, acting out of pique or worse out of some kind of obsessive revenge and uncontrolled anger. When critics of penal substitution go on to say that the theory represents God as one who acts in relation to his own Son in a morally dubious way, which in turn tends to represent the Son as a hapless innocent victim, this charge tends simply to be passed over by the proponents of the theory as a misunderstanding. It is said to carry no real weight because it in fact deals with a kind of caricature. The suggestion is that such criticisms therefore need not to be taken seriously.

For example, despite the 2010 Sydney Doctrine Commission Report's own appeal to the alleged "wrath of God" that is said to issue in a demand

PENAL SUBSTITUTION AND THE CARICATURE OF GOD 107

for justly punitive or "deserved justice" of a kind that can only really be satisfied by the death of God's own incarnate Son, the report argues that Steve Chalke's characterization of God's dealing with his Son in terms that are unfortunately reminiscent of a form of child abuse, seriously misrepresents the authentic biblical doctrine (see paras. 24, 29, and 36). The implication is that, if it is understood rightly and biblically, and provided unfair caricaturing is carefully avoided, penal substitution may be seen to be morally and theologically acceptable.

This kind of response to criticisms of the theory is regularly heard. Indeed, Joel Green and Mark Baker note that the contention that it is a caricature "is the *usual* defence of the model of penal substitution."[1] A historical paradigm example of this kind of defense was articulated by John Stott in his response to the criticism of penal substitution of Sir Alister Hardy. Stott charged that Hardy "caricatured the Christian understanding of the cross in order the more readily to condemn it."[2]

In alleging that criticisms of penal substitution exhibit an incurable and unfair tendency to deal with a mere caricature, the authors of the Sydney Doctrine Commission Report rely heavily on the work of Garry Williams, who, in his spirited presentation in support of penal substitution at the London Symposium of July 2005, also accused the critics of the theory of dealing with a caricature in order to dismiss it. In that address Williams insisted that "it is not enough for critics of penal substitution to engage with such caricatures of the doctrine; they have a responsibility to distinguish more carefully the crude from the sophisticated, and to deal with it at its best."[3]

Similarly, N. T. Wright, in a vehemently forthright response to Jeffrey John that was published on the Fulcrum website on April 23, 2007,[4] accused John of presenting not just "a sad caricature" of "the atonement itself" but of "the biblical doctrines of God's wrath" and "God's moral providence" as well. After accusing Jeffrey John of being guilty of "rejecting a caricature of the biblical doctrine," Wright went on to argue that if John found his own self-generated caricature offensive and entirely out of kilter with the character of God as revealed, not just in the life and death of Jesus but in the biblical tradition as a whole, then he might draw upon the same understanding of the character of God to attend to a more accurate alternative version of the theory, which might well be found to be perfectly acceptable. Thus, Wright

---

1. Green and Baker, *Recovering the Scandal of the Cross*, 47 (my italics).
2. Stott, *Cross of Christ*, 112.
3. Williams, "Penal Substitution," 78.
4. Wright, "Cross and the Caricatures."

contends that John's rejection of traditional approaches to the atonement on the basis of a false caricature is entirely unwarranted: "To throw away the reality because you don't like the caricature is like cutting out the patient's heart to stop a nosebleed." It is thus not the notion of penal substation itself but the promotion of a popular and unsophisticated caricature that is regularly said to be at fault.

On the other hand, N. T. Wright points out with equal vehemence and with some regret that it is not only the critics of the theory, like John, who are guilty of dealing with a non-biblical caricature. He openly acknowledges that "many Christians have spoken, in effect, of the angry God upstairs and the suffering Jesus placating him"[5] and that misrepresentations of this general kind abound even in positive presentations of the theory that are earnestly designed to defend it. To Wright's mind, this is very notably the case, for example, in the published attempt of Michael Ovey and two students at the Oak Hill Theological College, who sought to defend the penal substitutionary theory of the atonement explicitly in the face of Steve Chalke's criticism of it.[6] Thus, though Wright is critical of popular caricatures, of which Jeffrey John's serves as a kind of paradigm, he grants that even those, like Ovey and his colleagues, who have come to the defense of penal substitution, also fail because they produce a version of it that is unbiblical.[7]

In the face both of caricatures generated by the theory's critics, and the biblically unsophisticated attempts of many who have sought to defend it, Wright therefore contends that it may be restated in a more acceptable "biblical way." Wright's own presentation of what he contends is a more biblical way of looking at things turns out to be a somewhat idiosyncratic restatement that is significantly different from the classical expressions of traditional evangelicalism, even though he believes it may reasonably still be called penal substitution.

This alternative is based on Wright's reading of Isaiah 53, and his personal belief that Jesus himself used Isaiah 53 to interpret his own looming

---

5. Wright, "Cross and the Caricatures." Wright says: "So we must readily acknowledge that of course there are caricatures of the biblical doctrine all around, within easy reach." Joel Green and Mark Baker also observe that "this sort of caricature is held by many Christians." Caricatures are not only confined to the theory's critics. (*Recovering the Scandal of the Cross*, 47).

6. Jeffery, Ovey, and Sach, *Pierced for Our Transgressions*, 1.

7. Indeed, Wright pulls no punches. The attempted defense of penal substitution in *Pierced for Our Transgressions* is declared to be "deeply, profoundly, and disturbingly unbiblical." ("Cross and the Caricatures," Section 3.)

death in a penal and substitutionary way as one who was going to be wounded for the transgressions of others. Though Wright does not refer to the historical shadow of federal theology in much contemporary evangelicalism, especially that of the Westminster tradition, it is clear that he provides a corrective to the tendency of contemporary conservative evangelical theology to overemphasize the contractual need for a just penalty to be paid as recompense for the failure of Adam and of all subsequent humanity. He believes he succeeds in his quest for an acceptable form of penal substitution by placing his consideration of the meaning of Christ's cross in the broader context of the story of Israel, starting with God's covenant promise to Abraham. Distortions that are suggestive of a merciless, cruel, and even vindictive pseudo-god are said to creep into expositions of penal substitution because of a failure to take sufficient account of the generous love and mercy of God, as expressed in God's (unconditional) covenant promises to Abraham. Hence, the prevalence of caricatures at the hands of critics, and unsophisticated and misleading defenses of the theory at the hands of its would-be defenders, all of which fall short of Wright's own version of penal substitution rightly and biblically understood.

There is a sense in which those who lament the tendency of the theory's critics unfairly to caricature the doctrine appear inclined to think that, simply by pointing this out, they have sufficiently answered its chief alleged difficulties. In other words, simply by identifying the regular criticisms by and large as "caricatures" and pointing to a more biblical alternative they have dealt with the theory's chief problems and laid them to rest. However, just to categorize them as "caricatures" is in fact only to indicate the nature of a continuing problem. Of course, the representation of the Christian God as a cosmic abuser of children is a caricature. That is what is entirely wrong with it: it is a caricature that misrepresents the true nature of God. Surely, nobody imagines that the Christian God is rightly compared with those of this world who are guilty of abusing and mistreating innocent children. To point out that this is a caricature does nothing more than restate the problem.

This was precisely Steve Chalke's point (at least initially), when he in fact declared that "God *is not* an abuser of children."[8] In the ensuing controversy Chalke's continuing complaint with regard to the idea of penal substitution was that, in his experience of the practice of ministry, this theory of the atonement almost inevitably gives rise to such caricatures, and that these must be called for what they are—misleading and untrue distortions of the gospel. This missiological concern is exactly what he believes makes

---

8. Chalke and Mann, *Lost Message of Jesus*, 182, my italics.

the theory unhelpful to the cause of the proclamation of the Christian message. And although N. T. Wright also admits this while expressing the hope that a more sophisticated and accurate content of meaning might deliver the theory from this tendency of critics to caricature it, Steve Chalke's view is that it might be best simply to abandon notions of penal substitution altogether as flawed, unbiblical, and destructive in relation to the proclamation of the gospel.[9]

The crucial question facing those who wish to defend penal substitution, therefore, is whether this kind of caricature can be effectively answered by articulating a rehabilitated and more truly biblical account of the theory.

The 2010 Sydney Doctrine Commission Report also insists that, when it is rightly and biblically understood, penal substitution may be delivered from all unfair caricatures and distortions of it. In response to such misrepresentations it is contended that what "protects the biblical teaching regarding Jesus' penal substitutionary death from needless caricature" is in the first instance the "voluntary nature of Jesus' self-offering" (para. 24). In other words, in a correct and biblical understanding of things, it is contended that there is "no sense in which the Father inflicts punishment on an unwilling, uninvolved or unsuspecting Son, or in which the Son persuades a reluctant Father to forgive" (para. 36). Rightly understood, then, the penalty of death is therefore not imposed to placate a vindictive and "vengeful Father" (para. 34) who is hellbent on exacting an undeserved recompense upon a dutifully compliant Son as an unfortunate third party (para. 22).

When we ask what Garry Williams believes is the best and most sophisticated version of the theory that makes it possible to avoid the misrepresentations that unfairly caricature a correct and more biblical understanding of it, the essence of his answer is also that the response of the Son is not coerced. Rather, the Father's demands (or perhaps better, his "proposals") are freely and willingly accepted by the Son out of his love both for the Father and for all humankind. In support of this contention Williams quotes the seventeenth-century theologian John Owen, who referred to "an authoritative imposition of the office of Mediator, which Christ closed withal by his voluntary susception of it, willingly undergoing the office."[10] By *willingly* paying the required penalty for the systemic fracture of human obligations

---

9. See Wood, "Penal Substitution in the Construction of British Evangelical Identity," 215.

10. Owen, "Death of Death," I. 3, 10; quoted by Williams, "Penal Substitution," 77n25.

to God that was precipitated by the disobedience of Adam, the Son himself may therefore be said to act out of his love for humanity.

Yet an appeal to the concept of "willing obedience" or the uncomplaining compliance of the Son with what the Father requires of him is capable of answering the charge that the penal substitution theory unhelpfully and unjustifiably misrepresents or caricatures God the Father, may be somewhat illusory. After all, a wife who is psychologically and physically abused by her husband, but who is nevertheless prepared or willing to remain within the family home because she feels bound by her marriage vows to do so, and also because she believes that it would ultimately be in the best interests of her children, hardly makes the husband's behavior somehow less reprehensible. The appeal to the willingness of Jesus as God's incarnate Son to comply with the Father's wish, whether it be represented as a divine command/demand/request/or manipulative suggestion, still leaves the misleading impression of grossly immoral behavior on the part of the Father hanging uncomfortably in the air.

It is important to note, however, that defenders of penal substitution take this purported defense a step further than an appeal to the mere *willingness* of the Son as we see this being played out in the economy of salvation, especially in the passion narrative. It is not just that objections to the mistaken image of God the Father are neutralized by the fact that the historical Jesus was willing to undergo what was required of him out of love for "the many" who would benefit from his passion and death on the cross. It is not, in other words, just that the human Jesus of Nazareth did not strike back at his persecutors, and in a spirit of nonviolence willingly allowed himself to fall into the hands of those who crucified him in a conscious decision of will of his *human nature*. Rather, we are bidden by proponents of "eternal functional subordination" to remember that the Son is the Second Person of the Trinity. There is a sense in which it is contended that, by willingly undertaking what is required of him, his divine will is involved. It is the *divine Son* who takes upon himself the necessity of suffering the punishment that is required of him. In a sense it is suggested that the Son appreciates the need for *someone* to pay the price that punitive justice is said to demand in return for the reconciliation of humanity to be accomplished. Thus, when Garry Williams argues that the Son is not an unwilling human victim, who is dragooned into something against his will, it is in the interests of securing the rehabilitation of penal substitution on the basis of Trinitarian considerations: "The Persons of the Trinity covenant with each other in eternity to act together in all of their purposes."[11]

Williams argues forcefully that because the crucified Jesus is not just a third party or an ordinary human being, but the Second Person of the Trinity, the burden of paying the penalty for the sins of humanity is in a sense assumed by God himself. His point is that, at its best, the theory does not suggest the caricature of a God who unjustly inflicts suffering on his own Son as an entirely unwilling innocent victim, because a more accurate reading of the biblical tradition suggests that there is a sense in which God nobly takes the burden of paying the required penalty for the misdeeds of disobedient humanity upon *himself*. Jesus is not just a hapless and unwilling human victim who, as a third party, is dragooned into something against his will.

Following the lead of Williams's appeal to the doctrine of the Trinity, the Sydney Doctrine Commission also argues that any suggestion "that the Son is merely the 'object' of the Father's action" is exposed as a caricature by the fact that the incarnate Son is "of one being with the Father" in his divine nature (para. 36). Since (quoting Williams) "conscientious advocates" of penal substitution form the doctrine "within a conscious, mature doctrine of the Trinity" the members of the commission thus contend that it cannot be thought that the Son is simply "the object of the Father's action" (para. 36, note 11). In other words, the Father is not to be thought to treat the Son as a mere object, in a callous quest to accomplish his own plan of human reconciliation with himself by requiring that a just penalty be paid on account of human disobedience and sin. At the same time, God is not just preserving the integrity of his own righteousness character at the expense of the Son by expressing his wrathful indignation in this kind of way. The Sydney Report therefore does not just argue that the theory may be restated and made acceptable by saying that the imposition of a penalty on the undeserving and innocent Jesus may be rendered inoffensive and untroublesome, so as to become perfectly acceptable, just by insisting that the Son willingly complies with the Father's requirements out of a shared concern for the redemption of humanity. Rather, because "Love is the motivation both of the Father's sending of the Son (John 3.16) and the Son's self-sacrifice (Eph. 5.2)," it can be argued that "the atonement is a loving act of the triune God, whose life and purpose are undivided" (para. 36). Therefore, far from the Father acting

---

11. Williams, "Penal Substitution," 77. T. C. Hammond also conjectured that there was a kind of contractual covenant between the Father and the Son by virtue of which the Son was sent by the Father; the Son in turn agreed to come into the world in order to achieve the world's redemption. See the companion volume to this, *Arius on Carillon Avenue*, chapter 2, 75–76.

on the Son merely as "object," the Son is also a willing subject, and because the Son is not just a human Son, but the divine Second Person of the Trinity, there is thus a sense in which God (if not explicitly "the Father") takes the penalty for human sinful disobedience on himself in the Person of the Son.

It is important for the report to say that the burden of paying the penalty "is borne by *God* himself in the person of his Son"[12] and not that "God *the Father*" takes this burden upon himself, for it is acknowledged that this would fall into the ancient error of "patripassionism," the view that the Father suffered upon the cross. This is rightly and explicitly denied in the Sydney Report (para. 36, note 12). Nevertheless, the report comes perilously close to suggesting that the Father does also suffer. It contends that "we must also reckon with the cost to the Father, his giving of his Son and what might be called the forsaking-ness (John 3.16; Rom. 8.32)." I am not entirely sure if I understand what this "forsaking-ness" might involve, but if it is the case that this indicates a kind of divine suffering, the difficulty might certainly ensue that this calls into question the impassibility of God, by compromising the perfection of the absolute ontological independence and non-relativity of God as absolute in all respects. Indeed, this might even therefore introduce change into the changelessness of God. Even so, at the end of the day, it is said that the appeal to the doctrine of the Trinity "all adds up to just one certain fact: because the triune God himself (Father, Son, though the eternal Spirit [Heb. 9:14]) has entered into his own wrath on our behalf." (para. 36).

In proposing his own somewhat idiosyncratic version of the theory that he contends may nevertheless "reasonably be called penal substitution," N. T. Wright also argues that Jesus' death is to be understood as a substitutionary death, and even a penal substitutionary death, yet without any of the problems that caricatures and unsophisticated non-biblical misrepresentations unfortunately carry. Generally speaking, his chief complaint is, for example, that Michael Ovey and his would-be champions of the theory fall short of biblical truth because they fail to place their understanding of it in the context of the whole narrative history of Israel from Abraham onwards, as the story of the love and mercy of a God who is faithful to his covenant promise to his people. Wright's appeal to the love and mercy and faithfulness of God is essentially what he believes is needed to deliver atonement theory from

---

12. That the Father himself suffers is explicitly denied in the report, para. 22: it is not that God the Father "takes this burden upon himself, for this would not only play into the hands of the caricaturists, but also fall into the ancient error of 'patripassionism.'"

unsophisticated misrepresentations of a vindictive and punishing autocrat acting upon a hapless, submissive victim. Likewise, the overarching mercy and love of God is also said to be what delivers penal substitution from the "bizarre (if sadly still well known) caricature" of a psychotic that Jeffrey John leveled against it. Ultimately, this means that Wright also appeals to the doctrine of the Trinity. As he himself puts it:

> The propitiatory effect of Jesus' death is seen as the result of God's overarching and overwhelming mercy and love, and in which the persons of the Trinity are held in extremely close union.[13]

In other words, the argument is that we can move beyond mere caricatures and unsophisticated misrepresentations of God by appealing to the unified loving purpose and mercy of the Persons of the Trinity in willing the redemption of humanity and acting "in extremely close union." The significance of the cross does not just depend upon a decision of will exercised in the economy of salvation and within boundaries imposed by the historical Jesus' human nature; it is grounded in a divine decision, rooted in the doctrine of the Trinity. In his response to Jeffrey John, Wright was therefore able to quote Charles E. B. Cranfield with approval:

> God, because in His mercy He willed to forgive sinful men and, being truly merciful, willed to forgive them righteously, that is, without in any way condoning their sin, purposed to direct against His own very Self in the person of His Son the full weight of that righteous wrath which they deserved.[14]

Clearly, Wright believes that Jeffrey John's caricature may be effectively avoided once it is acknowledged that God does not impose a penalty as the remedy for Adam's disobedience on a third party, but out of his own love and mercy, takes this burden upon himself. This is believed to deliver the theory's critics from thinking of God as a fearsome and psychotic potentate unjustly inflicting suffering on his own Son as an entirely unwilling innocent victim. Insofar as the Son is the Second Person of the Trinity who acts willingly in union with the Father, the required penalty may be said to be paid, not just by the historical human Jesus, but in a sense by God himself. The Son willingly lays down his own life in response to the Father's proposals, precisely as the substitute for sinful humanity in the interests of securing humanity's reconciliation and peace with God. In a sense both Father and Son in their different ways act together out of love. Again, as N. T. Wright puts it, in love and mercy "the persons of the Trinity are held in extremely close union."

---

13. Wright, "Cross and Caricatures," Section 2.
14. Cranfield, *Commentary on the Epistle to the Romans*, 1.217.

Wright's language of "extremely close union" here may appear uncomfortably ill-defined. This deficit is made up, however, by Garry Williams, who has accepted the challenge of finding support for the theory of penal substitution in the doctrine of the Trinity in more helpfully precise and technical terms. In his presentation at the London Symposium in 2005, Williams pursued this Trinitarian possibility, first by taking issue with the critique of penal substitution that was mounted in 2000 by Joel B. Green and Mark D. Baker in *Recovering the Scandal of the Cross*. In that book Green and Baker had argued that the problem with penal substitution is the idea of Jesus as the *object* of the Father's action, and that "any atonement theology that assumes, against Paul, that in the cross God did something 'to' Jesus is . . . an affront to the Christian doctrine of the triune God."[15] At this point they note that Stephen Sykes had correctly pointed out that "the New Testament juxtaposes two principal narrative sequences in its representation of Jesus' death as a sacrifice, each of which has its own primary actors—for the one, God; for the other, Jesus."[16] Consequently, the theology of the story of the cross, operates both with Jesus as subject and God as subject.[17] Following Stephen Sykes, Green and Baker therefore explain that:

> The New Testament portrays Golgotha along two story lines—one with God as subject, the other with Jesus as subject. It will not do, therefore, to characterize the atonement as God's punishment falling on Christ (i.e., God as subject, Christ as object) or as Christ's appeasement or persuasion of God (Christ as subject, God as object).[18]

In this way they reach their conclusion that the problem with penal substitution lies with the idea of Jesus as the *object* of the Father's action. Specifically in relation to the thinking of Paul they therefore say categorically that "Paul does not treat God as the subject and Jesus as the object of the cross."[19]

To this point, Williams agrees that if penal substitution depicted the cross as simply "God as subject, Christ as object," as Green and Baker characterize it, then it would indeed be problematic. However, Williams then

---

15. Green and Baker, *Recovering the Scandal of the Cross*, 57.

16. Green and Baker, *Recovering the Scandal of the Cross*, 113; see Sykes, "Outline of a Theology of Sacrifice," 122.

17. Sykes, "Outline of a Theology of Sacrifice," 122. This is cited in Green and Baker, *Recovering the Scandal of the Cross*, 96.

18. Green and Baker, *Recovering the Scandal of the Cross*, 113.

19. Green and Baker, *Recovering the Scandal of the Cross*, 96.

argues that, when it is rightly understood, penal substitution does not fall into this error: "no thoughtful proponent of penal substitution has ever portrayed it in this fashion." On the contrary, Williams appeals to some cautionary words of John Stott: "We must never make Christ the object of God's punishment or God the object of Christ's persuasion, for both God and Christ were subjects not objects, taking the initiative together to save sinners."[20]

Thus, while registering this initial agreement with Green and Baker, and accepting the subject-object terminology inherited from Stephen Sykes by noting the point about the historical Jesus and God both being subjects in the passion narrative, Garry Williams nevertheless insisted that, *provided Jesus is understood as a willing subject* and not just the object of the Father's wrath, there is a sense in which Jesus *is* the object of the Father's action after all. Indeed he even once again summoned John Stott to his aid to make this point by appealing to the tenor of Stott's writing elsewhere. While noting Stott's contention that Jesus is subject and not *just* an object of the divine action, Williams insists that "given Stott's position as a whole" this statement may be understood "to exclude only the notion that Christ was the object *without* being the subject, not the notion that he was in any sense the object."[21] In other words, Garry Williams's view is that the insistence that Jesus was a willing subject and not just the object of the Father's action, does not preclude the Son's also being the (subjectively willing) *object* of the Father's action. His contention is therefore that the Father "acted upon" the crucified Son (as object of his action) so as to accomplish the reconciliation of humanity, and that this was achieved precisely by the mechanism outlined in the theory of penal substitutionary atonement.

It is of some significance that the authors of the 2010 Sydney Doctrine Commission Report openly acknowledged their reliance on Williams's London Symposium defense of 2005 in also insisting that the Son is not *just* the "object" of the action of the Father as subject because he is also a willing subject.[22] Moreover, like Williams, they also argue that the Son nevertheless remains the object of the Father's action. In other words, Williams's argument is unchallenged and uncritically accepted by the authors of the Sydney Doctrine Commission Report, who, without denying that the Son is the willing subject of the redemptive action of the cross, also insist that the Son

---

20. Stott, *Cross of Christ*, 151.

21. Williams, "Penal Substitution," 77n22.

22. Sydney Doctrine Commission, "Penal substitutionary atonement," para. 36, note 11.

remains the object of the Father's action: "there is plain biblical testimony to the Father's acting on the Son at the cross" (para. 36, note 11).

Though the report does not itself explain or cite instances of this "plain biblical testimony," this information was unpacked in some detail by Williams in his London Symposium presentation upon which they rely. Williams catalogued a list of biblical quotations, all designed to illustrate not just the subject-object nature of the relation of Father and Son, but quite explicitly the Father's *acting upon* the Son as object to achieve the objective of the redemption of humanity through the mechanism of penal substitution. He pointed out that there are "multiple activities where the Father is the subject and the Son the object in Scripture: 'the Father loves the Son' (John 3:35); the Father 'sent the Son into the world' (John 3:17); the Father 'has granted the Son also to have life in himself' (John 5:26); the Father set forth the Son as a sacrifice . . . (Rom 3:25)." As a consequence of such texts, Williams therefore declares, "No one can deny that the Father acts on the Son, provided we are clear that the Son also wills the action."[23]

Williams is quite explicit, moreover, when he points out that the Father may be understood to "act upon" the Son as object when the Son is employed as substitute for sinful humanity in paying the penalty of death that is required to make atonement. In support of this contention, he argues that "Isaiah 53 speaks of the suffering of the 'Servant of the Lord,' which is understood in the NT as a description of the suffering of Christ (e.g., 1 Pet 2:21–24), and that verse 6 (of Isaiah 53) says that 'the Lord has laid on him the iniquity of us all.'"[24] Clearly, Christ is here understood not just as the willing subject but the object of the divine saving action. A burden is "laid upon" him. Moreover, verse 10 of Isaiah 53 says that "it was the will of the Lord to crush him with pain."

Williams sums up this argument in support of the contention that the Father as subject "acts upon" the Son as object, even though, also as subject, the Son becomes a *willing* object of the Father's action:

> [I]n Isaiah 53, it is evident from the connection with sin and the suffering of the Servant that they have a penal connotation. Thus we find in verses 6 and 10 statements that the Lord willed the suffering of the Servant in a context where that suffering is defined as being penal, and indeed atoning (v. 5). Likewise, in the NT we read that the Father "condemned sin in the flesh"

23. Williams, "Penal Substitution," 78.
24. Williams, "Penal Substitution," 78.

(Rom 8:3) of his Son. There is therefore biblical testimony to the action of the Father toward the Son, specifically in laying iniquity on him and condemning it in him.[25]

In addition, Williams goes on to point out that in Mark 14:27 and Matthew 26:31 Jesus himself is said to quote Zechariah 13:7: "You will all become deserters; for it is written, 'I will strike the shepherd, and the sheep will be scattered.' But after I am raised up, I will go before you to Galilee." In relation to this text, Williams registers interest in the fact that "the Hebrew and the LXX have a second person imperative here, addressed to Yahweh's sword: 'Awake, O sword . . . Strike.' But as quoted in the Gospels this passage from Zechariah is changed to the first person future, . . . thus actually emphasising the personal involvement of Yahweh rather than the more impersonal image of the sword: 'I will strike.'"[26] It seems that Williams, in insisting that the Son is the object of the Father's action is prepared to endorse the view that God the Father, acting as subject, and acting upon the Son as object, "strikes" the Son!

Williams thus says that in Isaiah 53 and Zechariah 13 we have "two statements that the Father purposes the suffering of the cross, indeed that he wills the crushing and striking of the Son, who also wills the same acts."[27] The Father not only "crushes and strikes" the Son, but thereby, for some unexplained reason, scatters the flock.

It needs to be noted that all the biblical quotations from the New Testament as illuminated by these Old Testament texts that are said by Williams to illustrate the contention that the Father as subject acts upon the Son as object, are taken from the context of the economy of salvation. They have to do with the relation of God the Father in his dealings with the humanly incarnate Son, the historical Jesus. In this case, God as subject may be said to relate to Jesus as object (and vice versa) in this divine-human relationship. But Williams wants to say more than this. In doing so he simply lifts this evidence out of the context of the economy of salvation and drops it into Trinitarian description of the eternal life of the immanent Trinity. Thus, quoting John Owen once again, Williams declares:

> The agent [i.e., the subject] in, and chief author of, this great work of our redemption is the whole blessed Trinity; for all the

---

25. Williams, "Penal Substitution," 79.
26. Williams, "Penal Substitution," 78.
27. Williams, "Penal Substitution," 79.

works which outwardly are of the Deity are undivided and belong equally to each person, their distinct manner of subsistence and order being observed . . .[28]

Thus, for Williams, the "Reformed conception of the covenant of redemption between the Persons in eternity shows how Christ is in every action of God ad extra the subject." And so he arrives at this contention that "The Persons of the Trinity covenant with each other in eternity to act together in all of their purposes."[29]

It is clear that, in order that the Father's "acting upon" the Son is not understood just to involve an action upon the historical and human Jesus in the economy of salvation, so as in addition to ensure that in some sense God acts upon himself, it is important to Williams that the *eternal* relationship of Father and Son is also understood in subject-object terms. Obviously, this can be sustained if one divine *hypostasis* can be said to act upon another: the eternal Father as subject commands and the Son as object of the Father's willing, even as the eternal Son as subject dutifully and willingly obeys. In this way humanity is said to have been reconciled to the Father as the result of the Son's redeeming work, and at the same time, in the Person of the divine Son, God himself is said to pay the penalty required to satisfy the need for his righteous character to be sustained through the public demonstration of his condemnation of sin. Furthermore, as though to clinch his point, Williams says that unless this eternal subject-object dynamic is maintained within the immanent Trinity we end with a sub-Trinitarian modalism, in which, instead of maintaining three distinct and identifiable *hypostases*, or Persons, the one God is said to act in different modes (the heresy of Sabellianism). Thus, Williams: "Ultimately, the logical implication of the denial that one Person of the Trinity can act on another is the denial of the distinction between them, namely modalism."[30]

---

28. Williams, "Penal Substitution," 77, quoting Owen, "Death of Death," 1.3, 1. There is at least an echo here of the contractual understanding of the Father-Son relationship reminiscent of T. C. Hammond's particular version of federal theology in which the Father enters into a contractual agreement with his Son for the purpose of redeeming the world from its enthrallment to sin. For his part, the Son agrees to the proposal of the Father in a "covenant of redemption." This is not just a contract made with the human Jesus in the economy of salvation, but with the eternally begotten Son in the immanent Trinity. The Father sends the Son into the world for this salvific purpose and the Son in full agreement freely consents to go, and thus gives himself "as a ransom for many." The divine Son is said not to be commanded by a vindictive potentate and made to go under duress, but goes of his own accord, being motivated by love for humanity and its need of redemption.

29. Williams, "Penal Substitution," 77.

30. Williams, "Penal Substitution," 79.

Alas, sadly for Williams's argument, this is certainly not so. As has regularly been noted in discussions of the doctrine of the Trinity,[31] in orthodox Trinitarian theology the fallacy of modalism is avoided, and the respective *hypostatic* identities of Father, Son, and Spirit are distinguished and protected, by defining their relations in terms of origin. In other words, the incommunicable property that is essential to the Father's specific identity *as* Father has to do with his *begetting* of the Son. Likewise, the incommunicable property essential to the identity of the Son has to do with his *being begotten by the Father*. His distinct *hypostatic* identity is that he is the "*only begotten Son.*" In the case of the relation of the Father with the Spirit, the relevant incommunicable properties are respectively those of *spiration and procession*, which likewise express a relation of origin. The Holy Spirit proceeds *from* the Father. The three *hypostases* are thus identifiable and distinguishable by reference to these considerations of origin. This is what renders the notion that God may be conceived as simply one God who operates in three modes untenable.

Beyond these biblically based dogmatic assertions relating to *hypostatic* origin, an apophatic reserve operates in relation to our claims to know more than the limits of our finite minds will allow in relation to the inner identities of the three divine *hypostases*. As they are in themselves they are unknowable or incomprehensible to finite minds. Certainly, the distinct and distinguishable identity of each of the three divine *hypostases* does not depend upon mythical assertions relating to continuing operations of the Father as subject with respect to the other two *hypostases* as objects of his action, and *vice versa*.

We also have to be very wary of the pitfall of falling into anthropomorphism—the idolatry of forming God in our own image, simply by assuming that the divine *hypostases* are psychological centers of personality barely distinguishable from those we know amongst human beings. Understandably, it is primarily for this reason that the early church fathers resisted attempts to move beyond the scripturally based distinctions between the *hypostases* of Father, Son, and Spirit that are secured by appeal to the criteria of the incommunicable properties established according to their relations of origin.

Moreover, by contrast with the incommunicable properties that identify each of the three *hypostases* by reference to considerations of origin, the divine moral properties that have been revealed in the course of the economy of creation and redemption as properties of the divine nature to which Scripture bears witness, particularly those involving the perception

---

31. As for example, in chapters 4 and 5 of *Arius on Carillon Avenue*.

of the exercise of the divine will in divine action, are *not* in orthodox Trinitarian theology attached to the distinguishable *hypostases* respectively of Father, Son, and Spirit. Rather, these moral properties are not incommunicable but eminently communicable and, in fact equally shared by all three *hypostases* together, who thus as a consequence may be said always to act indivisibly in accordance with them. Indeed moral properties of this kind attach to the very same substance (*ousia*) that is equally shared by all three *hypostases* together, and thus secure the unity of the single and undivided divine nature of all three identifiable *hypostases*. There is as a consequence not a multiplicity of individual wills in God, but one single and indivisible divine will. This is quite fundamental to the understanding of the unity of God. Though this is at one point acknowledged by Garry Williams himself, he unfortunately loses sight of it as he pursues his defense of penal substitution, which necessarily implies two wills—the commanding will of the Father and the obediently submissive will of the Son. He is on safer ground when, quoting Augustine, he affirms that there is but one divine will, and as a consequence one indivisible divine action. Thus, he declares: Augustine's celebrated principle is that "since the Father, the Son, and the Holy Spirit are inseparable, so they work inseparably."[32]

Insofar as Williams insists, however, that the Father as subject "acts upon" the Son as object "specifically in laying iniquity on him and condemning it in him" (and not *vice versa*) in order to achieve his redemptive purpose, even though the Son (to avoid all caricatures) is said also to be a (subjectively) willing object, this unfortunately raises some very serious problems. It is not possible, in order to try to defend the penal substitutionary theory of the atonement, to argue that the reconciliation with God the Father won by the cross of Christ involved an act of the *hypostasis* of the Father, acting as subject upon the *hypostasis* of the Son as object, with one exercising a commanding will, and the other responding with a willing obedience, because individualized willing of this kind is not associated with the *hypostases* of the Trinitarian identities as distinct from their shared divine nature.[33] In other words, an identity-specific will is not an incommunicable and unique *hypostatic* property attaching to each individual Trinitarian identity. A specific or individual kind of willing is not an incommunicable and thus identifying property of the Father, acting, for example, as the

---

32. Augustine, *On the Trinity* I, iv. 7: "[T]he Father, and the Son, and the Holy Spirit intimate a divine unity of one and the same substance in an indivisible equality; and therefore . . . they are not three Gods, but one God: . . . as they are indivisible, so work indivisibly."

33. A detailed examination of this point may be found in *Arius on Carillon Avenue*, chapter 6: "Sidestepping the *Homoousion*."

commanding subject, over against the Son as object, even with the allegedly incommunicable, and identifiably compliant, individualized willing of the Son (as subject). This would lead, quite disastrously, to a kind of tritheism, involving three individual *hypostases*, each with their own individualized center of willing.[34] Even more disastrously, insofar as the Son (as object) is the *subordinate* of the Father (as subject) obediently doing the Father's will, this obviously and inevitably leads to a form of neo-Arianism. The Son cannot be the object of the Father as subject in a relation of domination and submission without the Son becoming the subordinate of the Father. This would be so even despite his alleged subjectively willing entry into his subordinate role. Whether his obedience is willing or unwilling is immaterial.

On the other hand, if we seek to rescue Williams's argument from these disastrous sub-Trinitarian outcomes by arguing that the subjective exercise of a willing compliance by the Son, does not attach to the *hypostasis* of the Son as an incommunicable identifying property of the Son as Son, but to the *ousia* and its divine nature that he shares with the Father and the Spirit, as a moral property of the divine nature, then we have essentially the same problem. The same problem arises if the commanding will of the Father is detached from the *hypostasis* of the Father as an identifying incommunicable property of the Father as Father. When detached from the *hypostases* and located in the equally shared same substance or *ousia* and its divine nature, willing and acting are communicable properties, equally shared by all three Trinitarian identities. As such, these communicable properties of the divine nature are not individualized and unique to each of the three Trinitarian identities, but single and indivisible and equally shared.[35]

This means that, insofar as the Son's divine will might be understood in Williams's account of penal substitution to be the will explicitly of the Son as subject, that is responsive and complementary to, but different from, the exercise of Father's subjective will with respect to the Son as object, we apparently have on our hands two divine wills as properties of the divine nature (one the commanding will of Father and the other the obediently responsive will of the Son). Unfortunately, the expression of these two different wills, even if they were understood to be harmoniously congruent, would disastrously fracture the essential unity and indivisibility of the divine action. First, we have the action of the Father who as subject "acts upon" the Son as object, "laying iniquity on him and condemning it in him" (as Williams says) and, secondly, we have the action of the Son who, as subjectively

---

34. This is not to mention the problem of anthropomorphism that seems implicit here.

35. As Augustine is at pains to expound in detail in *On the Trinity*, 5.7.

willing object, "bears this penalty" by his suffering and death on the cross.[36] Unfortunately, this talk of a diversity of wills is inimical to the indivisible and equally shared communicable property of the one single divine will. Insofar as the same divine nature and will is equally shared by all three *hypostases*, along with the consequent indivisible unity of the divine action, this is vitally important to the unity of God. As Augustine said, in "the divine unity of one and the same substance" there is "an indivisible equality." The three Trinitarian identities are not three Gods with three individual wills, but one God, sharing equally and indivisibly the same substance (*ousia*) infused with the same divine nature, willing and acting together in indivisible unity. Otherwise, we unfortunately once again end with a form of tritheism. Insofar as one will is subordinate to the other, this unfortunately once again also heads in a neo-Arian direction.

It is important to remember that Williams gets himself into this disastrous predicament in his quest to demonstrate that, far from the usual alleged caricatures, a true and biblical presentation of penal substitution ensures that the Son bears the iniquity of all humanity since Adam, not only willingly, and not just as a function of his human nature, but as a function of his divine nature. In order to avoid the usual caricatures, there is an important sense in which the Son is not an innocent third party. Rather, in paying the penalty for human iniquity and disobedience God bears the burden himself "in the person of the Son." It is thus a willing entry of the Son into this role in which his divine nature, including therefore the alleged exercise of his divine will, that must necessarily come into play. Hence, Williams is unfortunately led into talk of a form of divine willing that is unique to the Son. Alas, the orthodox doctrine of the Trinity allows for no such thing. There is but one indivisible divine will, equally shared by all three *hypostases* of the Trinity, for there is but one divine substance that secures a single divine nature in which willing is a communicable property.

Insofar as in expositions of penal substitution the Son is said to be responsively subordinate and obedient to the Father, not just in his human nature, but from all eternity in his divine nature, then it follows that we have on our hands talk, not only of two divine wills, but (alarmingly) talk of one of these divine wills being subordinate to the other. Clearly, we then once again end with a form of neo-Arianism. Against this, we are obliged to affirm that there are not two (or three) identifiably different individualized wills within the divine nature in a hierarchy of willing, but one single and

---

36. Williams, "Penal Substitution," 79.

indivisible divine will that is equally shared. All three Persons of the Trinity are of the same substance (*ousia*), and thus equally share the same indivisible divine nature and its (necessarily communicable) properties. Moreover, the equally shared communicable properties of willing and acting are what characterize and secure the unity of God and thus cannot be compromised if Christianity is to claim to be a monotheistic religion.

All this means that the attempt to deliver a truly biblical version of penal substitution from mistaken caricatures, by appeal to Trinitarian principles, leads to the abandonment of the caricature in favor of an alternative that, whatever way we look at it, appears to end in the abandonment of the doctrine of the Trinity. In its place we end with a kind of tritheism that is also at the same time unavoidably neo-Arian. The contention that the Father as subject, exercising his divine will by "acting upon" the Son as object, even if the Son as subject exercises his divine will by willingly obeying and bearing the penalty imposed upon him, cannot escape the charge of introducing a hierarchy of divine natures and wills into the godhead. Thus, the attempt to argue that the penal substitutionary theory of the atonement cannot legitimately be assailed on the ground that criticisms regularly only deal with a mistaken caricature, such as the gross image of God the Father as a psychotic who to all intents and purposes appears to be involved in a kind of child abuse, itself seriously compromises orthodox Trinitarian belief.

The attempt to rescue the penal substitution from unfair caricaturing by appealing to Trinitarian principles therefore actually backfires, and results in a disastrously sub-Trinitarian outcome. Whether identifiable individual wills are assigned to the three *hypostases* as incommunicable properties in the belief that the alternative is modalism, which is certainly not correct, or whether identifiably different wills are said to inhere in the same substance or *ousia*, which, although it is said to be *equally the same*, actually introduces a differential of willing into what becomes a now unequal and differentiated divine nature, we run into essentially the same set of problems. Either way, the indivisible divine unity of God is inevitably compromised, if not disastrously fractured. Whatever way we look at it, this means that the attempted answer to the caricaturing of the Father-Son relationship at the hands both of critics and of unsophisticated exponents of penal substitution by explicitly appealing to the doctrine of the Trinity must be judged to be a failure. If this applies to Garry Williams's attempted defense of penal substitution it equally applies to the work of the Sydney Doctrine Commission, which is obviously dependent upon and echoes Williams's thinking.

We are now in a position to return to Williams's discussion of the *eternal* relationship of Father and Son in the immanent Trinity in subject-object terms, for there are yet more difficulties that must be pursued. In defending his contention that the eternal Father as subject "acts upon" the eternal Son as object of his action in the immanent life of the Trinity, Williams says:

> We must also note that the reverse is the case with the Persons of the Trinity. Just as the Son cannot be the object in an unqualified sense, but he can be the subject and the *willing* object, so the Father cannot be the object in an unqualified sense, but he can be the subject and the willing object.[37]

Then, in attempting to illustrate the alleged truth of this contention, Williams argues that

> This emerges most clearly in the intercessory work of the Son and the Spirit. The Son intercedes with the Father for us (Rom 8:34). So, too, the Holy Spirit intercedes for us (Rom 8:26). The Father is the willing subject and object of the intercessory work of the Son and the Spirit.[38]

The first thing to note here is that these references to the intercessory functions of the Son and the Spirit actually belong in the economy of salvation, insofar as their intercession is "for us." Thus, apart from these Pauline statements from Romans that Williams quotes, the Epistle to the Hebrews also affirms that as a consequence of Jesus' death and resurrection, God has highly exalted him to sit at God's right hand where "he ever lives to make intercession *for us*" (Heb 7:25). Even so, if we are to extrapolate the subject-object relation between the Father and the crucified and victoriously exalted Son from the economy of salvation, and import it into the discussion of eternal intrapersonal relations of the immanent Trinity, it does seem unexceptional to say that the Father addresses the Son, as subject to object *and vice versa*. Though it would probably be more felicitous to say that the Father is subject with respect to the Son and the Spirit as *shared* object, and the Son and the Spirit are the shared subject with the Father as object, and so on around in the perichoretic circle: The Father and the Son are the shared subject, with the Spirit as object, and the Spirit is subject with Father and Son as shared object, and so on. In any event, the point is that the absolute mutuality of reciprocal self-giving love between the Persons of

37. Williams, "Penal Substitution," 79.
38. Williams, "Penal Substitution," 79.

the Trinity may be spoken of utilizing subject/object language in this kind of way.

The appropriateness of this subject/object language initially and primordially seems to be implied insofar as interpersonal or *hypostatic* relationality is important to the distinctive identities of Father, Son, and Spirit and the definition of their incommunicable properties. A fundamental form of subject/object relationality is implicit in the discussion of the incommunicable properties of the *hypostatic* identities that come to definition in the consideration of matters pertaining to eternal origin. In Trinitarian description it is thus possible to say that the Father as subject eternally begets the Son as object and also that the Spirit eternally proceeds as object from the Father as subject of the spiration of the Spirit.

In addition, we might well argue that subject/object language is appropriate in relation to the discussion of the mutual exchange of *communicable* moral properties. If part of what it means to be a person is to address another and to expect a response of a similar kind, then as Persons/*hypostases* as distinct from individuals, the three Trinitarian identities may be said not only to "address" one another, but to love and honor one another. This interpersonal relationality is essential to their unity. The intercession of the Son and the Spirit on our behalf in the economy of salvation may be understood against the background of this Trinitarian context. Thus, we may take Williams's point that subject/object language may be appropriate in reference to this aspect of Trinitarian relationality.

Williams, however, takes this kind of Trinitarian description a step further than this. He says "if we deny that the Persons of the Trinity can be at once the willing subject and object of one another's actions, then we must deny not only penal substitution, but also the love of each Person for the others, and the sending of the Son, who comes willingly."[39] As we have noted above, we may not necessarily wish to deny the legitimacy of using subject/object language either in Trinitarian description, but there is a problem insofar as Williams suggests that there is a kind of univocal parity in the understanding of subject/object relations that obtains both in intra-Trinitarian description and in his exposition of the theory of penal substitution. Williams seems to be suggesting that if we were to affirm our belief in the mutual exchange of love between the Persons of the Trinity using subject/object categories, and likewise speak of the "Father's sending of the Son," also presupposing subject/object categories, then this somehow not only legitimates the specific use of subject/object categories in expositions

---

39. Williams, "Penal Substitution," 79.

of penal substitution, but somehow legitimizes the theory of penal substitution itself.

It is important to note, however, that there is a huge difference between the understanding of subject-object relations and *vice versa* in the shared *mutuality* and *equal reciprocity* of the eternal exchange of love between the *hypostases*/Persons in the immanent Trinity in the unity of the single divine nature of one and the same divine substance (*ousia*), and talk of the Father as subject "acting upon" the Son as willing object in such a way as to accomplish an outcome in the condemnation of sin through the suffering of the Son, which is explicitly said to be "in the flesh" (Rom 8:3) and as such something occurring in the economy of salvation.

A serious problem is in fact to be reckoned with if it is assumed that the subject-object relationship is somehow identical in both these areas of discourse. Furthermore, to argue that the use of subject/object language in one area of discourse legitimizes its specific use in the other, simply compounds the problem. This is because, in the case of the exchange of the equally shared communicable property of love amongst the Persons of the Trinity, the mutually reciprocal subject-object relation expresses the single and undivided will to love of the (equally shared) divine nature with which the divine *ousia* is said to be infused. However, in the case of penal substitution, the subject/object relation expresses a requirement of suffering and death with which the Son is obliged to comply, but which, even if this is undertaken willingly, is *in no way* mutually reciprocal or equally shared. Nor is it the expression of a single undivided will. In the case of penal substitution there is a differentiation of willing—the commanding will of the Father and the obediently submissive will of the Son.

This fundamentally significant difference is camouflaged when both of these areas of discourse, one pertaining to the immanent Trinity and the other to penal substitution in the economy of salvation, are lumped together, as examples of subject/object relations. In one case a mutually reciprocal self-giving love is understood as a defining communicable property of the equally shared divine nature; in the other an *unequal* interpersonal dynamic is said to operate as one Person obediently does the will of another *and not vice versa*. Even if this is said to be harmoniously complementary, this necessarily implies two different and radically unequal wills.

In other words, the absolutely balanced mutuality of the exchange of love of the kind that we might find in the discussion of interpersonal subject/object relations of the immanent Trinity (if we choose to use this subject/object language) is necessarily absent from expositions of the theory of penal substitution in subject/object terms (if we choose to use this language in this area of discourse). On the contrary, the subject-object relationship involving the imposition of suffering "in the flesh" that is required by the theory of penal substitution, means that the absolute mutuality and reciprocity between equals that characterizes the interpersonal relations of the Persons of the Trinity is seriously compromised. Even when the crucified Son is said to be also a willing object who (as subject) agrees out of love to accept what is required of him by the Father, the problem is that this transaction nevertheless involves the imbalance of an entirely unequal power differential. This imbalance is obvious when we recall that the Son suffers horrendously, while the Father does not suffer in any way at all. The Father certainly does not suffer "in the flesh" for the Son is incarnate and the Father is not. In classical Christian theism, furthermore, the divine nature, being changelessly perfect, is impassible, unaffected, and nonrelative with respect to what happens outside of the divine life as it is in itself. This essential power differential between the Father and the incarnate Son is underlined by the authors of the Sydney Doctrine Commission Report insofar as they insist that it would be a mistake to fall into the ancient heresy of patripassianism, for the Son suffers on the cross but the Father does not.

All the talk of the compliance of the Son as object, and the *willing* compliance of the Son as subject, with the demands/requirements/requests of the Father simply as subject, does not alter the fact that the theory of penal substitution introduces a seriously troublesome imbalance in the subject-object relationship between Father and Son. This must obviously be the case when the Son but not the Father is treated as object. This is inevitably a factor, not just in the so-called caricatures but even in what are claimed to be biblically sophisticated versions of the theory. Indeed the inescapable fact is that even the "best" and most sophisticated expositions of the theory of penal substitution introduce a thoroughly objectionable interpersonal power differential, which means that the subject/object relationship between Father and Son necessarily ceases to be a mutually reciprocal relationship between equals. Unfortunately, this moral power differential cannot be eliminated from the theory.

Furthermore, the imbalance of the interpersonal power differential that cannot be avoided in expositions of penal substitution, but which is absent from talk of the mutual exchange of love between the persons of the Trinity, is also absent from the affirmation that the "Father sent the Son into the world." Despite Williams's suggestion that one legitimizes the other, just because both are conceived in subject/object terms, the imbalance of the power differential that is implicit in the theory of penal substitution cannot be said to be present in the Father's sending of the Son into the world. As Augustine was at pains to point out, the unity of willing and of acting found in the Trinity entails that, insofar as it is correct to say that the Father "sent the Son" into the world for the redemption of humanity, it is also correct to say that the eternal Word, sharing the very same will, and thus also willing the redemption of humanity "came" into the world.[40] Clearly, this is not to be mistaken for a straightforward literal or monopolar subject-object sending. Augustine points out that although the Son was sent into the world, we have to remember also that the Word through whom all things were made was already in the world. "He was sent therefore thither, where He already was. For consider that, too, which is written in the prophet, that God said, 'Do not I fill heaven and earth?'" Augustine also notes that Paul says of "God the Father 'Who spared not His own Son, but delivered Him up for us all' while elsewhere Paul also says of the Saviour Himself, 'Who loved me, and delivered Himself for me.'"[41] His point is that in all things Father, Son and Spirit, sharing a single will, always act together in the economy of salvation. Instead of the sharing of the same will by Father and Son equally and together, such as might be said when the willing of the redemption of humanity is said to be the equally shared will of both Father and Son (and Spirit), penal substitution has to work, even at its best, with a complementarity of two different and unequal wills, the Father's commanding will and the Son's willing compliant response. This is in no way reciprocal, given that the Son does not command the Father in a way that requires the Father's compliant response. It is not too difficult to appreciate that this is a subject/object relationship of an entirely different kind from the mutual expression of love and the exercise of a single undivided will in the jointly mounted project of the redemption of humanity in which Father and Son (and Spirit) act indivisibly together in unity. Certainly, the denial of the theory of penal substitution does not mean that we must therefore also deny the Father's sending of the Son, any more than we must deny the expression of love between Persons of the Trinity simply because of the use of "subject/object" categories to conceive and speak about these things.

It is clear that a fundamental problem in expositions of penal substitution is not with subject/object language as such, but with the specific dynamics of the subject/object relationship that is alleged to hold between Father and Son. The problem with the use of subject/object categories in the interests of defending the theory of penal substitution is that talk of the Father as subject "acting upon" the Son as object, introduces a morally objectionable interpersonal power differential in a relationship of domination and submission that has no part in the exposition of the interpersonal

---

40. Augustine, *On the Trinity*, II.5. The subject/object relation of Father and Son is not simply monopolar.

41. Augustine, *On on the Trinity*, II.5. See the discussion of Augustine on the relation of the Father and the Son in Carnley, *Arius on Carillon Avenue*, 112–14.

relations of the *hypostases* in the unity of the same substance and the sharing the very same divine nature of the immanent Trinity. Insofar as they share equally and with mutual reciprocity in self-giving love, which gives all unconditionally and demands nothing in return, they relate as equals. If this is discussed using subject/object categories it involves a subject/object relationship of a uniquely distinctive kind, that is significantly different from what is involved in the theory of penal substitution.

This of course is exactly why the critics of penal substitution are prone to draw an analogy with the sad experience of interpersonal abuse in this fallen world where a notorious interpersonal power differential becomes disgracefully unequal, self-interested, and exploitative. When Williams says that the Father as subject "crushes and strikes" the Son as object, this surely plays directly into the hands of those who insist that expositions of the theory of penal substitution make it sound remarkably like a form of cosmic child abuse. The fact is that the defenders of penal substitution may find it impossible to avoid the implicit logical pressure that suggests this kind of caricature. It is understandable that Steve Chalke, as already noted, is inclined to the view that the penal substitutionary atonement should profitably be abandoned as "flawed, unbiblical and destructive to the proclamation of the Gospel."

Perhaps it is time to admit that the penal substitutionary theory of the atonement has reached its shelf life. Its congenital difficulties cry out for it to be abandoned. If it is still held to be a quite essential doctrine that is necessary to a certain kind of conservative evangelical identity, then that kind of evangelicalism is clearly in serious trouble. Intellectual integrity demands that this theory should be allowed quietly to pass into dignified desuetude.

6

"THE GOOD NEWS OF GOD'S WRATH"

The somewhat confronting title of this chapter is taken from a brief article which was published by Archbishop Peter Jensen in *Christianity Today* on March 1, 2004, having been adapted from an address originally delivered at the National Evangelical Anglican Congress in September 2003.[1] It starkly reminds us of the importance for conservative evangelical Christianity of the fundamental requirement that God must act, not just in accordance with an abstract set of legal principles derived from the rough and ready administration of justice in this world, but in accordance with his very own character as this has been revealed to us. In this case, the alleged character of "the divine wrath" is the key to fathoming what penal substitutionary atonement it is really all about.

Talk of the "wrathful anger" of God is in the first instance confronting because, as Novatian of Rome already saw in the middle of the third century, it appears inappropriate to attribute to God something that we find sinful in ourselves. Novatian's advice is that if we read of God's wrath "and consider certain descriptions of His indignation, and learn that hatred is asserted of Him" in Scripture, "we are not to understand these to be asserted of Him in the sense in which they are human vices."[2] Novatian argued that a scriptural reference to God's anger "arises from no vice in him"; rather, by such threats "men are recalled to rectitude."[3]

---

1. Jensen, "Good News of God's Wrath."
2. Novatian, *On the Trinity*, 5.
3. Novatian, *On the Trinity*, 5: "For that God is angry arises from no vice in Him. But He is so for our advantage; for He is merciful even then when He threatens, because by these threats men are recalled to rectitude. For fear is necessary for those who want the motive to a virtuous life, that they who have forsaken reason may at least be moved by terror."

In a similar vein some examples of contemporary biblical exegesis attempt to rationalize the biblical tradition of the "wrath of God" by accommodating it to God's righteousness and justice. The conservative evangelical commitment to the penal substitutionary theory of atonement is based upon the contention that a just and wholly righteous God is incapable of acting contrary to his very own nature: before (or at least at the same time as) God acts to reconcile sinful humanity to himself, his essential righteousness must therefore ensure that it is made perfectly clear that he is not acting in a way that compromises an abiding and unalterable divine commitment to the ultimate value of justice. This means that God cannot just turn a blind eye towards the many injustices of the world, thus blurring good and evil. Rather, he must express his wrathful condemnation of all that is evil. Likewise, the selfishness of rebellious and sinful humanity must necessarily be shown to be what it is—something entirely alien and offensive to the standards of justice demanded by the character of a righteous God. The wrathful condemnation of evil, indeed, is essential if a righteous God is to remain true to his very own nature. The demonstration of righteousness that is said to be essential to God's nature, which is exhibited when God acts in judgment upon all that is evil and unjust, is thus held to be what is meant by talk of the exercise of the "wrath of God."

It is held that God's wrath must necessarily be expressed in the face of human sinfulness, for, if behavior that is deserving of punishment and correction were simply left to go unpunished in a *laissez faire* kind of way, the moral integrity of the divine might well be called in question. In this way, the righteousness of God and the wrath of God go hand in hand, for there is a sense in which a righteous and just God *must* of necessity act in judgment by actively condemning human rebelliousness and sin. This means that God could not do otherwise than pronounce a verdict of "guilty" and impose a penalty, not only on the self-assertive disobedience of Adam, but upon all sinful humanity after him. God's own character requires that the ultimate penalty be paid for human rebelliousness from Adam onwards—and this happens to be the penalty of death, just as God is said to have solemnly forewarned in Genesis 2:17.

From this conservative evangelical point of view, the good news of the cross is that this justly deserved penalty has been paid once and for all by Christ himself, acting representatively for all humanity, thus releasing all the guilty from the burden of apprehensiveness and fear that would otherwise necessarily fall as a shadow upon them as potential objects of the wrath of God. Accordingly, all who appropriate the sacrifice of Christ to themselves in faith are able to walk tall in thankfulness for the loving mercy of God, rejoicing in a kind of reprieve or deliverance from the otherwise justly deserved punishment of eternal death. It follows that the redemption won by Christ did not just involve the satisfaction of the legal requirements of an abstract principle of justice, specifically of the kind found in the "law of contract" of federal or "contractual" theology, according to which the disobedience of Adam had necessarily to be punished. Christ's redemption also involved his work "as a Saviour who interposed His sacred Person between us and the just wrath of God."[4]

Dr. Jensen represents this general point of view, therefore, when he argues, "The New Testament again and again connects the death of Christ to our sins. And when it does, it means that God himself is one who actively punishes; it is not merely a matter of sin being its own reward." He goes on to explain that this means that, when Paul speaks of death as the "wages of sin," it is not to be imagined that death is simply the natural outcome of seeking to live autonomously in self-assertive independence of God, thus severing all connection with the source of all life, but rather that death is actively imposed by God as a punishment. It is an intentional and deliberative determination of the divine. Thus, he says, "the New Testament speaks of Christ 'bearing sin,' of him 'becoming a curse,' even of him 'becoming sin.'"[5]

From the perspective of this line of reasoning, it may be said that when Christ died, he therefore did not just pay the penalty normally reserved for the punishment of those who have committed the most serious of offenses, as though this simply fulfilled a juridical requirement, understood as some kind of purely theoretical and impersonal legal abstraction. Rather, as Jensen says, Christ "fell under the curse of God." Likewise, he says, "When Israel went into exile, that is precisely what was happening. As the story unfolds, every sign of God's wrath is experienced by Jesus: the betrayal, the abandonment of friends, the twofold negative judicial verdict by those who were God's agents of justice, the darkness at noonday, the great cry of dereliction from the cross." This seems to suggest that the abandonment of Jesus by his friends, and even the active involvement of Caiaphas, the religious leaders and high priest, and Pilate the highest official of the local Roman civil authority, as those immediately responsible for his crucifixion, may be thought to embody "signs of God's wrath," for in a sense they were all doing the work of God as "God's agents of justice."[6]

---

4. Hammond, *New Creation*, 72.
5. He has in mind such texts as 1 Peter 2:24, Galatians 3:13, and 2 Corinthians 5:21.
6. Jensen, "Good News of God's Wrath."

This theological position in fact has a long historical pedigree. John Calvin embraced the notion that those responsible for Jesus' arrest, trial, and crucifixion were in a sense the earthly agents of the justice of God, even to the point of claiming that Christ's death would have been of no avail for our salvation had he been killed by bandits.[7]

In the scholastic Calvinism of the next generation Pilate was understood to have played a role in the realization of God's good purposes as the earthly representative of the heavenly Judge. The Heidelberg Catechism taught that Jesus, even being innocent, was "yet condemned by a temporal judge" in order that "he might thereby free us from the severe judgment of God."[8]

Even if unwittingly, contemporary proponents of the penal substitutionary theory of the atonement are heirs to this aspect of the tradition of federal theology.

It is apparently not to be imagined that God was simply able to bring forth a good result, even from a diabolical set of humanly contrived historical circumstances, by salvaging at least something of a good and positive nature from out of it, despite its obvious evil—for example, by raising Jesus from the dead and vindicating him, and thus ultimately demonstrating his victory not only over his enemies but over death itself. Rather, there is a sense in which the historical evil of Jesus' crucifixion is itself explicitly in accordance with the will of God. It was not just God's will in the permissive sense that Caiaphas, Pilate, Judas, the crowd who cried "Crucify him!" were all exercising a God-given human freedom to act as they did. Rather, something more than the permissive will of God appears to have been involved insofar as those who were instrumental in bringing about the crucifixion of Jesus are said to have actually been the agents of the divine redemptive purpose. In a sense they were "acting out" or expressing God's very own wrathful judgment on all human sinfulness.

In this way, even something so obviously unjust in this-worldly terms as the condemnation and crucifixion of an innocent victim, and something as morally reprehensible as the abandonment of Jesus by his own friends, is all made to serve the purposes of God's justice by effecting the payment of the penalty that is said to be necessary to satisfy the "wrath of God" by the graphic condemnation of human sin and evil.

Some might think it unfortunate that this seems to mean that something that would normally be regarded as a gross miscarriage of justice, is, by a paradox, made to serve the good purposes of God's justice, as the expression of the divine wrath. Even so, Jensen declares, "It is useless hoping

---

7. Calvin, *Institutes*, II.16.5.

8. Heidelberg Catechism, Lord's Day 15, question and answer 2.

that there is no such thing as punishment in a just universe. It is useless hoping that you will not merit punishment in a just universe. You can only hope that somehow, someone will lovingly bear your punishment, and that the universe will still be just."[9] In a sense, the other side of the penny of the righteousness of God in upholding all that is good and beautiful, is, as it were, the shadow side of a God, who must condemn and punish what is sinful and unjust at the same time as he upholds and commends what is just and good. In relation to all that is evil, a just God must therefore be wrathful.

Henri Blocher seeks to justify this by contending that Paul taught that civil authorities generally are to be obeyed as agents of the administration of God's justice in the world. He points out that in Romans 13:1–7 the civil magistrate is regarded as God's servant and minister. Indeed, a civil magistrate is understood to act as a "vindicator of wrath" (Rom 13:4).[10]

Even if, generally speaking, human judges may be understood to have been instituted by God for the administration of God's justice, it is quite another thing, however, to claim God's approval for the miscarriage of justice constituted by the execution of the innocent and, indeed, sinless Jesus at the hands of Judas, Caiaphas, Pilate, and the crowd that called "Crucify him!"

This uncomfortably fearsome characterization of God as "wrathful" is regularly heard in expositions of penal substitution. A freelance pastor of a lively evangelical community in Perth, Rory Shiner, who would probably himself assent to the general characteristic commitments of Carillon Avenue theology, does not hesitate, for example, to commend belief in penal substitution by speaking of redemption and salvation in essentially this same way—as a deliverance from "the divine wrath." Indeed, he speaks in remarkably graphic and apparently literal terms. Shiner explains that the salvific effect of the cross of Christ was achieved because "the full wrath of God has already been spent" at Calvary. He illustrates what he means by employing the analogy of an Australian bushfire and the practice of seeking refuge from danger in an already burnt-out piece of forest: "When the bushfire comes it cannot burn what has already been burnt." Likewise, "Christ becomes the place of refuge, the place in the world where the full wrath of God has already been spent. Therefore, to stand in Christ is to stand in a place where the wrath of God will never be felt, because it has already been there."[11] Insofar as it is assumed that the suffering and death of Christ on the cross was deemed by

9. Jensen, "Good News of God's Wrath."
10. See Blocher, "Biblical Metaphors," 642–43n71.
11. Shiner, *One Forever*, 36.

God to have paid the penalty for humanity's sinful disobedience, this is not just in the cause of fulfilling the requirement of a kind of retributive justice abstractly conceived. Rather, Christ becomes our savior by bearing the full force of "the wrath of God" instead of us.

Sometimes, the theological exposition of the notion of the "wrath of God" as a property of the divine character tends to be understood by assimilation with the common human experience of the emotional response of anger. J. I. Packer, for example, speaks forthrightly of the "divine anger" apparently as the semantic equivalent of "the divine wrath": "It is the sacrificial death ('blood') of Jesus, God's incarnate Son, that quenches divine anger against sinners, just because Christ's death was a vicarious enduring of the penalty that was our due."[12]

For some of us, however, the representation of God's character in this kind of way by appealing to notions of "wrath" or "anger" immediately triggers some misgiving. For example, Joel Green and Mark Baker observe that expositions of penal substitution suggest that "Since Jesus has paid the penalty for us, God can regard us as not guilty." However, they further observe that this unfortunately "sounds as though Jesus died, not to save us from our sins, but to save us from God—God's wrath."[13]

It has to be said that what Green and Baker are reacting to is, of course, the somewhat unsophisticated view of the God of popular expressions of the penal substitution theory, and it must in fairness therefore be noted that this is exactly what defenders of penal substitution insist is nothing more than a mistaken caricature. N. T. Wright, in response to Jeffrey John's controversial Lent address on "the wrath of God" pointed out, for example, that it was not just that John was responding to a caricature and that, when rightly understood, a more positive and authentically biblical alternative will turn out to be much more acceptable. In addition he said that, when rightly understood, the doctrine of the "wrath of God" may be appreciated as a "massive biblical doctrine." It is obviously thought to be of considerable importance. We are urged to take it very seriously and to resist unfair and inaccurate caricatures of it lest the "true and authentically biblical doctrine" be lost.[14]

Wright's contention, therefore, is that a more nuanced and theologically sophisticated biblical understanding of "the divine wrath" may be achieved, and all unfair caricaturing avoided, by acknowledging that it is actually grounded "in the doctrines of God as creator and as the one who will restore his creation at the last." He explains what he means:

---

12. Packer, "Anger," 382.
13. Green and Baker, *Recovering the Scandal of the Cross*, 167.
14. Wright, "Cross and the Caricatures."

"THE GOOD NEWS OF GOD'S WRATH"

The biblical doctrine of God's wrath is rooted in the doctrine of God as the good, wise and loving creator, who hates—yes, hates, and hates implacably—anything that spoils, defaces, distorts or damages his beautiful creation, and in particular anything that does that to his image-bearing creatures. If God does not hate racial prejudice, he is neither good nor loving. If God is not wrathful at child abuse, he is neither good nor loving.[15]

In support of this approach to the love/wrath of God, Wright calls up an early twentieth-century report of the Church of England, dating from 1938. The report, entitled *Doctrine in the Church of England,* summed up the general position which Wright wishes to commend in a special note "On the Wrath of God against Sin." The report comments:

> It is to be observed . . . that in the New Testament the "love" and the "wrath" of God in relation to sin and forgiveness are closely connected . . . and that is an important sense in which the assertion of God's "wrath" against sin is the indispensable presupposition of any properly Christian doctrine of forgiveness. There can be no forgiveness where there is indifference towards either the offender or the offence.[16]

The report points to a possible biblical warrant for drawing a kind of parallel between God's love and God's wrath in a footnote reference to Romans 5:8 (in which it is said that "God commended his love toward us, in that, while we were yet sinners, Christ died for us") and Romans 1:18 (in which "the wrath of God" is said to have been "revealed from heaven against all ungodliness and unrighteousness . . ."). The report then goes on to explain that "wrath" as distinct from the response of anger is an ethical rather than an emotional quality:

> "Wrath" in this ethical sense is not only compatible with love, but in its purest form cannot exist apart from love. Righteous wrath cannot be based on self-concern, nor at its best is it consistent with any loss of self-control such as characterises the primitive emotion of anger.[17]

---

15. Wright, "Cross and the Caricatures."
16. Church of England Doctrine Report, *Doctrine in the Church of England,* 71.
17. Church of England Doctrine Report, *Doctrine in the Church of England,* 71.

The report is therefore able to emphasize that God's love "is a holy love, and therefore always actively affirms itself both in condemning sin and also in striving to restore and to remake the sinner."[18]

In the light of this association of the wrath of God with the love of God, the report declares, "The Cross is a satisfaction for sin in so far as the moral order of the universe makes it impossible that human souls should be redeemed from sin except at a cost. Of this cost the death on the Cross is the expression . . . Thus the Cross is a 'propitiation' and 'expiation' for the sins of the whole world."[19]

In other words, in the face of caricatures of the notion of the "wrath of God," N. T. Wright, following the argument of this 1938 report, insists that by aligning the love of God and the wrath of God together, a modified and more sophisticated outcome is achieved by contrast with any tendency to speak of the love of God as the polar opposite of God's wrath. This is said to be the basic mistake of Jeffrey John among critics of penal substitution generally. It is not that one excludes the other; rather the one helps define the true nature of the other. Thus, Wright says: "You can't play off the juridical account of atonement, so called, against an account which stresses God's love." He insists that "they belong together. If God is love, he must utterly reject, and ultimately deal with, all that pollutes, distorts and destroys his world and his image-bearing creatures."[20] This rejection of all that pollutes the world and the lives of those created in God's image is what is meant by "the wrath of God."

On the other hand, the "wrath of God," understood in this more refined ethical sense as something inseparable from the love and justice of God, is said to be placated or neutralized by the sacrificial offering of Christ's life. Whatever we may think about the notoriously disputed meaning of the Pauline use of the term *hilasterion* in Romans 3:24–26 (whether it be "propitiation," "expiation," or simply "mercy-seat"), Wright points out that in the preceding section of the letter (Romans 1:18–3:20) God's wrath is said to have been revealed against all ungodliness and wickedness, and at the end of the passage, in accordance with the "justice" of God, those who were formerly sinners and under God's wrath are said now to be justified freely by grace through faith. Wright therefore contends that "the logic of the whole passage makes it look as though something has happened in the death of Jesus through which the wrath of God has been turned away."[21] This allows

---

18. Church of England Doctrine Report, *Doctrine in the Church of England*, 91.
19. Church of England Doctrine Report, *Doctrine in the Church of England*, 92.
20. Wright, "Cross and the Caricatures."
21. Wright, "Cross and the Caricatures."

him to massage the meaning of *hilasterion* so as to avoid any suggestion of the human propitiation of an angry God understood in crudely emotional and anthropomorphic terms, by bringing it into conformity with his more refined and acceptable understanding of the love/wrath of God. It is at this point that he cites the passage of Charles E. B. Cranfield, already quoted in the previous chapter:

> We take it that what Paul's statement that God purposed Christ as a propitiatory victim means is that God, because in His mercy He willed to forgive sinful men and, being truly merciful, willed to forgive them righteously, that is, without in any way condoning their sin, purposed to direct against His own very Self in the person of His Son the full weight of that righteous wrath which they deserved.[22]

On the basis of what is presented as this more sophisticated understanding of the love/wrath of God, as against all caricatures, Wright engages in an earnestly defensive apologetic in which he not only expounds his understanding of Paul's atonement theology against the background of the cultural context of the sacrificial worship of the ancient Jewish world, but appears to believe that, by a kind of "direct transference," it is possible to drop it into the modern world as though we may just as easily understand it as a way of explaining the atonement. He thus notes that in Romans 8:3, Paul says explicitly that "God condemned sin in the flesh of Jesus Christ." Even so, Wright apologetically, though it must be said, somewhat equivocally, explains that it is important to note that "Paul does not say that God condemned Jesus; rather, that he condemned sin; but the place where sin was condemned was precisely in the flesh of Jesus, and of Jesus precisely as the Son sent from the Father. And this, we remind ourselves, is the heart of the reason why there is now 'no condemnation' for those who are in Christ Jesus (Romans 8.1)."[23]

In this way, it is hoped that any suggestion that God the Father directed his wrath at Jesus as an unsuspecting innocent human victim in the manner of the caricature of "the angry God upstairs and the powerless suffering Jesus downstairs" will be avoided. If it is understood that a penalty has been paid according to juridical practice, or a sacrificial offering has been made according to cultic ritual purpose, it is precisely as the divine Son "sent from the Father." In this way, Wright seeks to maintain the view, against all caricatures, that the whole story is directed by the love of God for the redemption of humanity, and that there is a sense in which God takes

---

22. Cranfield, *Commentary on the Epistle to the Romans*, 1:217.
23. Wright, "Cross and the Caricatures."

upon himself the punishment necessary to demonstrate the divine hostility to all evil in the divine person of the Son, even if it nevertheless actually involved the agonizing suffering in the human flesh of Jesus.

Wright's appeal to what he believes is an authentic biblical understanding of the love/wrath of God, in this way ultimately brings us back to the doctrine of the Trinity. Alas, as we already noted in the previous chapter, insofar as the compliant will of the divine Son, "sent from the Father," must obey the commanding will of the Father so as to satisfy the divine wrath/love of the Father, we once again seem to be dealing with a notion of God with two divine wills. The Father exercises his will in sending his Son into the world for the explicit purpose of demonstrating his love/wrath. The Son exercises his will by acting in obedient compliance to the Father's directive. As was noted previously, in orthodox Trinitarian doctrine there is but one divine will, fully and equally shared by all three divine identities as a property of the single undivided divine nature.

Insofar as it may be said that the value of justice is a shared property of the divine nature, and that this necessarily involves the condemnation of all injustice as contrary to the divine will, we may therefore say that all three persons of the Trinity equally share this communicable moral property. However, once the divine wrath, understood as a kind of righteous anger, is attributed to one person of the Trinity, as subject, and directed against another Person of the Trinity, as object, we are no longer talking of a communicable and equally shared moral property, but rather are attributing this property to one person of the Trinity (the Father) which is said to be exercised at the expense of another (the Son). Clearly, we have a problem here, which seriously undermines the unity of the single and undivided divine will of God, fully and equally shared by all three persons of the Trinity.

This is not to be confused, of course, with the dyothelite teaching of Maximus the Confessor, endorsed by the Third Council of Constantinople, that postulates two wills, a human will and a divine will, in the *hypostatic* union of the incarnate Jesus. As Chalcedon made clear, the two natures of which these two wills are key elements are not to be confused. Nevertheless, it would be appropriate to say that "wrath," even as a kind of purely ethical and unemotional "righteous anger" was exhibited by the incarnate Jesus in the episode of the casting out of the thieves from the temple, as a property of his human nature. It is in the spirit of Maximus to say that this was congruent with, and to some degree reflective of, a corresponding, eternal property of the divine nature, and thus revelatory of it. However, in this case it is a property that is equally shared by all three Trinitarian identities that was at least partially revealed in space and time through the human nature of the incarnate Jesus so as to suggest a kind of coincidence of human and divine willing.

On the other hand, a theology of conscience might appropriately speak of the moral pressure of the divine will in human experience in the process of identifying and speaking against all that is unjust in the world. Further, this might well be understood as an illuminating work of the Holy Spirit. In this case, it could be argued that this also illustrates something of the way in which people of faith at least partially perceive the divine "wrath" understood as an ethical posture of condemnation towards evil of the divine nature of God. However, in this case the perception of the "divine wrath" in relation to all that is evil must, once again, be understood as a shared property of the divine nature, not an incommunicable property of the Father alone directed towards the Son.

It is important to be alert to a difficulty that is regularly raised in relation to the doctrine of the Trinity by expositions of the "wrath of God." In the course of defending the doctrine of penal substitution, its proponents face a very serious problem that attaches to the fundamental contention that the true biblical understanding of "the wrath of God" as an ethical property of the divine nature cannot be separated from an understanding of the divine love also as a shared property of the same divine nature. For once these two moral properties are brought into such close association, almost as two sides of the one penny, it is very easily assumed that the logical behavior of the concept of God's wrath parallels the logical behavior of the concept of God's love. This is not the case.

The divine love, as a property of the divine nature that is equally shared by all three Persons of the Trinity, can be said to flow from the Father to the Son, and also equally and reciprocally from the Son to the Father. The same may be said of the relation of the Son to the Spirit, and of the Spirit to both Father and Son, and so on. An interpersonal set of loving relationships expresses the perichoretic reciprocity within the immanent life of the Trinity. It is this divine love, furthermore, that characterizes the communion of God that is also generously shared with the people of God in the communion of the church, where it is perceived and known by faith.

By contrast, the shared ethical property of the condemnation of evil in the world cannot likewise be imported into the internal life of the Trinity as something directed by one *hypostatic* identity towards another. Some kind of condemnatory attitude of one Trinitarian identity towards the others would seriously disrupt the internal unity of the Trinity. Unlike love, there is no sense in which wrath can be said to be a property that is reciprocally directed from one to the other by all three persons in the internal life of the Trinity. The three Persons may share the ethical attitude of condemnation towards the evil *of the world*, so as to be of one heart and mind, but it would be inappropriate to line up a similar attitude of condemnation between the Persons themselves, for whom evil is an entirely alien property.

Expositions of the penal substitution theory of the atonement, however, regularly insist that in the economy of salvation the payment of a penalty by the Son propitiates the wrath of the Father. This is not to be mistaken for "the wrath of God" understood as an ethical hostility to evil in the world that might be said to be directed by Father, Son, and Spirit acting indivisibly together in condemnation of the sinfulness of humanity. There is no sense, on the other hand, in which it may be said that the divine wrath in this shared sense, may be attributed uniquely to the Father as an incommunicable property of the Father alone, that is somehow satisfied by the payment of a penalty by the Son. It is clear that the appeal to the notion of the "wrath of God" as way of speaking of the ethical hostility of God towards all that is unjust and sinful in the world is one thing; to turn it into an incommunicable property of the Father alone which is then turned on and borne by the Son in the internal life of the Trinity is quite another.

It seems reasonable enough to argue that a righteous God must be understood to adopt a posture of ethical hostility to evil in the world, as Jensen and Wright in different ways contend. It is quite another thing to argue on the basis of this that the Father may be understood to direct the ethical hostility of his wrath on to his entirely innocent Son as the "object" of the Father's wrath, to use the language of Garry Williams. Indeed, if this were to happen in the world it would be judged precisely to be an example of sinful and unjust behavior of the kind that an ethical and righteous God should rightly condemn.

In other words, God's love as a communicable property that is shared by all three of the divine *hypostases* is entirely reciprocal. God's righteousness and God's ethical hostility (wrath) is, like love, equally shared by all three divine *hypostases*. The divine wrath understood in this ethical sense may be a shared property of all three Persons of the Trinity that any one of them, or better all three together, might direct towards evil and the injustices of the world in the economy of salvation. However, insofar as an appeal is made to the concept of "the wrath of God" in expositions of the theory of penal substitution, it is clearly not regarded as a reciprocally shared property of the divine nature (falling under the provisions of the *homoousion*).

Instead, it is made into an incommunicable property of the Father, that has to be propitiated by the Son. But if it is said to be directed by one Person of the Trinity towards another in a monopolar way, the reciprocity of communicable and equally shared moral properties is entirely lost, with the very serious implication that the unity of the Godhead is seriously compromised.

It is also very difficult to see how a troublesome subordination of the will of the Son to the commanding will of the Father can be avoided here. Indeed, as has already been noted in the discussion of the question of the "eternal subordination of the Son to the Father,"[24] to begin to think in this way is already to step on to the dangerous path to a kind of tritheism. Insofar as the obediently compliant will of one Trinitarian identity is necessarily subordinate to the commanding will of another Trinitarian identity, we are once again already on the equally dangerous path to neo-Arianism.

It is, of course, arguable that the property of the divine wrath, when it is understood as the ethical posture of the condemnation of sin and evil, is not just thought to be an essential property of a righteous God that is exercised in relation to the evil of the world, but that it was actually revealed as such in the economy of salvation—in the life, death, and resurrection of the human Jesus. For, it may fairly be said that Jesus displayed something of the divine hostility or "wrath of God" in the face of sin and evil when, in a notable act of his human will, he turned the money changers out of the temple.[25]

Furthermore, this display of righteous anger or wrath by the human Jesus in turning out the money changers in the economy of salvation might naturally be said to echo (or harmoniously to be of a piece with) an *eternal* quality of divine righteous anger as a divine property of God, the holy, just, and righteous Trinity. What we see in the incident in the temple might, in other words, therefore be said to be not just a *human* display of anger understood as an act of the human will of the historical Jesus, but essentially also a manifestation of the divine will, the unwavering and consistent divine wrath expressed as the condemnation of sin and evil in the world. The resurrection of the human Jesus by God may in turn rightly be interpreted as it certainly was amongst the first Christian believers—as the vindication of Jesus and as God's judgment on all those who had unjustly condemned and crucified him.

All this seems reasonable enough. However, it is hardly an attractive proposition from the point of view of the proponents of the penal

---

24. Initially in *Arius on Carillon Avenue*, chapter 3.

25. Accounts of Jesus driving the money changers from the temple are found in all four Gospels: Mark 11:15-18; Matthew 21:12-13; Luke 19:45-46; and John 2:13-17.

substitution theory of the atonement. For, as the theory has it, it is not the eternal Son or divine Word whose righteousness is demonstrated by adopting a posture of condemnation towards the sin and evil of the world; rather it is God the Father whose righteousness is at stake. It is explicitly said that the Father's wrath (admittedly even understood as an ethical attitude of hostility to all that is sinful and evil in the world) that is said to be in need of propitiation by the willing obedience of the Son. Alternatively, it is in this way that the Son is said to pay the alleged penalty required by the Father in order to make it clear that sin and evil cannot be lightly passed over and not taken seriously. Exponents of the theory contend that the Father's righteousness is demonstrated when he sends the Son to die upon the cross; it is the merit of the Son that he is obediently submissive to the Father's will. This means that, if sin and evil is to be dealt with appropriately, the theory holds that the Son's role is to be the "object" of the Father's wrath by paying the penalty that the Father's justice demands, as Garry Williams has insisted.

In this case, however, if the righteous anger exhibited by Jesus in the economy of salvation by casting out the thieves from the temple is to be taken to reveal something of the divine wrath *of the Father* rather than of the equally shared divine nature, this at the very least appears to be somewhat arbitrary. It would surely be more in accordance with orthodox Christian belief to say that the incarnate Jesus reveals a communicable property of the eternal God as such, rather than a uniquely incommunicable property necessarily and explicitly associated with the Father.

Admittedly, the proponents of the penal substitution theory of the atonement also regularly support the "eternal functional subordination" of the Son to the Father as a related belief. Indeed, the Father's sending of the Son into the world not just "so that the world might believe" but explicitly so that Jesus might die upon the cross with the explicit intention that the world might be redeemed. This is regularly said to demonstrate the revelation of the "eternal functional subordination" of the Son to the Father in the historical context of the economy of salvation. Obviously this novel belief of Trinitarian complementarianism is intimately related to the willing obedience exhibited in the alleged penal substitution of his historical life for others. Indeed, his suffering and death is said to be the ultimate exemplification in time of his alleged eternal subordination and submissiveness to the Father. He is indeed "the subordinate substitute." The *human* submissiveness of Jesus in subordination to the Father is thus of a piece with his alleged "eternal functional subordination" in the internal life of the immanent Trinity. This in turn is said to be complementary to the Father's allegedly unique power of command.

In the cause of consistency it is therefore said, as a matter of principle, that what is humanly revealed by the Son in the economy of salvation may be said to reflect a parallel property in the eternal Son.²⁶ In parallel with this, it only seems consistent to say that the righteous anger of the human Jesus exhibited in the casting out of the thieves also points towards the eternal paradigm of this same, or at the very least analogous, righteous anger or wrath as a property of the eternal Word rather than as an incommunicable property that is said to be unique to the Father.

It might be argued, furthermore, that in the tradition of Christian orthodoxy, the understanding of the revelatory significance of the historical Jesus is that he "shows us the Father." In this case, it might be argued that the righteous anger exhibited by Jesus in the temple incident would lead to the association of the property of wrath, understood as an ethical hostility to evil, with the Father rather than with the eternal Son. This might therefore be judged to be in order and in theological terms perfectly admissible.

Even so, whether even this judgment can be judged to be correct as it stands, and whether it holds any joy for the proponents of the penal substitutionary theory, is another matter. For insofar as the historical Jesus "shows us the Father" this is because "he and the Father are one"; he reveals something that he possesses *in common with* the Father. It is not an incommunicable property in the sense that it is something unique to the Father's identity alone. This, after all, is what provided Athanasius with the biblical grounding for the articulation of the *homoousion*.

Thus, the ethical posture of the condemnation of sin and evil perceived in the story of the casting out of the thieves from the temple actually reveals something of an analogous divine property of the "righteous anger" of God as such.²⁷ All three Trinitarian identities may be said to share, fully and equally, the same just and righteous nature. Hence, in "showing us the Father" the historical Jesus may be understood to reveal something of the nature *of God*.

Here we have an example of the need to avoid a simplistic application of Rahner's Rule whereby an insight grounded in the economy of salvation is unthinkingly imported without caution or qualification into an understanding of the immanent life of the Trinity. We are wise to be "restricters" rather than "radicalizes" before assuming that the perception of righteous

---

26. This is Robert Doyle's line of argument, using Rahner's principle that the economic Trinity is the immanent Trinity, but applied specifically to the identity of the Son, as we observed in chapter 1.

27. The Council of Chalcedon stipulated that the two natures of Christ were not to be "confused," but as Maximus clearly taught, the human will of the incarnate Christ and his divine will, while not being confused, were not at odds with one another, but were in some kind of synergy or harmony; only so could the human nature of Christ reveal something of the divine nature of God.

anger exhibited in the actions of Jesus in casting out the thieves from the temple may "show us the Father" in the sense of indicating an incommunicable quality that is unique to his *hyperstatic* identity (and that might even be exercised at the expense of the Son), rather than a communicable quality of the divine nature that the Father shares equally with the Son and the Spirit in accordance with the *homoousion*.

The problem with the penal substitutionary theory of the atonement from the perspective of the orthodox doctrine of the Trinity is that it tends to treat the ethical property that is condemning of sin and evil in the world, and that is revealed by Jesus in the explicit example of the casting out of the thieves from the temple, not as a shared or communicable property of the Trinity, but as an incommunicable property that is unique to the Father. The property of wrath *has* as a matter of logic to be associated with the Father rather than the eternal Son (or the Spirit) precisely in order to meet the demands of the penal substitution theory itself. The righteous anger or wrath of the Father, and his need to uphold principles of justice in the imposition of a penalty, has to be propitiated through the death in perfect obedience of the Son.

In a sense, therefore, the property of wrath has to be associated uniquely with the *hypostatic* identity of the Father alone for the purpose of providing the rationale for explaining why it was necessary for the Father to send his Son into the world to die upon the cross and not *vice versa*. According to this story-cum-theory it was not that the eternal Son needed propitiating, or that the eternal Son needed to demonstrate a posture of hostility in the face of the sin and evil of the world. According to the theory of penal substitution it is the Father who has to engage in the public demonstration of his righteousness, by upholding principles of justice that might otherwise be thought to be compromised by him in "turning a blind eye" and passing over sin and evil in a *laissez faire* kind of way and not taking it seriously. Jesus' death on the cross therefore becomes the means whereby *the Father* demonstrably shows unequivocally that sin and evil are being taken seriously and dealt with satisfactorily so that his justice might prevail. Thus, the Father ensures that the appropriate penalty is paid by the Son *instead of* the rest of humanity in what is essentially a transaction between the Father and the Son. The Father is the subject of the story; the Son is the submissively obedient object of the Father's alleged commanding will and redemptive action.

This, however, is out of kilter with the orthodox theology of the Trinity, which invites us to observe the truth that what is revealed by the incarnate Jesus, specifically for example in relation to the display of righteous anger in the story of the casting out of the thieves from the temple, is not something unique either to the Eternal Word or to the Father. What is revealed by Jesus in the economy of salvation is something fully and equally *shared* by the Son with the Father. This means, in other words, that what the Son reveals is something of the character and good purpose *of God*—what is revealed is the divine nature equally and indivisibly shared by all three Persons of the Trinity.

Insofar as the divine will is understood to be exercised in upholding the moral values of justice and goodness through the condemnation of sin and evil, it is shared in a way that is single and indivisible, rather than something distributed to one or other of the Trinitarian identities. It follows that the property of the divine wrath is not an incommunicable property that is unique to the identity of the Father, nor is it a property that might be thought to be is unique to the identity of the eternal Son.

Given that the penal substitution theory deals with a kind of transaction in which the Father requires the death of his own Son for the redemption of the world through the payment of a penalty for Adam' disobedience, and at the same time thereby demonstrates his justice and wrath in the ethical sense of his condemnation of sin and evil, it is implied that wrath is and must be a property of the Father. At least for the purposes of the story-cum-theory of the atonement it is unique to the identity of the Father.

This means, unfortunately, that when this divine property of wrath is dissociated from the shared divine nature and associated instead with the *hypostasis* or person of the Father, it has the consequence of becoming yet another example of sidestepping the *homoousion;* through dissociating the property of the divine wrath from the shared divine nature and the Nicene requirement that it is of necessity equally and fully shared, it is associated instead with the *hypostasis* of the eternal Father.[28]

This is why it is more amenable to Christian orthodoxy to say that, if the concept of the divine wrath is to be understood in the more refined way suggested to us by the proponents of penal substitution as the ethical posture of hostility and condemnation of evil, then it has to be defined simply as a divine property of God the Holy Trinity. There certainly seems to be no

---

28. This theological maneuver is discussed in *Arius on Carillon Avenue*, chapter 6, in relation to the eternal Son's alleged property of "subordination" which is likewise unfortunately detached from the equally and fully shared nature of the persons of the Trinity (as a kind of other-regarding mutual submissiveness), and associated instead exclusively with the *hypostasis* of the Son, so that the property of authority and the power of command may be associated exclusively with the *hypostasis* of the Father. In this case the property of divine wrath is associated with the *hypostasis* of the Father, rather than being treated as a property of the equally shared divine nature. This amounts to a "sidestepping of the *homoousion*."

objection to thinking of "the wrath of God" as a way of expressing the defining property of God's righteousness that entails that such a God must take evil seriously and deal with it. But in this case, it must be an equally shared property of the divine nature and subject to the requirements of the *homoousion*. All three Persons of the Trinity may be said to share the righteous abhorrence and condemnation of the evil in the world. If this is referred to by the use of the code word "divine wrath," so be it. But, in this case, it is not amenable to treatment as an incommunicable property that is unique to the Person of the Father as is unfortunately necessarily presupposed by the penal substitution theory of the atonement.

On the other hand, the attribution of "wrath" to God the Holy Trinity (as distinct from the Father alone) must surely be balanced by the very opposite biblical tradition of the perception of God as "long-suffering" and "slow to anger." Indeed, just how the tradition of the "wrath of God" is to be accommodated to this biblical tradition of a God who is to be celebrated for his long-suffering forbearance is a good question that should properly be addressed. For, apart from the tradition of the "wrath of God," which is understood to be exercised in relation to those who are deemed to be deserving of punishment, the God of the Hebrew-Christian tradition is equally said to be patient and long-suffering, and mercifully slow to anger, in relation to his dealing with wayward and sinful humanity. And this is specifically the case in his dealing with his covenant people who justifiably rely on their God to be steadfastly merciful and faithful to his promise, even despite their own shortcomings.

For example, Psalm 86:15 aptly defines this aspect of the divine character: "But you, O Lord, are a God merciful and gracious, slow to anger and abounding in steadfast love and faithfulness." Likewise, the prophet Hosea noted the promise of a God who is understood to be faithful to his covenant people, even in the face of the fact that they were incurably "bent on turning away" from God.[29] Although "the more he called them the more they went from him"; "they kept sacrificing to Baals and offering incense to idols." As a consequence, the sword of their enemies rages in their cities and their schemes end in social chaos.[30] Even so Hosea perceives that God is a God who is faithful to his covenant promise: "I will not execute my fierce anger, I will not again destroy Ephraim, for I am God and not man, the Holy One in your midst, and I will not come to destroy (or in wrath)."[31] There is an

---

29. Hos 11:7.
30. Hos 11:2.
31. Hos 11:9.

implicit warning here of the dangers of anthropomorphism: God will not act in the way that mere mortal men might be anticipated to act.

This tradition of the merciful forbearance of God, even in the face of uninhibited human sinfulness, is also very clearly expressed in the story of Jonah and his mission to the people of Nineveh. In obedient response to his calling to go up to Nineveh to proclaim the word of the Lord, Jonah eventually arrived at his destination, despite the rerouting of his travel plan via the instrumentality of the whale, and so dutifully delivered the not-so-good news that "in forty days Nineveh will be overthrown" (Jonah 3:4). When this prompted the king of Nineveh to lead a city-wide expression of repentance in the hope that God might "turn from his fierce anger" (Jonah 3:9) we are told that "God saw what they did, how they turned from their evil ways," and then, as a consequence, God is said to have "changed his mind about the calamity that he had said he would bring upon them; and he did not do it" (Jonah 3:10). This was apparently a surprise even to Jonah, who seems to have believed that the people of Nineveh justly deserved the punishment that God originally had in store for them.

In the ancient theological tradition expressing the specific aspect of the divine nature expressed in this story, despite the obvious need to acknowledge the anthropomorphism involved in talking of God's "change of mind," we note that there is no suggestion that God was turned from his wrathful condemnation of evil by anything other than sincere and abject repentance. There is certainly no suggestion that some kind of penalty or cost had necessarily first to be paid in order to ensure that God's forgiveness might not be mistaken for a liberal-minded *laissez faire* acceptance of their evil.

While there is no suggestion that the divine character is in any way compromised, there is every indication that we are to understand that God is by nature generously merciful. Jonah himself thus affirms faith in "a gracious God merciful, slow to anger, and abounding in steadfast love who turns away from evil" (Jonah 4:2). This is so even if Jonah himself found it difficult to feel sorry for people who in his view justly deserved the punishment that he had originally said was coming to them.[32] Furthermore, though the people of Nineveh experienced the merciful kindness of God who does not impose punishment on them, there is no suggestion that they were in any way confused about the divine righteous condemnation of evil; their abject demonstration of repentance is itself a sufficient sign of their clear appreciation of the gravity of their wrongdoing.

---

32. Hence God has to teach Jonah to be sorry for the Ninevites in their ignorance, which appears to be viewed by God as an extenuating circumstance deserving of pity, for they "do not know their right hand from their left" (Jonah 4:11).

Given the continuity of Jewish and Christian monotheism, it is understandable that Christians have likewise appreciated and celebrated God's marvelously commendable forbearance and mercy. Jesus' own teaching about the desirable extent of forgiveness, not just a complete number of times, but seventy times seven times, points, for example, to a divine paradigm that cannot be less than this human norm of the teaching of Jesus.[33] Also, far from thinking of God in terms of hastening to condemn and punish, let alone to be driven by a kind of necessity in publicly venting his alleged hostility to evil as a dictate of his own unalterable character, the author of 2 Peter exhorts those who were expressing their impatience at the apparent tardiness of God in coming in eschatological judgment to be patient: for God "a thousand years are but as a day, and a day a thousand years." God is "not slow about his promise, as some think of slowness, but is patient (or long-suffering) with you, not wanting any to perish, but all to come to repentance."[34]

This aspect of the New Testament tradition alerts us to the truth that the discernment of the character of God may not be quite as straightforward as some proponents of penal substitution often appear to assume. Clearly, given the diverse richness of biblical language about God, we must at least seek to balance talk of "God's wrath" with talk of God's love and his long-suffering "merciful forbearance." Otherwise, we would, once again, be in danger of falling into a kind of naive biblical literalism of the highly questionable kind that defenders of penal substitution themselves bid us not to take seriously by forthrightly dismissing it as mere caricature.

It seems imperative that we need to attend to the whole of the biblical tradition about the nature of God, rather than just a part of it. Those who seek to distance themselves from grotesque caricatures of "the wrathful God" by attending to the love and justice of God are surely therefore on the right track. They are also rightly motivated in their nuancing of the concept of "God's wrath" so as to speak of it as a kind of ethical posture involving the rejection of all that is evil and unjust by milking it of the anthropomorphic coloring suggestive of something akin to an emotional outburst of rage.

However, if the property of the righteousness of God and its logically necessary accompaniment of "the divine wrath," correctly understood as an ethical posture that is condemnatory of sin and evil, is to be "balanced" by the love and mercy of a long-suffering and patient God, the question is how more exactly may these divine properties be understood to operate together?

And if the property of divine wrath, along with the divine love and forbearance, are both understood as communicable properties of the kind

33. Matt 18:22.
34. 2 Pet 3:9.

that are equally shared by all three hypostatic identities in accordance with the *homoousion*, rather than an incommunicable property that is unique to the identity of the Father alone, what impact would this have on the internal logic of the penal substitution theory of the atonement?

In conclusion, I think we are obliged to say that the attempt to avoid caricatures of God by placing the theory of penal substitution in the context of the doctrine of the Trinity and the love of God is unsuccessful. This is because as soon as the notion of the "wrath of God," even if understood as an ethical disposition of the condemnation of sin and evil," is associated with the *hypostasis* of the Father, with the Son being obediently submissive as the object of the Father's "wrath," the *homoousion* is implicitly challenged. In the orthodox Christian theology of the Trinity the property of the divine wrath (understood in this ethical sense) is a property of the divine nature, not of the Father alone. It is an illicit theological maneuver to try to "sidestep" the *homoousion* by disengaging it from the requirements of the *homoousion* and associating it uniquely with the Father as an incommunicable property unique to the Father's personal identity. It is in fact a communicable property of all three Trinitarian identities, equally and fully shared. It is not amenable to being associated with the *hypostatic* identity of the Father, in a relationship of domination and submission of the kind exemplified in the Father's requirement that the Son pay the penalty demanded by his alleged "wrath."

We have to take note of the fact that as soon as we speak of the "divine nature" we are speaking of something that is equally shared by the Father, Son, and Holy Spirit. If we are to remain true to the dogmatic norms of Christian orthodoxy, the divine nature is something that must meet the requirements of the *homoousion*. Unfortunately, the penal substitutionary theory of the atonement commandeers the divine property of righteousness with its need to be condemning of sin and evil and all that is unjust, and effectively disengages it from the divine nature and ascribes it uniquely to the Father, who is then said to act in accordance with it in imposing the penalty of death on his obediently submissive Son. When the implicit dichotomy between the commanding will of the Father and the obediently submissive Son is imported into the understanding of the immanent life of the Trinity so as to speak of the "eternal functional subordination" of the Son to the Father we end not only with a form of tri-willing tritheism, but with a form of Arianism.

7

GOD'S JUSTICE:
Punitive, Retributive, or Restorative?

Those who have sought to defend the penal substitutionary theory of the atonement have made two basic proposals that have yet to be addressed. The first of these arises from the fact that expositions of the theory hasten to assure us that, in carrying through his redemptive purpose by sending Jesus to die upon the cross, God was only following the dictate of "the law of his own nature." In other words, the exponents of the theory regularly allege that a God who is righteous by nature is *constrained* by the very quality of his own character to act in such a way as to express his "divine wrath" in relation to the rebellious sinfulness of the world. The "divine wrath" is understood, of course, not as an uncontrolled outburst of emotion, but as a dispositional attitude of an ethical kind that is condemnatory of sin and evil. In a sense this dictates the divine behavior.

In the words of the Sydney Doctrine Commission's 2010 Report on Penal Substitutionary Atonement, it is not just that God *will not* tolerate evil; rather, God's "personal divine revulsion to evil" means that he "cannot" do so.[1] In other words, the nature of God's action in the world is something that even God cannot change, for there is a sense in which, by virtue of his own

---

1. Sydney Doctrine Commission, "Penal substitutionary atonement," para. 4: "There is thus no tension between God's love and his holiness, between his goodness and his righteousness. Nor should God's wrath against sin be understood as mere personal pique. The same evil which constitutes an attack upon his person also represents an attempt to overthrow his purposes, purposes which secure the lasting welfare of his creation, especially humanity. For this reason, God cannot and will not tolerate that which stands opposed to all he is and does. His wrath is a powerful expression of his love for the world he has made as well as a 'personal divine revulsion to evil.'" (Quoting Morris, *Cross in the New Testament*, 190).

GOD'S JUSTICE: PUNITIVE, RETRIBUTIVE, OR RESTORATIVE? 153

eternal and unchanging nature, God is programmed to express his judgment on evil as a matter of necessity. It is therefore said that "the necessity of a penal substitution arises from God's own holy character rather than any law or code external to his person. Indeed, God is not bound by anything apart from his own nature."[2] In this way evil is taken seriously as something with which God necessarily had to deal.

A second basic proposition regularly found in defenses of the theory, and implicit in what has just been said, has to do with the necessary imposition specifically of a punishment in condemnation of sin and evil as distinct from other logical possibilities.[3] It is thinkable, for example, that the righteousness of God and his just condemnation of sin and evil might well be demonstrated in other logically possible ways. Not least among these is the regular way in which God communicates his ethical stance against all that is evil and unjust, through the moral pressure of his will as this is revealed in human experience though the "still small voice" of conscience. This is not to mention the human impact of the hearing of the insistent call of the word of God to repent of sin and evil. When this triggers a profound sense of guilt, and initiates repentance and amendment of life, it is clear that God's judgment has had its effect. It is significant, however, that more than the expression of a general theoretical or verbal condemnation of evil is said to be required as an implicit element of the understanding of the righteous nature of God's character. Following upon the alleged imposition of the death penalty on Adam, a similar deserved punishment for continuing human rebelliousness leaves an unresolved legal issue that calls for a legal solution in the form of positive action.

The logic of the penal substitutionary theory assumes, therefore, that it is necessary, in order to preserve the integrity of God's righteous nature and to make it clear that he is by nature inimical to the world's sinfulness and evil, that God's expression of this condemnation of evil must be objectively and decisively explicit and of a penal and substitutionary kind. As N. T. Wright has observed, this point of view may be grounded in Paul's statement in Romans 8:3, where it is said that a juridical or penal element is implicitly included in God's "No" to sin and evil: "For Paul, Jesus' death clearly involves (in e.g. Romans 8.3) a judicial or penal element, being God's proper No to sin expressed upon Jesus as Messiah, as Israel's and therefore

---

2. Sydney Doctrine Commission, "Penal substitutionary atonement," para. 21. This is accounted for as a consequence of God's holiness: "His demand for holiness in his creatures, therefore, is precisely because he is holy (Lev. 11:44–45; 1 Pet. 1:16). For this reason *he could not* ignore or set aside the penalty our sin deserves without injury to his own character as the holy and just judge of all (Hab. 1:13)." (My italics).

3. By "logical possibilities" I mean "thinkable without self-contradiction."

the world's representative."[4] Perhaps, however, it is v. 4, where Paul speaks of God's sending of Jesus "that the just requirement of the law might be fulfilled" that Wright has in mind when he speaks of an alleged "penal element."

In this way, it is contended therefore that "penal substitution" arises from God's character: the imposition of an appropriate punishment is really the *only logically possible* outcome for a God who must uphold the ultimate value of justice. This contention therefore provides the explicit reasoning that explains why it was that God necessarily imposed the penalty of death on the sinless Jesus *instead of* the rest of humanity, although as rebellious and sinful all humanity is deserving of punishment (2 Cor 5:21).

Even if the imposition of a penalty was not just at the whim of an over-emotionally conceived, angry, and capricious God, as in the alleged caricatures that are said to be manufactured by the critics of the theory, those who insist upon the validity of speaking of the "wrath of God" as an ethical property therefore speak of it as a property of the *nature* of God. The penal substitutionary death of Christ was not just the outcome of some abstract juridical principle relating to the operation of deserved or punitive justice that might be understood almost in separation from the being and nature of God. This is why it is appropriate to speak of the *propitiation* of God. Sins might be expiated, but a person has to be propitiated.[5] The contention therefore is that God *must* act in this specific way in accordance with an understanding of the divine nature. The issue thus becomes a matter of the integrity of a righteous God. It is grounded in the demand for the reliability and consistency of God's acting in accordance with his very own nature.

In the words of Robert Doyle, it is a matter of God's work in the world being "limited by the law of his own being."[6] This specific approach to the understanding of God and his nature is not limited, however, to the expression of his will only in relation to the atonement. It is a matter of general principle that applies in a variety of other spheres as well. For example, Doyle apparently believes that it also applies to the possibility that God might call women to ministerial priesthood or to the episcopate in the church. This is simply declared not to be possible because Doyle contends

---

4. Wright, *Evil and the Justice of God*, 59. Despite this alleged penal reference, Wright himself, however, declares his preference for the motif of the Christus Victor, as having more overall appeal in the interpretation of the significance of the cross of Christ. For example, Hebrews 2:14–15 speaks of Christ's victory over death and the devil and of deliverance from the lifelong bondage to death.

5. The helpful distinction of Jensen, "Good News of God's Wrath," Core Words 3: *Propitiation*.

6. Doyle, "Reflections in Glass, Chapter 7," Intro.

GOD'S JUSTICE: PUNITIVE, RETRIBUTIVE, OR RESTORATIVE? 155

that the subordination of women to men is a matter that must conform to the law of God's own character: "God's work in the world being limited by the law of his own being." Thus he says that "God's will is not arbitrary, it expresses his nature and his purposes for the world."[7]

On the other hand, if in the course of defending the necessity of God's redemptive action in terms of penal substitution, the defenders of the theory argue that a just and righteous God cannot act contrary to his nature, there is also a sense in which, in relation to his dealing with sinners, God has no alternative than to exercise his love, mercy, and forgiveness. Apart from the contention that God is constrained by his own righteous nature and is therefore unable to do otherwise than carry through the terms of the penal substitution theory, he must also act in a way that is loving and merciful, for love and mercy are also qualities of the divine nature and God must of necessity also act in accordance with them. Even if he wished it otherwise, this is said to be something that God cannot avoid because it is also dictated by his own character. This provides the reason for sending his own Son to pay the penalty required by God's very own commitment to justice. Rather than impose on a third party there is a sense in which by necessity he must therefore take the burden upon himself out of love. In other words, it is suggested that God is caught in a kind of catch-22. In addition to being righteous and therefore having to act in a way that is expressive of the condemnation of sin and evil, he also has to act lovingly and mercifully for, by nature, God is merciful and loving. This means there is a sense in which God must necessarily "suffer punishment" by lovingly accepting the burden of paying the penalty for human sin and evil.

Those who claim a more "sophisticated" or "biblically authentic" understanding of "God's wrath," by interpreting it in ethical terms in association with God's justice, therefore have to face the task of balancing it against, or combining it with, an understanding of his merciful and loving character. The precise way in which this is achieved poses a theological issue for us to examine.

The first question to be tackled is whether it is theologically acceptable to say that God is constrained by his own righteous nature to demonstrate his condemnation of sin and evil by taking it seriously and imposing an appropriate penalty in judgment upon it. This contention raises a serious theological issue: Is God, as a matter of necessity, bound to act in accordance with his perceived nature in this kind of way? In other words, is it

7. Doyle, "Reflections in Glass, Chapter 7."

as a matter of general principle in fact true that God must always act in accordance with "the law of his very own being" so that the expression of this nature in the form of penal substitution may be conceived specifically as something to which even God is bound?

There is, unfortunately, a fundamental theological and logical flaw in this thinking. The first problem with this concentration on the divine *nature* is that natures do not do anything. Nor do they will anything. A kind of willing is an integral part of human nature, for example, but human nature does not itself will anything. It is persons, as distinct from their nature, that will things and act in the expression of that will. Despite all the emphasis on the role of the Father in relation to the Son in defenses of the penal substitutionary theory, it is not the *Person* of the Father so much as the divine nature that is brought into prominence when the theory is actually defended. Indeed, the emphasis on conformity to the God's perceived divine nature in discussions of penal substitution almost suggests that the concept of divinity is reducible to the idea of a divine nature. It is as though the divine nature drifts about, as though detached from any specifically identified person, even the Person of the Father as the operative subject of the theory, for it is the divine nature of the Father, rather than the Person of the Father, upon which the argument heavily relies. Indeed insofar as the Father features in the presentations of the theory he tends to be regarded as an individual representative of the divine nature rather than as a Person.

It is clear that a good deal hangs upon the distinction being made here between God the Father as an individual and God the Father as a Person. What exactly is the difference? Though there is an obvious danger of falling into a form of anthropomorphism, we may best illustrate this theological distinction between the divine nature and person of the Father by first considering the equivalent phenomenon when found amongst humans—by exploring the difference between human *nature* and the concept of human *personhood*.

Those who belong to the species *homo sapiens* behave in many ways that conform to an inherited human nature. Each human individual is a representative of that nature. This ensures that his or her human nature is distinct from "other natures." This distinct and identifiable nature is genetically determined; conformity to it is a matter of necessity. A "nature" in this way specifies the defining boundaries of a species. For example, by nature rather than by choice, lions roar and chase down deer and eat meat raw; it is natural to lions to be "red in tooth and claw." Human beings, by contrast, by nature do not roar and prowl, or stalk their prey exactly as lions do, and if they eat deer at all, it is more in keeping with their nature that this will be in a restaurant, where it may appear on a menu as "venison." Similarly, by nature honey bees return to their hive on discovering a source of supply of honey and do a "tail wagging dance" that communicates the location, the distance to it, and the quality of the supply of honey. This is part of their nature; it is programmed for them as a matter of necessity. By contrast with honey bees, humans communicate meaning through the *conventionally agreed upon* meanings of a language. Linguistic behaviors that are specific to humans are in this kind of way defining properties of human nature, no less than the natural animal behaviors that are specific to lions and bees and so on. A human individual like a lion or a bee is thus a representative of a species, and this means that the nature he or she shares with other human individuals is a given. It is a matter of necessity.

If a human individual is a representative of a human nature, and if nature requires conformity as a matter of necessity, then, by contrast a human *person* has the capacity to be and to act within boundaries set by his or her human nature, but in ways that are unique to him or herself, and that are *not* necessarily determined by his or her inherited nature. They are not simply individual instances of behaviors that are necessarily common to their species. In other words, uniquely distinctive human persons are not bound by the necessities imposed by their inherited nature, but are able to step beyond the boundaries that nature normally imposes upon them. It is in this sense that they are free to be the unique persons they are. This is especially the case in relation to their moral, spiritual, behavioral, and lifestyle commitments. For example, as users of language, unlike lions and bees, human persons are able to "hear the word of God" and are able to step beyond the necessities imposed by their nature, so as with the help of God's grace, to "make something of themselves." They are not just individual instances of a nature, but human *persons*.

Vladimir Lossky points out that the concept of a "person" signifies the irreducibility of a human *person* to his or her human nature.[8] For while an individual being is distinct from "another nature" as a human *person* he or she is in another sense not bound to conform to the characteristics of others of the distinct species whose nature he or she shares, and is thus not just genetically unique, but personally unique. Within limits human persons are thus free to make of themselves what they will in a way that goes beyond their inherited nature.

As human *individuals*, they may be countable representatives of a nature; but as *persons* they are able to "stand apart" from the inherited nature to which they otherwise conform. In this sense a human person is *free* from the necessities imposed by his own nature. As a person he or she

---

8. Lossky, "Theological Notion of the Human Person," 120.

does not exist apart from a nature, but he or she nevertheless exists in a sense "beyond" this shared human nature and the need to conform to it, by overstepping it, and so constantly exceeding it. As Lossky puts it: a human person exists "beyond the nature which he 'enhypostasizes' and which he constantly exceeds."[9]

If this were not so there would be no possibility of human persons achieving moral or behavioral excellence; it would not be possible for them to exceed their "sinful nature" so as to live new and redeemed lives that move beyond the imperfections of their inherited human nature. Thus, in pursuing this insight, Lossky points out that "the idea of person implies freedom vis-à-vis the nature. The person is free from its nature, is not determined by it."[10] This grounds a kind of antinomy between nature-as-necessity and *hypostasis*-as-freedom.[11] As Aristotle Papanikolaou, following Lossky, puts this: "Nature is, thus, identified with a kind of necessity that personhood ecstatically overcomes and transcends."[12]

Now, very importantly, Lossky believes that this person/nature distinction has its origin in the Trinitarian reflection of the early church fathers, especially the Cappadocians of the fourth century, precisely in the course of working out the doctrine of the Trinity when they drew a clear distinction between *ousia*/essence (and its nature) and *hypostasis*/person. Moreover, if we were originally concerned not to fall into a kind of anthropomorphism by fashioning God in a human image, we are delivered from that danger by just the opposite thought: human persons as distinct from mere individual representatives of a nature, are "made in the image of God." As Lossky says: "Personhood belongs to every human being by virtue of a singular and unique relation to God who created him 'in His image.'"[13] As persons made in the image of God and in distinction from other species of animal,

---

9. Lossky, "Theological Notion of the Human Person," 120.

10. Lossky, *Mystical Theology of the Eastern Church*, 122. See also his *Orthodox Theology*, 72: "The Person . . . is then man's freedom with regard to his nature, 'the fact of being freed from necessity and not being subject to the domination of nature, but able to determine oneself freely.'" (Lossky claims here to be dependent upon Gregory of Nyssa.)

11. According to Aristotle Papanikolaou, "The antinomy, however, between nature-as-necessity and hypostasis-as-freedom is actually attributable to Sergius Bulgakov, even if Bulgakov never developed a theology of personhood with which we are now all familiar." ("From Sophia to Personhood," 9). See Bulgakov, *Bride of the Lamb*, 127–28.

12. Papanikolaou, "From Sophia to Personhood," 4.

13. Lossky, "Theology of the Image," 137.

humans are able to hear the word of God and to respond to it in prayer and worship. In other words, while human individuals are representative of a nature, human persons are "made in the image of God" and precisely as persons are uniquely able to respond to God in interpersonal relationality and so to represent God in the world in a way that other animals do not.

The Christian theology of God therefore requires that, apart from the shared divine nature, an important emphasis has also to be put on the Persons of the Trinity, and their freedom to exercise the divine will and to act in the world indivisibly in the expression of that will. Initially, the personal freedom of God is exercised quite simply as the freedom to be, in the sense that God is not answerable to or dependent upon anything other than himself for his being. God is self-existent. This absolute ontological independence is the *aseity* of God—his being from himself. Consequently, it is the *Person* of the Father as "origin" and "cause" of the other two Trinitarian identities, that in logical terms is the font of divinity; divinity does not originate from an impersonal "substance" and its divine nature. This initial exercise of the personal freedom to be, is matched by an eternal and uniquely personal freedom, within obvious boundaries set by the divine nature, to be and to act as God wills.

As important as the concept of the divine nature is to Trinitarian description, it is also of huge importance that the concept of a *hypostasis* or Person is not marginalized, if not virtually excluded from the discussion. This is for the obvious reason that God cannot be reduced to a nature. Neither is God hostage to the necessities of his perceived nature. Indeed this free "going beyond" the necessities imposed by a perceived nature may be in ways that may surprise us.

Once again, this overreliance on the concept of the divine nature and what it is said necessarily to entail illustrates the sub-Trinitarian matrix of thought out of which the theory of penal substitution emerges. It is not just a matter of introducing two wills, a commanding will of the Father and the obediently submissive will of the Son, so as to end in tritheism. It also has to do with a shortfall in relation to the Trinitarian interplay between the concepts of the divine nature on one hand and the divine Persons on the other. We must therefore take a little more time to attend to the truth that God is not reducible to the equally shared divine nature to the exclusion of an equal, and in fact logically prior, emphasis on the divine *hypostases* or Persons.

While the concept of a nature signals a boundary-defining necessity to which each individual representative of that nature must conform, the freedom to be and to act associated with personhood allows for the necessary constraints of a nature to be transcended. Within a set of boundaries set by our human nature, for example, as human *persons* we are *free* to act in a variety of ways. A set of boundaries are likewise set by the concept of the divine nature that is equally and fully shared by all three of the Trinitarian identities, but as Persons they are also free to will and to act in a variety of ways.

Even if the property of "divine wrath" is an equally shared communicable property of the divine nature, and if it is understood to mean that there is a sense in which God is bound of necessity to pronounce judgment upon all that is unjust and that sinfully disfigures human nature, this does not mean that the divine Persons are not free to do as they will in specific ways that "go beyond" that nature. The divine Persons, even sharing the self-same nature, may act together in ways that do not conform to the expectations that might be generated by the human perception of their shared nature; they may in fact go beyond the finite human perceptions of their nature. In going beyond the perceived necessities said to be imposed by the shared divine nature, as divine *hypostases* they exercise the freedom to be and to act as they will.

Some behaviors are not appropriately predicated of God because by nature God has no body, party, or passions. It is obviously not within those boundaries of God's nature for God to be understood to sit down to eat a steak sandwich, for example, yet within the boundaries set by the divine nature of God, God as personal is understood to be free to act in a wide variety of ways. Far from being constrained always to act in accordance with a single perception of what is appropriate to his nature, there is a sense in which God as a Person, or more correctly as three Persons, is *free* to act not necessarily and predictably but even surprisingly.

In the face of this distinction between individuals and persons, it is possible to appreciate that there is an obvious tendency in expositions of penal substitution to emphasize the notion of the divine nature, and the *necessity* of God's acting in accordance with it, that the personal freedom of God to act as God wills tends either to be minimized or even overlooked entirely or implicitly denied. Instead, presentations of the theory tend to represent God the Father as an individual rather than a Person—in other words, a representative of a nature rather than as a Person.

The idea that nature may rightly be linked to the concept of *necessity*, while the idea of a person is to be linked to a kind of self-defining *freedom*, means that the contention of defenders of penal substitution "that God must act in accordance with his nature" is urgently in need of revision. The personal

GOD'S JUSTICE: PUNITIVE, RETRIBUTIVE, OR RESTORATIVE? 161

freedom of God means that, precisely as a Trinity of *hypostases* or Persons in one unity of being, and not just three instantiations of a divine substance and its nature, God is free to act in a variety of ways—all within but at the same time going beyond the parameters prescribed by his nature. Given this distinction between "nature" and "person," the usual attempt to explain why it was allegedly necessary for God to act punitively falls to the ground.

To the extent that the theory of penal substitution holds that God is *constrained* to act in accordance with the just and righteous character of his own divine nature *in an explicitly punitive way* is therefore problematic. The very specific set of penal conclusions of the penal substitutionary theory do not follow with any kind of logical necessity from the premise of the argument—that God must act in accordance with a "wrathful" disposition, understood as ethical stance with respect to human sin and evil. When we ask if statements outlining the various elements of the penal substitution theory follow with logical necessity as the *only* possible way in which this ethical understanding of the "wrath of God" *might* achieve its public expression, we have frankly to admit that this is not so. There are other possibilities.

Even if it were to be conceded that God cannot act contrary to his nature as righteous—by demonstrating the quality of character by maintaining an ethical stance of condemnation towards all that is sinful, evil, and unjust—God remains personally free to act in specific terms as God wills. Even within parameters set by the perceived need for God to be righteously condemning of sin and evil, as a person with freedom God may choose to act in an indeterminate variety of other ways. All this flows from the Trinitarian contention that God in not just an individual representative of a nature who is bound by the necessity of conformity to a nature, but an indivisible unity of *hypostases* or *Persons* with freedom to act as God wills.

That the imposition of penalties may not be the only way of registering his condemnation of sin and evil is already implicit in the regular defense of the theory itself. Indeed the proponents of penal substitutionary atonement are quick to point out that it is a caricature of God to assume that he expresses his condemnation of sin and evil in a furiously angry and vindictive way, as though he is hellbent on retribution. In other words, the exercise of retributive justice is ruled out of court in the defense of a more 'sophisticated" and "biblical" understanding of things. A preference is then registered for a purely punitive non-retributive form of justice, from which the emotional fury is excluded. This, however, is itself an acknowledgment of the fact that the administration of the divine justice may take a variety of forms. By saying "No" to retributive justice and "Yes" to punitive justice this variety is clearly demonstrated. But this inevitably then raises a question as to whether a purely punitive form of justice might in turn itself also be modified so as to give way to a form of justice less wedded to the concept of punishment. This is particularly so when we remember that love, mercy, and forgiveness are also a part of the divine nature that has also to be brought into play.

We may rightly anticipate that a righteous and just God will be prone to act in way that expresses the divine condemnation of sin and evil in the world. But exactly *how* in precise personal terms God will express this, God alone is free to determine. Humans cannot assume to know precisely what form the expression of God's righteousness might take.

Clearly, finite human creatures dare not presume to dictate to the divine Persons, who are free to be themselves, to create beyond themselves, and to redeem and renew their creation in whatever way they will, and freely to enter into communion with those beyond themselves. This is certainly not something that is already determined by God's just and righteous nature. As Persons with freedom to step beyond the necessities that might be said to define the divine nature, they are able act together in ways that are beyond our human perception of their nature, even if in ways that may not be contrary to it.

Clearly, apart from hesitating to draw a set of detailed conclusions from a very general perception of God's wrathful character, we have to face the fact that, once we bring the notion of the "wrath of God" into association with the tradition of the long-suffering and loving forbearance of God, a punitive kind of justice may no longer commend itself any more than a retributive kind of justice. A righteous God might well be said to be obliged to uphold the value of justice by condemning sin and evil of the world, but clearly, it does not *necessarily* have to be a demonstration of a punitive or a retributive kind.

Once again, the basic theological problem facing the proponents of the penal substitution theory of the atonement in their contention that God cannot act contrary to his nature, is that God cannot be reduced to a nature. An equal importance must be accorded to the Trinitarian definition of a *hypostasis* or Person, and the freedom to be other than the necessities dictated by a nature. Amongst other things, the consideration of the implications of the orthodox doctrine of the Trinity with regard to this particular issue well illustrates Karl's Rahner's point that a Trinitarian matrix of thought out of which the doctrine of redemption comes naturally exercises a kind of continuing control on what may or may not be said.

The contention that the specifically *penal* and *substitutionary* theory of the atonement does not *necessarily* arise out of this requirement of a righteous God to act justly in accordance with his righteous nature's requirement to condemn the sin and evil of the world does not mean, however, that a case has been made to justify its abandonment. If it were even to be true that God was constrained by his natural righteousness to demonstrate his condemnation of sin and evil, the question is whether there are good and sufficient reasons why a punitive administration of divine justice might commend itself as something to which the proclamation of the Christian gospel of redemption is bound. On the other hand, there may well be good reasons for abandoning it. This is yet to be demonstrated.

The first issue that might mitigate against accepting the penal and substitutionary understating of the cross of Christ arises from the problematic nature of the presence of a penal understanding of death in the texts of Scripture. The truth is that a penal view of death is missing from the Old Testament. It has already been observed[14] that, despite God's warning in Genesis 2:17, the punishment of Adam and Even was not death, but expulsion from Eden. This admittedly separated them from access to the tree of life in the middle of the garden and therefore from the possibility of immortality. However, they were not created immortal and then deprived of immortality by the imposition of the penalty of death.

In order to reach a more clearly penal understanding of death we have, like St. Paul himself, to go to the book of Wisdom. But, as we have also already noted,[15] even this is a problematic reading of the view that "the wages of sin is death." This does not necessarily mean that death was imposed as a penalty on Adam and all sinful humanity after him. Rather, as was noted in the previous chapter, it is more true to say that the wages of sin is death in the sense of a premature death, the failure to experience the blessing of "length of days." This blessing from God is the reward of those who strive to live according to "wisdom." The fate of the wicked rather than all humanity is to be deprived of this blessing, not so much as a punishment but as a consequence of their own foolish fault.

Moreover, when we go to the New Testament Scriptures in search of the actual texts that pin down what Paul may have had in mind when he said in 1 Corinthians 15:3 that Christ "died for our sins according to the scriptures," exactly what Scriptures are being referred to is not entirely clear.

---

14. See, for example, 63, 69, 81 above.
15. See, 69–70, 93 above.

We know that, as the first Christians searched for words to explain all that had happened so cruelly and unjustly to Christ, phrases of Isaiah 53 immediately came to mind: "he suffered for our transgressions."[16] In the light of the fact that the first Christians had themselves contributed to Jesus' death by hailing him as "messiah" and "king" (prompting Pilate's question: "Are you a king?"[17]), this would have made the words "he died for our transgressions" immediately poignant. But whether Isaiah actually had Jesus Christ in mind when he wrote some six centuries earlier that "he suffered for our transgressions" is another thing altogether. Whether Isaiah's expression of hope at the prospect of peace in Israel with the help of Cyrus of Persia after the Babylonian captivity can by a process of direct transference be made to speak predictively of the peace with God won by Christ on the cross is surely questionable. Even if early Christians could naturally appropriate his words in relation to their own experience, a predictive reading of Isaiah is surely a big ask. Indeed, Old Testament scholars regularly point out that when Isaiah spoke of the "Suffering Servant" he was actually referring to Israel.

It is unfortunate that proponents of the penal substitution theory of the atonement tend simply to slide past this problem by assuming the legitimacy of a straightforward predictive reading of Isaiah's prophecy. Peter Jensen says quite categorically, for example, that Christ's penal and substitutionary death was somehow anticipated by Isaiah:

> He endured a punishment by becoming this substitute for us. This of course, was prefigured in Isaiah 53: "He was pierced for our transgressions, he was crushed for our iniquities; the punishment that brought us peace was upon him, and by his wounds we are healed."[18]

Similarly, Peter Brain in a brief article in *Essentials*, the publication of the Evangelical Fellowship of the Anglican Church in Australia, has argued that the "scriptures must be allowed to speak for themselves" and then simply lists Isaiah 53 along with a number of other prooftexts that are said to secure a penal understanding of the atonement.[19] Some of these texts

---

16. Isaiah 53 may have been in mind, for example, in the writing of such texts as 1 Peter 2:24 and 3:18 and at a stretch 2 Corinthians 5:21.

17. There is a sense in which the sign pinned to the cross—"King of the Jews"—should not have been altered to say "He said he was King of the Jews" but, more properly, "By word and action he inspired others to hail him as King of the Jews" (even despite the fact that Jesus actively proclaimed "the kingdom of God" or "the kingdom of Heaven" and is himself reported to have declared that his kingdom was "not of this world").

18. Jensen, "Good News of God's Wrath," Under Core Words 2, Punishment

19. Brain, "Could I talk to you?," 4–5.

GOD'S JUSTICE: PUNITIVE, RETRIBUTIVE, OR RESTORATIVE? 165

have an obvious general bearing on the redemption achieved by God in and through the life, teaching, suffering, death and resurrection of Jesus, but whether they really have to do explicitly with a "penal" and "substitutionary" understanding of things is problematic.[20]

Among the texts that might be thought to offer some support for the penal view of Jesus' death, Brain lists Galatians 3:13: "Christ redeemed us from the curse of the law, having become a curse for us—for it is written, 'Cursed be every one who hangs on a tree.'" This unfortunately asks us to accept the view that Jesus was cursed by God insofar as God sent him into the world to undertake the penalty of death by crucifixion instead of us.[21] Paul's whole argument in this section of Galatians, however, is not about the curse of God, but about the curse of the law and its inability to justify a person before God (v. 11). A person who is righteous[22] by being justified by faith in Christ Jesus, by contrast receives the blessing promised to Abraham—the gift of the Spirit through faith (v. 14). This is what delivers a person from the "curse of the law." And very significantly, Paul's point is that this blessing is available not to Jews who keep the law, but to Jews of faith and Gentiles as well. In this way Jesus redeemed humanity from the curse of the law, even by becoming subject to the curse of the law himself. There is no joy for those who seek to wring a punitive understanding of God's administration of justice here.[23]

Whether such a theory springs directly from Scripture "speaking for itself" without its being read through the preconditioning lens of some kind of dogmatic schema seems entirely improbable. Rather, the quest to assemble a few texts that might help support belief in the penal substitutionary theory is explicable from the point of view of pre-Barthian evangelicalism, and especially in the light of the federal theology of the scholastic Calvinism of Ursinus and the Heidelberg Catechism. This style of theology, which swept across Europe through the first half of the seventeenth century, and became

---

20. For example, Mark 10:45; John 3:36 and 4:10; Romans 3:24–25; 2 Corinthians 5:21; 1 Peter 3:18.

21. This is also the view of Peter Jensen: "When Christ was handed over by his own people to the pagan occupying power, it was understood to be a mark of judgment. He fell under the curse of God." Jensen, "The Good News of God's Wrath," Core Words 2: Punishment.

22. Significantly, not "accounted righteous."

23. For a full discussion of the exegesis of Galatians 3:13–14, see Donaldson, "Curse of the Law," and Hamerton-Kelly, "Sacred Violence and the Curse of the Law." Also, Bonneau, "Logic of Paul's Argument on the Curse of the Law in Galatians 3:10–14".

enormously important in British Puritanism and in the development of the Westminster tradition, subsequently reached significant levels of popularity in America in the nineteenth century and in Australian, notably in Carillon Avenue theology, from 1936 onwards.[24] The residual influence of federal theology's contention that God made a contract with Adam in the alleged "covenant of works" that was conditional upon Adam's obedience, but which was broken by Adam's rebellious insistence on "going it alone," entailed that, as with breaches of contract generally, it brought with it a penalty.

According to the ensuing penal substitutionary theory of the atonement the payment of this penalty was discharged effectively by the "covenant of grace" that was said to have been sealed with the blood of Jesus Christ. From this perspective when God is said to demonstrate his "wrathful" condemnation of sin and evil, it is naturally understood in strictly juridical and punitive terms.

Given the problematic nature of the insistence on a moral and penal view of death instead of an ontological view of death as a necessary implication of life in finite space and time, we have to ask whether a penal view of the atonement is really necessary. This also becomes a pressing issue when we seek an answer to the theological question of what may be understood to happen when God's righteous nature, and his need to express his unequivocal condemnation of sin and evil and all that is unjust in the world, is brought into association with his loving, merciful, and forgiving nature. The answer of the proponents of the penal substitution theory is that God's graciously loving and merciful character finds expression in the very fact that God himself in a sense paid the required penalty for Adam's sin and of all humanity after him, by providing the victim who felt "the curse of the law" in suffering and dying on the cross. But an alternative answer might conceivably be that God's loving and merciful character entails that his righteous commitment to uphold the principle of justice in condemning sin and evil, is expressed in a way that actually modifies a straightforwardly punitive outworking of justice rather than simply being an instance of it.

It is perfectly understandable that those who wish to defend penal substitution as a way of explaining the saving significance of the cross are naturally anxious to distinguish the caricatures of God that they say the critics of the theory employ, from what they themselves understand to be a more "sophisticated" and "biblical" and therefore acceptable image of God. This

---

24. A more detailed examination of federal or contractual theology and its history may be found in Carnley, *Arius on Carillon Avenue*, chapter 2.

is achieved by placing the penal substitutionary theory of the atonement in the wider biblical context of God's loving and merciful nature and the story of his steadfast dealing with his covenant people. In this case, the broader context of the theme of the love and mercy of God of the biblical revelation is brought to bear in theological reflection on the meaning of the cross in such a way as to modify and soften the caricatures of an emotionally wrathful and fiercely angry God. In this way the God of the alleged caricatures who is cast in the role of an agent of retributive justice, is helpfully modified in the hope of becoming less morally objectionable and more acceptable.

The strategy of attempting to hold apparently disparate images of God together in this way is not unusual in the doing of systematic theology. Theological discourse about the nature of God, as a matter of regular practice, seeks to hold various images together in a kind of balance. Images of God as a Father, for example, or as a shepherd, are held together with the images of God as a rock or a wind. In the attempt to lay out the grammar of "God" the task of systematic theology is to seek to explain something of the meaning of these images in such a way as to allow them to be held together so as at least to allow them to point toward the nature of divine truth. Thus, classical theism has been quick to point out that God is obviously not literally a rock, but that this metaphor is nevertheless helpful in pointing towards God's character: God's stability and reliability is rocklike, and therefore steadfast and dependable. This may then be harmonized, for example, with the fatherly image of care and love, to suggest the kind of relational stability and reliability of a God who is trustworthy and faithful to his promise, analogous to that expected of fathers in this world. In this way the images of "Father" and "rock" though in one way so obviously disparate become mutually interpretative. One image modifies the other. The proponents of penal substitution rightly bring the love, mercy, and forgiveness of God to bear upon the biblical tradition of the "wrath of God" so as to make it acceptable by modifying it so as to avoid the alleged caricatures of the theory's critics.

However, this methodological procedure then raises the crucial question of what happens theologically when the love, mercy, and forgiveness of God as this is perceived in faith to have been revealed in the life, teaching, and manner of dying of Jesus Christ is brought to bear, not just on the notion of the "wrath of God" but on the concept of a God whose nature is said to require him to act punitively.

In other words, we have to ask what happens theologically when the perception of the love, mercy, and forgiveness of God is brought into conjunction, not now with the concept of the "wrath of God" so as, in a sense, to demythologize it, so that it heard as an ethical principle of condemnation with regard to the sin and evil of the world, but into conjunction with the presentation of an understanding of the exercise of God's justice. If the love, mercy, and forgiveness of God and the "wrath of God" are mutually interpretative, what are we to say about the outcome of the mutually interpretative conjunction of the love, mercy, and forgiveness of God with the penal substitutionary theory of the atonement? Is God to be understood as one who is necessarily committed to a punitive form of the administration of justice? Is it thinkable they are mutually interpretative in the sense that one may condition or qualify the understanding of the other?

The theoretical possibility that the understanding of the divine righteousness, and the consequent need for a righteous God to adopt an ethical disposition that is condemning of sin and evil, may be modified and rendered more acceptable by association with values of love and mercy, may legitimately be demonstrated analogically by reference to the current experience of the administration of justice in the world. In the course of explaining the outworking of the wrathful divine character in the economy of salvation, so as to achieve the key outcomes of the penal substitution theory, a number of concrete images are either inevitably presupposed and implied or overtly called into play. When expositions of this theory of the atonement contend, for example, that God demonstrates his own righteous commitment to justice by wrathfully pronouncing Adam and all rebellious humanity guilty, then allegedly followed by imposing the death penalty upon Adam and all sinfully humanity after him, it is hard to avoid imagining these alleged divine acts in some concrete form of juridical imagery. Inevitably, an image drawn from this world is projected onto a heavenly screen. Hence, T. C. Hammond conjured up the earthly image of a civil magistrate: "Punishment is an inevitable sequel to sin" that may be understood on analogy with "a form of judicial dealing" such as the "punishment prescribed by a human magistrate."[25]

In modern courts of law, however, in the process of handing down verdicts and thus upholding all that is just in the face of the forces of evil, a range of sentencing options is regularly considered. Without compromising the cause of upholding the values of justice, and ensuring that "justice is duly done," mandatory sentencing is in fact rare. Instead, contemporary legal practice allows for a variety of sentencing options to be summoned into play. A judicial discretion is normally accorded to the presiding judge, who, as a matter of principle, is usually free of any necessary legal or logical

---

25. Hammond, *In Understanding Be Men*, 85.

pressure to opt for one sentence rather than another. The range of options available in the legal work of sentencing does not compromise the fundamental principle of the commitment to the just condemnation of what is patently evil and unjust. Certainly, the death penalty is not universally and unwaveringly imposed, even in trials of those accused of the most serious of offenses, or when it might normally be regarded as being well deserved. Indeed in many countries of the world capital punishment is regarded as morally unjustified, and even as crudely reprehensible as the ancient rough and ready justice based on principles of vengeance and retribution—the maxim "an eye for an eye and a tooth for a tooth" is not only understood to put a limit on the degree of retribution that may be sought, but is interpreted as an inhibition on seeking retribution of any kind.

Today sentencing judges take account of the mental capacity of those convicted of crimes in assessing degrees of responsibility and culpability. Moreover, the justice systems of the world regularly work, not just punitively let alone in the way of retributive justice, but often (and most would say mercifully and rightly) in the way of restorative justice. In all this the ethical and judicial commitment to upholding the seriousness of an offense is sustained, so that the legal system is still condemning of evil. It does not take evil lightly. Nevertheless values of mercy and forbearance are brought to bear in the hope of the restoration of those guilty of crimes, with a corresponding diminished concern for the imposition of harsh penalties or social retribution. In this way the administration of justice operates to modify and soften what would otherwise be an uncompromisingly merciless, hard-nosed, and harsh outcome.

It is important to say that all this is without minimizing the seriousness of the original wrongdoing. Rather, it is precisely when the seriousness of the offense is sincerely recognized and owned by defendants themselves, that those who administer the law feel free to be more lenient and merciful in dealing justly with them. Lighter sentences and even suspended sentences, not to mention good behavior bonds, become possible sentencing options in the wake of a verdict of guilty when genuine remorse and regret is expressed, and when defendants honestly own up to their crime and plead guilty rather than seek to wriggle out of the predicament in which they have trapped themselves. Certainly, when guilt is admitted, penalties are, generally speaking, less harsh, and opportunities are made for amendment of life.

Once an offender is judged to be guilty of an offense, for example, sentencing judges take careful account of victim impact statements, but they also consider the mitigating circumstances surrounding the committing of an offence. In other words, in the administration of justice in this world the need for a penalty to be paid in order to uphold the value of justice is in these ways often modified or tempered by the values of love and mercy and the desire for restoration over a purely punitive retribution. This raises a question as to whether the perception of the ethical need of a righteous God to uphold justice, may be thought to fall short of the administration of justice in this world. Indeed the opposite may be the case: we have to take account of the possibility that it is the biblical tradition of the love and mercy of God, the divine forbearance and the ultimate values of restoration over unbending retribution, so as to turn sinners from their wickedness to live in repentance and forgiveness, that has actually acted historically to temper and modify the administration of justice even in the secular world.

This means that, even when God's wrath is understood as an ethical disposition of a condemning kind against all that is sinful and unjust, the conclusions of the penal substitution theory do not follow with logical necessity as the *only* conclusions that might be warranted by this initial ethical insight into the character of the divine nature. If we are able to learn something about the administration of justice from contemporary secular experience of the administration of justice the suggestion is that, in association with the love, mercy, and forgiveness of God, the exercise of justice may take the form of a justice that relies less on the imposition of penalties and more on the restoration of sinners to wholeness of life. In other words, God's justice in the face of the sin and evil and all that is unjust in the world may not only avoid the retributive justice of the alleged caricatures of penal substitution, but the punitive justice of the substitutionary theory of the atonement even in its alleged more "sophisticated" and "biblical" form as well.

It might be objected at this point that Scripture itself specifically ascribes a kind of punitive if not actually a retributive justice to God. Ephesians 5:6, for example, might be interpreted as scriptural warrant for thinking of a kind of retributive justice in association with God's wrath: "Let no one deceive you with empty words, for because of these things the wrath of God comes upon the sons of disobedience." But Romans 12:19 is even more direct. Quoting Deuteronomy 32:35, Paul says: "Beloved, never avenge yourselves, but leave it to the wrath of God, for it is written, 'Vengeance is mine, I will repay, says the Lord.'"[26]

We may be well advised, however, to exercise a little caution before using prooftexts of this kind to ground the assertion that God is necessarily a God of punitive or even retributive justice, rather than of what today is in human terms called restorative justice. This appears somewhat problematic,

---

26. Quoting Deuteronomy 32:35; see also Hebrews 10:30.

given that this Pauline text is clearly in the first instance an exhortation to humans not to take retributive vengeance into their own hands. Rather than a specific attribution of vengeance-taking to God, it is at least thinkable that Paul is simply urging his readers not to take vengeance to themselves, and instead to leave the administration of justice to God—without necessarily committing God to act revengefully. In other words, it is at least thinkable that Paul's meaning is that we should leave it to God to deal with evildoers in whatever way he deems appropriate; and who is to presume that it is not open to God to act in a more merciful kind of way?

After all, while Deuteronomy 32:35 may suggest that God may act revengefully and punishingly so as to warn against evil, Proverbs 25:21–22 lays down an alternative strategy in dealing with those have been wronged by others: "If your enemy is hungry, give him food to eat, and if he is thirsty, give him water to drink. For in so doing, you will heap burning coals on his head, and the Lord will reward you." In any event, the encouragement of righteousness in the form of the warnings of the punishment that might well await evildoers in the justice of God, is another thing from attributing vengeance-taking to God of the kind which imposes a "one-size-fits-all" death penalty *upon all humanity* by God in the wake of Adam's disobedience.

It is also relevant to note once again, that in the theological work of discerning the divine character we may have to balance this kind of statement with other texts whose meaning points in an altogether different direction. There is even a hint that considerations of a mitigating kind already operate in the story of Jonah, where God tutors Jonah to be sorry for the Ninevites in their confused ignorance. "After all," God is made to say, they can hardly distinguish "their right hand from their left"(Jonah 4:11). Another relevant text would obviously be Matthew 5:45, where God is spoken of as one who "makes his sun to rise on the evil and on the good, and sends rain on the just and on the unjust." And did not the followers of Jesus himself, remember him as one who spoke of the need to love, not just "your neighbor as yourself," but even to love "your enemies, and to pray for those who persecute you," rather than seek to ensure that they were (even if perhaps deservedly) punished for their misdeeds: "Bless those who persecute you; bless and do not curse. Do not repay anyone evil for evil" (Matt 5:43–48)?

This must surely mean that, without sacrificing the general principle that a righteous God must necessarily be thought to adopt a negative and condemning stance in relation to sin and evil, it may at least be said that God might well be free to choose to act in a manner that is restorative rather than purely punitive or retributive—and in the light of the revelation of God in Christ to be more likely to do so. Indeed, this is exactly the kind of justice one might expect from a God who is also understood to be infinitely loving and merciful, long-suffering, and of great forbearance. In other words, the exercise of divine judgment may be less concerned with the imposition of punishment than the proponents of the penal substitutionary theory would have us believe, and more concerned to effect a kind of restorative justice that rehabilitates a repentant sinner. Even if sinners might themselves expect God to act in righteous judgment in accordance with his perceived nature by acknowledging that they deserve to be punished, God is free to act mercifully as one who "does not require the death of a sinner, but rather that he should turn from his wickedness and live."[27]

Furthermore, it cannot be denied that the general drift of the teaching of Jesus on the importance of forgiveness, not just seven times, but seventy times seven, and his exhortation not to seek retribution or even to seek the satisfaction of the payment of a penalty for a wrong done, but rather to "forgive your enemies," suggests that we would be remiss to elevate a punitive form of justice to a place of centrality in the mind and character of God. Indeed, in the death, resurrection, and glorification of Jesus we have if anything a paradigm of restorative justice. Justice is done in the sense that Jesus the victim of "the curse of the law" was vindicated by restoration to life. As a consequence, his oppressors were implicitly judged for their crime. Furthermore the early proclamation was that Jesus returned victoriously, but not to condemn those who had persecuted him, or to seek legal redress, let alone revenge or retribution, but lovingly, with the proffer of salvation even to those who had crucified him. In all this Jesus revealed something of the love, mercy, and forgiveness of God.

In any event, it is clear that the conclusion that God *must* act in judgment by imposing the penalty of death on all humanity for the inherited sinful disobedience since the fall of Adam, is not the *only* logically possible way of demonstrating his righteousness commitment to justice. It is thinkable that God could act according to "an ethical posture of a negative and condemning kind in relation to all that is sinful, evil and unjust" in other ways.[28] None of the sentencing options that are brought into consideration in the contemporary administration of justice compromises the need to act in a way that is demonstrably and consistently just. If restorative justice and amendment of life may be pursued even in this world with a seriousness that clearly does not diminish or "pass over" the gravity of criminal activity, then in this case, the alleged requirement of the imposition of the death

---

27. Words from the *Book of Common Prayer*, 1662.

28. Once again, by "logically possible" here I mean "thinkable without self-contradiction."

penalty does not follow with logical necessity from statements describing the righteousness, and therefore at the same time the necessarily "wrathful" character of God. This means that the penal substitutionary theory of the atonement loses a fundamental element of the usual attempt to furnish it with a rationale.

One good reason for doubting the appropriateness of opting for a punitive form of the administration of justice in relation to God's demonstration of his righteous and just nature arises from the train of historical events leading to Jesus' passion and death. The fundamental logic of expositions of the penal substitutionary atonement inevitably suggests that those who had persecuted Jesus, although acting out of cruelty and self-interest at the expense of an innocent victim, were in another sense doing the work of God. After all, God is said to have sent his Son into the world with the specific mission to redeem the world by offering himself in submissive obedience to die upon the cross, thereby paying the penalty required to propitiate the offense of Adam and all humanity after him. Inevitably the logical implication of this is that Caiaphas, Pilate, and the mob baying for blood were, without knowing it, acting as agents of the redemptive purpose of God. In other words, God's "sending" of the incarnate Son into the world as the one designated to undergo the punishment that his justice is said to require, leads to the suggestion that God was "using" Caiaphas, Pilate, and the crowd shouting for blood as his agents in achieving his own "wrathful" purpose.

Presentations of the penal substitution theory are often somewhat coy in drawing attention to the role of Caiaphas, Pilate, and others as instruments of God in achieving his alleged overall purpose in this way. Indeed the uncomfortable suggestion that Caiaphas, Pilate, and the baying crowd act in God's behalf as active agents of the divine purpose is often effectively suppressed in presentations of the substitutionary theory. Obviously, this is a somewhat awkward idea, because the joint action of Caiaphas, Pilate, and the crowd appears to constitute a concrete example of evil in the world of the very kind that needs to be condemned by God rather than being positively used by God as an intentional part of his redemptive plan. This unfortunately appears to mean that God uses evil as a positively intended means of achieving his own redemptive ends—as though the end justifies the means.

It is understandable that this may raise questions as to whether this is really any advance on the so-called caricatures of a viciously revengeful God "hellbent" on exacting retribution out of pique and uncontrolled anger.

But what is the alternative? One possible alternative would be to argue that the suffering and death of Jesus was not a penalty intentionally imposed by God, with its execution orchestrated by God through the agency of Caiaphas, Pilate, and the crowd. Instead it may be viewed essentially as a human evil, for which human beings were entirely responsible. In this case, it was not something that was actively and positively willed by God, though it has to be conceded that it was in accordance with God's *permissive will*, given the creation of humans with the freedom to do evil. In this case, it is not just that in achieving his general plan for the redemption of humanity by sending the incarnate Jesus into the world, it was within the foreknowledge of God and in accordance with his permissive will that he would be persecuted, but that this was positively intended by God in order to achieve his own wrathful purpose.

Given that God's original creation of humans with freedom to do good also necessarily involved the freedom to sin and do evil, there is a sense in which sin and evil must always be in accordance with God's permissive will. This takes its place in a theodicy in which it may be argued that only in a reasonably tough "vale of soul-making" with the real possibility of human sin and evil, could humans "learn obedience"[29] and so mature as morally responsible persons.[30] In the case of the evil of Calvary, God's role, rather than the active exercise of will in carrying out of a purposive plan, falls within his permissive will. By vindicating Jesus, however, through raising him from the dead, followed by his glorification and the transforming gift of his living Spirit to constitute the communion of the redeemed, God's role becomes one in which good was by grace brought out of evil.

Rather than something positively intended, planned, and actively carried through by God through the agency of Caiaphas, Pilate, and the crowd, God's role was to turn their evil to good effect. The cross takes its place as a human evil, the historical preliminary which God turned to a positive result with an eternal redemptive effect.

The vindication of Jesus may in turn then be understood as a demonstration of God's triumph over evil, by putting the reign of death to an end, and offering new life for all humanity. When Jesus returned from the grave, however, he came not vindictively to punish and condemn those who had unjustly treated him. Rather, he came with the proffer of forgiveness "even to those who had crucified him."[31] But this does not mean that those who

---

29. Heb 5:8.

30. As argued in the theodicy of the great William King early in the eighteenth century in *De Origine Mali*, and by John Hick in the twentieth century parallel to this in *Evil and the God of Love*.

31. Acts 2:36.

crucified him were not judged, nor that they were not made aware of the patent wrongfulness of the cruel crucifixion of an innocent victim at their hands. Thus, in the early sermon of Peter in Acts 3 it is declared that the very ones who had crucified Jesus who had "acted in ignorance" (v. 17) were now being called to repentance: "God having raised up his servant sent him to you first." But the raised Christ came not to punish or to seek legal redress, but with the proffer of forgiveness. He is declared to have come "to bless you in turning every one of you from your wickedness" (v. 26). Those who had crucified him were not thanked for their actions in carrying out the ultimate good purposes of God; they were not thanked but forgiven. If the theory of penal substitution, with its unfortunate implication that Caiaphas, Pilate and the lynch mob were used by God to accomplish his redemptive ends, is judged to be abhorrent to the good purposes of God, the alternative suggestion is that the death of Jesus becomes a demonstration of triumph over the human injustice and evil of those who persecuted him, while God is said to have been able to turn this evil to a positive result. In this way, there is a sense in which God's justice was done through the vindication of Jesus the victim, and its implicit judgment on those who had rejected and victimized him by crucifying him.

This account seems to offer at least the possibility, therefore, of abandoning the penal theory altogether so as to allow the unjustly cruel and politically manipulated act of crucifying Jesus to be seen as it is, starkly confronting and abhorrent, without trying to sanitize it by incorporating it into the intentional will and purposes of God. Although, as an uncompromising evil that is not in accordance with the active will of God but in fact contrary to it, through the good purposes of God it is turned to good effect by God's vindication of Jesus by raising him from the dead, exalting him to glory, and designating him to be Lord and Messiah of his people.

I think we are obliged to conclude that punishment is not the only way of dealing with human sin and rebelliousness. As Steve Chalke observed in the context of responding to the proposals of proponents of the penal substitution of the subordinate Son, "we're much better off abandoning it altogether and starting again with a clean sheet of paper."[32]

The clean sheet that is set before us as we begin to rethink the doctrine of redemption is, however, never entirely blank. We may do well at the outset to heed Karl Rahner's plea that the doctrine of the Trinity should be

---

32. Chalke, "Cross Purposes," in which he is somewhat more definite in his criticisms than his original "not a form of child abuse" remark.

brought into play. When it is remembered that the penal substitution of the Son to the Father in the economy of salvation has been linked historically with the sub-Trinitarian, and indeed Arian belief in the "eternal functional subordination" of the Son to the Father, we may be forgiven entertaining some foreboding concern. When it is further remembered that in the orthodox doctrine of the Trinity all three Persons act together indivisibly in the world, no less than in its creation, according to the single will of their equally shared divine nature, alarm bells begin to sound.

We may have some reservations about the unqualified application of the second half of Rahner's Rule—that the economic Trinity quite simply *is* the immanent Trinity—because of the danger of projecting imperfect human epistemological defects relating to the perception of God in the economy of salvation into the immanent life of the Trinity. If, on the other hand, we may comfortably reaffirm his basic point about the fundamental importance of revelation of God in the economy of salvation as the ground not just a straightforward monotheism but belief in the Holy Trinity of eternal Persons in one unity of being, we may also accept his plea about the importance of bringing this genuine Trinitarianism to the consideration of the doctrine of redemption.

For starters, if Rahner's fundamental contention that we have first to attend to salvation history as the context within which we may perceive the undivided operation of all three Trinitarian identities in the economy of salvation, then we may wisely exercise some caution before automatically preceding to work on a metaphysical level. It has already been noted that those who originally declared that Jesus died "for our sins" (in the genitive plural), in the tradition quoted by Paul in 1 Corinthians 15:3 were in the first instance uttering a historical truth of their experience the economy of salvation before it came to be projected onto a heavenly screen as a metaphysical truth with eternal dimensions. In terms of historical truth, Jesus had died "*because* of their sins" in the immediate sense that they had been indirectly guilty of precipitating the unjust charge against Jesus that he claimed to be messiah and king. In the course of his triumphal entry into Jerusalem (even if it was actually on a lowly donkey) their action in heralding him as messiah and king seems to have triggered a negative response in the minds of the governing authorities. In addition one of their number then betrayed him to those authorities, some of them had apparently deserted him in the quest to save their own skins, and others, most notably Peter, had actually denied him. In a historical sense he had literally died not just because unjustified and unfounded charges were laid by those whose authority was threatened, but in another less direct sense, in the traumatized minds of the perspective his followers also because of "their sins." It is understandable that in guilt they came to interpret his death retrospectively as being of benefit "for their sins." In the next generation of believers, represented for example by Paul, who had not been party to the historical betrayal, a less historical and more clearly metaphysical interpretation of Christ's dying "for their sins" naturally followed.

By attending in the first instance to the historical truths of the "economy of salvation" we might first also exercise a little caution before rushing to speak of Jesus being "made sin" in the metaphysical sense that God was prepared to upload the sin of the world onto Jesus when he died on the cross. Defenses of the theory of penal substitution tend to suggest that, at least in some notional sense, God made him the "bearer of our sins" in a kind of sacrificial offering with an eternal effect on humanity's behalf, and so as to fulfil the need for a penalty to be paid for the disobedience of Adam and all humanity after him. By giving priority to the economy of salvation, however, we may wisely first attend to the historical reality of Jesus' "becoming sin." Speaking historically, the coming of Jesus into the world in the economy of salvation involved Jesus' entry into the imperfection of a world "gone wrong." As a matter of historical fact Jesus entered a world disfigured by sin, evil, social injustice, and that was inevitably overshadowed by the ultimate trauma of death in some form, often at a very young age by our contemporary standards. In a sense Jesus "became sin" and subject to the harsh reality death by entering fully into this world of sin.

It is in this sense that Paul often speaks of "sin" as distinct from "our sins" (in the genitive plural). For Paul sin is an all-pervading "gone-wrongness" with the whole world. Although he speaks of "our sins" in the genitive plural when he quotes words he had received from others (as notably in 1 Corinthians 15:3), this is his own more usual and characteristic phraseology. "Sin" is a general and inclusive failure of the whole creation to meet the mark that God intended for it. Thus, for Paul "the whole creation groans in travail until now."[33] It was a Jewish world, furthermore, in which the keeping of the law as an attempt to deal with sin "in the flesh" ultimately led only to death. This was the world in which Jesus became "sin" in the sense that he became "subject to sin." Hence God did what the law could not do when he redeemed the world though the life, death, resurrection, and glorious exaltation of Jesus and the gift of his Spirit. In this way the doctrine of redemption is in the first instance worked out in the historical context of the economy of salvation, before it can be lifted on to a metaphysical level with eternal implications.

---

33. Rom 8:22.

Certainly, when an orthodox Trinitarianism is brought into association with the usual expositions of the penal substitutionary theory of the atonement, some concerning difficulties immediately begin to surface. At this point the relevance of the doctrine of the Trinity to the understanding of God's redemption has to be taken with the utmost seriousness. For it soon becomes apparent that, insofar as this theory involves an overconcentration on a behind-the-scenes transaction of a metaphysical kind between the Father and the Son, this is regularly at the expense of the Holy Spirit.

If, according to Rahner's Rule, the Trinitarian nature of God is revealed in the economy of salvation, then we should anticipate that all three Trinitarian identities are involved in the drama of human redemption in a complex series of events: the call of the gospel to repentance and faith in the life and teaching of Jesus through to his suffering and death, his vindication by the Father by resurrection, glorification, and exaltation to "God's right hand," *and ultimately the gift of the Spirit*. This is a logically and causally connected composite whole. We proclaim Jesus Christ and him crucified; but at best this is only half of the Christian good news. We also proclaim the good news that the Crucified One was raised from the dead and exalted to glory and, furthermore, that we now know his living presence though the transformative gift of his Spirit. This immediately signals that we should resist theological methodologies that are quick first to account for the justification of sinners in a purely juridical way with a concentration of interest on the meaning of the cross with its focus on the Father and the Son but in a way that is effectively exclusive of any mention of the Holy Spirit, only then to bring the Spirit into play in a separate chapter of the theology of redemption on "the sanctification of sinners."[34]

---

34. This is the methodological arrangement of T. C. Hammond in *In Understanding Be Men* and in *New Creation*. Indeed, when Hammond moves from the doctrine of the redemption to consider the work of the Holy Spirit, the Spirit is said to be "the Executor of the counsels and purposes of God." Hammond briefly mentions that the Spirit "mediates Christ to the church and the individual" and then hurries to speak of the inspiration of the Scriptures by the Holy Spirit (*In Understanding Be Men*, 134). In *New Creation*, the sanctifying work of the Holy Spirit is described as "God's gracious working in the souls of those who have entered into new and saving relation to him" (121). That the Holy Spirit might have a part in achieving this "new and saving relation" to God does not come into consideration. Rather, as the divine Agent of sanctifying grace he is brought in by God to complete "the whole process of his regeneration." That the gift of God's Spirit in Christ might have an originative role in achieving humanity's entry into the "new and saving relation with him" is displaced by Hammond's fundamental reliance on a legal mechanism to achieve this outcome.

When the gift of Holy Spirit is admitted to a part in a more integrated and Trinitarian understanding of the story of God's redemption of humanity we are invited to contemplate a less juridical and more participative approach to soteriology in which reconciliation and peace with God is ultimately achieved in concrete human experience through the receiving of the gift of God's very own life. As John V. Taylor once said in the title of a notable book, the Spirit is the "go-between God" with an explicit role in bringing fractured humans together by reconciling them to himself.[35]

It is surely not just a fortuitous coincidence that the very texts that are most often cited in support of belief in the theory of penal substitutionary atonement, Galatians 3:13 and Romans 8:2, actually include a direct reference to the role of the Spirit in achieving reconciliation with God through the fulfillment of his covenant promise to Abraham. Galatians 3:13 reads:

> Christ redeemed us from the curse of the law, having become a curse for us . . . that in Christ Jesus the blessing of Abraham might come upon he Gentiles, that we might receive the promise of the Spirit through faith.

Romans 8:2–4, which N. T. Wright explicitly cites as a possible indicator of a penal approach to the atonement, reads:

> For the law of the Spirit of life in Christ Jesus has set me free from the law of sin and death. For God has done what the law weakened by the flesh could not do: sending his own Son in the likeness of sinful flesh and for sin, he condemned sin in the flesh, in order that the just requirement of the law might be fulfilled in us, who walk not according to the flesh, but according to the Spirit.

Indeed, even here in Roman 8:3, with the "penal element" to which N. T. Wright refers, Paul consciously juxtaposes the concepts of "flesh" and "Spirit" in seeking actually to describe the radical experiential change that the new and reconciled life with God in Christ involves. It is significant that here it is not unequivocally said that the requirements of the law had been fulfilled in Christ's death on the cross, but that in sending the Son sin had been condemned in the flesh, and that the just requirements of the law had been *"fulfilled in us* who walk not according to the flesh but according to the Spirit."

Clearly, the cross and resurrection and the gift of the Spirit are to be held together as constituent elements of a composite redemptive event. It was as though the first Christian believers remembered the poignant quality

---

35. Taylor, *Go-Between God*.

of Jesus' nonviolent surrender of his life on the cross by laying down his life for his friends as a token of the remembered uniquely personal self-giving that had characterized his entire time with them, which they interpreted in faith as the revelation of the self-giving of God. But then miraculously they found in concrete experience that through the gift of his Spirit they received his life again as something in which they participated "in Christ" as a consequence of his resurrection from the dead.

Thus, it is understandable that the author of 1 Peter, in writing to early Christian believers, apparently in the context of their own persecution and suffering, sums up this redemptive experience:

> [I]t is better to suffer for doing right, if that should be God's will, than for doing wrong. For Christ also died for sins once and for all, the righteous for the unrighteous, that he might bring us to God, being put to death in the flesh but made alive in the Spirit.[36]

The redemptive outcome of the words and works of Jesus that "he might bring us to God" is not to be understood in a crucicentric way, as though something was achieved in a behind-the-scenes transaction of a juridical kind between the Father and the Son, exclusive of the Holy Spirit. Rather, his "bringing us to God" in reconciliation and peace was achieved by the composite whole of his "being put to death in the flesh but made alive in the Spirit."

Gordon Fee, in a splendidly helpful treatment of Paul and the Trinity, points to the actual experience of the raised Christ and the Spirit for Paul's understanding of God: "to be a trinitarian of the Pauline kind means to be a person of the Spirit: for it is through the Spirit's indwelling that we know God and Christ relationally, and through the same Spirit's indwelling that we are being transformed into God's own likeness 'from glory to glory' (2 Cor. 3:18)."[37]

This means that atonement is not just a theory of an abstract kind in which to believe, but a concrete experience of the economy of salvation in which by faith humans may actively participate. It is entered into in an empirical way by faith and baptism into Christ whereby we are admitted to the life of reconciliation and peace with God though sharing in the interpersonal communion of the Trinitarian life of God.

---

36. 1 Pet 3:17–19.

37. Fee, "Paul and the Trinity," 72.

It is of some interest to note that N. T. Wright, in his response to the alleged unfair caricatures of the atonement produced by the critics of penal substitution, and even in response to more sophisticated attempts to develop positive defenses of the theory that he also believed to be essentially unbiblical, pointed out that when Jesus was approaching his coming death "to help his disciples get the full meaning and benefit of what was about to happen, he didn't give them a theory, he gave them a meal." Wright went on to say that this meal contains "the means by which theories can be turned into real life. Personal, practical, political life. Kingdom-of-God-on-earth-as-in-heaven life. And that, after all, is what 'atonement' ought to be about."[38]

In other words, even though Wright himself attempted to produce his own allegedly "more biblical" *theory*, which he believed could still reasonably be called "penal substitution," at the end of the day he pointed (if somewhat enigmatically) to the mistake of becoming exclusively and rigidly committed *just* to abstract theories. It is the concretely experienced reality of humanly sharing together in the communion of God through the reconciled life in Christ that is of more importance. And this is most poignantly perceived as an "inward and spiritual grace" encountered in the "outward and visible sign" of the characteristic worship of the eucharistic community in the breaking and sharing of bread.

In the economy of salvation what was understood to have been initiated by the death of Christ upon the cross was brought to fruition in his resurrection from the dead in fulfillment of the covenant promise made to Abraham—now extended, as St. Paul would be quick to say, beyond the narrow confines of Israel to include the entire Gentile world as a sharing in the interpersonal communion of God in love and peace. The concretely participative experience of the mystery of redemption in the economy of salvation in this way provides the basic ingredients of the doctrine of the Trinity which in turn, in a mutually interpretative way, then informs the church's understanding of the doctrine of redemption. A participative understanding of the achievement of reconciliation and peace with God through the sharing of the divine life "in Christ" by the gift of the Spirit are all integral elements of the Christian good news.

---

38. Wright, the closing words of "Cross and the Caricatures."

8

METAPHORS AND MYSTERY

In the course of the examination of the interrelated doctrines of the Trinity and of God's redemption of humanity two theological principles have emerged that may wisely be kept in sight.

The first is that whatever is said in understanding of "the definite plan and foreknowledge of God"[1] in his dealing with sin and the fulfillment of the covenant promise made to Abraham, it has to be clearly affirmed that the first Christians understood God's redemption of humanity to be an objective reality that was perceived and known by faith in concrete human experience. They were not just dealing with an abstraction of thought or a kind of legal fiction that by default then came to be celebrated as the primary object of Christian belief. Reconciliation with God is a concrete reality of interpersonal experience rather than something purely notional or theoretical. The object of their faith is not a theory but a person through whom, by his death and resurrection to life and gift of his Spirit, they believed they had gained access to reconciled fellowship with God the Father in a way that overcame the alienation created by sinful disobedience.

Paul speaks from his own concrete experience, for example, when, in Romans 8:3-4, he says that "God has done what the law, weakened by the flesh, could not do, by sending his own Son in the likeness of sinful flesh, in order that the just requirement of the law *might be fulfilled in us, who walk not according to the flesh but according to the Spirit*" (my italics). It is not insignificant that Paul says here, not that the just requirement of the law was satisfied in some abstract or theoretical sense—for example, by the notional application by God of Christ's death for the payment of a penalty *instead* of those who really deserved to die. Rather Paul says that God sent his Son to

---

1. Acts 2:23.

do what the law could not do by ensuring that it might actually be fulfilled, effectively, as a matter of historical fact *"in us"*—i.e., not in assigning some abstract kind of value to the death of Jesus but by actually achieving something in the lives of the first Christians as a consequence of the unlawful death of Jesus—something of an empirical and tangible kind in the lives of those "who walk according to the Spirit."

T. C. Hammond was of the view that the problem with what he identified as "liberalism" and "modernism" was that the life and manner of dying of Jesus was presented only as exemplary—at best it was something to be emulated. But he noted that this meant that nothing was actually done about the sin and the evil of the world. Hammond therefore insisted that, according to Paul, something had happened through the death of Jesus by which the "wrath of God" has been turned away from sinful humanity. Hammond's mistake was to assume that the legal fiction of a kind of self-imposed punishment to turn away "the wrath of God" and to express the righteousness and justice of God was the only objectively real way of conceiving the meaning of the cross. This is parallel to his assumption, that was noted in the previous chapter, that God's justice could be assumed to be only of an explicitly punitive kind. In any event, he assumed that if God did not achieve something of this juridical and forensic kind, then we are left with an essentially Pelagian attempt on the part of humans merely to emulate Jesus.[2]

A more clearly Trinitarian approach to the mystery of the redemption of humanity by God, perceived in the economy of salvation through the nexus of Jesus' death/resurrection and glorification/and the gift of his life-giving Spirit, offers an alternative of an "incorporative" and "participative" kind that is no less real—if not more real. The achievement of human reconciliation and peace with God in the history of salvation, as something positively created amongst Jews and Gentiles alike in the wake of the suffering and death of Jesus through his resurrection and the gift of the Spirit, is an objective state of human affairs. It is a reality that is empirically and concretely known in human experience by faith. It is in this experiential sense that it can be said to be something that is objectively real.

It certainly seems right that, in order to be true to the New Testament witness, the meaning of the cross cannot be reduced just to a way of "looking at" it, or to a matter of interpreting it in a purely speculative and notional kind of way. It is more than a matter of a theoretical "on-look" even relating to an alleged covenant arrangement between God the Father and God the Son that is said to have been put in place "behind the scenes." It involves,

---

2. Hammond, *New Creation*, 71–72.

rather, the creation of a new state of affairs in the history of salvation in which the covenant promises to Abraham were understood to have been fulfilled amongst both Jews and Greeks, who were in turn conscious of "standing" in it[3] or "walking" in it[4]. It involved an empirical experience of life in which alienation from God by the all-pervading disfigurement of sin and evil was understood to have been positively overcome.

Though Hebrews speaks of Christ as "the pioneer[5] and perfecter of our faith" (Heb 12:2), he is more than merely exemplary. Our assessment of the importance of his mission has nothing to do with the Pelagianism of a purely human achievement of striving to live in imitation of Christ, understood only as an ideal. Rather, the active participation in the divine life of God to which we have access though the offering of Christ and his subsequent resurrection and gift of his Spirit is by his grace alone. The Christian consciousness of "walking no longer according to the flesh but according to the Spirit" was accompanied by a consciousness of the fact that this was enabled by "the gift of the Spirit." This is obviously understood as a thoroughly objective achievement of the redemptive work of God in Christ.

The new life in Christ into which we are called by the gospel is quite positively not just a life which Christians seek earnestly to emulate by treating Jesus as an ideal to follow. This has nothing to do with Pelagianism, for it is not a human achievement. Only with God's help, by grace alone, appropriated by faith alone, do those who die with Christ in the waters of baptism rise with him to a new kind of life in him and walk according to the Spirit. All this is God's achievement through raising Jesus Christ from the dead.

The second basic theological principle to which we might wisely attend is that the redemptive experience of reconciliation and peace with God, precisely because it is perceived by faith to be the gift of the generosity of God in admitting humanity to a share in his very own life, is ultimately to be understood as a surpassing mystery. In the first instance, when early Christians described this concretely experienced reality of the gift of the Spirit, they spoke of their knowledge of it in faith as something that was necessarily understood to be partial and incomplete. They therefore interpreted the gift of the Spirit in eschatological terms as promissory of more to come. From the perspective of the present what had yet to be fulfilled in

---

3. See Romans 5:1–2: "we are justified by faith, we have peace with God through our Lord Jesus Christ, through him we have access to this grace in which we stand . . ."

4. Rom 8:4.

5. Sometimes translated "author."

future time came to be is seen as a reflection in a mirror, something seen dimly, not face-to-face.[6] For this reason, justification by faith and access to the grace of peace with God in which Paul was conscious of "standing" or "walking" was interpreted as the basis of hope. As St. Paul said, "we rejoice in our hope of sharing in the glory of God."[7] This means that, pending the "full revealing" of the mystery of God when we humans will know even as we ourselves are already known,[8] all finite human attempts to express the concrete experience of the redemptive mystery of God fall short of precise, clear, and distinct specification. We "do not hope for what is already seen."[9]

As the first Christian believers searched for a language to describe their newfound experience while awaiting clarity of perception in the time to come, they inevitably resorted to the genre of metaphor. Just as analogies and metaphors are employed to speak of God himself as King, shepherd, Father, judge, rock, wind, or consuming fire, so analogies and metaphors are used to envisage something of the nature of God's dealing with his creation and specifically its redemption. Obviously, the gift of God's own Spirit as an integral element of his redemptive activity is not the finite kind of gift that comes "gift wrapped" and delivered from a department store, but something transcendent and essentially elusive and difficult to pin down. We speak of the "gift of the Spirit," but when we come to envisage it or to describe the nature of the experience of it, we have necessarily to resort to images of "wind" and "fire" (as in Acts 2), or we speak of it as something "poured out" into our hearts (as in Romans 5:5), or of the "fruit" of the Spirit (as in Galatians 5:22–23). Or, borrowing a commercial image, we speak of it as a "down payment" or "guarantee" of a greater yield to come (as in 2 Corinthians 1:22; 5:5; and Ephesians 1:13–14). All this is clearly metaphorical language. Likewise, the humanly transformative consequences of the nexus of Christ's passion, death, and resurrection that in historical time preceded the gift of his Spirit were also necessarily expressed in metaphorical images—Christ's offering of his life to God was understood as a propitiatory sacrifice on analogy with rituals of the temple in Jerusalem. Alternatively, it was spoken of as the payment of an outstanding and burdensome debt incurred through commercial misadventure, or as securing fallen and sinful humanity's release from confinement in a kind of imprisonment. Or it was conceived on analogy with the payment of a ransom to secure the release

6. 1 Cor 13:12.
7. Rom 5:2.
8. 1 Cor 13:12.
9. Rom 8:24.

of those taken into captivity by an enemy, or the achievement of victory in battle with the forces of evil.

As N. T. Wright says, the language of Paul grounds a "multilayered" theology of redemption.[10] But, if the language on which this redemptive theology is based was initially intended to be heard descriptively, given its use for the primary purpose of indicating something of the quality of a concrete experience, perhaps that multilayered tradition of images and metaphors was not intended to be developed into a theory or theories of the atonement and still less elevated to a semi-dogmatic status and proclaimed as the "essence of the gospel." Paul's redemptive language may be best left as we find it in the New Testament—as a "multilayered" assemblage of images and metaphors that may be used today for the very same purpose as that for which they were originally used—that is, to express something by way of interpretative description of the experienced reality of the surpassing mystery of the redemption of God.

Normally the metaphors that we use in day-to-day discourse may be unpacked in more precise, clear, and distinct, literal, and prosaic language. But because humanly devised linguistic tools are designed to come to terms with life in the finite world, they have to be tailored or "stretched" to refer to the infinite mystery of God and his dealing with his creation and its redemption. This application of finite images in a quest to conceive of the infinite means there is a sense in which God is always beyond the images that are formed to refer to him. It is understandable that there is an immediate difficulty when images taken from this finite world are projected onto a heavenly screen and used to refer to a surpassingly transcendent religious Object that is by definition Infinite and therefore in an important sense "beyond words." In order to handle this difficulty the tradition of classical theism has highlighted the fundamental importance of the *apophatic* or "negative way": when positive affirmations are made about the divine reality with which faith has to do they must immediately be qualified by a negative "but not" statement, so as to avoid the mistaken implication that language is being used literally or univocally. Hence, as Aquinas put it, statements about God and his ways are not univocal, nor entirely equivocal, but analogical or metaphorical, and furthermore that they cannot be reduced to literal or absolutely clear and distinct specification.[11] Even when God reveals himself it is not that a mystery is entirely resolved, as in an Agatha Christie novel; rather, God

10. Wright, "Redemption from the New Perspective."
11. Aquinas, *Summa Theologiae*, I.13.5.

reveals his essential nature *as* mystery—as transcendently awesome, remote, sublime, and ultimately incomprehensible to finite human minds.

This means that when Christians address God as "Father" it is not being suggested by this analogy that God is in all respects like a human father of this finite world—he has no body, parts, or passions; he obviously does not "father" offspring as the fathers of this world do; nor does he have a beard in the way so often depicted in stained glass windows. But this same need for negative qualification applies to any finite or positive image that may be used of the Infinite God. God is by definition Infinite, a transcendent and surpassing mystery who is always "beyond" our images of him, whether they be material or verbal, metal or mental.

The same applies to the transformative impact of his gracious action on his creation and specifically to his redemptive activity within creation. The experienced reality exceeds the capacity of the linguistic tools that are brought to the task of dealing with it. When Job, for example, says that God (as it happens, metaphorically speaking, acting as milkmaid) has "poured me out like milk" or "curdled me like cheese" (Job 10:10), this metaphor is not immediately open to being reduced to a clear and literal specification. Or when the prophet Malachi says that God will operate at "the day of his coming" *like* "a refiners' fire and like fullers' soap" it is clear enough that he is resorting to a simile. When he goes on to say that God "will sit as a refiner and purifier of silver, and he will purify the descendants of Levi and refine them like gold and silver, until they present offerings to the Lord in righteousness" (Mal 3:2–4), this metaphor of God as a purifier of silver is employed to describe a hoped-for divine activity of refining and cleansing of his human children. However, a degree of imprecision is obviously left to the religious imagination in relation to the actual details of the divine production of righteousness in those whom he will spiritually and morally "refine" and "purify" and precisely how this will be accomplished.

The metaphors and images of God with which faith has to do, and with which theology has to deal, are therefore *irreducible* metaphors and images.[12] At best religious language points towards the divinely transcendent reality with which it has to do. Understandably therefore, for Paul "the peace

---

12. Sarah Coakley questions this by pointing out that to speak of Christ metaphorically as a rock can be unpacked in more literal language by saying that he is "reliable, unchanging." But the precise way in which he is "reliable and unchanging" may nevertheless remain elusive. He is not "reliable and unchanging" in the precise way a rock may be. Nor is he reliable in the literal way an omnibus line might be said to be reliable by always showing up on time. The divine reliability is less easily pinned down in finite terms. See Coakley, "'Persons' in the 'Social Doctrine' of the Trinity," 138.

of God passes all understanding."[13] Similarly, in praying that his readers might "be filled with all the fulness of God," Paul (or the anonymous author of Ephesians in the Pauline tradition) expresses the hope that they might have "power to comprehend" the love of their shared experience of new life in Christ, and to know "the love of Christ which surpasses knowledge."[14] As Paul himself certainly expresses his sense of this surpassing mystery in Romans 11:33: "O the depth of the riches and wisdom and knowledge of God! How unsearchable are his judgments, and inscrutable his ways!" At the very least this should strike a cautionary note in the work of formulating theories of the atonement by rushing in overconfidently where angels fear to tread.

While this incapacity of metaphorical images to yield a more clear and distinct literal or prosaic specification is regularly acknowledged as something that is peculiar to their use in a theological or religious context,[15] some have argued that similar interpretive issues impact upon the use of metaphor more generally. The French philosopher Paul Ricoeur has argued, for example, that even preceding the difficulties of the function of metaphor in a theological context, all metaphors necessarily suffer from a degree of imprecision, which means that their interpretation is not ever straightforward. As Aristotle observed, "A good metaphor implies an intuitive perception of the similarity in dissimilars."[16] This is something of an art.

Assumptions have to be made about exactly what a specific metaphor is meant to communicate simply because metaphors are multilayered or multifaceted and do not come bearing labels that explain exactly how they are to be interpreted. Ricoeur is of the view that justice is not done to "metaphorical truth" when specific possible aspects of their supposed meaning are selectively, and somewhat arbitrarily, isolated from others. This means that he is not at all sanguine about the straightforward reducibility of metaphors to literal paraphrase. It follows that the capacity of metaphor as an instrument of communication of truth invites some serious questioning.

Ricoeur is of the view that an irreducible "metaphorical truth" may be discerned using the strategy of placing a metaphorical image in the context of the whole sentence in which it is used, but even this necessarily leaves

---

13. Phil 4:7; see also Isa 40:13; 55:8.

14. Eph 3:18–19.

15. A paradigm example in relation to the theology of atonement is Gunton, *Actuality of Atonement*. On his distrust of conceptual clarity, see 17, 38, 167.

16. Ricoeur notes and endorses Aristotle's point about the importance of perceiving resemblances. See Ricoeur, *La Métaphore vive*, 10.

a degree of imprecision given that there is always a "surplus of meaning" that cannot simply be reduced to some literal paraphrase.[17] Similarly, Janet Martin Soskice, who is also somewhat resistant to the possibility of reducing metaphors to a precise form of literal specification while celebrating "the irreducible power of metaphors for knowledge," highlights the importance of the living context of the use of metaphors, and not just the verbal context of a sentence. Soskice points out that more than a sentence may be required insofar as *speakers* rather than words use metaphors, particularly in order to refer to and describe realities of their living experience. The extra-linguistic context is therefore important for the identification and interpretation of metaphorical meaning; certainly, the living context of the speech-act, or illocutionary act, is not to be ignored.[18]

Obviously metaphors have an important descriptive role in the communication of aspects of experience, or in pointing to aspects of reality in a kind of ostensive way, that would otherwise go unnoticed, otherwise we would not use them. Some are therefore more optimistic about the possibility of reducing some of the meaning communicated by metaphors in literal paraphrase, while acknowledging that not everything that could be said is actually said. Max Black, for example, accepts that, at least in relation to trivial cases, there may be minimal loss of cognitive content when metaphors are paraphrased. For Black what is lost is merely "the charm, vivacity, or wit, of the original."[19] This means that whether metaphors are thought to be entirely irreducible as in the thinking of Ricoeur, or only partially so, metaphors should not be peremptorily dismissed as of little significance; they are improperly spoken of as "mere metaphors," as though they are next to meaningless.

On the other hand, some have been beguiled into the mistake of assuming that a positive assessment of the value and function of metaphors in their general day-to-day use may be uncritically imported into theological and religious discourse. Henri Blocher tends to slip into this error in his article explicitly on "Biblical Metaphors and the Doctrine of the Atonement."[20] After helpfully reviewing the contemporary discussion of the functioning of metaphors in human communication generally, Blocher expresses a personal disinclination to dwell on "types of metaphors" on the ground that he believes "a radical divide between sub-kinds is not very likely."[21] He then goes

17. Ricoeur, *Interpretation*, 46–53.
18. Soskice, *Metaphors and Religious Language*, 134.
19. Black, *Models and Metaphors*, 46.
20. Blocher, "Biblical Metaphors," 637.
21. Calling on the support of Soskice, *Metaphors and Religious Language*, 94–95.

on to argue that, while we may "feel" that a metaphor cannot be replaced by any other form of discourse, whether some great artist might one day come up with an appropriate paraphrase may always remain a rhetorical possibility. His assumption is that "Reasonably adequate paraphrases . . . are not beyond reach"[22] and then that even in theology, and despite the hallowed apophatic tradition of classical theism, this also holds true. At this point he relies heavily on Kevin Vanhoozer's contention that the interpretations of metaphors, like other texts, "are determinable enough to convey stable meaning without being exhaustively specifiable" and that "Interpretation is not a matter of interpreting all figurative language into clear and distinct propositions. Our interpretations may adequately, though not exhaustively, grasp the metaphorical and textual meaning."[23] This means that interpretations, "while not arbitrary, are revisable and incomplete."[24] Unfortunately, there is a latent difficulty lurking here insofar as metaphors are said by Vanhoozer to be both "determinable enough to convey stable meaning" and at the same time to be "revisable and incomplete." Clearly, the capacity of metaphorical images to furnish information with sufficient cognitive precision and stability to constitute the first premises of a theoretical argument begins to look somewhat problematic.

In any event, on the basis of the belief that devising metaphors "is more than mere passive recording or imaging,"[25] and in the firm belief that interpretations of metaphors "inevitably take the form of paraphrases"[26] (at least in the case of metaphors of a trivial or mundane kind), Blocher quickly moves from a commonsense understanding of the capacity of metaphors to yield to literal paraphrasing to the assumption that the New Testament metaphors of atonement also conform to the same possibility. The element of theological indeterminacy thus tends to be passed over and minimized.

Blocher, as "one who proceeds to *build a theology* of Christ's work of redemption,"[27] explicitly expresses his interest in justifying and promoting the use of metaphorical function in this system-building enterprise. Clearly, the use of metaphors in the speculative work of "building a theology" goes well beyond the use of metaphors simply in the process of talking descriptively about the perceived nature of the Object of concrete religious experience with which faith has to do. Likewise, I. Howard Marshall, quoting

22. See Vanhoozer, *Is There a Meaning?*, 130.
23. Vanhoozer, *Is There a Meaning?*, 139.
24. Vanhoozer, *Is There a Meaning?*, 140.
25. Blocher, "Biblical Metaphors," 637.
26. Blocher, "Biblical Metaphors," 638.
27. Blocher, "Biblical Metaphors," 631 (my italics).

Blocher's article, contends that the metaphorical language of the New Testament does convey truth and is to be taken seriously.[28] However, Marshall does not pause to ask what kind of truth it is that is taken seriously, or what kind of truth is appropriately expressed through the use of metaphors in their religious function, or more explicitly whether metaphors might be of descriptive use in the communication of religious experience while being less amenable to providing the fundamental premises of a speculatively theoretical doctrinal argument. In other words, what remains necessarily problematic is the question of whether metaphors are irreducible to a sufficiently clear and distinct literal specification for theoretical explanations of the redemptive working of the mind of God.

Blocher is not unaware of the apophatic traditions of classical theism but is surprisingly dismissive of them. It is somewhat curious that he is prepared to admit that "the rules of language themselves depend on experienced reality: they have been shaped . . . by the actual intercourse of human groups in and with the world."[29] But he is obviously disinclined to countenance the possibility that the experience of human groups in their intercourse with the surpassing mystery of God has shaped the specific rule that theological and religious language is always analogical or metaphorical and is irreducible to clear and distinct finite specification.

Blocher is not at all fazed by the diversity of New Testament atonement metaphors, which he groups in four categories—sacrificial metaphors, judicial metaphors, and metaphors of ransom and victory—the first two of which are the most often used and are identified as the most important. Nor are the apparent divergences among this variety of metaphors troublesome to him. On the contrary, he says, "This abundant evidence is best explained by the hypothesis of an underlying doctrinal scheme."[30] As the first Christians sought to communicate the nature of their newfound experience of reconciliation and peace with God in Christ, they naturally resorted to metaphorical images. Notwithstanding that Paul had said that this was something that "passes all understanding," the first Christians are said by Blocher to have been confident that "the various representations had direct doctrinal cash value."[31] While admitting that their metaphorical language does not say everything that could be said, and is not exhaustive of truth, it tends to be assumed even so to be "good enough" for the theoretical development of doctrines. Indeed, for Blocher this becomes an "effortless task," for the

---

28. Marshall, *Aspects of the Atonement*, 12.
29. Blocher, "Biblical Metaphors," 636.
30. Blocher, "Biblical Metaphors," 640.
31. Blocher, "Biblical Metaphors," 641.

various New Testament atonement metaphors "fittingly complement each other; they exhibit the same structure (isomorphism), so that they naturally *translate* into one another—hence the intertwining in so many passages."[32]

In purporting to transcend the difficulties of the apophatic tradition, however, Blocher tends to part company with Vanhoozer, who declares, "It's metaphors all the way down. There is no non-metaphorical word that can be said of God. The pragmatists' 'God' is indeterminate."[33] However, Blocher does not actually argue a case against the apophatic method; he is simply derogatory and dismissive of it. We are encouraged not "to flee across the misty spaces of apophatic theology" even with its "air of wisdom and its celebration of God's transcendence, and the humbling of theological reason."[34] This is said to be "of no use against the mind of the flesh." Indeed, it "may camouflage the arrogant refusal to let God speak in intelligible terms to his people."[35]

This abandonment of the cautionary tutelage of the apophatic tradition thus comes at the cost of refusing to acknowledge the implications of the surpassing mystery and transcendence of God, and the limits of religious thought. This is even summarily dismissed with the declaration, "It finds very little encouragement in Scripture."[36] Alas, this may come as a surprise to those of us who venture to put our feet in Moses's shoes and then find ourselves taking them off as we venture on to holy ground. The alleged lack of a biblical warrant for any need to take account of the surpassing mystery of a God who is "wholly other" and transcendent is difficult enough to sustain in the face of the prophetic invective against the idolatry of fashioning God in a finite image. St. Paul, on the other hand, will have something more to say about the need to acknowledge the fundamental importance of the concept of mystery that confronts those who seek to "speak humanly" about the ways of God and what "passes all understanding."

But first let us examine some examples of the functioning of metaphors by those committed to the use of them in the construction of explanatory theories of the atonement. We may profitably focus on the two sets of

---

32. Blocher, "Biblical Metaphors," 643–44. At this point Blocher is following Vanhoozer: "The canon of the Old and New Testaments, as well as that of the Bible as a whole, encloses a space within which texts deemed authoritative can interact and inform one another." (Vanhoozer, *Is There a Meaning?*, 134).

33. Vanhoozer, *Is There a Meaning?*, 134.

34. Blocher, "Biblical Metaphors," 644.

35. Blocher, "Biblical Metaphors," 644.

36. Blocher, "Biblical Metaphors," 644.

metaphors that Blocher himself privileges—the sacrificial and the judicial—which are said "to have a special relationship to the event they interpret."[37]

It is understandable that the proponents of the penal substitutionary theory of the atonement encounter some difficulty in handling the sacrificial imagery that appears to have come so naturally to the lips of those who were faced with processing the meaning of the traumatic experience of the suffering and death of the innocent Jesus.[38] It could fairly easily be appreciated that there was "no greater love" than that demonstrated by the sacrificial self-giving of Jesus' own life on behalf of his friends. That was a reasonably straightforward moral judgment. But the more metaphysical question of how this death operated as a sacrifice that overcame the alienation of humanity from God, given the sinful disobedience that was so obviously contrary to the divine will, was much more of a conceptual challenge.

For a start, as Andrew McGowan has pointed out, a compelling explanation of exactly how the sacrificial systems in the ancient world actually worked is notoriously ill-defined. It was not just a simple matter of placating an angry God, as might be popularly believed. It is clear that there was no one overarching sacrificial theory capable of explaining the working mechanism of sacrifices even in ancient Judaism, let alone in the Hellenistic world. Given the variety of sacrifices, meal offerings as well as the sacrifice of living animals, and the differences between the burning of sacrificed flesh and consuming it, and just how this had its desired effect, whether it either "took away" or "expiated" sin or "propitiated" the divine wrath, or simply expressed thanksgiving, and whether the laying on of a hand was to transfer sins to the sacrificial animal or simply to identify the worshipper with the victim, and so on. All this is far from clear.

This general lack of clarity in relation to the working of sacrificial systems is compounded by the fact that in the New Testament the single use of the term *hilasterion* by Paul in Romans 3:25 is persistently resistant to interpretation, given that it can mean "expiation," "propitiation," or simply "mercy seat"—the place of the temple presence of God where atonement was effected. Precisely how Christ's sacrificial death on the cross had its effect as a *hilasterion* remains elusive.

Part of this difficulty arises because the appearance of *hilasterion* in the text of Romans 3:25 is in fact a Pauline *hapax*, with no parallels elsewhere

---

37. Blocher, "Biblical Metaphors," 641.

38. As we have it in a developed sense in the Epistle to the Hebrews, but also scattered through the writings of Paul.

in Paul to help our understanding of his exact meaning. Although the word does appear once again in the New Testament in Hebrews 9:5, its translation from the Greek both in Romans and Hebrews, and also the related *hilasmos* in 1 John 2:2 and 4:10, remains less than clear. This deficit in understanding is compounded by the fact that interpretative difficulties arise precisely because Paul's use of the term *hilasterion* in Romans 3:25 is apparently metaphorical; Christ's sacrificial offering of himself is being thought of in a relation of comparison with a ritual practice of the temple in Jerusalem. But exactly how those temple sacrifices were understood to work remains obscure.

While it has to be admitted that the sacrificial system of the ancient world comes from a culture remote from ours, with unfathomable difficulties,[39] at the very least it is possible to discern that the offering of the temple sacrifice on the Day of Atonement falls into two distinct parts. First, it obviously involved the death of a sacrificial victim. However, the killing of the victim did not necessarily accrue some kind of virtue in and of itself; it was rather the necessary preliminary to the taking of the blood of the victim by the high priest, through the temple and into the holy of holies where it was splashed on the mercy seat—the gold plate on top of the ark of the covenant between the cherubim, the symbolic place of the presence of God.

The Hebrew language equivalent of *hilasterion* is *Ha-Kapporeth*, which is usually translated "mercy seat" or "lid of the arc" (following Ezekiel 43: 14, 17, 20)—the place where Yahweh is said to have "appeared." Indeed, the "place of atonement" or "mercy seat" that is the usual translation of the same word in Hebrews 9:5 could also be the intended meaning of Paul's use of *hilasterion* in *Romans*. If it is understood simply as the mercy seat or "lid of the ark," the reference is a metaphorical way of identifying the cross as the place of the sacrificial shedding of Christ's blood, or "place of atonement." But that leaves many unanswered questions.

Just how the sprinkling of the blood by the high priest achieved the intended result of securing reconciliation and peace with God remains something of a residual mystery. The Hebrew root *Kaphar*, from which we get *Kapporeth*, which becomes *hilasterion* in the Greek translation of the Old Testament (the Septuagint), and then *propitiatorum* in the Latin Vulgate, and finally becomes "propitiatory atonement" in English, appears originally to have actually meant simply "to cover sins." It might well therefore be translated, as is often in fact the case, to mean the "expiation" of

---

39. See Ullucci, *Christian Rejection of Animal Sacrifice*, and McClymond, *Beyond Sacred Violence*. Philo's defense of the sacrificial cult perhaps went some way towards generating a coherent "theory." See McGowan, "Philo and the Materialization of Sacrifice."

sins. However, as soon as this word is placed in the conceptual context of transactional relations between individuals, the sense of expiation gives way to propitiation, and hence unavoidably to thoroughly noxious notions (especially from a Trinitarian point of view) of the appeasement of one individual by the action of another.[40]

It is understandable that proponents of penal substitution therefore conveniently switch to the forensic language of the payment of a required penalty to satisfy the demands of justice so as to display the righteousness of God. Though some feel that they are free to say more exactly what Paul meant by *hilasterion* by placing it in the context of the justice of God and the operation of legal principle in the hope of explaining how God was propitiated in a way that satisfied the wrathful demands of his righteousness, there is logic in returning the term to the context of the sacrificial cult of the temple in which it properly belongs.

Before doing that, however, it is important to pause to note that this process of bringing together sets of metaphors drawn from contexts as different as the temple and the courthouse in the hope that they may be mutually interpretative, allows us to discern something of the detail of what may actually be involved when Blocher speaks of the fact that the New Testament atonement metaphors are "intertwined with one another."[41] Indeed, Blocher speaks of the interpretation of their cognitive meaning as the "effortless task" of "coordinating them" so that "they naturally *translate* into one another."[42] As it turns out, in fact, in this process juridical elements drawn from the context of the court of law tend to rise to the surface in order to exercise a kind of control over alternative sets of metaphors, which tend to be subordinated to them. In the case of the sacrificial imagery of the high priestly ministry on the Day of Atonement, the metaphor is pressed well beyond drawing the analogy of the high priestly ministry of Christ in our behalf as both the sacrificial victim and the priest who ever lives to make intercession for us. To this imagery is added the speculative theory that purports to explain why it was necessary for Christ to do so as to bear the alleged punishment for Adam's disobedience, how it was that God was bound to act in accordance with his own justice, how it was that God threatened death should Adam be disobedient and why it was that God had to be true to his promise, why death is alleged always to be a penalty, why it was necessary for God to demonstrate his righteousness and justice and even his

---

40. The notion of propitiation was coined in English only in 1536, then conditioned the Comfortable Words of the English Prayer Books from 1549 onwards, and then the texts of King James Version of the Bible, which was commissioned in 1604.

41. Blocher, "Biblical Metaphors," 640.

42. Blocher, "Biblical Metaphors," 643–44.

wrath in this way (perhaps with wrath understood in a moral sense as a hostile attitude toward sin and evil) by ensuring that a penalty was in fact paid, why God's forgiveness could not be extended to humanity without such a penalty first being paid, how Christ assumed the burden of this penalty and died as a substitute for sinful humanity, how it was that God sent his own Son into the world with this specific plan and purpose in mind, and how it was that Judas, Caiaphas, Pilate, and the crowd acted as agents of God in carrying through this plan—and so on. Hence, the "penal substitutionary theory" of the atonement.

At this point we need to be alert, however, to the fact that in this "interpretative" process a subtle transition is made by a kind of logical sleight-of-hand from the descriptive function of metaphors in the business of communicating aspects of the newfound experience of reconciliation and peace with God actually experienced "in Christ," to the more speculative and theoretical explanation of this earthly experience in terms of the mechanics of an otherworldly transaction between the Father and the Son. It is important to notice that in the course of the "interpretative" exercise, metaphors have morphed into metaphysics.[43] Instead of *describing* the experience of redemption in Christ they are tortured into producing "paraphrases" that are said to be "good enough" for what then becomes a highly speculative explanatory account of a behind-the-scenes intra-Trinitarian transaction of a juridical kind. This means that, if we are in the business of the distribution of arrogance (which in any event may not be very advisable), a move has been made from what Blocher speaks of as "the arrogant refusal to let God speak in intelligible terms to his people"[44] to the equivalent arrogance of finite human minds presuming to be capable of giving counsel to the Infinite and transcendent God—something that St. Paul suggests we should not presume to do!

The second half of the imagery of the sacrificial system that the author of the Epistle to the Hebrews takes and applies to the heavenly pleading of Christ's own self-giving sacrifice is understood to endow the role of the Mediator with an eternal significance: "he holds his priesthood permanently, because he continues forever" (Heb 7:24). This apparently gives the historical death of Christ on the cross a timeless dimension, through the *eternal* pleading of the sacrifice before the throne of grace. He died "once and for all" but as the resurrected and glorified One he now lives forever. As Great High Priest

---

43. Something about which Vanhoozer warns; see *Is There a Meaning?*
44. Blocher, "Biblical Metaphors," 644.

the raised and glorified Christ at the "right hand of the Father" exercises his ministry as Mediator by representing humanity to God in prayer.

Henri Blocher puts a somewhat idiosyncratic spin on this in a way that effectively eliminates the consideration of Christ's eternal and otherworldly ministry as an integral element of his work of atonement. Blocher's interpretation of the use of the sacrificial metaphor in Hebrews shifts the focus of interest away from Christ's going into the heavenly sanctuary and instead concentrates on the return of the earthly high priest from the most holy place to his former life in this world. He argues that because the high priest "risked his life on behalf of the people," given that drawing near to the presence of God was a matter of life and death, "His safe return could be called a resurrection *en parabolê* like that of Isaac."[45] In other words, the return of the high priest to his normal life is said to be the representation of "a kind of resurrection," which is said to establish Jesus as the antitype of both "victim and priest." Even though this effectively bypasses the imagery of the raised Christ's eternal ministry "at the right hand of the Father," Blocher believes that his focus on the return of the high priest to this world in this way means that the "sacrificial type is remarkably complete, and the 'metaphor' highly adequate."[46]

It is somewhat ironic that Blocher's idiosyncratic use of the extended metaphor of the high priest aptly illustrates Ricoeur's point about the imprecision of metaphors generally and their indeterminate openness to the arbitrary exploitation of being pulled in novel directions. On the other hand, Blocher's presentation of the high priest's alleged "near-death" experience and restoration to life in the mundane world may not be particularly helpful to Christian resurrection belief, given that it might be thought to suggest that Jesus did not actually die, but was somehow resuscitated in the tomb and returned to this world.[47] We may prefer the emphasis of the Epistle to the Hebrews itself on drawing an analogy between the high priest's entry into the most holy place and the redemptive significance of Christ's eternal and heavenly ministry beyond death not instead of us but "for us"—on our behalf.

In Hebrews the raised and glorified Christ who "passed through the heavens" on analogy with the high priest passing through the veil of the temple into its inner sanctuary, and into of the nearer presence of God (Heb 4:14), then takes his place "at the right hand of God" where he "ever lives to make intercession" for us (Heb 7:25). Paul had already anticipated this

---

45. Blocher, "Biblical Metaphors," 642.
46. Blocher, "Biblical Metaphors," 642.
47. The thesis of Ernst Renan in the nineteenth century.

thought in Romans 8:26–27, where the Spirit is understood to be a continuing help for the Spirit "helps us in our weakness" and "intercedes for us" *according to the will of God.* The same sentiment is repeated in Romans 8:34 where it is Christ who "intercedes for us."

Interestingly, in Hebrews the estimate of the status of the law also resonates with that of Paul: the law is "weak" and "useless" for it makes nothing perfect (Heb 7:18). Thus, "a better hope is introduced through which we draw near to God." Certainly, Paul's own understanding of things "drawing near to God" is achieved by the gift of the Spirit, perceived in faith as the ground of the better hope of things to come.[48] The gift of the Spirit that is received in faith ensures the grace of ongoing assistance. Indeed, "anyone who does not have the Spirit of Christ does not belong to him" (Rom 8:9).

The Epistle to the Hebrews makes the point a little more clearly that, in the context of the temple sacrifices of ancient Judaism, it was as though the ultimate sacrifice had been offered by Christ in a way that fulfilled all the sacrificial impulses of the ancient world, however it was that these were imagined to work. Certainly, Hebrews makes it patently clear that Christ's ultimate sacrificial offering of his life could be understood to have put an end to all futile offerings of the sacrifice of "bulls and goats."[49] For Paul, it is more characteristic to say that it put an end to "walking according to the law."[50]

Of course, the metaphorical images drawn from the temple by the author of Hebrews and also by Paul constitute a kind of mythological device by attempting to envisage and understand the continuing eternal life and mediatorial work of Christ beyond this world—his heavenly life in a hidden world that can only be imagined. Even in this case, however, this imagery is not *purely* speculative. For insofar as the work of Christ is understood to involve the concrete gift of the Spirit in which believers participate in historical time, it touches down in the living substance of the primitive Christian Easter experience. In a sense the references of Hebrews and in Romans 8:34 to Christ's sitting at God's right hand helps account for the gift of the Spirit by tracing it to its heavenly origin. As Paul also says, the Spirit actually helps to bridge the gulf between earth and heaven by assisting us in our weakness, teaching us to intercede as God wills, and indeed, interceding on our behalf. To this extent this extended metaphor from the sacrificial system was obviously used as a heuristic device to interpret and come to terms with a concrete reality of the early Christian experience of life and worship.

48. Hence the Spirit is itself the down payment or guarantee of what is hoped for in the coming eschatological future (2 Cor 5:1–10).

49. Heb 10:3–4.

50. For example, in Romans 10:4 Paul says, "For Christ is the end of the law so that there may be righteousness for everyone who believes."

It seems clear that this sacrificial approach to the understanding of reconciliation with God that was achieved as a consequence of the cross and resurrection of Christ relies less on belief in the propositional truth of matters of justice and legal principle, and more on the experience of reconciliation with God by incorporation and participation in the communion of God through the gift of the Spirit. For Paul, the raised and exalted heavenly Christ's giving of the gift of his Spirit to his faithful ones in the fellowship of the church is what is to be understood eschatologically, as "the promise" of more to come for the salvation of the world.[51]

Even Romans 8:3, which N. T. Wright cites as a possible example of Paul's sustained use of the juridical language that is characteristic of Romans 1 through 4 with its alleged, although somewhat minimal, "penal element," is not without a reference to the Spirit. God's action in sending the Son "to do what the law, weakened by the flesh, could not do" is said by Paul to have been accomplished by condemning sin in the flesh "in order that the just requirements of the law might be fulfilled *in us* who walk not according to the flesh but according to the Spirit" (v. 4). Indeed a little earlier he had declared that he had been freed from the law of sin and death by "the law of the Spirit of life in Christ Jesus" (v. 2). It is as though, for Paul, the new order of walking according to the Spirit has simply bumped the law of sin and death aside and replaced it with walking by the "law of the Spirit of life in Christ Jesus." Then, Paul sustains this participative sentiment by celebrating the newfound sense of justification and freedom from the condemnation of God (v. 33), and declaring his confident affirmation that, given that the Christ who died has been raised from the dead, now at the right hand of God intercedes for us (v. 34). Once again, the resonances with these views of Paul also in Hebrews is not to be overlooked. It is the analogy with this additional high priestly action that furnishes us with some possible insight into Paul's reasons for his apparently metaphorical use of the term *hilasterion*. The end result of all this for Paul is that nothing "will be able to separate us from the love of God in Christ Jesus our Lord" (v. 35; repeated in v. 39). It appears that reconciliation with God is understood to have been positively achieved as a concrete reality of Christian experience by the joint action of Christ as victim and as high priest.

---

51. 2 Cor 1:22; see also Eph 1:13, 14.

By contrast with this extended use of sacrificial imagery in the Epistle to the Hebrews, the penal substitutionary theory of the atonement is itself remarkably crucicentric. Unfortunately, a concentration on the first half of the process of the offering a sacrifice—the death of the victim—in the way exemplified by presentations of the penal substitution theory[52] is to underestimate the importance of the second part of the temple ritual—the pleading of the sacrifice by the high priest. If the cross is conceptually separated, however, from its causal relation to what followed in the economy of salvation so that it is no longer seen as the necessary presupposition of resurrection, ascension, and the gift of the Spirit, then some kind of intrinsic meaning has to be found in the death of Christ considered by itself. Hence the penal substitutionary theory with its reliance on Paul's juridical language, even though this is alien to the context of the temple, has somewhat arbitrarily to be called into play.

The retreat from the context of the temple to the law court by proponents of the penal substitutionary theory is in a sense understandable, especially in the modern world in which the sacrificial systems of ancient religious cultures survive only as incomprehensible relics of past history rather than as meaningful and living elements of contemporary culture. It is therefore understandable why it is felt that the New Testament's sacrificial imagery has to be complemented by images of punitive justice from the law court. At least this furnishes us with a language with which the modern world is familiar. It can be appreciated that recourse to the concept of penal substitution helps make up the shortfall experienced in trying to comprehend the detailed working of the sacrificial system. Whether this is a theologically legitimate procedure without acknowledging this switch of context is, however, problematic. After all, the strategy of simply combining the metaphor of sacrifice when it is used to interpret the death of Jesus on the cross, with the juridical metaphor of the payment of a penalty for an offense, or the settlement of an outstanding debt, in order to explain the meaning of the sacrificial term *"hilasterion"* that is otherwise difficult to construe, is hardly convincing.

Even so, some exponents of the theory go on to argue that the penal substitutionary theory may be said to exercise some kind of heuristic control over other atonement images and metaphors. In this case, it does not just bring some more definite meaning to the lack of definition of a sacrificial understanding of things, but is itself of more fundamental importance. Thus, theologians of the atonement often turn to the penal substitution theory as

---

52. Of which T. C. Hammond's *New Creation* is a prime example. Hammond explicitly denies the eternal offering of the sacrifice that he locates wholly on Calvary.

the "primary controlling model" of the atonement so as to explicate alternative theories. Indeed, it is argued that the other models of atonement on their own, and without an overriding and controlling juridical framework, are inadequate:

> [O]ther aspects of the atonement cease to make sense if penal substitution is denied . . . penal substitution is essential to Christ's victory over evil powers . . . to his restoration of the relationships between sinners and God (reconciliation) and to the liberation he brings from captivity to sin and Satan (redemption or ransom). Far from being viable alternatives to penal substitution, they are outworkings of it.[53]

However, apart from the theological impropriety of bypassing the obvious difference of context between temple and court of law, as we have already seen, we cannot be overconfident about assuming that it is possible to produce a clear and distinct, let alone logically coherent and morally acceptable presentation of penal substitution itself. As we have already seen, its problematic standing in the world of contemporary theoretical reflection on so many different levels suggests that we need to be aware of the theory's limitations. Whether it is capable of furnishing some clarity to the sacrificial theory of the atonement remains problematic.

There is a tendency among proponents of the penal substitutionary theory to treat Paul primarily as a theoretician. Indeed, often it is as though the chief quest of contemporary Pauline studies generally is simply to get into the mind of St. Paul. Even Paul's participative concept of being "in Christ" tends to be treated less as descriptive of concrete experience and more as a theoretical concept whose meaning is to be found in notions of the "corporate personality" of the king in ancient Israel whose personal destiny overflowed into the destiny of all his people. We should not be beguiled into thinking, however, that Paul actually had Old Testament references to being "in the king" in mind when he allegedly "worked out" what being "in Christ" might mean in a purely abstract and theoretical sense.

Even so, the contemporary theological task appears then to be conceived in terms of following Paul's *argument* and then expounding the logical coherence of his points, perhaps by relating them to more general themes—creation or covenant or whatever. This in turn seems to assume that the atonement metaphors and images can be given more clarity of

---

53. Jeffery, Ovey, and Sach, *Pierced for Our Transgressions*, 156.

meaning and so made more intelligible and acceptable by being coupled with the help of additional theoretical "wraparound" concepts, such as the meaning of messiahship inherited from Second Temple understanding of the "corporate personality" of the king, crocheted together into one composite theological theory using the overarching concept of the covenant. Whatever nuggets of truth may be found in this, whether the resulting complexification of Paul's alleged theoretical understanding of things is really necessary is a reasonable question given that it all seems so speculative—and ultimately beyond proof. Perhaps the atonement language should be taken in the opposite direction so that it is less speculative and theoretical and more descriptive and interpretative of concrete experience.

Often Paul's purpose in writing his letters, for example, has a more practical and pastoral orientation. It is basically to remind those to whom he wrote to uphold and cherish the fundamental realities of the new life in which they had been incorporated, and in which they continued to participate, by living according to its distinctive qualities and norms. His task is descriptively to interpret the theological significance of something that has actually happened in their lives rather than to lay down the basics of a theory for the entertainment of those interested in the study of theology in the twenty-first century.

Sometimes Paul's descriptive passages therefore naturally become exhortatory: In writing to the Philippians, for example, when Paul links the "comfort of love" and the "communion of the Spirit," he is once again clearly not just theorizing—he exhorts the Philippians to strive to uphold their interpersonal unity in both heart and mind: "So if there is any encouragement in Christ, any comfort of love, any participation in the Spirit, any affection and sympathy, complete my joy by being of the same mind, having the same love, being in full accord and of one mind" (Phil 2:1–2).

Even some of the passages that are often used to ground the more speculative development of a metaphysical "theory" of atonement, such as Colossians 2:14–15, regularly include specific references to the realities of concrete Christian experience that point to an understanding of atonement of a more incorporative and participative and less speculative kind. This Colossians passage, for example, reminds those to whom it is addressed that, as a consequence of the death and resurrection of Christ, "God made you alive *together with him* [i.e., with Christ]." Then this is expanded upon by saying that this being "made alive" happened "when he forgave us all our trespasses, *erasing the record that stood against us with its legal demands.*" Although this last phrase is regularly seized upon in the process of developing the penal substitutionary theory, we should then note the use of yet another metaphor. In relation to this juridical statement about the "legal demands of the law" Paul says in reference to God: "He set this aside, nailing it to the cross"—just as Jesus was literally nailed to the cross.[54] We do not need to unpack the exact literal meaning of the metaphor of God's erasing or canceling of the human record of sinfulness and "its legal demands" by "nailing it to the cross." Just how this disarmed the principalities and powers and triumphed over them by making a public example of them is not entirely clear, though this might well be a reference to the resurrection and vindication of Jesus (Col 2:15). The point is that in the first instance this metaphorical language is used in a valiant attempt to describe the experience of God's grace—his apparent setting aside of the law to allow for the incorporative and participative experience of the Spirit of Christ and of "being made alive together with him."

One only has to read Colossians 2 to appreciate that its fundamental participative language was descriptively interpretative and grounded in an actual shared experience. Colossians 2 exhorts those "who have received Christ Jesus the Lord" to "continue your lives *in him,* rooted and built up *in him*" for just as "*in him* the fullness of deity dwells bodily . . . you have come to fullness *in him* . . . when you were buried *with him* in baptism, you were also raised *with him* through faith in the power of God, who raised him from the dead . . . God made you alive together *with him.*"[55] In this passage Paul is clearly not engaging in the construction of a theoretical argument of a metaphysical kind, or even toying with the notion of "corporate personality" as the key to the representative role of the Messiah in relation to Israel and then the rest of the world (a favorite theme of N. T. Wright), but actually describing a new state of affairs that his hearers could in faith identify as a living reality of their own experience.

In epistemological terms he is pointing to something known not by theoretical description, but by actual acquaintance. This is the context that allows him to draw upon the juridical metaphors, which do not so much explain the detailed working of how this state of affairs was achieved by the action of God, as to point towards the originating causal event which issued in the state of affairs in which they participatively stood—the event of the cross to which the catalogue of human fault was said (metaphorically speaking) to have been "nailed" to (Col 2:15).[56]

Clearly, Paul is not just to be cast as a theoretician—laying out a theoretical argument about justification and the need for a righteous God to

---

54. Col 2:14.

55. Col 2:6–15.

56. The interpretation of this text is notoriously difficult on lexical and syntactical grounds. See Yates, "Colossians 2.15."

uphold principles of justice in a show of his wrathful condemnation of sin, or whatever. Nor is he talking about some theological propositions abstractly conceived that are simply to be "believed" as though the object of faith is purely propositional. He is not just passing on some theologically speculative information. Rather, he is describing and interpreting the theological significance of something concretely perceived and appropriated in faith by actual acquaintance.

One reason for the historical tendency to develop an attachment to speculative theories of the atonement by contrast with speaking of atonement more concretely as an experience of actual life and worship into which believers are incorporated, or in which they participate by actual acquaintance, has to do with the way in which the church has received the Epistle to the Romans. This is particularly the case in the theological tradition of the Reformation with its focus on justification by faith and its abhorrence of "good works."

In order to avoid false stereotyping, it is important to say that this emphasis on salvation by "incorporation" or "participation" "in Christ" as a concrete experience and not just as a theoretical legal fiction is not to be assumed to be entirely missing even from Reformation thought. Wolter Huttinga has noted that while Calvin, for example, "does not offer anything like a 'doctrine' of participation, participation in the divine is a very important theme of his work."[57] Similarly, Todd Billings has pointed out that while a metaphysical-speculative development of the theme is not to be expected in Calvin's work, "the theme of communion with God through Christ in terms of participation is clearly important for him 'largely because it is a biblical and patristic category.'"[58] Calvin borrowed the language of Christ as the Second Adam, who fulfills and restores creation by uniting humans to God, from Irenaeus, and eucharistic insights relating to the vivification by the life of Christ from Cyril of Alexandria, so that participatory language takes its place in Calvin's theology "if understood as a soteriology that affirms the unity of humanity and divinity, such that redemption involves the transformation of believers to be incorporated into the Triune life of God, while remaining creatures..."[59]

Nevertheless, Luther's emphasis on justification by faith alone and his hostility to an approach to salvation through a reliance on "good works" has

---

57. Huttinga, *Participation and Communicability*, 66.

58. Billings, *Calvin, Participation and Gift*, 18. See Calvin, *Institutes of the Christian Religion*, IV, 17, 9, on the Lord's Supper.

59. Billings, *Calvin, Participation and Gift*, 54.

led to a focus on the theoretical mechanisms of God's justification of sinners. This difficulty arises because the Epistle to the Romans has historically been treated, particularly since the Reformation, as the primary document for the development of the doctrine of the atonement, especially given the use of juridical language that is concentrated in chapters 1 through 4. Indeed Paul's Epistle to the Romans has long been received as Paul's mature reflection on the themes of justification and sanctification that he had only touched on in his earlier letters. Günther Bornkamm, for example, spoke of it as "Paul's last will and testament," as though it contains material that he felt constrained to get down on paper before he died. In this respect it is assumed that Paul wrote Romans with a fundamentally different purpose from his motivation in writing his other epistles insofar as they were apparently intended to address locally identified pastoral issues. This therefore tends to lift Romans from its possible relation to an actual historical context, so as make it fair game for a somewhat abstract and theoretical treatment that simply assumes that it provides the raw material for the exposition of a theological "argument."

A reading of Romans with an eye to its more practical and pastorally oriented face, however, may be achieved by placing it in the historical context in which Paul wrote it. This appears to have had to do with the emergence of early Christianity from the life and worship of the Jewish synagogue around the middle of the first century.[60] According to the historian Suetonius, in the year 49 Emperor Claudius expelled the Jews from Rome because of civil disturbances in the synagogues over somebody called "Chrestus"—almost certainly a mishearing of "Christus."

The use of this rather blunt instrument of social control apparently had traumatic implications not just for the Jewish community in Rome, but for the life of the city itself. One can imagine the commercial impact in ancient Rome of the removal of Jews from the city by considering what would happen if this kind of thing were to occur in the modern context of Melbourne or New York. After Claudius's death in 54 the dispossessed Jews were allowed back by the incoming administration, apparently for economic reasons. In any event, the effect of this traumatic decision of Claudius was that law-observant Jews were emptied out of their synagogues, possibly leaving them in the hands of gentile Godfearers.[61] When the Jews were al-

60. The thesis of Karl Donfried in *Romans Debate*.

61. The importance of the attraction of Jewish monotheism amongst gentiles in the ancient world cannot be underestimated. One interesting indication of this is the impressive list of Godfearers who had contributed to a building restoration program, that may still be seen engraved into the wall of the ancient ruins of the synagogue in Aphrodisias in Turkey.

lowed back to Rome in 55 this situation did not change, for their return was on condition that it was without the right of public assembly—a not insignificant historical fact in relation to Paul's Letter to the Romans, given that he sends greetings in chapter 16 to what appears to be a network of scattered household communities.[62]

The really interesting thing about this set of historical circumstances, however, is that it provides the context of social tension between Jews and the emerging worshipping communities of Christians within the synagogue, for the asking of an important theological question: how is it that God's promises to Abraham appear to be being fulfilled amongst gentile Godfearers, and not amongst those of us who think of ourselves as the covenant children of Abraham who faithfully keep the Jewish law? Paul's answer to this question was that justification is not by observing the law, but by faith— God accounts humans righteous, whether Jews or gentiles, not by works of the law but by the fact that they have a faith like Abraham's.

In other words, Paul may be less a purely theoretical and speculative thinker, and much more the missionary to the gentiles, taking responsibility for the well-being of worshipping communities around the Mediterranean, and addressing concrete pastoral situations by interpreting them theologically. The motivation for writing the Epistle to the Romans in this case is of a piece with his fundamentally pastoral reasons for writing his earlier letters. The fulfillment of the covenant promises of God in the life, death, resurrection, ascension of Jesus, and the gift of the Spirit among people of faith by the creation of the integrated community of Jews and gentiles as the outworking of God's redemptive plan, is a matter of practical importance demanding hands-on maintenance and care. It is not just a purely speculative and theoretical matter.

The covenant, furthermore, that was in the forefront of Paul's mind was naturally the covenant made with Abraham, rather than an alleged covenant originally made with Adam, which is said to have been fractured by Adam's disobedience that therefore attracted the penalty of death. This might trigger the kind of speculative theory that explains Jesus' death on the cross as the penalty paid by the obediently subordinate substitute for the whole spectrum of sinful humanity. However, it was in fact the covenant promise to Abraham that gave rise to the explanation that it was by faith in Jesus Christ and what had happened as a consequence of his death and resurrection was accounted righteous rather than the works of the law. This

---

62. The "church in the house" of Prisca and Aquila, for example (Rom 16:3) or "those in the Lord who belong to the family of Narcissus" (Rom 16:11).

naturally prompts reflection on the function and status of law itself, such as we find Paul engaging in Romans 7.

It is understandable that in chapter 11 of Romans Paul then has some cautionary words for gentiles who might understandably have been basking in the glow of divine favor, given the benefits of the fulfillment of the promises of God to Abraham to which they had been admitted. Paul's message to them is that they are not to be too full of themselves, because they should remember that if God could incorporate them, "a wild olive," into the stock of Abraham, how much easier would it be for God to reincorporate those who had been lopped off from the original stock. It is not insignificant that the archaeological discovery of a recycled stone lintel in the Roman Forum bears the title "Synagogue of the Olive Tree." But that is another story.

The point is that Paul wrote his Letter to the Romans with the practical and pastoral purpose of upholding the vision of the new order in which members of the emerging Jewish/gentile community of faith in Rome could grasp their identity as inheritors by faith of the promises made to Abraham in the concrete experience of reconciliation, love, and peace that flowed to them as the gift of the Spirit. It is thus the concrete experience of reconciliation and peace with God of an understanding of atonement of an incorporative and participative kind, in the inclusive community of Jews and gentiles "in Christ," rather than an abstract and speculative theory that Paul is committed to articulate and defend. His interests are *descriptive* and theologically *interpretative* of experience rather than purely *theoretical* and *speculative*.

Certainly, in more recent New Testament studies a purely abstract interest in theories of the atonement has given way to the more serious consideration of Paul's interest in themes of "incorporation" and "participation."[63] Although N. T. Wright acknowledges the possibility that the historical context of Paul's writing to the Romans may be of some interest and significance, he passes over it in pursuit of the interest in unpacking the details of Paul's "argument." However, he represents something of the emerging balance between "theories" of the atonement and the concrete experience of atonement amongst contemporary New Testament scholars, insofar as he is anxious to point out that for Paul juridical and forensic considerations relating to the understanding of God's righteousness and "justification" that occupy his attention in the argument of Romans chapters 1–4, are not to be separated from the incorporative material of chapters 5–8. It is not that Paul

---

63. See for example Hays, *Faith of Jesus Christ*.

"gave up talking about 'righteousness' and so forth in chapter 4, and that in chapters 5–8 he was no longer dealing in 'juristic' or 'forensic' categories, but now in 'incorporative' or 'participatory' ones."[64] The work of the Messiah is not twofold. Rather "the language of the law-court belongs intimately, in Paul's mind, with the language of incorporation into the Messiah and his people."[65] These chapters (5 though 8) are to be seen, not as an alternative way of conceiving of salvation, but as the continuation of the same argument given that juridical references continue to appear even in these chapters (for example in Romans 8:31–39). Wright, indeed, insists that Paul's emphasis is on the integration of forensic considerations of a theoretical nature about the meaning of righteousness/justification derived from the context of the law court, and more experiential incorporative material. Those who are justified by faith are those who are "in Christ" or "in the Messiah" as Wright prefers to put it. Righteousness or justification (as a legal consideration) and a more experiential incorporation into the life of Christ go hand in hand.[66] Hence, he says, "The people who are declared to be 'in the right' are the people *who are incorporated into the Messiah*."[67]

Furthermore, Wright is very clear in insisting, "All this comes true in personal reality *because of the work of the spirit.*"[68] Wright acknowledges that "The place of the spirit in all this is often either misunderstood or not even grasped, but is fundamental for Paul." Although Wright tends to conceive of the Spirit not as the perceived object of resurrection faith but as an agent who "works through the proclamation of the good news of the Messiah, to generate faith in humans" he adds that the Spirit's work is also "to constitute all those who believe as the single forgiven family promised to Abraham."[69] The implication of this appears to be that what was positively achieved through the death, resurrection, and ascension of Christ and the gift of the Spirit is not just a theoretical matter but a reality of the economy of salvation that was concretely experienced.

It follows that the Christian gospel is not just the good news of a theoretical kind *that* something happened "behind the scenes" on the initiative of God whereby the death of Christ was used as an adequate punishment

---

64. Wright, *Paul and the Faithfulness of God*, 891.

65. Wright, *Paul and the Faithfulness of God*, 891. Wright points out that this integration of language is also true of Galatians 3 and Philippians 3.

66. Wright, *Paul and the Faithfulness of God*, 950. Wright points out that this is the case in each of Paul's major expositions of justification: Romans 3:24; Galatians 2:17; and Philippians 3:8–11.

67. Wright, *Paul and the Faithfulness of God*, 950.

68. Wright, *Paul and the Faithfulness of God*, 952.

69. Wright, *Paul and the Faithfulness of God*, 952.

for the disobedience of humanity so as to achieve human reconciliation and peace with God, but rather the good news of a set of events that carry an invitation to transformation through the gift of the Holy Spirit, which is perceived in faith and received in trusting acceptance, and sealed by baptismal incorporation into the community of the new humanity. This means that conservative evangelical Christianity's elevation of the theory of the penal substitution of the atonement to a place of centrality in its proclamation of the Christian good news, as the "pulsating heart of the Gospel" may be a mistake. The crux of the gospel is less the understanding and acceptance of the mechanisms that are alleged to have achieved reconciliation and atonement that are communicated in the form of the propositional truths of an abstract theory involving a hidden transaction between the Father and the Son "behind" the historical event of the cross. Instead it involves, as a direct consequence of the cross, the possibility of a participatory engagement in a concretely experienced living reality of reconciliation and peace with God "in Christ," in whom trusting faith is personally placed with thanksgiving.

The consciousness of what is perceived in faith to be the reconciling love and peace of God that has overcome the alienation caused by human sin and evil is understood to be the direct consequence of a nexus of interrelated events in the economy of salvation: the life, passion, and death of Jesus, his resurrection and ascension, and the gift of his Spirit. These interrelated elements are all integral parts of a Trinitarian understanding of God's redemptive activity. In other words, the redemption of humanity is achieved though the help (or grace) of our Lord Jesus Christ in granting unimpeded access to the love of God the Father, by the removal of the impediment of sin, which is displaced through the gift of the Holy Spirit.

Of course, the cross of Christ was crucial in the economy of salvation—if I may put it this way. Without the faithful obedience of Christ that resulted in his death upon the cross there would have been no possibility of his being raised from the dead by the Father. Without the cross there would not have been an ascension to heaven to the right hand of the Father, or the gift of his Spirit to transform and redeem fallen humanity. But in this nexus of events all three Trinitarian identities are involved in verbally identifiable ways and the outcome is incorporation and participation in the interpersonal divine life. The theology of redemption is in this way grounded in the doctrine of the Trinity as it was revealed in the economy of salvation.

On the other hand, if the New Testament's metaphorical images of atonement are to be received as *descriptive* and theologically *interpretative* of the experience of what has happened in the economy of salvation, it has to be acknowledged that those metaphorical references and images may not have really been intended to be put to the *speculative* use that purports to be informative of some kind of heavenly behind-the-scenes transaction between the Father and the Son. This is not to mention the illegitimate use of these metaphors and images to try to prove that the death of the Son was somehow necessary so as to allow God in his righteous "wrath" to deal satisfactorily with the outstanding punishment allegedly incurred by Adam's disobedience.

The New Testament metaphors of atonement may rightly be used to describe and interpret the redemptive nature of the experience of being "in Christ." In terms of Rahner's Rule we may in faith justifiably argue that this experience of the economy of salvation is an experience of God, the eternal Trinity, but we may exercise some caution before embracing the reverse of Rahner's Rule: we would be unwise to draw inferences from these metaphors and images and then presume to claim to know the mind of the Lord or to be his counselor in the manner of much contemporary fundamentalism and naive biblicism. We cannot assume that our thoughts are simply God's thoughts.

In other words, at this point the work of theology may wisely be governed by a prudent apophatic reserve. The exploration of what has been discerned to be a "participative" or "incorporative" doctrine of human redemption, developed from the perspective of the doctrine of the Trinity, has clear implications for the assessment of the nature of the language that is necessarily called into use in relation to it. For a start, when it is acknowledged that much of the raw material furnished by the atonement traditions of the New Testament are clearly metaphorical, it is important to recognize the limitations of the genre of metaphor. By nature metaphors are descriptively helpful, but they have to be acknowledged to suffer from limitations if they are pressed into service in the hope that they might deliver a fully-fledged and systematically organized explanation or theory in the hope that it might be rationally compelling and persuasive. Gregory of Nazianzus warned of this difficulty in the course of explaining his Trinitarian use of the analogy of Adam, Eve, and Seth, to illustrate how different persons could nevertheless be of the same substance. Adam as a creature, Eve as fragment (created from Adam), and Seth as begotten by them both are said to be "objects of thought alone." As an analogy of the distinguishable Trinitarian identities, however, this threefold image is of limited usefulness: "For it is not possible to trace out any image exactly to the whole extent of the truth."[70]

---

70. Gregory of Nazianzus, *Oration 32*, (Fifth theological oration) 11. (*Nicene and Post Nicene Fathers*, II, 7, 321).

Given that the New Testament witness to the atonement is patently metaphorical, we may therefore justifiably entertain serious reservations about the capacity of the metaphors and images to which this religious language necessarily has resort to deliver clear and distinct propositions that might be capable of grounding a speculative argument of a logically conclusive kind. The very nature of these images and metaphors of atonement, precisely because they are images and metaphors, inhibits their more speculative and theoretical use. In other words, such speculative theorizing asks more of this metaphorical language than can reasonably be demanded of it.

If the divine redemption of humanity, furthermore, is a mystery of God the Holy Trinity of three Persons in one unity of being, then it follows that even what is revealed to human perception in the economy of salvation in principle remains *a mystery* that passes all understanding. For finite minds it is something that may be *apprehended* in faith but not *comprehended*. There is therefore a necessary sense in which the conceptual expression of the surpassing mystery of the experience of the reconciliation and peace of God, and of the unconditional generosity of his love and forgiveness, is not available to ultimate scrutiny.[71] As with Solomon's knot, this mystery is ultimately impenetrable.

As a consequence the metaphors and images that are used to point towards this mystery are irreducible to clear and distinct, literal, and prosaic specification. Even juridical references to justification understood as being "accounted righteous" by God, or "put in the right" that are based upon the analogy of the announcement of a verdict in the operations of a court of law, have in principle to do with a reality of religious experience that "passes all understanding." We cannot envisage exactly how God does this, for the inner life of God is incomprehensible to finite minds—remote, sublime, and ultimately unknowable. This language cannot in principle be reduced to a clear and distinct set of black-and-white propositions so as to form the basis of a neatly worded and logically persuasive "theory." Instead these metaphors and images are by nature essentially descriptive. They do not purport to explain *how* the impediment of human sin was blotted out or removed by the death of Christ so as to be a grace or help to humanity in gaining unimpeded access to the love and reconciliation of God. The use of such metaphors in describing the experiential replacement of "walking by the law of the flesh" by "walking by the law of the Spirit" is one thing; it is another matter to explain the inner working of the divine in dealing with sin in flights of speculative thought by following entailments that are alleged to

---

71. Phil 4:6–7.

flow with logical necessity as implications of the metaphors and images that account for this experience "in Christ."

The best we can do is refer in images and metaphors to the concrete experience of reconciliation and peace with God "that passes all understanding" and that "guards our hearts and minds in Christ Jesus" (Phil 4:7). To know reconciliation with God in faith and release from the disfiguring human sinfulness that otherwise spoils and goodness and beauty of life, may rightly be said to be like release from prison; it is as though a debt has been paid on behalf of sinful humanity, so as to ward off the insistent anxiety created by the possibility of future condemnation; it is as though humanity has been released from a kind of imprisonment to the necessity of sin and death. Or, it is as though a ransom has been paid to secure release from the clutches of an enemy, or even better, that an ultimate victory has been won over the enemy.

The New Testament metaphors relating to what God is believed to have positively achieved through the death and resurrection of Jesus seek to describe what is essentially a divine mystery. This accounts for their rich diversity and the variety of contexts from which they come and from which they draw whatever insight of meaning may be drawn from them. As Joel Green and Mark Baker remark: "So infinite is the mystery of God's saving work that we need many interpretive images, many tones, many voices."[72] Recourse to a variety of metaphors became necessary amongst the first generation of Christians "in order to portray for them something of what in the end cannot be captured by language or images, the mystery of the saving significance of Jesus' death."[73]

N. T. Wright in turn refers to this as Paul's "multilayered" theology of the cross. This many-layered linguistic tradition of metaphorical references and images that are used in the New Testament to describe the surpassing mystery of the redemptive experience of being "in Christ" and so being justified by God cannot therefore be reduced to clear and distinct specification whose logical threads might then be carefully teased out and woven into a neat theoretical account of what went on in the inner life of God to achieve the atonement of humans with God. If the atoning work of God in Christ is a mystery of God that surpasses all human understanding, then it follows that the metaphors and images that are used to describe the experience of reconciliation and "peace with God" that in faith is understood to have been won by Christ on the cross are irreducible.

72. Green and Baker, *Recovering the Scandal of the Cross*, 139.

73. Green and Baker, *Recovering the Scandal of the Cross*, 140. "This is because of the limitations of human language, and of even our most impressive metaphors, to account fully for this mystery, the cross of Christ" (240).

Unfortunately, the speculative theories that are erected upon the basis of these New Testament's atonement metaphors mistakenly seek to draw out logical implications with far more confidence than the metaphors themselves will allow, and end with a deceptively clear and distinct set of abstract propositional beliefs that are said to flow, even from acknowledged metaphors, almost with logical necessity.[74] Consequently, in an instant, we have on our hands not only a full-blown and overconfidently proclaimed explanation of the mechanics of what God achieved in and through the death and resurrection of Christ, but a detailed explanation of exactly *how* he achieved it.

We have to face the fact, however, that the metaphorical language of atonement may not be amenable to either oversimplification (by its reduction to clear and distinct literal and prosaic language) or overdevelopment (by extending it into the abstractions of a theory). When it is remembered that the speculative superstructure of a theory of atonement is erected on the basis of the first Christians' recourse to such descriptive metaphors as "release from prison," the "payment of a ransom," and "victory in battle" as ways of illustrating the declaration that Christ's death was "for many" or "for our sins," we may be forgiven for judging it to be a massively mistaken exercise in over-belief. This is why we must conclude that such speculative theorizing asks more of this metaphorical language than can reasonably be demanded of it.

Even though the metaphors and images of the language of the redemption are received as essentially *descriptive* of concrete religious experience rather than ultimately theologically informative, they nevertheless serve an important purpose. It is important to appreciate that even if the New Testament's atonement metaphors are irreducible metaphors, they nevertheless point towards the nature of something concretely real. Even if by definition this reality of human experience passes all understanding, and thus defies all human attempts to reduce it to a clear and distinct literal specification, the language seeks to describe something of enormous human significance. The language of the atonement may be admitted to be finite, partial, and incomplete, and less than clear and distinct, and therefore incapable of grounding a logically coherent and tightly argued theory with persuasive power. This language is nevertheless *sufficient for all practical purposes* in the living of our religious lives. In other words, the atonement metaphors and images

---

74. By "logical necessity" I mean the kind of necessity by which we confidently conclude that if Tom is a bachelor, then he must be unmarried.

may be understood to be *regulative* rather than *theologically informative*. They allow us to respond in thanksgiving for the life and teaching of Jesus, his suffering and death, and for all the consequences for us of his resurrection and ascension to glory and the gift of the Spirit in overcoming human alienation from God. They descriptively *interpret* the resulting experience of reconciliation and peace with God, and they allow us to worship and to pray in thanksgiving and to seek to live lives worthy of our calling.

This means that the metaphorical references and images that the first Christians used in their halting attempts to describe something of the newfound reconciliation and peace with God that they understood to have resulted from the death, resurrection, and ascension of the vindicated Jesus and the gift of the Spirit, are to be received for what they are—images and metaphors. We use them today in exactly the same way as the first Christians originally used them, but we mistakenly torture a preferential selection of some of them into the production of a juridical theory of a kind that then requires all other images of the many-layered verbal response to this fundamental Christian experience into conformity with it. Instead of being put to work in the interests of producing a highly speculative and theoretical account of what might be believed to have occurred of a transactional kind between the commanding Father and the submissively obedient subordinate Son "behind the scenes" or "in parallel with" the historical event of Christ's self-offering on the cross in the economy of salvation, they have a more modest purpose of identifying the nature of a lived experience; they allow for the cherishing of it and for inviting others into it. The religious object of Christian faith is not a theory to be believed in, but rather a person in whom we place our faith and trust. And the *revelation of God* in the economy of salvation that is concretely experienced "in Christ" is not something abstract and propositional so much as something concrete and personal. We can readily understand why the church at large has steadfastly resisted the temptation to define any specific theory of the atonement as a required article of Christian belief.

Finally, the understanding of the atonement from the perspective of the doctrine of the Trinity in terms of an essentially experiential "incorporation" and continuing "participation" in the divine life that is not earned but graciously and freely shared through the gift of the Holy Spirit, coincides with the creation of the community of the redeemed to which St. Paul referred as the "fellowship" or "communion of the Spirit."[75]

---

75. 2 Cor 13:14.

In other words, this approach to atonement has ecclesiological implications. When the reconciliation and peace of God is described as the experience of an objective reality in which the first Christians were conscious of "standing" and "walking" as a consequence of the death and resurrection of Christ and the gift of the Spirit, they also spoke in a more institutional sense of the resulting reality of their continuing experience of life "in Christ" by participation in a humanly reconciled interpersonal "communion." The grace or help of the Lord Jesus Christ in gaining unimpeded access to the love of God the Father through the gift of the Holy Spirit results in the creation of an ecclesial reality with a distinctly Trinitarian coloring. The invitation of the gospel is to enter into the holy communion of God through participation in this effectual sign of his reconciling presence in the world.

Although to contemplate this is to enter the territory of the eschatological mystery of God which passes all understanding, we nevertheless dare to say something. And what we may say is this: we understand the church itself to be that part of God's creation where his kingdom is already dawning; it is the anticipation or *prolepsis* in the present of the future reign of God when God's Spirit will be poured out on all flesh.[76] The church finds its regular renewal in time and grasps again something of its identity and mission in the world in the liturgical consummation of its life in the event of the Eucharist. To quote N. T. Wright again: "Christ did not give us a theory; he gave us a meal." In continuity with the first generation of Christians God's living Word continues to be heard, addressing sinful human beings and, by calling them into reconciled fellowship with himself, graciously uniting them in the unity of heart and mind in an interpersonal communion of faith through the gift of his Spirit. The church is thus itself a sacramental sign, outward and visible, of an inward and spiritual grace known through incorporation and participation "in Christ."

This means that, when the reconciliation and peace of God is understood from a Trinitarian perspective as an incorporative and participative experience in Christ through the gift of the Spirit, the church "instituted by Christ and constituted by the Holy Spirit" may itself be understood as an integral element in God's plan of human redemption. It is a community that grasps its essential identity as it is inwardly energized by the gift of the Spirit of God's own life. And as Luke assures us, the persistent prayer for the gift of the Spirit is a prayer that never goes unanswered (Luke 11:13). Hence, as Cyprian of Carthage once famously said "*Salus extra ecclesiam non est*"—"outside of the church there is no salvation."[77]

---

76. Joel 2:28.
77. Cyprian of Carthage, *Collected Epistles*, Letter 72.

9

PERSONS IN COMMUNION

The New Testament witness to the understanding of human redemption suggests that, almost from the very beginning, what was interpreted in faith as the achievement of unimpeded access to the love of God the Father that had been won through the help (or grace) of the Lord Jesus Christ, in the communion of the Holy Spirit, provided a nexus of shared experiences for reflection on the Trinitarian nature of God. This same set of remembered experiences along with the continuing experience of the gift of the Spirit was sustained through the course of succeeding centuries to the fourth century, when the perception of the triune nature of God was brought into sharper definition by the Cappadocian fathers.

When the Cappadocian fathers sat down to sort out the doctrine of the Trinity in the middle of the fourth century, in other words, their mature reflection is not to be mistaken simply for a purely academic or wholly intellectual or theoretical enterprise. Rather, just as with Paul and the first generation of Christians, it was grounded in their own living experience of justification and of "incorporation" and "participation" "in Christ" in the communion of God. They worked as theologians but with a consciousness of living and worshipping in the eucharistic community. They did not just sit quietly in a corner and cast around for linguistic tools to sort out an intellectual problem. Instead, the work of mining and ordering the traditions of thought that they inherited from the Scriptures and the theological reflection of their immediate forebears was prosecuted in the context of the eucharistic experience of "persons in communion."

Though the christological formula of the *homoousion* had already defined Christ's divine status and authority using the concept of his sharing of the very same substance with the Father, there is an understandable sense almost of inevitability about the fact that the somewhat static concept of "substance" would give way to the more dynamic concept of *persons* sharing together in the life of the one "communion." Thus, John Zizioulas points out that when Basil of Caesarea came to speak about the unity of the persons of the Trinity, the Nicene language of "three *hypostases* and one substance" was already at hand. The divine substance and nature equally and fully shared by each of the three *hypostases* in one Unity of Being—as had been defined in the Nicene *homoousion*—was a given. However, when Basil wrote of these things in *Of the Holy Spirit* around 374 he displays an observable proclivity to speak of the unity of the three Trinitarian identities, not so much using the inherited static category of the sharing of the "same substance," but using the more dynamic category of participation in the one interpersonal "communion" created by the gift of the Holy Spirit. In other words, he showed a distinct preference for the formula of "three persons and one communion." The Three are of one heart and mind, sharing a common will and a common purpose, in an interpersonal communion of mutual self-giving love.

While appeal could be made to the analogy of three human individuals sharing the same substance, as in the case of Gregory of Nazianzen's talk of Adam the creature, and Eve created from the fragment of Adam's rib, and Seth their offspring, it was perfectly clear that this was nothing more than an analogy. Its limitations were already well recognized by Gregory himself. For one thing, this analogy tended to suggest three *individuals* sharing the same substance and nature, which raised the uncomfortable spectre of ending in a form of tritheism. The same may be said of Gregory of Nyssa's Trinitarian reference to Peter, James, and John, which is sometimes used even today to speak of the "social trinity."[1] The Persons of the Trinity are, however, not to be thought of as three individuals. Sarah Coakley has therefore signaled some helpful reservations about the social doctrine of the Trinity, which overuses Gregory of Nyssa's references to the analogy of Peter, James, and John all united by "manhood" and thus sharing the one nature. This too easily leads to the suggestion of three separate individuals as self-conscious centers of personality. As a corrective Coakley points out that Gregory in fact emphasizes the unity of the divine nature as the starting point of his apologia and insists that for Gregory the concept of a *hypostasis* "*does not denote consciousness or self-consciousness*" of the individualized kind that might be suggested by the analogy of Peter, James, and John.[2]

---

1. See Coakley's insightful discussion of this in "'Persons' in the 'Social Doctrine' of the Trinity," 132.
2. Coakley, "'Persons' in the 'Social Doctrine' of the Trinity," 133.

Instead, Coakley points out that Gregory of Nyssa's "favoured analogies of the Trinity stress the indivisibility of the 'persons' and even a certain fluidity in their boundaries."[3] Her point is that Gregory of Nyssa is misrepresented as a "social" trinitarian.

By distinguishing three *hypostases* and one divine substance, fully and equally shared, the early church could ensure that any Arianizing tendency to subordinate the Son to the Father could be held at bay.[4] It was only a matter of time, however, before the concrete experience of interpersonal communion would give way to a concentration on the mystery of persons in a more incorporative and participative human unity, a unity of a dynamic kind as distinct from three individuals sharing the same static "substance."

John Zizioulas therefore credits the Cappadocian fathers with being responsible for moving the Trinitarian discussion beyond the difference between *hypostases* and the equally shared *ousia* and its divine nature. Zizioulas believes that, because of a fundamental interest in the unity of the Trinity, the Cappadocians are to be celebrated effectively for paving the way for the making of a distinction between individuals and persons—the basic difference in Zizioulas's mind being that while an individual is necessarily conceived in separation from others, simply as a countable representative of a shared human nature, persons know themselves to be persons in relation to others, or in sharing in the relationality of interpersonal communion with others. The Father has his *hypostatic* or personal identity, for example, from the fact that he eternally begets the Son; the Son likewise has his identity by being eternally "begotten" by the Father; the same applies in relation to the Spirit who proceeds from the Father. The being of God as Trinity is to be understood in the first instance in terms of *relations* of origin. In order to be identifiable Persons there must be an essential relationality.

The nub of the distinction between an individual and a person as Zizioulas thinks of it lies in the fact that the very concept of an individual necessarily involves some kind of separation from others. An individual is defined over against other individuals of the same class, who share the same nature. In other words, he points out that individuals may be "enumerated"—in the sense that by being separated from the group they can be counted. By contrast, a person is by definition not separated out from

---

3. Coakley "'Persons' in the 'Social Doctrine' of the Trinity," 134.

4. In response to the subordinationism of Eunomius, Gregory insisted that the nature of God was "simple, uniform, incomposite" (*Conta Eunomium, Nicene and Post Nicene Fathers*, v. 61).

others but conceived *in relation to others* of the same nature. The chief defining property of a human person as distinct from a mere human individual therefore has to do with relationality.

The celebrated thesis of John Zizioulas in the theological world of the second half of the twentieth century was therefore that the Cappadocians actually stumbled upon an important discovery about the relational nature and identity of persons, as something essential to their *being* as persons. Hence, his signature theology of the "ontology of persons" as he set this out in his very influential *Being as Communion*, which was published in 1985.

John Zizioulas, as the unchallenged champion of the ontology of "persons in communion," has repeatedly made the point that, in the process of expounding the doctrine of the Trinity during the course of the fourth century, the Cappadocian fathers therefore made a very significant discovery. In the first instance, in distinguishing the three *hypostases* from the shared divine *ousia* and the essential properties of the divine nature (*physis*), the Cappadocians used the inherited term from Greek theater—*prosopon* or face, for which the Latin counterpart was *persona,* (a term that also connoted an individual with legal rights).

Explicitly the *prosopon* was the mask used by the actor to speak through in performing a role, which then came to signify the role itself.[5] Even though it is more Fate than a "Thou" that the dramatic "I" had to face, the characters of Greek tragedy possibly contributed to the development of the concept of personhood through the interpersonal dialogue of the characters.

However, even though the determination of an interpersonal element was a feature of the dialogue of Greek tragedy, the concept of the *prosopon* with this meaning was hardly a likely candidate for sustained use in relation to the Father, Son, and Spirit. The problem was that in logical terms this would lead directly into a kind of modalism—inevitably suggestive of one God, who acts out different roles (the heresy of Sabellianism that so worried Novatian). To imply that the one God might have acted first as Creator, then as Redeemer, and then as Sanctifier, was quite positively *not* what the Cappadocians had in mind.[6] Furthermore, as István Bugár observes, the

---

5. Informed by Boëthius, St. Thomas Aquinas could still recall in the Middle Ages that the Greek *prosopon* originally meant characters of a drama, which were marked by the mask (*prosopeion* or *prosopon*). Thomas Aquinas, *Summa*, I q29a3. His reference to Boethius is *De persona et duabus naturis contra Eutychen et Nestorium*, 3 (*Patrologiae Latina*, 64, 1343).

6. This was in fact the heresy of Sabellius early in the third century. Basil identified

roles in a drama are necessarily temporary in the sense that a dramatic role is something an actor assumes superficially and which by nature he or she must exchange.[7] Bugár also notes that the fact that characters in Greek drama are mainly of mythical origin also signals that they are roles temporally assumed by the actors.

In addition Bugár alerts us to the fact[8] that, apart from the notion of the *prosopon* or mask/face drawn from the world of Greek drama, its use in translation by the Latin term *persona* added further complications, for *persona* also carried legal connotations. The term *persona* was used, especially in the Roman Empire, to express a set of legal entitlements—a *persona* was an individual with legal rights, such as the right to enter into contracts, or to form *collegia*, or to own property, including the ownership of slaves, and the right to participate in civic affairs of government. However, the idea of an "individual with legal rights" was also unlikely to be attractive to the Trinitarian cause for the obvious reason that thinking of the persons of the Trinity as three individuals with equal rights would immediately lead to a kind of tritheism—in a sense the very opposite of the equally unwelcome possibility of the modalism of one *hypostasis* playing different roles that was entailed by the use of the term *prosopon*.

What the Cappadocians had in mind required them to *hypostasise* the *prosopon* so as to avoid modalism with its associations of a temporary nature, and at the same time to avoid talk of three entirely separate individuals.

As it has transpired their Trinitarian theology of the essential relational unity of three *hypostases* with "a certain fluidity in their boundaries," as Sarah Coakley has so felicitously put it, concealed an implicit distinction that can be drawn between an individual and a person. Whereas an individual is conceived in separation from others, a person, by contrast, has his or her personal identity in relation to others. Just as the eternal Father could not be called "Father" were it not for the eternal Son, and *vice versa*, as Athanasius had so forcefully emphasized, so as a matter of general principle a person has his or her identity in relation with others. As Zizioulas makes this distinction, relationality is to persons as separation from others is to individuals. He therefore contends that the resulting "ontology of persons in communion" that ensues from the interpersonal relationality essential to persons, precipitated by reflection on the doctrine of the Trinity of three

---

Sabellius as a Libyan from Pentapolis, though it is conjectured that this is because his teaching relating to three modes or manifestations of the one divine Person was said by Dionysius of Alexandria (ca. 260) to have flourished there. Some think he actually taught in Rome.

7. Bugár, "Making of Personhood," 33.
8. Bugár, "Making of Personhood," 33.

Persons in one unity of being, is thus to be celebrated as an abiding legacy of the work of the Cappadocian fathers.

His great contribution has been to point out that the Cappadocian quest to clarify the nature of God the Holy Trinity led to a huge advance insofar as theological anthropology is concerned. In other words, the contemporary concept of a person, defined in terms of relationality, was the great discovery of the Cappadocian fathers in the fourth century precisely as they worked out the doctrine of the unity of God the Holy Trinity. The Trinitarian definition of three identifiably distinct Persons, bound together in one unity of being as one indivisible interpersonal communion, he says, led to a discovery about the nature of persons generally as distinct from individuals, and this was a great step forward in the history of ideas.

Of course, it is recognized that the Cappadocians did not start with a blank slate. The idea of a person was not an invention that was exclusively their own. Insofar as the early fathers over the three centuries after Paul reflected upon the nature of God in the light of the revelation of Christ, and gradually worked towards the understanding of God as a Trinity of Persons, their thinking was grounded in the New Testament's participative language of both Paul and John.

When, already at the beginning of the third century, for example, Hippolytus sought an answer to the question of how Father, Son, and the Holy Spirit can be one and yet three, he immediately went to the participative language of John's Gospel. He pointed out that "When Jesus said, 'I and the Father are one' (John 10.30), it is to be understood that he is not just referring to different titles; nor did Jesus suggest that he and the Father were 'one and the same person.'" Rather, says Hippolytus, "he did not say, 'I and the Father am one, but are one.' For the word 'are' is not said of one person, but it refers to two persons, and one power."[9] For Hippolytus, this could be understood on analogy with human persons who become one in the power (*dynamis*) and disposition of unity of mind (*homonoia*) and so are one together.

Hippolytus found further reasons for this unity in power and disposition of mind in John's participative language. He says that Jesus "has himself made this clear, when he spoke to his Father concerning the disciples. 'The glory which you gave me I have given them: that they may all be one, even as we are one: I in them, and you in me, that they may be made perfect in one, that the world may know that you have sent me' (John 17.22–23) . . . In the

---

9. Hippolytus, *Contra Noetum*, 7.

same manner the Son, who was sent and was not known of those who are in the world, confessed that he was in the Father in power and disposition."[10]

Hippolytus was followed in a similar vein by Novatian of Rome, writing in Latin in the mid-third century.[11] Novatian took issue with the modalism of the Sabellians, who argued that the one God acted in three different ways, by insisting upon the separate identity as persons (*personae*) of the Father and the Son. Drawing on a human analogy, he also sought to explain how it was possible for two persons to be one:

> For when two persons have one judgment, one truth, one faith, one and the same religion, one fear of God also, they are one even although they are two persons: they are the same, in that they have the same mind.... And although they are not actually the self-same people, yet in feeling the same, they are the same; and although they are two, are still one, as having an association in faith, even although they bear diversity in persons.[12]

The Cappadocian fathers therefore did not start with a blank slate when they were confronted with the need to develop their understanding of the nature of God in the next century, though their thinking took the more ontological turn. Indeed, apart from the initial forays into the exploration of the relatedness and unity of Father, Son, and Spirit of thinkers of the caliber of Hippolytus and Novatian, they also inherited the christological advances resulting from the encounter of Athanasius with what had been identified as the heresy of Arius, not to mention the Nicene definition of three *hypostases* and one *ousia*/substance.

In the immediate lead-up to the Council of Constantinople in 381, however, as they began more and more to dwell upon the quality of the relatedness of the three *hypostases*, they were drawn more and more towards the identification of the terms *hypostasis* and *prosopon/persona* that had already been used by Hippolytus and Novatian, but with a distinctive twist of their own. As a consequence it became no longer possible to think of a *hypostasis* as though it were a coat hanger upon which the shared properties of the divine nature could be hung. Rather, in the thinking of the Cappadocians there was much more to being a "person" than that.

---

10. Hippolytus, *Contra Noetum* 7; *Library of Ante-Nicene Fathers*, v. 226.
11. Novatian, *De Trinitate*, 27.
12. Novatian, *De Trinitate*, 27.

Apart from the relationality said to be essential to the identity of persons as distinct from individuals, Zizioulas further argues that as separate "countable" individuals, they are necessarily conceived as particular instances of the class or group from which they come, to which they *necessarily* conform by nature. But, purely as individual instantiations of a nature there can be no guarantee of uniqueness, whereas a person by contrast is free to move beyond the constraints *necessarily imposed by nature* so as to establish an identity that is unique.[13]

This element of personal freedom is clearly of enormous importance to Zizioulas, who also wants us to understand that it is only as a person and not as a substance that God is "free to be"; for this reason a divine substance and its nature fails to explain the *being* of God. Thus, the Cappadocians insisted upon the *Person* of the Father as the "origin" and "cause" of the Son and the Spirit; a naked "substance" cannot be the origin or cause of anything.[14] Thus, for Zizioulas the key to understanding the Trinity is the monarchy (*arche*) of the Father. Unfortunately, this leads Zizioulas into a tendency to overplay the problem of an alleged dichotomy between Eastern and Western approaches to the doctrine of the Trinity, with Augustine being singled out to bear the burden of blame for focusing on the "unity of one substance" as the beginning point for reflection on the Trinity, whereas in the East the beginning point was on the person of the Father.[15]

In any event, in making this point he goes further than the bare affirmation that the Father is the "origin" and "cause" of the other two Trinitarian identities. Precisely as a *Person* (as distinct from an individual who is bound *by necessity* to conform to a nature), the Father is said to have been *free* to beget the Son and to bring forth the Spirit. This means that the begetting of the Son and the bringing forth of the Spirit are the result of the free and gracious act of will of the Father. Moreover, a primordial free act of the personal will the Father is said to account for the very existence of God as a divine being. The absolute ontological independence that by definition is unique to the divine nature whereby God is said to have his being from himself (in classical theism the *aseity* of God) is also a personal act of the Father's will. In this sense, God eternally wills himself to be by a free act of his Person.

---

13. As was argued in chapter 5, above.
14. Zizioulas, *Being as Communion*, 41, 88.
15. Unfortunately, at this point Zizioulas appears to be over-influenced by an illicit and now discredited reading of De Régnon's alleged thesis of a division between "Eastern" and "Western" approaches to the doctrine of the Trinity. See Barnes, "De Régnon Reconsidered," and Hennessy, "An Answer to De Régnon's 'Accusers.'"

At this point Zizioulas has been taken to task by his former teacher Thomas Torrance. Torrance identifies an initial problem insofar as this emphasis on the *arche* of the Father appears to suggest a kind of subordination within the life of the Trinity. The exercise of will by the Father in begetting the Son and bringing forth he Spirit puts them in a subordinate position to the Father. Given Torrance's own methodological commitment to the *homoousion* as the determinative organizing principle of his theology of the Trinity, this is hardly congenial.[16] On the other hand, talk of the Father's exercising of his will, both in begetting the Son and bringing forth the Spirit, and also with respect simply to his willing of his own self-determined eternal "being as God," seems to imply that the Son and the Spirit have wills of their own, whereas in traditional Trinitarian belief there is, of course, only one undivided will, and this is shared equally by all three Trinitarian identities. Indeed, the single and undivided will of God is important for the divine unity, not least in relation to the indivisibility of the divine action in the world. Torrance, for one, thinks that this Zizioulas's thought is a bridge too far.

The issue of the freedom of God the Father to be by an act of his will, and his eternal begetting of the Son by the free exercise of his will, appears to arise out of Zizioulas's reflection on the nature of persons. In his concern to make the perfectly valid distinction between a person and an individual, his reliance on the *free exercise of will* as a defining category of a person, and his concern to specify that God and one kind of animal (human beings) are persons, means that God, in this respect like a human person, must be free to act in a way that is not constrained by the necessary constraints of "a nature."

In other words, Zizioulas holds that the God in whose image human persons are made must also be characterized by the free decision of his will. Torrance's complaint is that speaking of the free act of will of the Father in begetting the Son and bringing forth the Spirit is to suggest not just that individual wills must be assigned to the Son and the Spirit in distinction to that of the Father, but their willing subordination to the will of the Father.

Torrance's criticisms of Zizioulas, however, are not insurmountable. It is true, for example, that the absolute ontological independence, or *aseity* of God, who is not dependent on anything outside of himself for his own existence, means that God does not exist contingently. But Zizioulas also wants to say that God's existence is not necessary either. Instead, God's eternal existence is the consequence of his own free determination to be by a personal act of will. Furthermore, God does not exist as a kind of inert

---

16. See especially Torrance, *Trinitarian Faith*, 110–90. Torrance thinks that Zizioulas's (and in fact the Cappadocians') concentration on the Father's *arche* is inimical to the *homoousion*. It is seen as a kind of maverick remnant subordinationism inherited from Origen, a thought that Torrance attributes to Karl Barth (179n46).

substance, for substances and their distinctive natural properties do not exist without a *hypostasis*. Therefore God the Father in having his being from himself means for Zizioulas that this is "by an act of his personal will": the Father's personal freedom means "that God, as Father, and not as substance, perpetually confirms through 'being' His *free* will to exist."[17] Torrance is concerned that this implies different individual wills for each of the other two Trinitarian identities who have their "origin" from the Father and are "caused" by the Father, and is thus inimical to the *homoousion*.

However, it could be argued that different individual wills do not necessarily have to be assigned to the Son and the Spirit. For it can be contended that apart from willing his own existence the Father simultaneously wills the begetting (and therefore the existence) of the Son and the bringing forth (and therefore the existence) of the Spirit, and further that "at the same time" he fully and equally shares his divine nature, inclusive of the property of willing, with the Son and the Spirit. In this case, it is not just that the "will to be" (in absolute ontological independence) is expressed by the Father alone insofar as he continues eternally to exist, but that this will to exist is expressed equally and fully by the Son and the Spirit, who share fully and equally this feature of divine nature. They too continue to exist by virtue of the same shared divine will. This means that *aseity* is not an incommunicable property of the Father alone, but a property of the nature of God as such. Indeed, the Father is never alone, but eternally with his only begotten Son and the Spirit that proceeds from him, all equally sharing the same divine "will to be" in absolute ontological independence.

Zizioulas argues that the monarchy of the Father is of crucial importance, for it is precisely as a person that the Father exercises his monarchy by a free act of will by begetting the Son and bringing forth the Spirit. In *Being and Communion*, Zizioulas therefore insists on the *causal* role of the Father in the immanent life of the Trinity, by drawing attention to *Epistle 38*, which he attributes to Basil, (though it could equally be attributed to Gregory of Nyssa), in order to support the view that "substance never exists in a 'naked' state, that is, without hypostasis, without a 'mode of existence.'"[18] There may be a problematic tendency here for Zizioulas to overemphasize the category of "person" as against "substance" in a way that is typical of the current fashion of assigning a (correct) concentration on the category of "person" as an Eastern approach to the Trinity as against the (incorrect) Western approach of beginning with "substance" that, rightly or wrongly, is regularly sheeted back to Augustine. Nevertheless, we can take his point that if willing is a

---

17. Zizioulas, *Being as Communion*, 41.
18. Zizioulas, *Being as Communion*, 41 and 88.

property of the divine nature of the substance of God, it is never exercised without a *hypostasis*; indeed it is never without *hypostases*. For if willing is a property of the divine nature that the Father, in the exercise of his monarchy, fully and equally shares with the Son and the Spirit, then, in this case, they too must share fully and equally in the Father's "will to be." Zizioulas himself declares, "The ontological monarchy of the Father, that is, of a *relational* being, and the attachment of ontological causation to him, serve to safeguard the coincidence of the One and the Many in divine being, a coincidence that raises otherness to the primary state of being without destroying its unity and oneness."[19] In other words, it has to be said in the case of the Trinity that if the divine nature is fully and equally shared from all eternity in the unity of the One and the Many, and if God the Father wills his own existence he wills it from all eternity with the Son and the Spirit, then all three equally share the same "will to be," even though this property is causally received from the Father.

It follows that the divine property of *aseity*, the defining characteristic of the absolute ontological independence of God, which means that the divine being of God is from God's self and no other source, is a property of *God*, and not just of the Father alone. "Outside the Trinity there is no God, that is no divine substance, because the ontological 'principle' of God is the Father. The personal existence of God (the Father) constitutes His substance, makes it hypostases. The being of God is identified with the person."[20]

It is not necessary or even appropriate to assign individualized wills to the other two Trinitarian identities. This means that the fear of subordinationism also disappears. If all three divine *hypostases* share the very same will, there can be no suggestion that one will is subordinate to the other. Torrance's concerns therefore fall away.

However, this aspect of Zizioulas's Trinitarian theology has also had to face critical scrutiny on other grounds.[21] As long ago as 1985 and again in 1990 John Panagopoulos and Savas Argourides spearheaded a challenge to Zizioulas's attribution of the relational ontology of Trinitarian personhood to the church fathers of the fourth century. They contended instead that it is a modern phenomenon, incorrectly projected back and unjustifiably attributed by Zizioulas to the Cappadocians. This criticism was then given

---

19. Zizioulas, *Communion and Otherness*, 35.

20. Zizioulas, *Being as Communion*, 41.

21. See the peer review articles by Colin Gunton, "Persons and Particularity," and D. Farrow, "Person and Nature."

its most acerbic voice by Lucian Turcescu, who in 2002 accused Zizioulas of modern personalism and even existentialism.[22] Among other things he claimed to have found instances in the writing of Gregory of Nyssa that indicated that a clear distinction between an individual and a person was not maintained and which proved that Zizioulas was "attempting to dress his philosophical personalism and existentialism with Cappadocian language and parade it as patristic."[23]

There is no doubting that Zizioulas's emphasis on the ontology of persons resonates with the personalism of twentieth-century philosophical movements. In modern times it was arguably Hermann Lotze in the nineteenth century who first anticipated the idea that was fully developed by Martin Buber in his *Ich und Du* of 1920. In Buber's famous formulation, the "I"—which was his term of preference for what we might prefer to call "a person"—is constituted only in his/her relations with an "other" whom the "I" addresses as a "Thou." On the other hand, although Nicholas Berdyaev already in 1933 appreciatively reviewed the German-Jewish thinker's work,[24] French personalism seems to have developed independently of Buber. Nevertheless, an emphasis on interpersonal communication is common ground. For Emmanuel Mounier, the founder and director of *Esprit*, which became the organ of the personalist movement in twentieth-century France, interpersonal relations were the most fundamental factor in the making of personhood. In *The Personalist Manifesto* he wrote: "Common opinion notwithstanding, the fundamental nature of the person is not originality, not self-knowledge nor individual affirmation. It lies not in separation but in communication."[25]

Given these modern antecedents, it is a fair question to ask whether Zizioulas was projecting a twentieth-century, even existentialist, understanding of things back on to the Christian thinkers of the fourth century.

In 2004 Aristotle Papanikolaou came to the defense of Zizioulas by pointing out, in the face of Turecscu's frankly confronting rebuke, that Ziziouslas did not in fact rely on the work of Gregory of Nyssa, and actually only quotes him very rarely. In developing his ontology of persons Zizioulas draws upon Gregory of Nazianzus, and even more on Basil of Caesarea, in

---

22. Turcescu, "'Person' versus 'Individual.'"

23. Papanikolaou's summing up of Turcescu's complaint in "Is John Zizioulas an Existentialist in Disguise?," 601.

24. Berdyaev, "Martin Buber."

25. Mounier, *Personalist Manifesto*, 17.

order to unpack the distinctively Cappadocian concentration on the importance of the unity of persons in interpersonal communion. Furthermore, it is not Zizioulas's thesis that all three Cappadocians were marching with jack-booted precision in strict formation;[26] it was rather that their discovery about the importance of relationality to the being and identity of persons was something they stumbled upon as they identified the concepts of *hypostasis* and *person* in their reflection on the interpersonal unity of God.

Zizioulas himself in turn responded to Panagopoulos and Argourides by providing a number of clear reasons why his own thought should not be assimilated to modern personalist movements, let alone existentialism. In an article entitled "The Being of God and the Being of Anthropos," he openly acknowledged some similarities, however, with the personalism of such modern thinkers as Mounier, Berdyaev, Buber, Maritain and Marcel, and even Kierkegaard. Specifically in response to the charge of Turcescu, Zizioulas points out that the distinctive starting point of the Cappadocian contribution to the doctrine of the Trinity remains the emphasis (especially of Gregory of Nazianzus) on the monarchy of the person of the Father as the "origin" and "cause" of the other two Trinitarian *hypostases*. This is what is ultimately crucial in providing a decisive criterion of difference between the Trinitarian understanding of the person and the personalist accounts of modern philosophy. While openly acknowledging his dependence on Martin Buber, in this specific respect Zizioulas was unlikely to have been heavily dependent upon the Jewish thinker.

In relation to Turcescu's attempt to associate him with twentieth-century existentialism, Zizioulas insisted that for the most part this modern phenomenon locates the defining qualities of personhood in subjectivity or consciousness rather than in relationality. The Cappadocian approach to the understanding of a person has to do with relations: this is what "precludes any philosophical-personalistic interpretation of God."[27] He thus confidently upholds the patristic Trinitarian insight of the monarchy of the Father as of crucial importance. It is this *relation* to the Son and the Spirit that is the determinative element in identifying the unique theological discovery of the fourth-century ontology of persons in communion.[28]

On the other hand, twentieth-century personalism can hardly be said to have itself dropped from the sky out of nowhere, detached as it were from the same biblical traditions that informed the thinking of the Cappadocians,

---

26. Sarah Coakley in fact warns against setting individual Cappadocians over against one another, and suggests a self-correcting cooperative model instead.

27. Zizioulas, "Being of God and the Being of Anthropos," 18.

28. Zizioulas, "Being of God and the Being of Anthropos," 18.

or from the ensuing historical tradition to which the Cappadocians themselves contributed. Ideas tend to migrate anonymously without declaring their identity or complying with the strict requirements of international border control. It is obvious, for example, that even Buber was not just a philosopher in a contemporary bubble but was heavily indebted to the Old Testament biblical tradition in which he clearly stood. The historical tradition behind modern personalism may also be illustrated by the fact that St. Thomas Aquinas, who, with the help of Boethius, could remember that the Greek *prosopon* and its Latin counterpart *persona* referred to the characters in a drama (*prosopeion* or *prosopon*).[29] But over and above this reference to this early use of these terms, Aquinas in his *Summa* 1 q29 a4, also referring to Boethius's declaration in *De Trinitate* that all terms connected with a person signify relations, asserts that "Boetius, in libro de Trin., quod omne nomen ad personas pertinens, relationem significat."[30] By this Aquinas means that there are real relations and not just purely logical or nominal relations in God; they are not merely incidental or temporary but relations that actually affect or make a difference to the terms said to be related.[31]

It can hardly be said that the concept of a person formed by reference to relationality with an "other" is a purely modern phenomenon of the twentieth century or that Zizioulas has simply dressed up modern personalism and existentialism in Cappadocian garb in order to parade it as patristic. In fact, just as soon as the *unity* of the *hypostatic* identities of the Trinity becomes a matter of discussion, the immediate implication of some kind of relationality presents itself as something that also has necessarily to be discussed. This can already be seen to be the case in relation to Hippolytus and Novatian as early as in the first half of the third century. In other words, the distinction between an individual and a person based upon the lack of relationality on one hand and the ontological necessity of it in the other, is already latently implicit in the discussion of the unity of the persons of the Trinity—where it lies in wait to receive the kiss of life just as soon the question of the unity of the Persons of the Trinity is reflected upon or perceived to be something to be defended. Interpersonal unity necessarily implies some kind of interpersonal *relationality*.

As István Bugár has pertinently observed, "[T]he unity of the Trinity warrants that the persons are not seen as individuals in isolation. They *are*

---

29. Aquinas, *Summa Theologica*, 1 q29 a3.

30. Boethius, *Quomodo Trinitas unus Deus ac non Tres Dii*, 5–6.

31. In a more modern philosophical idiom, they are internal relations as distinct from external relations.

one *all together.*"[32] It is the *unity of the Trinity* that ensures that the persons are not seen as mere individuals in isolation from one another. This is exactly the context in which this concept of a person was generated. Persons are not one, two, or three in the sense of being separate from one another, but are one by being together in unity. For this Trinitarian reason we may be confident in affirming that the ontology of personhood was developed largely as a consequence of the work of the Cappadocians in the fourth century as they reflected on the internal relations of the persons of the Trinity in one unity of being. As Bugár says: "[T]he concept of a person was formed in the theological context . . . that is to say, in the discourse about the Trinity."[33]

John Zizioulas rightly declares that the concept of a person applies only to God and one species of animal—human beings. Furthermore, we have to remember that reflection on the interpersonal communion of the Persons of the Trinity that is so essential to the understanding of their identity *as* Persons, was the product of reflection upon the interpersonal communion of humans with God that was claimed to be known in the economy of salvation. But this raises the important question as to whether the use of the term "person" both with respect to humans and to God is univocal or analogical. Zizioulas appears to think in terms of univocity. The fact that I myself usually refer to the divine "Persons" using an upper-case "P" already betrays the fact that I am myself inclined to favor the role of analogy at this point. The fact that the inner life of God as God is in God's self is known only to God, and must of necessity remain an ineffable mystery to finite minds, ultimately incomprehensible and unknowable, means that we might prudently exercise some reserve in such matters. After all, even though human persons are made in "the image of God," the use of the concept of a "person'" may signal an important similarity between human beings created in God's image and God that is not shared by the rest of the animal world, but without the requirement that the divine and human persons are univocally the same in every respect. The apophatic nature of the theology of God, in other words, precludes the possibility of a confident specification of the way the divine Persons are Persons as God is in God's self.

Zizioulas is, of course, perfectly aware of the need to abide by the conventions of the apophatic method, and registers all the necessary qualifications: "We are unable to use the concepts of the human mind . . . for

---

32. Bugár, "Making of Personhood," 33.
33. Bugár, "Making of personhood," 32.

signifying God . . . ; God 'is beyond affirmation and negation.'"[34] There is a cognitive gap that therefore has to be bridged. But then he goes on to suggest that categories of "love" and "communion" can bridge this gap, because God is love.[35] We might well add that this cognitive gap is transcended when we are addressed by God—when we hear the insistent call to repentance and faith as God's call to communion with himself, and when he positively justifies those who are "in Christ" through the gift of his Spirit. This experience is admittedly beyond clear and distinct expression in mere words even though known by acquaintance in concrete experience.

Very importantly, the relationality that is essential to being a human person means that with persons there is necessarily communicability. A person, as distinct from an individual, may be addressed by another and may expect a similar response from those whom he or she addresses. Interpersonal give-and-take in communion with others occurs *between* persons. This is why by contrast with a living human person behind the counter in a bank, an ATM machine is judged to be "impersonal."

If the relationality essential to persons means that there is the possibility of communicability, we might well add that it is as a consequence of this relationality that human persons share a common language by which they communicate, employing words with *conventionally agreed upon* meanings. There is no such thing as a language that is private to an individual. It is with this instrument of communicability that one person is able to relate to an "other." Although self-reflection tends to be the focus in contemporary, especially twentieth-century,[36] approaches to the individualistic understanding of a person, self-reflection actually presupposes a language that necessarily has a communitarian base. Although with this same language an individual is able to speak to him or her self in the same way as he or she speaks to another, the language itself is a corporately created tool. Words have *conventionally agreed upon* meanings, and languages operate in accordance with a commonly accepted set of rules—in what Wittgenstein called a "language game"—otherwise they do not operate at all. There is no such thing as a private language. Only with this corporately devised linguistic

---

34. Zizioulas, *Being as Communion*, 90.
35. Zizioulas, *Being as Communion*, 89–92.
36. Though strictly speaking it is already found in Plato's *Alcibiades* 1A (128e, 129b, 130d, 133), as was noted by Kierkegaard in *Sickness unto Death*: "A human being is a synthesis of . . . freedom and necessity. . . . The human self is such a derived established relation, a relation that relates itself to itself and in relating itself to itself relates itself to another." Kierkegaard, *Sickness unto Death*, 13–14. Perhaps Kierkegaard would himself be prepared to revise this to read that as a babe "a human self relates itself to another, and in so doing comes to relate itself to itself."

tool are persons thus able to communicate with others, and are also capable as persons of making something of themselves in their self-reflective awareness as persons.

This linguistic capacity of human communicability entails that humans are able to express what they discern as the moral pressure of the will of God in words, thereby understanding themselves to have been addressed by God, as the prerequisite then to codifying this in a coherent set of moral and ethical social norms. And as persons those who "hear the word of God" respond to God in a similar way in prayer and worship. As we know ourselves to be addressed by God who calls us to himself and, responding to that, address God in prayer and worship, we know ourselves to be persons, made in the "image of God" who are thus able to relate to God. The primordial communicability of human persons thus knows itself also in the communion of the God-human relationship.

It therefore becomes thoroughly understandable that when Genesis declares that God made man, he is said not only to have made more than one, not just *a* man, but in the first instance Adam and Eve, male and female, for it "was not good for man to be alone"—hence two, who are thus humanly capable of interpersonal communion. Persons can be of one heart and one mind, as Hippolytus and Novatian had already observed, sharing a common will and a common purpose. By virtue of the interpersonal vector of communicability they can be one in love by mutual self-gift. Strictly speaking, none of this is possible in the case of individuals *as* individuals, who are necessarily conceived in separation from others, but is only possible between persons *as* persons.

Furthermore, and very significantly, in Genesis God is also said to have made them "in his own image"—and so intentionally created humans *as* persons, capable of entering into interpersonal communion with himself. Thus, it is not an accident that just as soon as God creates Adam and Eve, he addresses them.[37] The concept of a "person" applies to God and one kind of animal (human persons) who are in this way distinct from every other species of animal. Though Aquinas (once again informed by Boethius) speaks of a human being as the rational animal; it would be more appropriate to say that humans are not the rational animal but, at least in the first instance, the praying animal.[38]

---

37. Genesis 1:28: "And God blessed them, and said to them . . ."

38. Jenson, *Systematic Theology* II, chapter 20. Jenson points out that the "image of God" does not refer to a resemblance. Rather it is a comprehensive phrase for humanity's distinctiveness so to mean "simply that we are related to God as his conversational counterpart" (II, 95).

Now, when this Trinitarian perspective is intentionally brought to the doctrine of human redemption there are a number of clear implications that may be drawn. In the first instance, we have to be prepared to acknowledge that, not least among the many shortcomings of the penal substitutionary theory of the atonement, is the obvious fact that it implicitly suggests the operation of two wills within the life of the Trinity, the alleged commanding will of the Father and the obediently submissive will of the Son, which in fact fractures the unity and simplicity of the divine life. The orthodox doctrine of the Trinity speaks instead of a single divine will of the one fully and equally shared divine nature of all three Trinitarian identities.

When it is acknowledged that a Trinitarian approach to the doctrine of redemption involves the restoration of the "image of God" in redeemed humanity of those who find themselves participating "in Christ" in the restored communion of the love of God through the grace of the Lord Jesus Christ and the gift of his Spirit, then a number of entailments follow. The first has to do with the nature of the language of atonement. An approach to the understanding of the atonement of an incorporative and participative kind in the economy of salvation in which unimpeded access is granted to the love of God the Father, explicitly through the help or grace of the Lord Jesus Christ, and through the gift of his Spirit, allows the metaphors and images of the New Testament that are expressive of the experience of reconciliation and peace with God to come into their own for what they are. As metaphors and images they are descriptive and interpretative of experience rather than the basis for the distillation of abstract propositions of the speculative and juridical kind required for the logical development of a "theory." Still less is it possible to make a case for the necessarily punitive nature of these propositions and the punitive nature of the theory that is based upon them.

Second, this Trinitarian approach means that the church, as the communion of those who in repentance and faith are "in Christ" through the gift of the Holy Spirit, is itself an element in the redemptive plan of God in which its members know themselves to be justified or "put in the right" by God. As inheritors of the covenant promises made to Abraham, those who are justified by faith "in Christ" live in reconciliation and peace with God and with one another, regardless of considerations of ethnic diversity, social status, or gender difference (Gal 3:28).

Third, if the restoration and renewal of human persons achieved by the redemptive action of God involves the restoration and renewal *in them* of the "image of God" of their original creation, they know themselves "in

Christ" not just as an aggregate of individuals but precisely as a communion of persons—persons who have the capacity for interpersonal communication with God through the hearing of his word, to which they respond in prayer and worship. If as individual representatives of a human nature they are bound by the disfiguring necessities of that nature that ends in death, as persons they are by faith and the free gift of God's grace helped to transcend the necessities of their inherited nature so as to embrace the hope of abundant life. In the words of Aristotle Papanikolaou, their restoration and renewal in the image of God means that their personhood is reclaimed "as an event of irreducible uniqueness and freedom from the necessity of sin that has distorted created nature."[39] This unique personal identity is grasped through the enjoyment of restored interpersonal relationality with others in the communion of the church, which is coincident with the enjoyment of reconciliation and peace *in* the communion of the God who is himself a communion of Persons. Accordingly, atonement with God is not an abstract theory to which we are called to give a purely notional assent, but a concrete reality of the new life "in Christ" in which we are invited through the generosity of God joyfully to participate by faith with thanksgiving.

---

39. Papanikolaou, "From Sophia to Personhood," 19.

BIBLIOGRAPHY

Abelard, Peter. *Exposition of the Epistle to the Romans*. (An Excerpt from the Second Book.) In *A Scholastic Miscellany: Anselm to Ockham*, edited and translated by Eugene R. Fairweather, 276–87. The Library of Christian Classics X. London: SCM, 1956.

Adam, Peter. "Honouring Jesus Christ." *St. Mark's Review* 1/198 (2005) 11–17.

Agourides, Savas. "Can the persons of the Trinity form the basis for personalistic understandings of the human being?" *Synaxis* 33 (1990) 67–78.

Alston, William P. *Divine Nature and Human Language*. Ithaca, NY: Cornell University Press, 1989.

Aquinas, Thomas. *Summa Theologiae*. Translated by C. Thomas Moore. London: Eyre and Spottiswoode, 1976.

Armitage, Chris. "The Memorialists." *The Anglican Historical Society, Diocese of Sydney, Journal* 55/2 (2010) 18–25.

Asslet, W. J. van. *The Federal Theology of Johannes Cocceius (1603–1669)*. Translated by Raymond A. Blacketer. Studies in the History of Christian Thought 100. Leiden: Brill, 2001.

Athanasius. "Discourses Against the Arians." In *The Nicene and Post Nicene Fathers of the Christian Church* (*NPNF*), edited by Philip Schaff and Henry Wace. Grand Rapids: Eerdmans, 1971.

———. *Letters of Saint Athanasius Concerning the Holy Spirit*. Translated by C. R. B. Shapland. London: Epworth, 1951.

———. *On the Incarnation*. St. Francis Bay: Gladdening Light, 2023.

———. *On the Opinion of Dionysius*. English translation in *The Nicene and Post-Nicene Fathers*, second series IV. New York: Cosimo, 2013.

Augustine of Hippo. *City of God*. Translated by Henry Bettenson. London: Penguin, 1984.

———. *On the Trinity*. In *A Select Library of the Nicene and Post-Nicene Fathers of the Christian Church*, translated by the Rev. Arthur West Haddan, with an introduction by William G. T. Shedd and edited by Paul A Böer Sr. Buffalo: Christian Literature 1886; vol. 3. Veritatis Splendor, 2012.

Awad, Najeeb G. "Between Subordination and Koinonia: Toward a New Reading of the Cappadocian Theology." *Modern Theology* 23/2 (April 2007) 181–204.

———. "Personhood as Particularity: John Zizioulas, Colin Gunton, and the Trinitarian Theology of Personhood." *Journal of Reformed Theology* 4 (2010) 1–22.

Ayres, Lewis. *Augustine and the Trinity*. Cambridge: Cambridge University Press, 2010.

———. *Nicaea and Its Legacy: An Approach to Fourth Century Trinitarian Theology*. Oxford: Oxford University Press, 2004.

Barnes, Michel René. "Augustine in Contemporary Trinitarian Theology." *Theological Studies* 56/2 (1995) 237–50.

———. "De Régnon Reconsidered." *Augustinian Studies* 26/2 (1995) 51–79.

Barnes, Michel René, and Daniel H. Williams. *Arianism After Arius: Essays on the Development of the Fourth Century Trinitarian Conflicts*. Edinburgh: T. & T. Clark, 1993.

Barth, Karl. *Church Dogmatics*, IV, *The Doctrine of Reconciliation*. Translated by G. W. Bromiley, edited by G. W. Bromiley and T. F. Torrance. London: T. & T. Clark, 1956.

Barton, John. *A History of the Bible: The Book and Its Faiths*. London: Penguin Random House, 2019.

Basil of Caesarea. *On the Holy Spirit*. Introduction by David Anderson. Crestwood, NY: St. Vladimir's Seminary Press, 1980.

Bauman, Michael. *Milton's Arianism*. Frankfurt: Peter Lang, 1987.

Berdyaev, N. A. "Martin Buber. Der Chassidischen Buecher: Ich und Du; Zwiespreche; Koenigtum Gottes." *Put'* 38 (May 1933) 87–91.

Bilezikian, Gilbert. "Hermeneutical Bungee-Jumping: Subordination in the Godhead." *Journal of the Evangelical Theological Society* 40/1 (1997) 57–68.

Billings, Todd. *Calvin, Participation and Gift: The Activity of Believers in Union with Christ*. Oxford: Oxford University Press, 2007.

Bird, Michael F. *Evangelical Theology: A Biblical and Systematic Introduction*. Grand Rapids: Zondervan, 2013.

Bird, Michael F., and Robert Shillaker. "The Son Really, Really Is the Son: A Response to Kevin Giles." *Trinity Journal* 30 (2009) 257–68.

———. "Subordination in the Trinity and Gender Roles: A Response to Recent Discussions." In *The New Evangelical Subordinationism: Perspectives on the Equality of God the Father and God the Son*, edited by Dennis W. Jowers and W. Wayne House, 288–310. Eugene, OR: Pickwick, 2012.

Bird, Michael F., and Scott Harrower. *Trinity without Hierarchy: Reclaiming Nicene Orthodoxy in Evangelical Theology*. Grand Rapids: Kregel Academic, 2019.

Black, Max. *Models and Metaphors: Studies In Language and Philosophy*. Ithaca, NY: Cornell University Press, 1962.

Blocher, Henri. "Biblical Metaphors and the Doctrine of the Atonement." *Journal of the Evangelical Theological Society* 47/4 (December 2004) 629–45.

———. *Original Sin*. Nottingham: Apollos, 1997.

Boersma, Hans. *Heavenly Participation: The Weaving of a Sacramental Tapestry*. Grand Rapids: Eerdmans, 2011.

Boethius. *Against Eutyches and Nestorius*. Translated by W. V. Cooper. Mishawaka, IN: Aeterna, 2016.

Boff, Leonardo. *Trinity and Society*. Maryknoll, NY: Orbis, 1988.

Bonneau, Normand. "The Logic of Paul's Argument on the Curse of the Law in Galatians 3:10–14." *Novum Testamentum* 3/1 (1997) 60–80.

Boyd, Gregory A. "Christus Victor Response." In *The Nature of Atonement: Four Views*, edited by James Beilby and Paul R. Eddy, 99–105. Downers Grove, IL: IVP Academic, 2006.

Brain, Peter. "Could I talk to you about Dr. Carnley's views?" *Essentials, the Journal of EFAC* (June 2000) 1–5.

Brent, Alan. *Hippolytus and the Roman Church in the Third Century: Communities in Tension before the Emergence of a Monarch-bishop*. Supplements to Vigiliae Christianae. Leiden: Brill, 1995.
Bromiley, G. W. "Eternal Generation." In *Evangelical Dictionary of Theology*, edited by Walter A. Elwell. Grand Rapids: Baker, 1984.
Bugár, István M. "The Making of Personhood: Crossroads around 400 AD." *Interdisciplinary Research in Humanities*, edited by Gergely Angyalosi et al. Constantine the Philosopher University. https://www.academia.edu/3816223/The_making_of_personhood_crossroads_around_400_AD?auto=download&email_work_card=download-pap.
Bulgakov, Sergius. *The Bride of the Lamb*. Translated by Boris Jakim. Grand Rapids: Eerdmans, 2002.
Bull, George. *Defensio Fidei Nicaenae*, I and II. Oxford: J. H. Parker, 1851–1852.
Burkert, Walter. *Homo Necans: The Anthropology of Ancient Greek Sacrificial Ritual and Myth*. Berkeley: University of California Press, 1983.
Butner, D. Glenn, Jr. "Eternal Functional Subordination and the Problem of the Divine Will." *Journal of the Evangelical Theological Society* 58/1 (March 2015) 131–49.
———. *The Son Who Learned Obedience: A Theological Case Against the Eternal Submissiveness of the Son*. Eugene, OR: Pickwick, 2018.
Cable, K. J. "Hammond, Thomas Chatterton (1877–1961)." *Australian Dictionary of Biography* 14 (1966) 376–68. https://adb.anu.edu.au/biography/hammond-thomas-chatterton-10406
———. "The Memorialists." *Anglican Historical Society, Diocese of Sydney, Journal* 58/2 (2013) 10–24.
Calvin, John. *Institutes of the Christian Religion*. Edited by John Thomas McNeill, translated by Ford Lewis Battles. London: SCM, 1961.
Carnley, Peter. *Arius on Carillon Avenue: More than a Memoir: A Trinitarian Saga*. Eugene, OR: Cascade, 2023.
———. "Godfellows." *The Bulletin*, May 22, 2001, 38–40.
———. "In the Beginning." *The Bulletin*, September 3, 2002, 34–35.
———. "In Praise of Hierarchy—a Response to Jürgen Moltmann." *Common Theology*, edited by Maggie Hellas, I/1 (July 2002) 9–15.
———. "Introduction to the Colloquium." *St. Mark's Review* 1/198 (2005) 3–4.
———. "King on a Cross." *The Bulletin*, April 17, 2001, 33–35.
———. *Reflections in Glass*. Sydney: HarperCollins, 2004.
———. "Such is Life." *The Bulletin*, April 16, 2002, 36–38.
———. "T. C. Hammond and the Theological Roots of Sydney Arianism." *St. Mark's Review* 1/198 (2005) 5–10.
———. "Theory of the Atonement Makes God Look Cruel." *Anglican Messenger*, Perth (March 1991) 12.
———. "The Rising of the Son." *The Bulletin*, April 25, 2000, 40–43.
———. "The Ultimate Sacrifice." *The Bulletin*, April 2, 2002, 26–29.
———. *The Yellow Wallpaper and Other Sermons*. Sydney: HarperCollins, 2001.
Carson, D. A. "A Little Introduction to Covenants." November 4, 2016. https://www.desiringgod.org/authors/d-a-carson.
———. "Review of *Evil and the Justice of God*, by N. T. Wright." *Review of Biblical Literature* (April 2007). http://www.bookreviews.org/pdf/5581_5877.pdf.

Cave, William. *Ecclesiastici: or, The History of the Lives, Acts, Death and Writings of the Most Eminent Fathers of the Church.* London: Printed by R. J. for Richard Chiswell, 1863.

Chalke, Steve. "Cross Purposes." *Christianity* (September 2004) 44–48.

Chalke, Steve, and Alan Mann. *The Lost Message of Jesus.* Grand Rapids: Zondervan, 2003.

Church of England Doctrine Report. *Doctrine in the Church of England.* London: SPCK, 1938.

Claunch, Kyle. "God is the Head of Christ: 1 Corinthians 11.3." In *One God and Three Persons: Unity of Essence, Distinction of Persons, Implications for Life*, edited by Bruce A. Ware and John Starke, 65–93. Wheaton, IL: Crossway, 2015.

———. "What God Hath Done Together: Defending the Historic Doctrine of the Inseparable Operations of the Trinity." *Journal of the Evangelical Theological Society* 56/4 (2013) 781–800.

Coakley, Sarah. "Afterword: 'Relational Ontology,' Trinity and Science." In *The Trinity and an Entangled World*, edited by John Polkinghorne, 184–99. Grand Rapids: Eerdmans, 2010.

———. "Introduction: Disputed Questions in Patristic Trinitariaism." *Harvard Theological Review* 100/2 (2007) 125–38.

———. "'Persons' in the 'Social Doctrine' of the Trinity: A Critique of Current Analytical Discussion." In *The Trinity: An Interdisciplinary Symposium on the Trinity*, edited by Stephen Davis et al., 123–45. Oxford: Oxford University Press, 2002.

Cocceius, John. *Summa doctrinae de foedere et testamento Dei* (1648). Lugdono-Batava: Ex Officina Elseviriorum, 1654.

Congar, Yves. *I Believe in The Holy Spirit: The Complete Three Volume Work in One Volume.* Milestones in Catholic Theology. New York: Crossroad, 1997.

Cranfield, Charles E. B. *A Critical and Exegetical Commentary on the Epistle to the Romans.* 2 vols. Edinburgh: T. & T. Clark, 1975.

Cross, F. L., and E. A. Livingstone, eds. *Oxford Dictionary of the Christian Church.* 3rd rev. ed. Oxford: Oxford University Press, 200?.

Cvetkovic, Vladimir. "The Oneness of God as Unity of Persons in the Thought of St. Maximus the Confessor." In *Maximus the Confessor as a European Philosopher*, edited by Sotiris Mitralexis et. al, 304–15. Eugene, OR: Cascade, 2017.

Cyprian of Carthage. *Collected Epistles.* Fig Classics Series. Merchantville, NY: Evolution, 2013.

———. *On the Unity of the Church.* In *The Complete Works of Saint Cyprian*, edited by Phillip Campbell. Merchantville, NY: Evolution, 2013. https://patristics.info/cyprian-on-the-unity-of-the-church.html.

Del Colle, Ralph. "'Persons' and 'Being' in John Zizioulas' Theology: Conversation with Thomas Torrance and Thomas Aquinas." *Scottish Journal of Theology* 54/1 (2001) 70–86.

Denaux, Adelbert. Nicholas Sagovsky, and Charles Sherlock, eds. *Looking Towards A Church Fully Reconciled.* Mahwah, NJ: Paulist, 2016.

Devlin, Patrick Lord. *The Enforcement of Morals.* Oxford: Oxford University Press, 1968.

Dillistone, F. W. *The Christian Understanding of Atonement.* Welwyn: James Nisbet, 1968.

Dixhoorn, Chad B. Van. *Minutes and Papers of the Westminster Assembly, 1643—53*. Oxford: Oxford University Press, 2012.
Donaldson, T. "The Curse of the Law and the inclusion of the Gentiles. Galatians 3.13–14." *New Testament Studies* 32 (1986) 94–112.
Donfried, Karl. *The Romans Debate*. Expanded and rev. ed. Peabody, MA: Hendrickson, 1991.
Dorner, I. A. *A History of the Development of the Doctrine of the Person of Christ*. Translated by D. W. Simon. Edinburgh: T. & T. Clark, 1889.
Doyle, Robert. "God in Feminist Critique." *Reformed Theological Review* 52/1 (1993) 12–22.
———. "Reflections in Glass, Chapter 7: Women in the Episcopate: ARIANISM: OF STRAW MEN AND FABRICATION." Anglican Media Sydney, September 3, 2004. https://sydneyanglicans.net/news/1679a.
———. "Sexuality, Personhood, and the Image of God." In *Personhood, Sexuality, and Christian Ministry, Explorations: Moore Papers No. 1*, edited by B. Webb, 43–46. Sydney: Lancer, 1987.
———. "Use and abuse of the fathers and the Bible in trinitarian theology." A review of Kevin Giles, *The Trinity and Subordinationism*. *The Briefing*, April 1, 2004, 11–19. http://thebriefing.com.au/2004/04/use-and-abuse-of-the-fathers-and-the-bible-in-trinitarian-theology/.
Dunn, James G. D. *The Theology of the Apostle Paul*. London: T. & T. Clark, 2003.
Eberhart, Christian. "Sacrifice? Holy Smokes! Reflections on Cult Terminology for Understanding Sacrifice in the Hebrew Bible." In *Ritual and Metaphor: Sacrifice in the Bible*, edited by Christian Eberhart, 17–32. Atlanta: Society of Biblical Literature, 2011.
Emerson, Matthew Y. "Response to Bruce A. Ware and Malcolm B. Yarnell III." In *Trinitarian Theology*, edited by Keith S. Whitfield, 157–73. Nashville: B & H, 2019.
Emerson, Matthew Y., and Luke Stamps. "On Trinitarian Theological Method." In *Trinitarian Theology*, edited by Keith S. Whitfield, 95–128. Nashville: B & H, 2019.
Erickson, Millard. *Who's Tampering with the Trinity? An Assessment of the Subordination Debate*. Grand Rapids: Kregel, 2009.
Faith and Order Advisory Group of the Church of England (FOAG). "*Church as Communion*: Briefing for General Synod." 2008, GS Misc 1713. www.churchofengland.org/media/1236810/gs1713.pdf.
Farrow, D. "Person and Nature: The Necessity–Freedom Dialectic." In *The Theology of John Zizioulas: Personhood and the Church*, edited by D. H. Knight, 109–24. Aldershot: Ashgate, 2007.
Fee, Gordon D. *The First Epistle to the Corinthians*. Grand Rapids: Eerdmans: 1987.
———. "Paul and the Trinity: The Experience of Christ and the Spirit for Paul's Understanding of God." In *The Trinity: An Interdisciplinary Symposium on the Trinity*, edited by Stephen Davis et al., 49–72. Oxford: Oxford University Press, 1999.
Fenner, Dudley. *Sacra theologia, sive veritas quae est secundum pietatem*. Geneva: Eustache Vignon, 1585.
Fiddes, Paul. *Past Event and Present Salvation: The Christian Idea of Atonement*. London: Darton, Longman and Todd, 1989.
Filonenko, Alexander. "The Theology of Communion and Eucharistic Anthropology." In *Philosophical Theology and the Christian Tradition: Russian and Western*

Perspectives, edited by David Bradshaw, 177–85. Washington: Council for Research in Values and Philosophy, 2012.

Fokin, Alexey. "Models of the Trinity in Patristic Theology." In *Philosophical Theology and the Christian Tradition: Russian and Western Perspectives*, edited by David Bradshaw, 31–52. Russian Philosophical Studies V, Christian Philosophical Studies III. Washington, DC: Council for Research in Values and Philosophy, 2012.

Forsyth, Robert, "It's Negative Theology." *Market Place* 8 (April 2004) 6–12.

Frame, John. *Systematic Theology, An Introduction to Christian Belief*. Phillipsburg, NJ: P & R, 2013.

Frame, Tom. *Anglicans in Australia*. Sydney: University of New South Wales Press, 2007.

———. "The Dynamics and Difficulties of Debate in Australian Anglicanism." In *Agendas for Australian Anglicanism: Essays in Honour of Bruce Kaye*, edited by Tom Frame and Geoffrey Treloar, 139–69. Adelaide: ATF, 2006.

Gathercole, S. J. "Justified by Faith, Justified by His Blood: The Evidence of Romans 3:21–4:25." In *Justification and Variegated Nomism*, vol. 2, edited by D. A. Carson et al., 147–84. Grand Rapids: Baker Academic, 2004.

Gilders, William K. "Jewish Sacrifice: Its Nature and Function (According to Philo)." In *Ancient Mediterranean Sacrifice*, edited by Jennifer Wright Knust and Zsuzsanna Varhelyi, 94–105. New York: Oxford University Press, 2011.

Giles, Kevin. *The Eternal Generation of the Son: Maintaining Orthodoxy in Trinitarian Theology*. Grand Rapids: Zondervan, 2012.

———. "In Praise of Egalitarianism." *Common Theology* 1/2 (Advent 2002) 13–15.

———. *Jesus and the Father: Modern Evangelicals Reinvent the Trinity*. Grand Rapids: Zondervan, 2006.

———. "Response to Michael Bird and Robert Shillaker: The Son is not Eternally Subordinated in Authority to the Father." *Trinity Journal* 30/2 (2009) 237–56.

———. Review of *The Holy Trinity in Scripture, History, Theology and Worship*, by Robert Letham. *Evangelical Quarterly* 78/1 (2006) 85–94.

———. *The Rise and Fall of the Complementarian Doctrine of the Trinity*. Eugene, OR: Cascade, 2017.

———. "The Trinity and Subordinationism." *St Mark's Review* 1/198 (2005) 19–24.

———. *The Trinity and Subordinationism: The Doctrine of God & the Contemporary Gender Debate*. Downers Grove, IL: InterVarsity, 2002.

———. "The Trinity without Tiers." In *The New Evangelical Subordinationism? Perspectives on the Equality of God the Father and God the Son*, edited by Dennis W. Jowers and H. Wayne House, 262–87. Eugene, OR: Pickwick, 2012.

Giles, Kevin, and Robert Letham. "Is the Son Eternally Submissive to the Father?" *Christian Research Journal* 31/1 (2008) 10–21.

Goligher, Liam. "Is It Okay to Teach Complementarianism Based on Eternal Subordination?" *Mortification of Spin*, June 3, 2016. http://www.alliancenet.org/mos/housewife-theologian/is-it-okay-to-teach-a complementarianism-based-on-eternal subordination#.WGGyLfB96Ul.

Gons, Philip, and Andrew Naselli. "An Examination of Three Recent Philosophical Arguments Against Hierarchy in the Immanent Trinity." In *One God in Three Persons: Unity of Essence, Distinction of Persons, Implications for Life*, edited by Bruce Ware and John Starke, 195–213. Wheaton, IL: Crossway, 2015.

Grabowski, John. "Person: Substance and Relation." *Communio* 22 (Spring 1995) 139–63.

Green, Joel B., and Mark D. Baker. "Must We Imagine the Atonement in Penal Substitutionary Terms? Questions, Caveats and a Plea." In *The Atonement Debate: Papers from The London Symposium on the Theology of Atonement*, edited by Derek Tidball, David Hilborn, and Justin Thacker, 153-71. Grand Rapids: Zondervan, 2008.

———. *Recovering the Scandal of the Cross*. 2nd ed. Downers Grove, IL: IVP Academic, 2011.

Gregg, Robert C., ed. *Arianism: Historical and Theological Reassessments: Papers from The Ninth International Conference on Patristic Studies*, Oxford, September 5-10, 1983. Philadelphia Patristic Foundation, 1985.

Gregory of Nazianzus. *On God and Christ: The Five Theological Orations and Two Letters to Cledonius*. Crestwood, NY: St. Vladimir's Seminary Press, 2002.

Grudem, Wayne. "Biblical Evidence for the Eternal Submission of the Son to the Father." In *The New Evangelical Subordinationism? Perspectives on the Equality of God the Father and God the Son*, edited by Dennis W. Jowers and H. Wayne House, 223-61. Eugene, OR: Pickwick, 2012.

———. *Evangelical Feminism and Biblical Truth, An Analysis of More Than 100 Disputed Questions*. Wheaton, IL: Crossway, 4004.

———. *Systematic Theology: An Introduction to Biblical Doctrine*. Leicester: Inter-Varsity, 1994.

Grudem, Wayne, and J. Piper, eds. *Recovering Biblical Manhood and Womanhood: A Response to Evangelical Feminism*. Wheaton, IL: Crossway, 1991.

Gunton, Colin. *The Actuality of Atonement: A Study of Metaphor, Rationality, and the Christian Tradition*. London: T. & T. Clark, 1998.

———. "Eastern and Western Trinities: Being and Person." In *Father, Son, and Holy Spirit: Toward a Fully Trinitarian Theology*, 32-57. Edinburgh: T. & T. Clark, 2003.

———. "Persons and Particularity." In *The Theology of John Zizioulas: Personhood and the Church*, edited by D. H. Knight, 97-108. Aldershot: Ashgate, 2007.

Gwatkin, H. M. *Studies in Arianism*. Cambridge: Deighton, Bell, 1882.

Halcrow, Jeremy. "Passionate response to atonement attacks." SydneyAnglicans. net, September 25, 2007. http://your.sydneyanglicans.net/sydneystories/cross_concern_debated/.

Hamerton-Kelly, R. G. "Sacred Violence and the Curse of the Law (Galatians 3.13): The Death of Christ as a Sacrificial Travesty." *New Testament Studies* 36/1 (1990) 98-118.

Hammond, T. C. "Authority in Religion." *Irish Church Quarterly* 9/36 (1916) 287-99.

———. *In Understanding Be Men*. Edited and revised by David F. Wright. London: Inter-Varsity, 1976.

———. *The New Creation*. London: Marshall, Morgan & Scott, 1953.

———. *One Hundred Texts of the Society for Irish Church Missions*. 3rd ed. Society for Irish Church Missions. London: Marshall, Morgan & Scott, 1950.

———. *Perfect Freedom: An Introduction to Christian Ethics*. London: InterVarsity Fellowship of Evangelical Unions, 1938.

———. "Post-Reformation Theology in the Church of Ireland." In *The Church of Ireland AD 432-1932: Report of the Church of Ireland Conference Held in Dublin, 11th-14th October, 1932*, (with an account of the Commemoration by the Church of Ireland of the 1500th Anniversary of the Landing of St Patrick in Ireland), edited by W. Bell and N. C. Emerson, 97-105. Dublin: Church of Ireland, 1933.

———. "The Significance of the Death of Christ." In *From the Manger to the Throne: Outstanding Events in the Life of Our Lord*, edited F. Donald Coggan, 39–49. London: InterVarsity, 1936.

Hanson, R. P. C. "The Arian Doctrine of the Incarnation." In *Arianism: Historical and Theological Reassessments, Papers from The Ninth International Conference on Patristic Studies*, Oxford, September 5–10, 1983, edited by Robert C. Gregg, 181–211. Philadelphia Patristic Foundation, 1985.

———. *The Search for the Christian Doctrine of God: The Arian Controversy 318–381*. Edinburgh: T. & T. Clark, 1988.

Harnack, C. G. Adolf. *History of Dogma*. Translated by Neil Buchanan et al. 7 vols. London: Williams & Norgate, 1894–99.

Hays, R. B. *The Faith of Jesus Christ: The Narrative Substructure of Galatians 3:1–4:11*. Grand Rapids: Eerdmans, 2002.

Hennessy, Kristin. "An Answer to De Régnon's 'Accusers': Why We Should Not Speak of 'His' Paradigm." *Harvard Theological Review* 100/2 (2007) 179–97.

Hick, John. *Evil and the God of Love*. Cambridge: Cambridge University Press, 1967.

Hilborn, David. "Atonement, Evangelism and the Evangelical Alliance: The Present Debate in Context." In *The Atonement Debate: Papers from The London Symposium on the Theology of Atonement*, edited by Derek Tidball et al., 15–33. Grand Rapids: Zondervan, 2008.

Hillis, Gregory K. "Pneumatology and Soteriology according to Gregory of Nazianzus & Cyril of Alexandria." *Studia Patristica* 67 (2013) 187–97.

Hippolytus of Rome. *Contra Noetum*. Edited by R. Butterworth. London: Heythrop College, 1977.

Hodge, A. A. *Outlines of Theology*. New York: Robert Carter and Brothers, 1866 / Princeton 1878. London: Banner of Truth Trust, 1972.

Holmes, Stephen R. "Christology, Scripture, Divine Action, and Hermeneutics." In *Christology and Scripture: Interdisciplinary Perspectives*, edited by Angus Paddison and Andrew T. Lincoln, 156–70. London: T&T Clark, 2007.

———. *Quest for the Trinity: The Doctrine of God in Scripture, History, and Modernity*. Kindle ed. Downers Grove, IL: IVP Academic, 2012.

Horrell, J. Scott. "Complementarian Trinitarianism: Divine Revelation is Finally True to the Eternal Personal Relations." In *The New Evangelical Subordinationism? Perspectives on the Equality of God the Father and God the Son*, edited by Dennis W. Jowers and H. Wayne House, 339–74. Eugene, OR: Pickwick, 2012.

House, H. Wayne. "The Eternal Relational Subordination of the Father to the Son in Patristic Thought." In *The New Evangelical Subordinationism? Perspectives on the Equality of God the Father and God the Son*, edited by Dennis W. Jowers and H. Wayne House, 133–82. Eugene: Pickwick, 2012.

Huttinga, Wolter. *Participation and Communicability: Herman Bavinck and John Milbank on the Relation of God and the World*. Academisch Proefschrift, Theologische Universiteit van de Gereformeerde Kerken in Nederland te Kampen, 2014.

Irenaeus of Lyon. *Against Heresies*. In *The Ante Nicene Fathers*, vol. 1. Edited by Alexander Roberts and James Donaldson. Grand Rapids: Eerdmans, 1973.

Ivánka, E. von. *Plato Christianus: Übernahme und Umgestaltung des Platonismus durch die Väter*. Einsiedeln: Johannes Verlag, 1964.

Jeffery, Steve, Michael Ovey, and Andrew Sach. *Pierced for Our Transgressions: Rediscovering the Glory of Penal Substitution*. Nottingham: InterVarsity, 2007.

Jensen, Michael P. *Sydney Anglicanism: An Apology*. Eugene, OR: Wipf & Stock, 2012.
Jensen, Peter. "The Good News of God's Wrath." *Christianity Today*, March 1, 2004. http://www.christianitytoday.com/ct/2004/march/5.45.html.
———. "T. C. Hammond No Arian: A Response to Peter Carnley." *St Mark's Review* 2/199 (2005) 44–46.
Jensen, Phillip. "Defining the Evangelical." August 12, 2008. SydneyAnglicans.net, http://www.sydneyanglicans.net/archive/indepth/defining_the_evangelical/.
Jenson, Robert. *Systematic Theology*. 2 vols. Oxford: Oxford University Press, 1997 and 1999.
Jewett, P. K. *Man as Male and Female*. Grand Rapids: Eerdmans, 1975.
John, Jeffrey. *Lent Talks: Jeffrey John*, BBC Radio 4 Lent Talks, April 4, 2007. https://web.archive.org/web/20070607085657.
Judd, Stephen, and Kenneth Cable. *Sydney Anglicans*. Sydney: Anglican Information Office, 1987.
Kariatlis, Philip. "The Exercise of Primacy in the Church: An Orthodox Theological Perspective." *Phronema* 26/1 (2011) 27–47.
———. "St Basil's Trinitarian Doctrine: A Harmonious Synthesis of Greek *Paideia* and the Scriptural Worldview." In *Cappadocian Legacy: A Critical Appraisal*, edited by Doru Costache and Philip Kariatlis, 131–154. Sydney: St Andrew's Orthodox, 2013.
Käsemann, Ernst. *Commentary on Romans*. London: SCM, 1994.
Kasper, Walter. *Theology and Church*. Translated by Margaret Kohl. New York: Crossroad, 1989.
Kelly, J. N. D. *Early Christian Doctrines*. Revised ed. San Francisco: HarperCollins, 1978.
King, William. *De Origine Mali*, 1702, translated into English with extensive notes by Edmund Law in 1731 as *An Essay on the Origin of Evil*. London: Printed by F. Stephens for W. Thurlbourn, 1739.
Kierkegaard, Søren. *Sickness unto Death: A Christian Psychological Exposition of Edification and Awakening by Anti-Climacus*. Translated with an Introduction by Alastair Hannay. London: Penguin Classics, 1989.
Kirk, Kenneth. *Commentary of the Epistle to the Romans*. Oxford: Clarendon, 1937.
Klawans, Jonathan. *Purity, Sacrifice, and the Temple: Symbolism and Supersessionism in the Study of Ancient Judaism*. New York: Oxford University Press, 2006.
Knight, Douglas H., ed. *The Theology of John Zizioulas: Personhood and the Church*. Aldershot: Ashgate, 2007.
Knox, D. Broughton. *Selected Works*, 1, *The Doctrine of God*. Edited by Tony Payne. Kingsford: Matthias Media, 2000.
———. *Selected Works*, 2, *Church and Ministry*. Edited by Kirsten Birkett. Kingsford: Matthias Media, 2003.
Knox, John. *The Death of Christ*. London: Collins, 1959.
Koch, Klaus. "Is There a Doctrine of Retribution in the OT?" In *Theodicy in the Old Testament*, edited by James L. Crenshaw, 57–87. Philadelphia: Fortress, 1983.
Koutloumousianos, Chrysostom. *The One and the Three: Nature, Person and Triadic Monarchy in the Greek and Irish Patristic Tradition*. Cambridge: James Clarke, 2015.
LaCugna, Catherine Mowry. *God for Us: The Trinity and Christian Life*. San Francisco: HarperCollins, 1991.

Lansdown, Andrew. "The Carnley Row." *Life News* 640008/00001 (August 2000) 4–5.
Lattier, Daniel J. "John Henry Newman and Georges Florovsky: An Orthodox-Catholic Dialogue on the Development of Doctrine." PhD diss., Duquesne University, 2012.
Leibniz, Gottfried Wilhelm. *Théodicée*. Chicago: Open Court, 1985.
Leslie, Charles. *History of Sin and Heresy* (1698). In *Milton: The Critical Heritage*, 2 vols., edited by John T. Shawcross. London: Routledge, 1970–2.
Letham, Robert. "The *Foedus Operum*: Some Factors Accounting for Its Development." *The Sixteenth Century Journal* 14/4 (Winter 1983) 457–67. https://www-jstor-org.libproxy.murdoch.edu.au/stable/2540578.
———. *The Holy Trinity, in Scripture, History, Theology and Worship*. Rev. and expanded ed. Phillipsburg, NJ: P & R, 2019.
———. "The Man-Woman Debate: Theological Comment." *The Westminster Theological Journal* 52/1 (2009) 65–78.
———. "Reply to Kevin Giles." *Evangelical Quarterly* 80/4 (2008) 339–45.
———. *The Westminster Assembly: Reading Its Theology in Historical Context* (Westminster Assembly and the Reformed Faith). Phillipsburg, NJ: P & R, 2009.
Letham, Robert, and Kevin Giles. "Is the Son Eternally Submissive to the Father?" *Christian Research Journal* 31/1 (2008) 10–21.
Libolt, Clayton. "Synod Affirms Penal Substitutionary Atonement, Does Not Call Denial Heresy." *The Banner*, November 9, 2022. www.thebanner.org/new/2022/06/synod-affirms-penal-substitutionary-atonement.
Lieb, Michael. "Milton and 'Arianism.'" *Religion & Literature* 32/2 (2000) 197–220.
Loke, Andrew T. Review of *The Reconstruction of Resurrection Belief*. *Journal of Theological Studies* 72/2 (2022) 1055–57.
Lossky, Vladimir. *Orthodox Theology: An Introduction*. Translated by Ian and Ihita Kesarcodi-Watson. Crestwood, NY: St. Vladimir's Seminary Press, 1989.
———. *The Mystical Theology of the Eastern Church*. Crestwood, NY: St. Vladimir's Seminary Press, 1976.
———. "Redemption and Deification." In *In the Image and Likeness of God*, edited by John H. Erickson and Thomas E. Bird, 97–110. Crestwood, NY: St. Vladimir's Seminary Press, 1974.
———. "The Theological Notion of the Human Person." In *In the Image and Likeness of God*, edited by John H. Erickson and Thomas E. Bird, 111–23. Crestwood, NY: St Vladimir's Seminary Press, 1974.
———. "The Theology of the Image." In *In the Image and Likeness of God*, edited by John H. Erickson and Thomas E. Bird, 125–39. Crestwood, NY: St. Vladimir's Seminary Press, 1974.
———. *The Vision of God* (*La Vision de Dieu*, 1961). London: Faith, 1964.
Louth, Andrew. "Recent Research on St Maximus the Confessor: A Survey." *SV Theological Quarterly* 42 (1998) 67–84.
Lubardic, Bogdan. "Orthodox Theology of Personhood: A Critical Overview, Part I." *The Expository Times* 122/11 (2011) 521–530.
———. "Orthodox Theology of Personhood: A Critical Overview, Part II." *The Expository Times* 122/12 (2011) 573–81.
Ludlow, Morwenna. *Gregory of Nyssa, Ancient and (Post)modern*. Oxford: Oxford University Press, 2007.
Lyman, Rebecca. "A Topography of Heresy: Mapping the Rhetorical Creation of Arianism." In *Arianism After Arius: Essays on the Development of the Fourth*

Century Trinitarian Conflict, edited by Michel R. Barnes and Daniel H. Williams, 45–62. Edinburgh: T. & T. Clark, 1993.

Mansell, E. L. *The Limits of Religious Thought*. 4th ed. London: John Murray, 1859.

Marshall, I. Howard. *Aspects of the Atonement: Cross and Resurrection in the Reconciling of God and Humanity*. Colorado Springs: Paternoster, 2007.

Matelescu, Sebastian. "Counting Natures and Hypostases: St Maximus the Confessor on the Role of Number in Christology." In *Studia Patristica* lxxxix: Papers presented at the Seventeenth International Conference on Patristic Studies held in Oxford 2015, 15: The Fountain and the Flood: Maximus the Confessor and Philosophical Enquiry, edited by M. Vinzent & S. Mitralexis, 63–78. 2017.

Maxwell, Paul C. "Is There an Authority Analogy between the Trinity and Marriage? Untangling Arguments of Subordination and Ontology in Egalitarian-Complementarian Discourse." *Journal of The Evangelical Theological Society* 59/3 (2016) 541–70.

McCall, Thomas. *Which Trinity? Whose Monotheism? Philosophical and Systematic Theologians on the Metaphysics of Trinitarian Theology*. Grand Rapids: Eerdmans, 2010.

McClymond, Kathryn. *Beyond Sacred Violence: A Comparative Study of Sacrifice*. Baltimore: Johns Hopkins University Press, 2008.

McGowan, Andrew. "Philo and the Materialization of Sacrifice." *Studia Philonica Annual*, 183–204. Atlanta: SBL, 2020.

———. "The Shadow of Arius: Subordinationism Then and Now." *St. Mark's Review* 1/198 (2005) 25–28.

McGowan, Andrew T. B. *The Federal Theology of Thomas Boston*. Dissertation Thesis, University of Aberdeen, 1990. Rutherford Studies in Historical Theology. Edinburgh: Paternoster, 1997.

McIntosh, John A. *Anglican Evangelicalism in Sydney, 1897 to 1953: Nathaniel Jones, D. J. Davies, and T. C. Hammond*. Australian College of Theology Monograph. Eugene, OR: Wipf & Stock, 2018.

McIntyre, John. *The Shape of Soteriology: Studies in the Doctrine of the Death of Christ*. Edinburgh: T. & T. Clark, 1992.

McWilliam, Joanne. "Augustine at Ephesus?" In *One Lord, One Faith, One Baptism: Studies in Christian Ecclesiality and Ecumenism in Honor of J. Robert Wright*, edited by Marsha L. Dutton and Patrick Terrell Gray, 56–67. Grand Rapids: Eerdmans, 2006.

Mercer, Calvin. "*Apostelein* and *Pempein* in John." *New Testament Studies* 36/4 (1990) 619–24.

Mesyats, Svetlana. "Does the First have a hypostasis? Some remarks to the History of the term hypostasis in Platonic and Christian Tradition of the 4th–5th cent. AD." *Studia Patristica* LXII, Papers presented at the Sixteenth International Conference on Patristic Studies held in Oxford, 2011, edited by Marcus Vinzent, 41–56. 2013.

Millare, Roland. "Towards a Common Communion: The Relational Anthropologies of John Zizioulas and Karol Wojtyla." *New Blackfriars* 98/1077 (August, 2016) 599–614. https://doi.org/10.1111/nbfr.12056.

Milton, John. *De Doctrina Christiana*. In *The Complete Prose Works of John Milton*, vol. VIII, edited by John K. Hale and J. Donald Cullington. Oxford: Oxford University Press, 2012.

———. *Paradise Lost*. Arranged and edited by G. M. Davis. London: G. Bell and Sons 1981.

———. *A Treatise on Christian Doctrine*. Translated by Charles R. Sumner. Cambridge: Cambridge University Press for Charles Knight, 1825.

Molnar, Paul D. *Divine Freedom and the Doctrine of the Immanent Trinity: In Dialogue with Karl Barth and Contemporary Theology*. Edinburgh: T. & T. Clark, 2002.

———. "The Function of the Immanent Trinity in the Theology of Karl Barth: Implications for Today." *Scottish Journal of Theology* 42/3 (1989) 367–99.

Moltmann, Jürgen. "Political Theology." *Theology Today* 28 (1971) 6–23.

———. *The Trinity and the Kingdom* (1980). Translated by Margaret Kohl. London: SCM Press, 1981.

Morris, Leon. "Atonement." In *New Dictionary of Theology*, edited by Sinclair B. Ferguson and David F. Wright, 54–57. Leicester: Inter-Varsity, 1988.

———. "Atonement." In *Evangelical Dictionary of Theology*, edited by Walter A. Elwell, 113–14. Grand Rapids: Baker Academic, 2001.

———. *The Apostolic Preaching of the Cross*. Grand Rapids: Eerdmans, 1965.

———. *The Atonement: Its Meaning and Significance*. Leicester: Inter-Varsity, 1983.

———. *The Cross in the New Testament*. Exeter: Paternoster, 1976.

———. *The Epistle to the Romans*. Grand Rapids: Eerdmans, 1988.

———. *New Testament Theology*. Grand Rapids: Zondervan, 1990.

Mortenson, Terry. "Genesis 2:17—'You Shall Surely Die.'" *Answers in Genesis* (blog). May 2, 2007; again featured on November 24, 2015. https://answersingenesis.org/death-before-sin/genesis-2-17-you-shall-surely-die/.

Moule, C. F. D. "Further Reflections on Philippians 2.5–11." In *History and the Gospel*, edited by W. Ward Gasque and Ralph R. Martin, 264–76. Exeter, UK: Paternoster, 1970.

Mounier, Emmanuel. *The Personalist Manifesto*. London: Longmans, Green, 1952.

Nelson, Warren. *T. C. Hammond: Irish Christian–His Life & Legacy in Ireland and Australia*. Edinburgh: The Banner of Truth Trust, 1994.

Newman, John Henry. *The Arians of the Fourth Century*. London: Basil Montagu Pickering, 1876.

Nicole, Roger. "Postscript on Penal Substitution." In *The Glory of the Atonement: Biblical, Theological and Practical Perspectives: Essays in Honor of Roger Nicole*, edited by C. E. Hill and F. A. James III, 445–52. Downers Grove, IL: InterVarsity, 2004.

Normann, F. *Teilhabe–ein Schlüsselwort der Vätertheologie*. Münster: Aschendorff, 1978.

Novatian. *On the Trinity*. In *Ante-Nicene Fathers*, vol. 5, translated by Robert Ernest Wallis, edited by Alexander Roberts et. al. Buffalo: Christian Literature, 1886. Revised and edited for New Advent by Kevin Knight. http://www.newadvent.org/fathers/0511.htm.

Nüssel, Friederike. "Die Sühneverstellung in der Hassischen Dogmatikund ihre neuzeitliche Problemutisierung." In *Deutengen des Todes Jesu in Neuen Testament*, edited by Jörg Frey and Jens Schriter, 73–94. WUNT 181. Tübingen: Mohr Siebeck, 2005.

Nuttall, A. D. *The Alternative Trinity: Gnostic Heresy in Marlowe, Milton and Blake*. Oxford: Clarendon, 1998.

O'Brien, P. T. "Was Paul a Covenantal Nomist?" In *Justification and Variegated Nomism*, vol. 2, *The Paradoxes of Paul*, edited by D. A. Carson et al., 249–96. Grand Rapids: Baker Academic, 2004.

Otto, Randall. "Moltmann and the Anti-Monotheist Movement." *International Journal of Systematic Theology* 3/3 (2001) 293–308.

Ovey, Michael. *Your Will Be Done: Exploring Eternal Subordination, Divine Monarchy and Divine Humility*. London: Latimer Trust, 2016.

Owen, John. "The Death of Death in the Death of Christ." *The Works of John Owen*, vol. 10, edited by William H. Goold. Edinburgh: The Banner of Truth Trust, 1967.

———. "The Federal Transactions between the Father and the Son" In *The Works of John Owen*, vol. 19, edited by William H. Goold, 77–97. Edinburgh: The Banner of Truth Trust, 1967.

Packer, J. I. "Anger." In *New Dictionary of Biblical Theology*, edited by T. Desmond Alexander and Brian S. Rosner, 381–83. Downers Grove, IL: InterVarsity, 2000.

———. "The Atonement in the Life of the Christian." In *The Glory of the Atonement: Biblical, Theological and Practical Perspectives: Essays in Honor of Roger Nicole*, edited by C. E. Hill and F. A. James III, 409–25. Downers Grove, IL: InterVarsity, 2004.

———. "What Did the Cross Achieve? The Logic of Penal Substitution." In *The J. I. Packer Collection*, edited by Alister McGrath, 109–11. Downers Grove, IL: InterVarsity, 1999.

Panagopoulos, John. "Ontology or Theology of Person." *Synaxis* 13–14 (1985) 35–47; 63–79.

Pannenberg, Wolfhart. "Divine Economy and Eternal Trinity." In *The Theology of John Zizioulas*, edited by Douglas H. Knight, 79–86. Aldershot: Ashcroft, 2007.

Papanikolaou, Aristotle. *Being with God: Trinity, Apophaticism, and Divine-Human Communion*. Notre Dame: University of Notre Dame Press, 2006.

———. "From Sophia to Personhood: The Development of 20th Century Orthodox Trinitarian Theology." *Phronema* 33/2 (2018) 1–20. https://aristotlepapanikolaou.academia.edu/.

———. "Is John Zizioulas an Existentialist in Disguise? Response to Lucian Turcescu." *Modern Theology* 20/4 (October 2004) 601–7.

———. "Personhood and its exponents in twentieth-century Orthodox theology." In *The Cambridge Companion to Orthodox Christian Theology*, edited by M. B. Cunningham and E. Theokritoff, 232–45. Cambridge: Cambridge University Press, 2008.

Pedersen, Johannes. *Israel: Its Life and Culture*. 2 vols. Translated by H. Milford. Oxford: Oxford University Press, 1926.

Perkins, Harrison. *Catholicity and the Covenant of Works, James Ussher and the Reformed Tradition*. Oxford: Oxford University Press, 2020.

Perkins, William. *The Works of Mr William Perkins*. Edited by Randall J. Pederson and Ryan M. Hurd. Grand Rapids: Reformation Heritage, 2017.

Peters, Ted. *GOD as Trinity, Relationality and Temporality in Divine Life*. Louisville: Westminster John Knox, 1993.

Peterson, Derrick. "A Forgetfulness Which Appears as Memory: The Invention of Classical Theism, the De Régnon Paradigm, and Augustine's Place in Contemporary Trinitarian Historiography." Thesis, Multnomah Biblical Seminary, 2014. PDF filed by bounce.academia-mail.com.

———. "A Loud Absence: T. F. Torrance in Light of Recent Patristic Scholarship." *Participatio: The Journal of the T. F. Torrance Fellowship*, forthcoming.
Peterson, Erik. *Der Monotheismus als politisches Problem: Ein Beitrag zur Geschichte der politischen Theologie im Imperium Romanum*. Leipzig: Jakob Hegner, 1935.
Philo of Alexandria. *De Specialibus Legibus*. In *Philo of Alexandria: An Annotated Bibliography, 1937-86, 1987-96, and 1997-2006*, edited by Roberto Radice and David T. Runia, Supplements to Vigiliae Christianae 8, 57, and 109. Leiden: Brill, 1992, 2000, and 2012.
Portaru, Marius. "Gradual Participation According to St Maximus the Confessor." *Studia Patristrica*, lxviii' Papers presented to the Sixteenth International Conference on Patristic Studies, Oxford, 2011, edited by Markus Vinzent, 281-93. Leuven: Peeters, 2013.
Porter, Lawrence B. "On Keeping 'Persons' in the Trinity: A Linguistic Approach to Trinitarian Thought." *Theological Studies* 41/3 (1980) 530-49.
Rahner, Karl. *The Trinity*. Translated by Joseph Donceel. Tonbridge Wells: Burns & Oates, 1970.
Reid, Duncan. "The Trinity and Subordinationism: The Doctrine of God and the Contemporary Gender Debate." In *The Australian Theological Book Review OnLine*. www.atbr.openbook.com.au.
Rengstorf, K. H. "*apostello (pempo).*" In *Theological Dictionary of the New Testament*, translated by Geoffrey W. Bromiley and edited by Gerhard Kittel, 1:398-406. Grand Rapids: Eerdmans, 1964.
Richardson, Alan, ed. *A Dictionary of Christian Theology*. London: SCM, 1969.
Ricoeur, Paul. *Interpretation Theory: Discourse and the Surplus of Meaning*. Fort Worth, TX: Texas Christian University Press, 1976.
———. *La Métaphore vive*. Paris: Seuil, 1975/*The Rule of Metaphor, The Creation of Meaning in Language* (1977), translated by Robert Czerny with Kathleen McLaughlin and John Costello. London: Routledge, 2003.
Rimmer, Chad. "Poetic Participation: Re-narrating a Lutheran concept of faith and works by comparing the writings of John Milbank and Tuomo Mannermaa." MTh diss., University of Edinburgh, 2010.
Rollock, Robert. *Tractatus de vocatione efficaci*. Edinburgh: Waldegrave, 1597. English trans.: *Select Works of Robert Rollock*, 2 vols., translated and edited by William Gunn. Edinburgh: The Wodrow Society, 1849.
Rosenthal, James M., and Nicola Currie. *The Virginia Report*. In *Being Anglican in the Third Millennium: The Official Report of the 10th Meeting of the Anglican Consultative Council*, 211-81. Harrisburg: Morehouse, 1997.
Rumrich, John P. *Milton Unbound: Controversy and Reinterpretation*. Cambridge: Cambridge University Press, 1996.
Rutledge, Fleming. *The Crucifixion: Understanding the Death of Jesus Christ*. Grand Rapids: Eerdmans, 2015.
Sanders, Fred. *The Image of the Immanent Trinity: Rahner's Rule and the Theological Interpretation of Scripture*. New York: Peter Lang, 2004.
———. "A Plain Account of Trinity and Gender." June 17, 2016. http://scriptoriumdaily.com/a-plain-account-of-trinity-and-gender/.
Schoonenberg, Piet. "'He Emptied Himself': Philippians 2:7." *Concillium* 1/1 (1965) 47-66.
———. "The Kenosis or Self-Emptying of Christ." *Concillium* 1/2 (1966) 27-36.

Schreiner, Thomas R. "Head Coverings, Prophecies and the Trinity: I Corinthians 11.2–16." In *Recovering Biblical Manhood and Womanhood: A Response to Evangelical Feminism*, edited by John Piper and Wayne Grudem, 124–39. Wheaton, IL: Crossway, 2006.

———. "Penal Substitution View." In *The Nature of the Atonement: Four Views*, edited by James Beilby and Paul R. Eddy, 67–98. Downers Grove, IL: InterVarsity, 2006.

Schreiner, Thomas R., and Andreas J. Koestenberger, eds. *Women in the Church: An Interpretation and Application of 1 Timothy 2:9–15*. 3rd ed. Wheaton, IL: Crossway, 2016.

Seifrid, Mark. "Paul's Use of Righteousness Language against Its Hellenistic Background." In *Justification and Variegated Nomism*, vol. 2, edited by D. A. Carson et al., 39–74. Grand Rapids: Baker Academic, 2004.

Shiner, Rory. *One Forever: The Transforming Power of Being In Christ*. Sydney: Matthias Media, 2015.

Shiner, Rory, and Peter Orr. *The World Next Door: A Short Guide to the Christian Faith*. Sydney: Matthias Media, 2021.

Skliris, Dionysios. "Synodical Ontology: Maximus the Confessor's proposition for Ontology, within History and in the Eschaton." In *Christian and Islamic Philosophies of Time*, edited by Sotiris Mitralexis and Marcin Podbielski, 85–117. Wilmington, DE: Vernon, 2018.

Smail, Tom. *Like Father, Like Son: The Trinity Imagined in Our Humanity*. Grand Rapids: Eerdmans, 2005.

Soskice, Janet Martin. Metaphor and Religious Language. Oxford: Oxford University Press, 1987.

Staff Writers. "Religions split on stem cell issue." https//www.labonline.com au/content/life-scientist/news/religions-split-on-stem-cell-issue-599169430.

Stamps, Luke. "The New Evangelical Subordinationism? Perspectives on the Equality of God the Father and God the Son." *Journal of the Evangelical Theological Society* 59/4 (2016) 874–81.

Steenson, J. N. "Basil of Ancyra on the Meaning of Homoousios." In *Arianism: Historical and Theological Reassessments, Papers from The Ninth International Conference on Patristic Studies*, Oxford, September 5–10, 1983, edited by Robert C. Gregg, 267–79. Philadelphia: Patristic Foundation, 1985.

Stott, John. *The Cross of Christ*. Downers Grove, IL: InterVarsity, 1986.

———. "The Patriarch (Abraham)." A Sermon from Genesis 12:1–9, preached on April 6, 1986. London: Langham Place Media, 1986.

Sullivan, F. A. "Comment on *Church as Communion*." Pontifical Council for Promoting Christian Unity, *Information Service* 77 (1991–1992) 97–102.

Swinburne, Richard. "Christ's Atoning Sacrifice." In *Philosophical Theology and the Christian Tradition: Russian and Western Perspectives*, edited by David Bradshaw, 21–29. Russian Philosophical Studies V, Christian Philosophical Studies III, Series IVA, Eastern and Central Europe, Volume 44, Series VIII, Christian Philosophical Studies 3. Washington DC: The Council for Research in Values and Philosophy, 2012.

———. *Revelation*. Oxford: Clarendon, 1992.

Sydney Doctrine Commission. "The Doctrine of the Trinity and its bearing on the relationship of men and women." Reports to Synod, document 18, 1999. https://www.sds.asn.au/reports-received-synod-1999.

———. "Penal substitutionary atonement." Report to Synod, Referral 36/07; 2010. https://www.sds.asn.au/sites/default/files/PenalSubstitutionaryAtonement.Doc Commission.%2836.07%29%20%282010%29.pdf?doc_id=NDE1NTA=.

Sykes, S. W. "Outline of a Theology of Sacrifice." In *Sacrifice and Redemption: Durham Essays in Theology*, edited by S. W. Sykes, 282–98. Cambridge: Cambridge University Press, 1991.

Taylor, John V. *The Go-Between God: The Holy Spirit and the Christian Mission*. New ed. London: SCM Classics, 2002.

Thompson, John. *Modern Trinitarian Perspectives*. Oxford: Oxford University Press, 1994.

Tidball, Derek, David Hilborn, and Justin Thacker, eds. *The Atonement Debate: Papers from The London Symposium on the Theology of Atonement*. Grand Rapids: Zondervan, 2008.

Tilling, Chris. *Beyond Old and New Perspectives on Paul: Reflections on the Work of Douglas Campbell*. Cambridge: James Clarke, 2014.

Tinkham, Matthew L., Jr. "Neo-Subordinationism: The Alien Argumentation in the Gender Debate." *Andrews University Seminary Studies* 55/2 (2017) 237–90.

Tollefsen, Torstein Theodore. *The Christocentric Cosmology of St Maximus the Confessor*. Oxford: Oxford University Press, 2008.

———. "Did St Maximus the Confessor have a Concept of Participation?" *Studia Patristica* 37 (2001) 618–25.

Torrance, Alan J. *Persons in Communion, Trinitarian Description and Human Participation*. Edinburgh: T. & T. Clark, 1996.

———. "The Trinity." In *The Cambridge Companion to Karl Barth*, edited by John Webster, 72–91. Cambridge: Cambridge University Press, 2000.

Torrance, James B. "Covenant or Contract? A Study in the Theological Background of Worship in Seventeenth-Century Scotland." *Scottish Journal of Theology* 23 (1970) 51–76.

Torrance, Thomas F. *The Christian Doctrine of God: One Being Three Persons*. Edinburgh: T. & T. Clark, 1996.

———. *The Trinitarian Faith*. Edinburgh: T. & T. Clark, 1988.

Treloar, Geoffrey R. "T. C. Hammond the Controversialist." *Anglican Historical Society, Diocese of Sydney, Journal* 51 (2006) 20–35.

Turcescu, Lucian. "'Person' versus 'Individual', and Other Modern Misreadings of Gregory of Nyssa." *Modern Theology* 18/4 (October 2002) 97–109.

Ullucci, Daniel C. *The Christian Rejection of Animal Sacrifice*. New York: Oxford University Press, 2012.

Ussher, James. *Answer to a Jesuit; With Other Tracts on Popery*. Cambridge: Pitt, 1835, reproduced by BiblioLife.

———. "Eighteen Sermons Preached at Oxford. 1640." In *The Whole Works of the Most Rev. James Ussher*, XIII. Miami: HardPress, 2017.

Vanhoozer, Kevin. *Is There a Meaning in This Text? The Bible, the Reader, and the Morality of Literary Knowledge*. Grand Rapids: Zondervan, 1998.

Wainwright, Geoffrey. *Doxology: The Praise of God in Worship, Doctrine and Life*. London: Epworth, 1980.

Ware, Bruce A. "Does Affirming an Eternal Authority-Submission Relationship in the Trinity Entail a Denial of *Homoousios*?" In *One God in Three Persons, Unity of Essence, Distinction of Persons, Implications for Life*, edited by Bruce A. Ware and John Starke, 237–48. Wheaton, IL: Crossway, 2015.

———. "Equal in Essence, Distinct Roles." In *The New Evangelical Subordinationism? Perspectives on the Equality of God the Father and God the Son*, edited by Dennis W. Jowers and H. Wayne House, 13-38. Eugene, OR: Pickwick, 2012.
———. *Father, Son, and Holy Spirit: Relationships, Roles, and Relevance*. Wheaton, IL: Crossway, 2005.
———. "The Trinity and Subordinationism: The Doctrine of God and the Contemporary Gender Debate by Kevin Giles." *Religious Studies Review* 4/29 (2003) 355.
Ware, Bruce A., and John Starke, eds. *One God in Three Persons: Unity of Essence, Distinctions of Persons, Implications for Life*. Wheaton, IL: Crossway, 2015.
Weir, David. *The Origins of the Federal Theology in 16th-Century Reformation Thought*. Oxford: Clarendon, 1990.
Whitefield, George. "Sermons Preached by the Rev. George Whitefield in the High Church-Yard, Glasgow." In *The Revivals of the Eighteenth Century*, edited by D. MacFarlan. Wheaton, IL: Richard Owen Roberts, 1980.
Whitehead, A. N. *Process and Reality*. New York: Harper and Row, 1929.
Whitfield, Keith S., ed. *Trinitarian Theology*. Nashville: B & H, 2019.
Wilckens, Ulrich. "Exkurs: Das Gerich nach den Werken I (Traditionsgeschichtliche Voraussetzungen)." In *Der Brief an Römer (Rom 1–5)*, 127–31. EKK, Evangelisch-katholischer Kommentar zum Neuen Testatment. Neukirchen-Vluyn: Neukirchener Verlag, 1978.
Wiles, Maurice. *Archetypal Heresy: Arianism Through the Centuries*. Oxford: Oxford University Press, 1966.
———. "In Defence of Arius." *Journal of Theological Studies*, n.s., XIII, 10/1962, 339–47.
Williams, Garry J. "Penal Substitution: A Response to Recent Criticisms." *Journal of the Evangelical Theological Society* 50/1 (March 2007) 71–86. Also in *The Atonement Debate: Papers from the London Symposium on the Theology of Atonement*, edited by Derek Tidball, David Hilborn, and Justin Thacker, 172–91. Grand Rapids: Zondervan, 2008.
Williams, Rowan. *Arius: Heresy and Tradition*. Rev. ed. Grand Rapids: Eerdmans, 2002.
Wood, Maxwell Thomas. "Penal Substitution in the Construction of British Evangelical Identity: Controversies in the Doctrine of the Atonement in the mid-2000s." PhD thesis, Durham University, 2011.
Wright, David. "Dr Carnley on T C Hammond and Arianism." *St Mark's Review* 1/199 (2005) 46–48.
Wright, N. T. "The Cross and the Caricatures: A Response to Robert Jenson, Jeffrey John, and a New Volume Entitled *Pierced for Our Transgressions*." Eastertide. https://www.fulcrum-anglican.org.uk/articles/the-cross-and-the-caricatures/.
———. *Evil and the Justice of God*. London: SPCK, 2006.
———. *Jesus and the Victory of God*. London: SPCK, 1996.
———. *Paul and the Faithfulness of God*. Minneapolis: Fortress, 2013.
———. "Redemption from the New Perspective? Towards a Multi-Layered Pauline Theology of the Cross." In *The Redemption*, edited by Stephen T. Davis, Daniel Kendall, and Gerald O'Collins, 69–100. Oxford: Oxford University Press, 2004.
———. *What Saint Paul Really Said: Was Paul of Tarsus the Real Founder of Christianity?* Oxford: Lion, 1997.
Yandell, Keith. "How Many Times Does Three Go Into One?" In *Philosophical and Theological Essays on the Trinity*, edited by Thomas McCall and Michael C. Rea, 151–68. Oxford: Oxford University Press, 2009.

Yang, Hongyi. *A Development Not a Departure: The Lacunae in the Debate of the Doctrine of the Trinity and Gender Roles*. Phillipsburg, NJ: P&R, 2018.

Yates, Roy. "Colossians 2.15: Christ Triumphant." *New Testament Studies* 37/4 (October 1991) 573–91. DOI: https://doi.org/10.1017/S0028688500021962.

Zachuber, Johannes. "Individuality and the Theological Debate about 'Hypostasis.'" In *Individuality in Late Antiquity*, edited Alexis Torrance and Johannes Zachhuber, 91–109. Taylor and Francis Group, 2014. ProQuest Ebookcentral,proquest.com/lib/oxford/detail.action?docID=1589641.

Zizioulas, John D. "The Being of God and the Being of Anthropos." *Synaxis* 37 (1991) 11–35.

———. *Being as Communion*. London: Darton, Longman and Todd, 1985.

———. *Communion and Otherness*. Edited by Paul McPartlan. London: T. & T. Clark, 2006.

———. "Human Capacity and Human Incapacity." *Scottish Journal of Theology* 28 (1975) 401–8.

AUTHOR INDEX

Adam, Peter, 235
Agourides, Savas, 235
Alston, William P., 235
Armitage, Chris, 235
Asslet, W. J. van, 235
Awad, Najeeb G., 235
Ayres, Lewis, 235

Baker, Mark D., 54, 54n66, 55n1, 59n9, 107, 107n1, 108n5, 115, 115n15/16/17/18/19, 116, 136, 136n13, 212, 212n72/73, 241
Barnes, Michel René, 223n15, 236, 245
Barth, Karl, 3–4, 9n11, 11n16, 20, 22, 22n34, 165, 224n16, 236, 246, 250
Barton, John, 236
Bauman, Michael, 236
Beilby, James, 236, 249
Bell, W., 241
Bilezikian, Gilbert, 236
Billings, Todd, 204, 204n58/59, 236
Bird, Michael F., 21n33, 236, 240
Bird, Thomas E., 244
Black, Max, 189, 189n19, 236
Blocher, H., 135, 135n10, 189, 189n20/21, 190–93, 190n25/26/27, 191n29/30/31, 192n32/34/35/36, 193n37, 195, 195n41/42, 196–97, 196n44, 197n45/4, 236
Boersma, Hans, 236
Boff, Leonardo, 236
Bonneau, Normand, 165n23, 236
Boyd, Gregory A., 99n72, 236

Brain, Peter, 164–65, 164n19, 165n20, 236
Brent, Alan, 237
Bromiley, G. W., 236, 237, 248
Bugár, István M., 219–20, 220n7/8, 229–30, 230n32/33, 237
Bulgakov, Sergius, 158n11, 237
Burkert, Walter, 237
Butner, D. Glenn, Jr., 237

Cable, Kenneth J., 237, 243
Carnley, Peter, ix, xiin5, xiv, 51, 236, 236, 237, 243, 244, 251
  elected Primate, 27–28
  Primatial inauguration, 32–33
  Arius on Carillon Avenue, xn3, 1, 1n1, 129n41, 166n24, 237
  Reflections in Glass, xii, xiin5, 10, 10n12, 11n13/14/15, 28, 29n6, 30–31, 49, 49n53, 50–51, 51n55, 55n1, 154–55, 239
  The Yellow Wallpaper and Other Sermons, 32n15, 237
Carson, D. A., 47, 47n51, 77–79, 78n13/14/, 84, 84n32, 91, 237, 240, 247
Cave, William, 238
Chalke, Steve, 25, 51–52, 51n58/59, 52n60/61, 53, 53n63, 106–07, 108, 109, 110, 130, 175
  on God and "cosmic child abuse," 107, 109, 109n8, 238
  "Cross Purposes," 175n32, 238
  The Lost Message of Jesus, 51, 51n58/59, 52, 109n8, 238

Church of England Doctrine Report
   (1938)
  Doctrine in the Church of England,
   137–38, 137n16/17, 138n18/19,
   238
Claunch, Kyle, 238
Coakley, Sarah, 187n12, 217, 217n1/2,
   218, 218n3, 220, 228n26, 238
Cocceius, John, 235, 238
Congar, Yves, 20, 21, 21n32, 238
Cranfield, Charles E. B., 114, 114n14,
   139, 139n22, 238
Cross, F. L., 238
Currie, Nicola, 248
Cvetkovic, Vladimir, 238

Davis, G. M., 24
Davis, Stephen T., 238, 239, 251
Del Colle, Ralph, 238
Denaux, Adelbert, 238
Devlin, Patrick Lord, 238
Dillistone, F. W., 238
Dixhoorn, Chad B. van, 239
Donaldson, James, 242
Donaldson, T., 165n23, 239
Donfried, K., 205n60, 239
Dorner, I. A., 239
Doyle, Robert, 8, 239
   his use of "Rahner's Rule," 8–16,
    9n11, 10n12, 11n13/14/15/16,
    20,23, 145n26
   on God being "limited by the law of
    his own being," 154–55, 154n6,
    155n7
   "Use and abuse of the fathers"
    (review of Giles's *Trinity and
    Subordinationism*), 239
   review of Carnley, "Reflections in
    Glass, Ch. 7," 154n6, 155n7, 239
Dunn, James G. D., 46–47,
   47n46/47/48, 48, 239

Eberhart, Christian, 239
Eddy, Paul R., 236, 249
Emerson, Matthew Y., 239
Emerson, N. C., 241
Erickson, John H., 244
Erickson, Millard, 239

Farrow, D., 226n21, 239
Fee, Gordon D., 180, 180n37, 239
Fiddes, Paul, 239
Filonenko, Alexander, 239
Fokin, Alexey, 240
Forsyth, Robert, 53n65, 240
Frame, John, 240
Frame, Tom, 28–31, 28n5, 29n6/7,
   30n9/10/11, 35, 49, 240

Gathercole, S. J., 78, 78n15/16, 79,
   79n17, 81n21, 85–100, 86n37,
   87n43, 88n44/45/46/47/48,
   89n49/50/51, 91n57, 93n59,
   94n60/63, 95n64/67, 103,
   103n75/76, 105, 240
Gilders, William K., 240
Giles, Kevin, 4, 6, 10, 236, 239, 240,
   244, 251
   Arianism of Sydney Doctrine
    Commission, xn1
   The Trinity and Subordinationism,
    xn1, 4n4, 6n7, 10
   Jesus and the Father, xn1
   *Rise and Fall of the
    Complementarian Doctrine of
    the Trinity*, xn1
Goligher, Liam, 1n1, 240
Gons, Philip, 240
Grabowski, John, 240
Green, Joel B., 54, 54n66, 55n1, 59n9,
   107, 107n1, 108n5, 115,
   115n15/16/17/18/19, 116, 136,
   136n13, 212, 212n72/73, 241
Gregg, Robert C., 241, 242, 249
Grudem, Wayne, 241, 249
Gunton, Colin, 46, 46n45, 48, 59, 59n8,
   188n15, 226n21, 235,241
Gwatkin, H. M., 241

Halcrow, Jeremy, 35, 51n55, 241
Hamerton-Kelly, R. G., 165n23, 241
Hammond, T. C., x, xn3, 237, 241,243,
   245, 246, 250, 251
   his federal theology, xn3, 41n30, 46,
    46n44, 70, 71, 112n11, 118–19,
    119n28, 133n4
   influence of James Ussher, xi

influence of A. A. Hodge, xi
influence on formation of "Sydney Anglicanism," x–xi, 71
In Understanding Be Men, 46n44, 168n25, 178n34, 241
on theological liberalism (as "Pelagian"), 44–45, 44n38/39,45n40/41, 183, 183n2
on theological importance of law and justice, 41n30, 44, 46, 168, 168n25, 178n34
denial of "eternal offering" of Christ's sacrifice, 200n52
on substitutionary atonement, 132–33, 133n4, 200n52
Hanson, R. P. C., 242
Harrower, Scott, 21n33, 236
Hays, R.B., 207n63, 242
Hennessy, Kristin, 223n15, 242
Hick, John, 64n16, 174n30, 242
Hilborn, David, 43, 43n37, 52n62,53n63, 241, 242, 250, 251
Hillis, Gregory K., 242
Hodge, A. A., xi, 242
Hodge, Charles, xi
Holmes, Stephen R., 13, 13n18, 21n33, 242
Horrell, J. Scott, 242
House, H. Wayne, 241, 242, 251
Huttinga, Wolter, 204, 204n57, 242

Ivánka, E. von, 242_

Jeffery, Steve, 25, 43, 43n33, 73–82, 73n2, 74n4/6/7, 75n8/9, 77n10/11, 81n24, 82n25/26, 84n29/30/31, 85n34, 108n6, 201, 201n53, 242
Jensen, Michael P., 242
Jensen, Archbishop Peter, 28n2, 29, 42, 42n31/32, 53, 56n3, 131–35, 131n1, 133n6, 135n9,142, 154n5, 164, 164n18, 165n21, 243
Jensen, Phillip, 36–37, 36n19, 42, 42n32
Jenson, Robert, 12, 15, 232n38, 243, 251
Jewett, P. K., 243

John, Jeffrey, (Dean of St Albans), 25, 51, 51n56, 107–08, 114, 136, 138, 243
Judd, Stephen, 243

Kariatlis, Philip, 243
Käsemann, Ernst, 86n36, 90–91, 90n53/54/55, 91n56, 95, 95n66, 243
Kasper, Walter, 20, 243
Kelly, J. N. D., 243
Kendall, Daniel, 251
Kierkegaard, Søren, 228, 231n36, 243
Kirk, Kenneth, 45n42, 243
Klawans, Jonathan, 243
Knight, Douglas H., 239, 241, 243, 247
Knox, D. Broughton, 243
Knox, John, 86n36, 97, 97n69/70/71, 102, 102n74, 243
Koch, Klaus, 87, 87n42, 88, 243
Koestenberger, Andreas J., 249
Koutloumousianos, Chrysostom, 243

LaCugna, Catherine Mowry, 15–20, 19n28/29/30/31, 243
Lansdown, Andrew, 244
Lattier, Daniel J., 244
Leibniz, Gottfried Wilhelm, 64n16, 244
Leslie, Charles, 244
Letham, Robert, 240, 244
Libolt, Clayton, 244
Lieb, Michael, 244
Loke, Andrew T., 244
Livingstone, E. A., 238
Lossky, Vladimir, 38n23, 157, 157n8, 158, 158n9/10/13, 244
Louth, Andrew, 244
Lubardić, Bogdan, 244
Ludlow, Morwenna, 244
Lyman, Rebecca, 244

Mann, Alan, 51, 51n58/59, 52, 52n60, 109n8, 238
Mansell, E.L., 245
Marshall, I. Howard, 190–91, 191n28, 245
Matelescu, Sebastian, 245
Maxwell, Paul C., 245

McCall, Thomas, 245, 251
McClymond, Kathryn, 194n39, 245
McGowan, Andrew, 193, 194n39, 245
McGowan, Andrew T. B., 245
McIntosh, John A., 245
McIntyre, John, 40n28, 245
McPartlan, Paul, 252
McWilliam, Joanne, 245
Mercer, Calvin, 245
Mesyats, Svetlana, 245
Millare, Roland, 245
Molnar, Paul D., 15n21, 20, 22–23, 22n34, 23n35, 246
Moltmann, Jürgen, 12, 15, 237, 246, 247
Morris, Leon, 152n1, 246
Moule, C. F. D., 246
Mounier, Emmanuel, 227, 227n25, 228, 246

Naselli, Andrew, 240
Nelson, Warren, 246
Newman, John Henry, 244, 246
Nicole, Roger, 43, 43n34, 246, 247
Normann, F., 246
Nüssel, Friederike, 246
Nuttall, A. D., 246

O'Brien, P. T., 73n2, 96, 96n68, 247
O'Colllins, Gerald., S. J., 251
Ovey, Michael, 25, 73, 73n2, 74n4/6/7, 75n8/9, 77n10/11, 78, 81n24, 82n25/26, 84n29/30/31, 85n34, 108, 108n6, 113, 201n53, 242, 247
Orr, Peter, 249
Otto, Randall, 247

Packer, J. I., 43, 43n35/36, 59n9, 136, 136n12, 247
Panagopoulos, John, 226, 228, 247
Pannenberg, Wolhart, 12, 15, 16–18, 16n22, 17n23/24/25/27, 20, 21, 23, 247
Papanikolaou, Aristotle, 158, 158n11/12, 227, 227n23, 234, 234n39, 247
Pedersen, Johannes, 86, 86n38/39, 87, 92, 247

Perkins, Harrison, 247
Peters, Ted, 247
Peterson, Derrick, 7n8, 247
Peterson, Erik, 32, 247
Portaru, Marius, 248
Porter, Lawrence B., 248

Rahner, Karl, 3, 5–24, 5n5, 6n6, 8n10, 11n16, 12n17, 15n21, 105, 145n26, 162, 176–78, 210, 248
Reid, Duncan, 248
Renan, Ernst, 197
Rengstorf, K. H., 248
Richardson, Alan, 248
Ricoeur, Paul, 188–89, 188n16, 189n17, 197, 248
Rimmer, Chad, 248
Roberts, Alexander, 242
Rosenthal, James M., 248
Rutledge, Fleming, 248

Sach, Andrew, 25, 43n33, 73, 74n4/6/7, 75n8/9, 77n10/11, 78, 81n24, 82n25/26, 84n29/30/31, 85n34, 108n6, 201n53, 242
Sanders, Fred, 7, 7n9, 15n21, 20, 22, 248
Shillaker, Robert, 236, 240
Schoonenberg, Piet, 15, 248
Schreiner, Thomas R., 79, 79n18/19, 99n72, 249
Seifrid, Mark A., 100, 100n73, 249, 249
Shiner, Rory, 135, 135n11, 249
Skliris, Dionysios, 249
Smail, Tom, 249
Soskice, Janet Martin, 189, 189n18/21, 249
Stamps, Luke, 239, 249
Starke, John, 238, 240, 250, 251
Steenson, J. N., 249
Stott, John, 66–67, 66n19, 67n20, 107, 107n2, 116, 116n20, 249
Sullivan, F. A., 249
Swinburne, Richard, 57n4, 249
Sydney Doctrine Commission, 1n1, 8, 11,49, 50, 50n54, 52, 53–55, 60n12, 63n13, 64, 66, 70–71, 73, 73n1/2, 85, 106–07, 110,

112, 116, 116n22, 124, 128, 152, 152n1, 153n2, 249
Sykes, S. W., 115, 115n16/17, 116, 250

Taylor, John V., 179, 179n35, 250
Thacker, Justin, 52n62, 241, 250, 251
Thompson, John, 250
Tidball, Derek, 52n62, 241, 242, 250, 251
Tilling, Chris, 250
Tinkham, Matthew L., Jr., 250
Tollefsen, Torstein Theodore, 250
Torrance, Alan J., 250
Torrance, Alexis, 252
Torrance, James B., 250
Torrance, Thomas F., 4, 20, 224–26, 224n16, 236, 238, 248, 250
Treloar, Geoffrey R., 240, 250
Turcescu, Lucian, 227, 227n22/23, 228, 247, 250

Ullucci, Daniel C., 194n39, 250

Vanhoozer, Kevin, 190, 190n22/23/24, 192, 192n32/33, 196n43, 250

Wainwright, Geoffrey, 250
Ware, Bruce A., 238, 239, 240, 250, 251
Weir, David, 251
Whitehead, A.N., 251
Whitfield, Keith S., 239, 251
Wilckens, Ulrich, 87, 87n41, 92, 251
Wiles, Maurice, 251
Williams, Daniel H., 236, 245, 251

Williams, Garry J., 25, 26, 107, 107n3, 110, 110n10, 111–12, 112n11, 115–26, 116n21, 117n23/24, 118n25/26/27, 119n28/29/30, 123n36, 125n37/38, 126n39, 128, 130, 142, 144, 251
Williams, Rowan, 251
Wood, Maxwell Thomas, 53n63, 110n9, 251
Wright, David F., 241, 246, 251
Wright, Jennifer, 240
Wright, N. T., 25, 26, 47, 47n49/50, 48, 51n57, 52n61, 60, 60n11, 107–10, 107n4, 108n5/7, 113–15, 114n13, 136–40, 136n14, 137n15, 138n20/21, 139n23, 142, 153–54, 154n4, 179, 181, 181n38, 186, 186n10, 199, 203, 207–08, 208n64/65/66/67/68/69, 212, 215, 237, 251

Yandell, Keith, 251
Yang, Hongyi, 252
Yates, Roy, 203n56, 252

Zachuber, Johannes, 252
Zizioulas, John D., 4–6, 217–31, 223n14/15, 224n16 225n17/18, 226n19/20/21, 227n23, 228n27/28, 231n34/35, 235, 238, 239, 241, 243, 245, 247, 252

SUBJECT INDEX

Abelard, Peter, 235

Abraham, 249
   his offering of Isaac, 60–61
   God's covenant with, 61–62, 67, 71, 75–76, 182
   unconditional nature of covenant with, 67, 71
   alleged contractual connotations (*Pierced for Our Transgressions*), 74–75, 76
   missing from Sydney Doctrine Commission Report, 62, 71
   importance of Abraham's faith for Paul, 75, 100–102, 165, 181, 206, 233
   importance for theology of N. T. Wright, 109, 113–14, 179, 207–8, 208n64/65/66/67/68/69
   his covenant inclusive of Gentiles, 179, 181, 184, 206–7, 206–7, 208, 233

Adam, as understood by Ursinus and federal theology, xi, 43–46, 61–62, 64n15, 71
   as understood by authors of *Pierced for Our Transgressions*, 74–79
   God's alleged covenant (of works) with, 61, 77
   allegedly incurring penalty of death, 2, 62–63, 67
   his alleged covenant broken by disobedience, 62, 74
   and Eve, originally immortals punished with mortality, 79, 80, 102, 163
   and Eve as originally mortals not immortals, 102, 163
   as mortals, punished not with death, but expulsion from the Garden, 63–66, 69, 81, 82, 89, 89n50, 163
   as mortals, denied access to the Tree of Life, 63, 65, 81, 89, 102, 163
   expulsion "a spiritual kind of death" (according to authors of *Pierced for Our Transgressions*), 82
   Christ's substitutionary death as penalty for Adam's disobedience, 2, 36, 41, 71, 74

Anselm, 188, 235
   on atonement 49–50, 50n54, 55n1
   Cur Deus Homo, 49, 50, 55, 235
   "satisfaction" as penance rather than penalty, 49–50, 50n54, 55, 55N1, 61

Anthropomorphism, 120, 122n34, 149, 156, 158
   leading to tritheism, 13, 121–22, 123, 143, 151, 217, 220
   and neo-Arianism, 123, 124, 151, 159

Aquinas, Thomas, 6, 7, 10, 55n1, 186, 186n11, 219n5, 229, 229n29, 232, 235, 238

Aristotle, (on metaphor), 188, 188n16

Arius, xn1, 222, 236, 237, 244, 245, 251

Arian, Arianism, 236, 237, 239, 241, 242, 244, 249, 251
   in relation to Carillon Avenue theology, x, 24, 49, 72, 105, 122–24, 143, 151, 159, 176, 218

SUBJECT INDEX

Athanasius, 4, 12, 65–66, 66n18, 145, 220, 222, 235
Atonement, not a required dogma, 37, 40, 40n28, 214
   a core belief of evangelical identity, 41, 48, 186
   an experience, not a theory, 37, 100–102, 180–81
   incorporative/participative, 26, 180–81, 199–204, 207–9
   understood from the perspective of the Trinity, 3, 5, 15, 178–80, 209–14
   See under Penal substitutionary theory
Augustine of Hippo, 4, 223, 225, 235, 236, 245, 247
   on the "sending of the Son," 10, 12, 129, 129n40/41
   City of God, 81, 81n22, 235
   on single, shared divine will and action, 12, 121, 121n32, 123, 128
   On The Trinity, 121, 121n32, 122n35, 129n40/41, 235

Bartlett, Lawrence, 32
Basil of Caesarea, 217, 219n6, 225, 227–28, 236, 243
Beasley, Christine, 32
Bishops, (of the Anglican Church of Australia) 27, 27n1, 35
   as guardians of truth, 29–30, 30n8
Boethius, 219n5, 229, 229n30, 232, 236
Bradley, F. H., 44n39
Bryan, William Jennings, 63n14
Bull, George, 237
The Bulletin, (Australian News Journal), 28, 28n3/4, 29–30n7, 31, 31n12, 33–37, 48, 48n52, 49, 237

Caiaphas (with Pilate), as agent of God's redemptive purpose, 103–4, 133–35, 173–75, 196
Calvin, John, 134, 134n7, 204
Cappadocian Fathers, on hypostatic identities and "relations of origin," 6–7, 120, 223, 224n16, 228
   on "*ousia*" and "*hypostasis*"/ nature and person, 158
   on persons and communion, 216–18, 221–23
   on distinction between individuals and persons, 218–21, 226–27, 228–30
Caricature of God, 51—52, 52n60, 106–7, 124, 150–51, 154, 161, 166–67, 170, 174
   Garry Williams on, 107, 107n3, 110–30, 115–30, 125n37/38, 126n39
   N. T Wright on, 25–26, 47n49, 51n57, 60n11, 107–10, 107n4, 108n5/7, 113–15, 114n13, 136–40, 136n14, 137n15, 138n20/21, 139n23, 154, 154n4, 251
   Sydney Doctrine Commission on, 107, 110–13, 116
Casting Out of Thieves from the Temple, as expression of righteous anger, 140, 144
   disclosing the divine nature, 140–41, 145–47
   not an incommunicable property of the Father alone, 144–48
Carillon Avenue Theology, its Sydney origins, x, xiii, 26, 41, 70
   dating from 1936 onwards, 166, 166n24
   as form of federal theology, xi, 165–66
   its Australian dispersal, xi
   and British parallels, 43–44 (Jeffery/ Hilborn)
   its defence of "penal substitutionary atonement" as "indispensable/non-negotiable," 36–46
   as not indispensable, (Gunton/ Dunn/Wright) 46–54
   See also entries for Federal theology, and Sydney Doctrine Commission Report, 2010.
Cave, William, 238

SUBJECT INDEX

Church of England Doctrine Report, *Doctrine in the Church of England*, 137–38, 137n16/17, 138n18/19, 238
Church of Ireland, 241
Christus Victor, 38, 47, 47n50/51, 99n72, 154n4, 236
Claudius, expulsion of Jews from Rome (AD49), 205
   their return after his death (AD54), 205
   providing the context for Paul's *Epistle to the Romans*, 206–7
Cocceius, John, 235, 238
Colloquium on the Trinity (Melbourne, 2004), 237
Common Theology, a journal, 237, 240
Complementarianism, xn1, 1, 8, 10, 24, 49, 71–72, 144, 240, 242, 245
Communion of God, 141, 162, 181, 215–17
   with God, 39, 65–66 141, 180, 181, 199, 202, 204 (Calvin), 204n58/59, 232, 234
   of the redeemed, 162, 174, 202, 214, 215, 216–18, 232–34, 239, 245, 247, 249
   ontology of "Persons in communion" (Zizioulas), 4–5, 219–31, 223n12, 25n17/18, 231n34/35, 226n19/20, 250, 252
   "Image of God" as "Persons in Communion," 22, 69, 158–59, 158n13 (Lossky), 233–34
Conscience, theology of, 90, 141, 153
Cowen, Sir Zelman, 32
Crucicentrism, 38, 38n23, 59–60, 59n9, 99, 99n72, 103, 180, 200, 200n52
Cyprian of Carthage, 215, 215n77, 238

Darrow, Clarence, 63n14
Death, penal view of, x, xi, 36, 38n23, 56, 56n2, 63–71, 63n13, 77–85, 80n20, 88–92, 213
   metaphorical/spiritual view of, 82, 83–84

   natural, not penal 63, 79–80, 85–88, 234
   penal view not found in OT, 69–70, 93, 163
   less a penalty; more a misfortune (in Paul), 92–93
   not imposed on a third party (Wright, following Cranfield), 113–14, 114n14
   imposed on Christ as the "object" of the Father's action (Williams), 17–23
   accepted by Christ as a (subjectively) "willing object," 121
   of Death (Owen), 247
De Régnon, 223n15, 236, 242, 247
Dyothelitism, See also under Maximus the Confessor

Ecumenical Movement, 4
Eternal functional submissiveness, xi, xii, 2
Eternal functional/relational subordination, x, 1, 2, 12, 13, 49, 71–72, 111, 144, 151, 176, 237, 242
Eunomius, 218
Existentialism, 226–30 (in criticism of Zizioulas)

Faith and Order Advisory Group of the Church of England, 239
Federal theology, xn3, xi, xin4, 36, 41n30, 43–44, 46, 46n44, 61–66, 70, 71, 73–79, 73n3, 74n5, 89, 109, 119n28, 133–34, 165–66, 166n24, 235, 245, 247, 251
Fenner, Dudley, 77, 239
   and alleged "Covenant of Works," 77, 89, 166

Gender, and the Trinity, x, 1–3, 236, 240, 248, 250, 251, 252
   contemporary gender politics, 1–2
   irrelevance of gender difference (Gal 3:28), 233

Goligher, Liam, 1n1, 240
Goodhew, Harry, 27–28, 28n2, 32, 32n14, 35n17
Green, T. H., 44n39
Gregory of Nazianzus, 210, 210n70, 227, 228, 241, 242
Gregory of Nyssa, 158n10, 217–18, 225, 227, 244, 250

Hardy, Sir Alister, 107
Heidelberg Catechism (1562–63), xi, n61–64, 64n15, 77, 134, 134n8, 165
    and Scholastic Calvinism, xi, 66, 71, 134, 165
    See also under Ursinus/Federal theology/Adam
Hilasterion, 45–46, 47, 60, 94–96, 94n61/62/63, 95n64/65, 96n68, 98, 99, 138–39, 193–200
    See also under Sacrifice
Hippolytus of Rome, 221–22, 221n9, 222n10, 229, 232, 237, 242
High Priest, 133
    on Day of Atonement, 39, 45–46, 60, 94, 95, 97–98, 194–95
    Raised Christ as, 39, 98, 196–97
    Blocher's view of, 197
    in Hebrews/Romans, 197–200
Holy Spirit, 7, 14, 21n32, 120, 121, 121n32, 141, 151, 178, 178n34, 221, 235, 236, 238, 241, 250, 251
    positive role in human redemption, 101, 125, 179–80, 198–99, 209, 214–15, 216, 217, 233
Hypostasis, 147, 151, 158n11, 159, 162, 218, 220
    "fluidity in boundaries" between (Coakley), 228, 245, 252
    Garry Williams on 119–24
    of the Father "acting upon" the *hypostasis* of the Son, 121
    essential equality of (in the Trinity), 121, 21n32, 122n35 (Augustine)
    willing not an incommunicable property of, 121–23
    danger of tritheism/neo-Arianism, 122, 123

Individuals. See entry under Persons
Irenaeus of Lyon, 81, 81n23, 204, 242

Jobbins, Boak, 32
John, Jeffrey (Dean of St Albans), 25, 51, 51n56, 106, 107, 108, 114, 136, 138, 243, 251

Kaye, Bruce, 32, 240
Kierkegaard, Soren, 228, 231n36, 243
King, William, 64n16, 174n30
Küng, Hans, 15

Leibniz, Gottfried Wilhelm, 64n16, 244
London Symposium (2005), 25, 26, 43, 52, 52n62, 107, 115, 116, 117, 241

Maru, Neil, 33
Mawaljarlai, Gideon, 32
Mawaljarlai, Luke, 32
Maximus the Confessor, 140, 145n27, 238, 244, 245, 248, 249, 250
    on two wills of Christ (dyothelitism), 140, 145n27
Metaphor, variety of, 26, 37, 37n21, 40, 43 (Jeffery), 46, 46n45 (Gunton), 47, 47n46/47/48 (Dunn), 58–59, 60–61, 71, 194
    on controlling status of penal metaphor, 42–43, 48; disputed by Wright, 47
    conflation of logically competing metaphors, 60, 60n12
    of High Priest in Hebrews, 39–40, 45–46, 47, 60, 94, 95, 97–98, 194–95
    of Raised Christ as High Priest, 39, 98, 196–99
    difficulty of interpretation of, 58–59, 166–68, 186–88, 187n12, 188n15 Gunton)
    difficulty of literal paraphrase, 186–88, 189
    irreducible in religious language, 186
    Paul Ricoeur on, 188–89, 188n16, 189n17
    Janet Soskice on, 189, 189n18/21

Blocher on, 189–96, 189n20,
190n25/26/27, 191n29/30/31,
192n32/34/35/36, 193n37,
195n41/42, 196n44, 197
descriptive of experience of
atonement, 185–86, 98–99,
209–14, 233
limitations of, 26, 37, 210–11
not amenable to theoretical
speculation, 26, 37, 59, 211–13
regulative rather than informative,
213–14
Metaphysics, 196, 245
Moo, Douglas J., 96
Moore Theological College, x, xi, 50,
73n2, 239
its location in Sydney, x–xi
its influence in Australia, xi
See also under T. C. Hammond
Mullen, Sean, 32
Mystery, 5, 12, 24, 37, 45, 103, 181, 183,
184, 185, 186–88, 191–92, 194,
211–12, 212n73, 215, 218, 230

Novatian, 131, 131n2/3, 219, 222,
222n11/12, 229, 232, 246

Owen, John, 74, 110, 110n10, 118–19,
119n28, 247
Oak Hill Theological College, 108

Pacific Hills Christian School, 53
Paul, a Covenantal Nomist?, 247
his use of righteousness language,
100, 249
not just a theorist, 100, 83–84,
201–7
his participative approach to
atonement, 101–2, 207–9
(Wright)
See also under Redemption
Parish of St. Mattias, 32n14, 36, 36n19,
243, 249
Penal substitutionary theory of
Atonement, x, xn2, xi, xii, xiii,
25, 26, 40, 140

as expression in time of "eternal
functional subordination," 23,
71–72, 144–45
as alleged "essence" of the Gospel,
25, 36, 40, 41, 42–43, 42n31/32,
43n33/34/35/36/37, 48, 53–54,
53n63, 79, 79n18, 130, 132, 186
other NT possibilities, 38–40
not to be elevated above other
theories (Gunton), 46, 46n45,
201–2
cultic sacrifice more prominent in
NT (Dunn), 47, 47n48
critically assessed by Chalke, 25,
51–62, 51n58/59, 62n60, 108–
10, 110n9, 130, 175, 175n32
revised in thought of Wright,
25–26, 47
fundamental difficulty of its
crucicentrism, 38, 59, 59n9, 99
confusion of "instead of" and "on
behalf of," 56–57, 56n3 (Jensen)
implied problematic view of God,
36, 36n20, 41n29, 51 (Jeffrey
John/Chalke and Mann),
51n56/57/58/59, 52n56
defended by Garry Williams,
107, 107n3, 110–12,
115–19, 116n21, 117n23/24,
118n25/26/27, 119n28/29/30
with sub-trinitarian implications
(tritheism/neo-Arian
subordinationism), 120–30,
123n36, 125n37/38, 126n39
said to be entailed by God's justice,
36, 131, 132–35, 138, 140, 144,
146–47, 154–55, 154n4
said to be expression of God's
wrath, 36, 131, 135–48
said to be expression of God's love,
112–13, 193; of "holiness and
love, 79, 79n19 (Schreiner); of
"a loving act," 112–13 (Sydney
Doctrine Commission),
of "mercy and love," 114,
114n13/14 (Wright/Cranfield);
of "goodness and wisdom,"
137–40 (Wright)

Penal substitutionary theory of
Atonement (*continued*)
    not necessarily entailed by God's
        "justice," 161–62, 163–66
    restorative justice a logically
        possible alternative, 166–73
    contrary to teaching of Jeremiah/
        Ezekiel, 38
    never dogmatically defined, 37, 40,
        214
    from perspective of the Trinity, 3, 5,
        124–30, 146–47, 151
    best left to pass into desuetude, 130
    See also under Caricature of God
Perkins, Williams, 247
Persons, 235, 238, 240, 241, 248
    distinct from individuals, 217–21,
        231n36
    capable of transcending necessities
        of a "nature," 159–61, 223–24
    and communicability, 231–32
    God as a communion of Persons,
        234
    See also under Communion
Personalism, 227–29
Petersen, Eric, 32
Philo of Alexandria, 194n39, 240, 245,
    248
Pilate, (with Caiaphas), as agent of
    God's redemptive purpose,
    103–4, 133–35, 173–75, 196
Puritanism, xi, 74, 166
    See under Federal theology
Praying animal, as distinct from
    rational animal, 232, 232n38

Quarmby, Mark, 32

Rahner's Rule, 5–6, 105, 176, 178
    Doyle's use of, 8–12
    its ambiguities, 12, 14–15
    radicalizers of, 15–20, 145n26
    restricters of, 20–24, 145, 176, 210
Redemption
    intimately related to the doctrine
        of the Trinity, 2–3, 105, 162–63
        (Rahner)

an experience rather than a theory,
    26, 181–86, 100–102, 181n38,
    198–99, 201–7, 209–10, 234
as "participation" in life of God, 102
    (John Knox), 183, 207–9
importance of resurrection for, 99–
    100, 99n72, 103, 104, 105, 181
as mystery, 181
ecclesial implications of, 214–15
as restoration of the "Image of
    God," 233–34
See also entries under Communion,
    and Persons
Renan, Ernst, 197n47
Rayner, Archbishop Keith, 27n1
Rodgers, Margaret, 35
Rollock, Robert, 248
Roman Catholic Church, 3–4, 15, 20,
    21
Rumrich, John P., 248

Sabellius, 219n6
Salier, Bill, 50–51, 51n55, 53
Sacrifice
    Christ's replacing animal offerings,
        38, 198
    Christ's eternal "pleading of," 57, 60,
        97, 196–97
    difficulties of definition, 45–46,
        96–97, 193–94, 194n39, 201
    sprinkling of blood (*hilasterion*),
        45–48, 60, 95–96 (cultic not
        juridical)194
    in Epistle to the Hebrews, 38–40,
        45, 98, 170n26, 184, 196–200
    in Ephesians and Colossians, 3
    in Romans, 39, 45, 98, 125
    in thought of Dunn, 46–47
    in thought of Wright, 47, 60, 199
    in thought of Aquinas, 55n1
    in thought of Swinburne, 57n4
    with juridical overtones, 45
        (Hammond), 195–96
        (proponents generally/Blocher),
        200–201
    without juridical overtones, 60,
        95–96
    See also under *Hilasterion*.

Sariola, Marice, 33
Scholastic Calvinism, See under Federal theology
Scopes, John Thomas, 63n14
Second Vatican Council (1962–65), 4
Subordination, See under "eternal functional subordination" of Son to the Father
Sydney Doctrine Commission, 49, 50–52, 249
    1999 Report "The Doctrine of the Trinity and its bearing on the relationship of men and women," 1n1, 8–9, 11, 49, 249
    2010 Report on "Penal Substitutionary Atonement," 50, 50n54, 52, 53, 53n63/64/65, 55–72, 63n13, 63–64, 66, 106–24, 116n22
    its synodical reception, 50, 53, 53n64/65
    its reliance on *Pierced for Our Transgressions*, 73, 73n1/2, 85
    its reliance on views of Garry Williams, 112–13, 116–24, 116n21/22, 124–30
    on God's acting "of necessity," 152–53, 152n1, 153n2
    on the alleged "penal" view of death, 63–64, 63n13, 66–70
    avoidance of "patripassionism," 113, 113n12, 128

Theology of the Trinity
    revival of, 3
    initiated by Barth, 3, 4
    pursued by Rahner, 3–4, Zizioulas and Torrance, 4
    complementarian doctrine of, 1–2, 8, 10, 24, 72
    "Eastern" and "Western" approaches to, 6–7
    De Régnon's thesis, 223n15, 236, 242, 247
    its bearing on the relationships of men and women, 1–2
    its relevance to contemporary gender politics, 2
    its relevance to the doctrine of redemption, 2–3, 162–63, 233–34
    shared or communicable properties of Persons (e.g. love), 141
    hypostases/Persons, not individuals, 217–20, 217n1/2, 218n3, 219n5
    unity of divine willing, 13, 25, 128 (Augustine)
    unity of as "communion of Persons," 217–18
    Persons in communion, 216, 219, 220, 228, 250
Third Council of Constantinople, 140
Tillich, Paul, 24
Thompson, Mark, (Doctrine Commission Chairman), 53n65, 73
Tritheism, danger of, 13, 122, 123, 124, 143, 151, 159, 217, 220

Ursinus, Zacharius, xi, 61, 62, 63, 64n15, 66, 77, 165
Ussher, James, xi, 247, 250

Wages of sin (Rom 6.23), 69, 85, 92, 133, 163
Weaver, Jacki, 32
Westminster Assembly, 239, 244
Will, divine
    discerned in "moral pressure" of conscience, 141, 153, 232
    discerned as "Word of God" in words of scripture, 153
    expressed in "positive action," 153
    single and undivided, 121, 123–24
    of the Son, 111–12, 122–23, 123n36
Willingness (alleged of the Son), 110–13, 121–24
Wisdom, Book of, 66, 69–70, 85, 163, 239
    Paul's reliance upon, 66
Wittgenstein, Ludwig, language games, 231
Women in the episcopate, not in accordance with divine will (Doyle), 154–55
Woodhouse, John, 31n13, 53n65

World Council of Churches, 4
Wrath of God, 36, 60, 96 97, 101, 135–36, 141, 170, 243
   "good news" of (Jensen), 131–35, 131n1, 133n6, 135n9, 154n5, 164, 164n18 (quoting Isaiah 53)
   depersonalised/ immanentist views of (Dodd/Pedersen), 86, 90, 90n53
   not depersonalized, 90–91 (Paul), 90, 90n54/55, (Käsemann), 91, 95–96 (Gathercole)
   as "dispositional ethical attitude" (Wright), 107, 136–40, 137n15, 138, 138n20/21, 152, 170
   as expression of God as "loving creator," 136–37, 137n15 (Wright)
   modified by "God's love," 137 (C of E Report 1938), 137n16/17, 155, 162
   civil authorities as instruments of, 133, 133n6, 165n21 (Jensen), 134 (Heidelberg Catechism), 135 (Blocher)
   unlike love, not an intra-trinitarian property, 141–42
   See also under Novatian.
Wright, J. Robert, 245

www.ingramcontent.com/pod-product-compliance
Lightning Source LLC
Chambersburg PA
CBHW022003220426
43663CB00007B/932